Imagined Empires

D0931080

Imagined Empires

TRACING IMPERIAL NATIONALISM IN EASTERN AND SOUTHEASTERN EUROPE

Edited by

Dimitris Stamatopoulos

Central European University Press

Budapest–New York

Published in 2021 by
Central European University Press
Nádor utca 9, H-1051 Budapest, Hungary
Tel: +36-1-327-3138 or 327-3000
E-mail: *ceupress@press.ceu.edu*
Website: *www.ceupress.com*

ISBN 978-963-3861-776 hardback
ISBN 978-963-3861-783 ebook

LIBRARY OF CONGRESS CATALOGING-IN-PUBLICATION DATA

Names: Stamatopoulos, Dēmētrios, 1969- editor.
Title: Imagined empires : tracing imperial nationalism in Eastern and
    Southeastern Europe / edited by Dimitris Stamatopoulos.
Other titles: Constructing ethnic nationalism in Eastern and Southeastern
    Europe
Description: Budapest ; New York : Central European University Press, 2021.
    | Includes bibliographical references and index.
Identifiers: LCCN 2020043770 (print) | LCCN 2020043771 (ebook) | ISBN
    9789633861776 (hardback) | ISBN 9789633861783 (pdf)
Subjects: LCSH: Nationalism--Balkan Peninsula--History. | National
    characteristics, Balkan. | Balkan Peninsula--Ethnic relations--History.
    | Balkan Peninsula--Foreign relations--History. | Balkan
    Peninsula--Politics and government. | Turkey--History--Ottoman Empire,
    1288-1918. | Religion and state--Balkan Peninsula--History. |
    Imperialism.
Classification: LCC DR38.2 .I57 2021 (print) | LCC DR38.2 (ebook) | DDC
    320.5409496--dc23
LC record available at https://lccn.loc.gov/2020043770
LC ebook record available at https://lccn.loc.gov/2020043771

Contents

Dimitris Stamatopoulos

Introduction

It is generally accepted that the long nineteenth century was an era of transition from the political entity of *empire* to that of *nation-state*. In the Balkans especially, the progressive break-up of the Ottoman Empire and the collapse of the Austrian Empire at the end of World War One shaped the contemporary nationalized landscape in that region. However, in historical studies usually this process has been interpreted as a linear course of development, a compelling or inevitable historical ending.

Nevertheless, national discourses in the Balkans, even in the latter part of the nineteenth century, were determined within, or in opposition to, imperial contexts. The empires of Eastern and Southeastern Europe within which these discourses developed belonged to the "old type" of continental empires: even if the arrival of modernity in the Balkans was already a reality—in a practical sense, modernity was identified with "westernization"—this did not mean that individual or collective subjects were prepared to adapt themselves to the new realities or even more, to comprehend the differences between a "traditional" and a "modernist" way of political entities's construction.

Subjects' historical "incapability" of distinguishing between an imperial type of domination and the nationalized forms of sovereignty had enormous effect on the formation of different modes of perception of "national time." Nation states imagined themselves as empires projecting their glorious past to an uncertain future (the case of the Greek *Great Idea* and the Serbian *Naçertaniye* being the most characteristic examples), and empires for their part attempted to adapt to the new circumstances by adopting versions of nation-building, although they themselves remained multi-national, multilingual, religiously diverse, and above all, pre-modern in regard to their political institutions (Ottomanism in the Ottoman Empires or different versions of Pan-ideologies in the Empires of Central and Eastern Europe are the best-known examples). If the Balkan states (and Balkan nationalist movements) fantasized their burgeoning on the basis of the prototype afforded by medieval empires, empires who had not realized their end was nigh, understood themselves through the logic of future homogenization of their various populations.

This contradictory yet mutually-intertwined ideological movement allowed a multitude of intellectuals who were resisting—or rather, who had not yet adapted to—the logic of the nation-state to recast their desire of preserving the empire. Although they identified themselves with the fortunes of the nation, they tried to overcome the necessarily limited temporal constraints of the national present and establish historiographic schemes of continuity, where either the medieval imperial past or the imaginary imperial future acquired immense importance.

The present volume brings together a collection of articles focused precisely on this use of imperial leitmotifs in the formation of national discourses. The appropriation of the imperial past as a historiographic argument is a core component of the schemes of continuity put forward by nationalist intellectuals in the Balkans during the nineteenth and twentieth centuries. Naturally, the issue of continuity is inextricably correlated with an understanding of the "nation" as a substantiated entity.

The articles endeavor especially to explore uses of the "nation" that are incompatible with ethnocentric models, something which produces eccentric or divergent perceptions of national historical time. From this point of view, the volume's contributions follow the logic of my *Byzantium after the Nation*,[1] which explores through the issue of continuity schemes' construction in the Balkan historiographies, the influence of different types of imperial nationalisms on the formation of the Balkan nationalist discourses. Moreover, they will insist not only on the modes that empire formed a constant reference for the emergence of the national imagined community in the historiographical narratives or in literary works, but also as the political present of the intellectual, political or cler-

---

[1] Dimitris Stamatopoulos, *Byzantium after the Nation: The Problem of Continuity in Balkan Historiographies* (Budapest: CEU Press, 2021).

ical elites in the Empires of Eastern and Southeastern Europe which were defending the imperial model even at the end of the nineteenth or the beginning of the twentieth century.

Consequently, the present collective work adds similar perspectives in the field of historiography while spreading this approach to the fields of literary, cultural and political studies, in an attempt understand how the re-invention of the memory of empire led to the re-construction of national identities. This approach differs from the related scholarship which focuses either on the issue of the survival of "imperial heritage" in the nation-states or the unidimensional development of irredentist nationalisms in opposition to empires.

Additionally, the volume explores Orientalist influences on the formulation of these schemes of continuity or modes of political intervention. Representatives of nationalist movements in Eastern and Southeastern Europe frequently relied on Orientalist schemes (or opposed them, producing Occidentalist responses). Orientalism often penetrated nineteenth century nationalist discourses horizontally, given that the latter developed the issue of a nation's recognition by the West as core motif: in the Balkans in particular, the issue of breaking away from whatever constituted "the East" formed the passport for admission into the chorus of "civilized nations," and an agenda item for the nation's organic intellectuals—even when anti-Westernism became a dominant trend in Eastern or Southeastern European public spheres, this constituted a negotiation weapon against the West for incorporating more effectively the nations of the "East." Loans from the Orientalist arsenal on the part of the Eastern European "modernizers" corresponded to Occidentalist narratives in which the invocation of the glorious imperial "Middle Ages" aimed to legitimize the East against the West. Consequently, the simultaneous appearance of these two ideological processes in the nineteenth century is not merely a temporal coincidence: Orientalism, as the dominant discourse of the Western hegemony, and nationalism, as an internalized discourse of Western modernization by the nationalist intellectuals of the East, appear to have functioned in complementary fashion in Eastern and Southeastern Europe.

This volume is arranged in four parts. The first includes articles which deal with imaginary—religious, historiographical or political—Ottoman

Empires. More specifically, my own contribution concentrates on the instrumentalization of the imperial and nationalist models on behalf of the Christian Orthodox clergy in the Late Ottoman Empire for reproducing its hegemonical position in the hierarchy of the *Rum millet*. It focuses on the cases of three cases of clerics to show that we cannot employ a holistic approach when we study the role of the highest-ranking clergy unless we consider three levels of analysis: the management of sentiments, the management of ideologies, and the management of identities, which constitute an indivisible field of social and political mediation. It was impossible for the prelates to abandon the role of political mediator in the name of some Westernizing reformation (Tanzimat), even more so in the name of the "nation" that necessarily promoted the dissolution of the empire. Neither the instrumental utilization of religion by the nation, nor the subjugation of the religious institution to the secular attitude could be easily accepted by them. At least this was not the case with this generation of bishops that learned how to weep on demand and did not consider that being a Janissary and being a Bishop were utterly incompatible.

In turn, Fujinami Nobuyoshi deals with the case of Pavlos Karolidis (1849–1930), a preeminent figure in the development of modern Greek historiography. Karolidis was born in Cappadocia and became a professor of history at the University of Athens, as successor to "the founder of modern Greek historiography," Constantine Paparrigopoulos. After the Young Turk Revolution of 1908, Karolidis was elected deputy from Izmir and participated in Ottoman constitutional politics, an experience that inspired him to develop a peculiar vision of Hellenizing the Empire. His geopolitical conception of the Greek East stretched far beyond the Hellenic borders; it was actually more conditioned by the existing borders of the Ottoman state, within which, in his view, the Orthodox Greeks had enjoyed their historical rights freely. His vision of a multi-religious Greek East accorded the Muslim Turks a very important place in its historical development from the time of the Byzantine to the Ottomans. In Karolidis' view, the Orthodox Greeks, together with the Turks as the leaders of all the Muslims, should be the co-leaders of the East, free from West European as well as Slavic intervention. His alliance with the Unionists was a means to achieve this goal; Karolidis had to safeguard the framework of the Ottoman imperial domain against the schismatic Bulgarian

Exarchists, and the Unionists were the sole administrators. Although his vision lost most of its significance after the Catastrophe of 1922, it is interesting to note that Karolidis was one of the most productive and politically active advocates of the vision of Hellenizing the Ottoman Empire.

In the final contribution of this section, Ariadni Moutafidou analytically describes the degree of identification of Muslim and Jewish populations with the ideal of Ottomanist co-existence, taking as paradigm the events of the Greek-Ottoman War of 1897. She investigates the reactions, and the mobilization of Muslim and Jewish communities and their solidarity with the Ottoman imperial ideal, and explores the functioning of control mechanisms and the strategies of power legitimation of the Hamidian regime during the crisis situation at the end of the nineteenth century, as a result of the war.

The second part focuses on the different modes that Balkan nationalisms choose to handle their relations with the imperial past. Bogdan Trifunović discusses the role poetry had in fostering and framing the collective memory of the medieval empire of the Serbs in the fourteenth century. This memory was partly an effort to connect the collective remembrance of the national "Golden Age" with the vision of a possible re-unification of most of the territories of the medieval Serbian empire of Emperor Dušan (1331–1355) within a modern Serbian state. He analyzes several major places of memory important for framing the mental map of an old empire and their reception in Serbian poetry in the early twentieth century.

Next, Nikolay Aretov seeks to interpret how the Ottoman conquest of Constantinople, a critical event in the history of the Balkans, left its profound imprint on the Bulgarians' notions of their past and their self-image. Behind the seemingly unambiguous evaluation of this event—a defeat of Christendom that has to do with the fall of Bulgarian Kingdom—the observer can trace a more complicated, ambivalent picture. Some of the premises of this paper are: a) The city was unsuccessfully attacked by Bulgarians several times in the past, and they still think of themselves through the prism of these wars; b) Byzantines (Greeks) and Ottomans (Turks) are the traditional enemies in Bulgarian national mythology; their conflict and their interrelations as a whole generate different reactions, and multiple plots; c) In the nineteenth century when the foundations of Bulgarian nationalism were laid, Constantinople (Istanbul) was probably the city with the largest Bulgarian population and the stage for many of the most important changes in Bulgarian society. This study offers a brief review of the main types of Bulgarian texts from the nineteenth and early-twentieth centuries dealing with the fall of Constantinople, comparing them with Byzantine sources and with some Greek and other interpretations of this event, focusing on one less popular dramatic work, written in verse by Svetoslav Milarov in the early 1870s. Here the ambivalent attitude of a part of Bulgarian society to the Ottoman conquest of Constantinople is more visible.

Finally, in this section, Naoum Kaytchev focuses on the manipulation of the dreams of Illyrianism on the part of Bulgarian nationalism. One often overlooked aspect of the Illyrian national model is its imagined "Turkish Illyrian" or Bulgarian dimension. Drawing on Illyrianist publications as well as on an unpublished manuscript by the main geographer of the movement, Dragutin Seljan, the article outlines and analyses the incorporation of the South Slavs of the Ottoman Empire by the Illyrianist national discourse. This inclusion significantly contributed to the multi-layered complexity and magnitude of the Illyrian ideologeme. Although, from the viewpoint of its promoters, the envisaged "Great Illyria" rested on a perceived linguistic and ethnic commonality and its possible political projection was a homogeneous nation-state rather than a composite empire. Nevertheless, the Illyrianist model could potentially have led to the creation of another full-fledged empire. Hierarchy and the multi-layering of its mental construction apart, Illyrianism in practice embraced widely diverging South Slav (and even Albanian) populations that could hardly adopt its ideal. On the other hand, from 1762 Paisii's *Slavonic-Bulgarian History* onwards, the nascent Bulgarian national model clearly separated the prospective nation from its only immediate Slav neighbour, the Serbs. In the 1830s–1840s, the emerging Bulgarian elite remained distant from, or unaware of, the Illyrianist constructions. The modern Herderian ideas of language nationalism combined with the historical capital of medieval Bulgaria provided the "awakeners" with enough ammunition for their mission. The immediate task of the Bulgarian nation-builders was not aimed at imperial appropriations but the other way around: they strove to achieve separation and emancipation from the far larger composite *Rum millet* community.

The third part addresses imperial imagined communities of the Russian world, including three articles which concentrate on the problem of the influences of Russian imperial ideology on the formation of Balkan national discourses, on a literary and political level, as well as an article on the early perceptions of the "Third Rome" theory by an hybrid religiously area between Catholic and Orthodox world.

Magdalena Żakowska examines the role played by Russian Slavophil and Pan-Slavistic ideologies in Balkan national discourses from the second part of the nineteenth century until the First World War, using the example of the Bulgarian myths about Dyado Ivan and Rayna, and the Serbian myth about the Battle of Blackbird's Field. The chapter also describes the similarities between the mythical image of Russia and the self-images of the Serbs and Bulgarians, as well as the correlation between the attitude of these nations towards Russia and their (and the Russians') inferiority complex towards Western Europe (as a symptom of a "self-orientalising process," in Edward W. Said's sense of Orientalism). It is highlighted that in both countries "Pro-European" narratives were created by adherents of gradual modernization, and Pro-Russian ones by both conservatives and revolutionaries. The text emphasises as well the similarities between the Russian ideology of "Russia-the-Third-Rome" and indigenous Balkan discourses about "Russia-the-Liberator" (Russia as an Orthodox Slavonic brother, liberating the Balkan peoples from the "Turkish yoke"). The author argues that the Serbian myth regarding Russia was significantly influenced by an important component of the Kosovo myth¾the cult of self-sacrifice and death. Consequently, the Serbian self-stereotype and the Serbian stereotype of Russia were similar, both containing messianic motifs. Bulgarian national myths, by contrast, tended to underscore the idea of Bulgaria and Russia as complementary entities. Russia was seen there as a protector and liberator, with Bulgaria as a victim pleading for aid.

In her contribution, Lora Gerd also examines Russian national policy in the Balkans during the years after the Crimean War, as it shifted from Panslavism to imperial nationalism and Pan-Orthodoxy. Among the ideologists of the new political line one can find both nationalists like M. N. Katkov and L. A. Tikhomirov and supporters of the pro-Greek tendency like K. N. Leontiev and Prof. I. I. Sokolov. The policy of the Russian Foreign ministry tended to support the Ecumenical Patriarchs—first and foremost Joachim III—who were loyal to other Orthodox nations and to Russian ambitions in the East. The second patriarchate of Joachim was, however, disappointing for the Russian government, because he preferred to take the side of the Greek nationalists on the Macedonian question, and the Bulgarian schism was not mended. The only short period when Russia managed to contribute to the unification of the Orthodox peoples of the Balkans was on the eve of the Balkan wars. But the revival of the Neo-Byzantine ideological scheme of a Pan-Orthodox union, proposed by the Russian government after 1878, could not work in an epoch of nationalism in the Balkans.

Finally, Liliya Berezhnaya deals with "New Romes" and "New Jerusalems" in the sixteenth to eighteenth century Polish-Lithuanian Commonwealth. The Ukrainian capital Kyiv as the New Jerusalem as juxtaposed to the Russian Moscow as the Third Rome is a currently recurring idea, particularly in the light of the recent political and military crisis in the region, but mostly within the post-Soviet reconceptualization of the Russian and Ukrainian past. Not only politologists, but also historians are taking active part in reconsidering the idea of "New Jerusalem" in East European history. Still, the number of studies on the "Moscow, the Third Rome" topic significantly prevail over the investigations on the "Ukrainian Jerusalem." The reason for this disproportion is an often conflation of political theory with religious myth. In fact, we are dealing here with two myths that were used at different times to define the basis for domestic and interstate goals. In fact, the topic of the "Ukrainian Zion" has yet to receive serious and ideologically neutral investigation. Particularly, it refers to its early modern implementations, and to its essential context—the rise of the "New Jerusalems" in the Polish-Lithuanian Commonwealth at the end of the sixteenth through the beginning of the eighteenth centuries. During this time was the competition between different "Romes" (Vatican, Cracow, and Warsaw) with several "New Jerusalems" (Vilnius, Mohylau, Luc'k, Zebryzdów, etc.). It is therefore more appropriate to speak about the competition between "Catholic" and "Orthodox Jerusalems" in Poland-Lithuania, and not so much about the juxtaposition of the Third Rome (Moscow) to the New Jerusalem (Kyiv). To put it more precisely, for the early modern period, the most valid ideological (and at the same time theological and imaginary) confrontation was between Warsaw/Cracow and Kyiv, and not between Moscow and Kyiv, as competing models in constructing sacral places. This article aims to find the grounds for, and the forms of expression, within this conflict.

Finally, the last part of our collection is dedicated to the negative (or occasionally positive) perceptions of the Ottoman past through the prism of the rising Balkan nationalisms (Ottoman utopias and dystopias).

Maro Kalanztopoulou's article discusses the idea of a Balkan interliterary network consisting of the different literary cultures of the region, the connections between which are analyzed from the point of view of their common political and cultural developments in a historical perspective. Such developments include the establishment of a common literary culture which goes back to the time of the Byzantine empire and continues through the Ottoman period, before the different Balkan literary cultures became increasingly influenced by Western models in the nineteenth century. The reluctance of scholarship to deal with parallel literary evolutions in the Balkans is discussed as being the result of historical developments that prevented the linguistic, religious and linguistic assimilation of the Balkan subjects of the Ottoman empire, as well as of a kind of internal Orientalism which consisted in the negative representations made of the Balkan peoples by their Balkan fellows. In addition, the article explores the representations of the respective Balkan national communities and their opponents—the representatives of the Ottoman/Muslim forces—as suggested in the most emblematic works of the "national" poets of Greece, Croatia and Serbia, namely in Dionysios Solomos's *The Free Besieged*, Ivan Mažuranić's *The Death of Smail-Aga Čengić,* and Petar Petrović-Njegoš's' *The Mountain Wreath*. More precisely, it discusses this question in terms not only of the poets' interest in the culture of their respective peoples, but, more importantly, of their adherence to the intellectual and literary currents that dominated Western Europe in the nineteenth century, and especially to German idealism and romanticism.

Eleonora Naxidou's paper deals in complementary fashion with the process of the creation of ethnic narratives in the Balkans during the nineteenth century, focusing on the differing interpretations of the ethnic past which were proposed by national leaders and intellectuals of the Bulgarian Revival. More specifically, two conflicting representations of the Ottoman era in the Bulgarian lands are discussed and related to different political, socio-economic and ideological milieus: the perception of Ottoman rule as the "Turkish yoke" by the national activists of the diaspora who espoused political liberation mostly by means of armed revolt, and the description of the Ottoman regime simply as domination by the national elite within the Empire who sought ecclesiastical autonomy and the perpetuation of the political status quo.

Konstantinos Giakoumis argues that the rise of Balkan nationalisms in the nineteenth century (Albanian nationalism at the last three decades of the nineteenth century) applied a powerful, divisive, elite-driven thrust into these groups. In the spirit of the Romantic exaltation of nationalism, the leaders of the Albanian national awakening movement who had been intellectually nourished in Turkish or Greek schools felt the urge to break with their educational and intellectual roots and to demonize Turks and Greeks alike as "enemies." At the peak of Albanian nationalism's momentum, all those who did not identify themselves in terms of ethnicity were labeled "Grecoman" (or Serbophiles) or "Turcoman." Such divisive thrusts were unconsciously fomented by local religious elites who called on their flocks to entrench Albanian nationalists outside religious enclaves. Giakoumis's chapter argues that as far as documentary and narrative sources permit us to sense from the worm's-eyes-view how the middle and lower strata of the local society felt, acted, interacted with other ethno-cultural groups and identified itself, the centuries-old symbiosis of diverse ethno-cultural communities was still deeply rooted in the region at the beginning of the twentieth century, until the centralized nation-state national-identity building processes maximized divisive thrusts by further demonizing the Greek and Turkish "enemies" and led to a certain degree of homogenization of the region's populations. It is noteworthy that for different reasons demonization stereotypes persisted throughout communist times almost to our own days.

In short, the present collective work explores the theoretical hypothesis that hybridity characterizes both the process of formulating national identities in the nineteenth century and national literatures in empires and nascent nation-states. Eastern Europe and the Balkans offer classic examples of how empires imagine they can transform into national states and how national states project themselves as future empires. This volume ex-

amines the interaction between these two projections. By detaching themselves from the established perception of a supposed complete differentiation of empire and national state, the articles study the effect of discourse
regarding imperial nationalisms on shaping Eastern European and especially the Balkan nationalisms in the nineteenth and twentieth centuries.

REFERENCES

Abu-Manneh B. *Studies on Islam and the Ottoman Empire in the 19th Century (1826–1876)*. Istanbul: The Isis Press, 2001.

Bakić-Hayden, Milica. "Nesting Orientalisms: The Case of the Former Yugoslavia." *Slavic Review* 54 (Winter 1995): 917–931.

Bakić-Hayden, Milica, and Robert Hayden. "Orientalist Variations on the Theme 'Balkans': Symbolic Geography in Recent Yugoslav Cultural Politics." *Slavic Review* 51 (Spring 1992): 1–10.

Barkey, Karen. "Changing Modalities of Empire: A Comparative Study of Ottoman and Habsburg Decline." In *Empire to Nation: Historical Perspectives on the Making of the Modern World*, edited by Joseph W. Esherick, Hasan Kayalı and Eric Van Young. Lanham, MD: Rowman & Littlefield, 2006.

———. *Empire of Difference: The Ottomans in Comparative Perspective*. Cambridge: Cambridge University Press, 2008.

Birtek, Faruk, and Dragonas Thalia, eds. *Citizenship and the Nation-State in Greece and Turkey*. New York: Routledge, 2005.

Deringil, S. *The Well-Protected Domains: Ideology and the Legitimation of Power in the Ottoman Empire, 1876–1909*. London and New York: I.B. Tauris, 1998. Distributed by St. Martin's Press in the USA and Canada.

Fleming, K. E. "Orientalism, the Balkans, and Balkan Historiography." *The American Historical Review* 105, no. 4 (2000): 1218–1233.

Hroch, M. *Social Preconditions of National Revival in Europe: A Comparative Analysis of the Social Composition of Patriotic Groups Among the Smaller European Nations*. Translated by Ben Fowkes. Cambridge and New York: Cambridge University Press, 1985.

Karpat, Kemal H. *The Politicization of Islam: Reconstructing Identity, State, Faith, and Community in the late Ottoman State*. Oxford and New York: Oxford University Press, 2001.

Kohn, H. *The Idea of Nationalism: A Study in its Origins and Background*. New York: The Macmillan Company, 1944.

———. *Pan-Slavism: Its History and Ideology*. Notre Dame, IN: University of Notre Dame Press, 1953.

Lieven, Dominic. "Dilemmas of Empire 1850–1918: Power, Territory, Identity." *Journal of Contemporary History* 34, no. 2 (1999): 163–200.

Meeker, Michael E. *A Nation of Empire: The Ottoman Legacy of Turkish Modernity*. Berkeley: University of California Press, 2002.

Motyl, Alexander J. *Imperial Ends: The Decay, Collapse, and Revival of Empires*. New York: Columbia University Press, 2001.

Okey, R. "Central Europe/Eastern Europe: Behind the Definitions." *Past and Present* 137 (1992): 102–133.

Said, E. D. *Orientalism*, London: Penguin, 1977.

Skopetea, Elli. *I Dysi tis Anatolis*. Athens: Gnosi, 1992.

Smith, A. D. *Nationalism and Modernism: A Critical Survey of Recent Theories of Nations and Nationalism*. New York: Routledge, 1998.

Stamatopoulos, Dimitris. "From Machiavelli to the Sultans: Power-Networks in the Ottoman Imperial Context." *Historein* 5 (2005): 76–93.

———. *Byzantium after the Nation: The Problem of Continuity in Balkan Historiographies*. Budapest: CEU Press, 2021.

Todorova, M. N. *Imagining the Balkans*. New York: Oxford University Press, 1997.

Part I

The Ottoman Empires

Dimitris Stamatopoulos

Prelates Weeping on Demand, Prelates Nationalists, Prelates Janissaries: Instrumentalist Discourses and Power Entanglements of the Christian Orthodox Clerical Elites in the Late Ottoman Empire

When the delegation of Admiral Menschikov arrived in Istanbul early in 1853 in order to assert the right to protect the Orthodox populations of the Ottoman Empire, the occasion sparking the Crimean War, the Holy Synod of the Ecumenical Patriarchate was convened in order to determine its claims. Then Dionysios, Bishop of Nicomedia addressed the other prelates and asked them, "without a humorous disposition": "Holy brothers, will there be a need to even weep?"[1] Because that was indeed the specialty of the said Bishop: weeping, deliberately of course, in order to induce the sympathy (but not necessarily the pity) of the Grand Vizier, the Minister of Foreign Affairs, and the Ambassadors of the Great Powers that were based in the Ottoman Empire's capital.

Let us not be hasty to accuse Dionysios of hypocrisy, nor should we praise him for submitting his sentiments in defense of the Ecumenical Patriarchate's institution. Dionysios, as Bishop of Nicomedia, came to be one of the most powerful prelates in the nineteenth-century Ottoman Empire.[2] Along with Joachim II, Bishop of Cyzikus and later Ecumenical

---

1 Manuel I. Gedeon, *Aposimeiomata Chronografou* [Notes of a chronographer], Athens 1932, 238.

2 Regarding to the Patriarchate's administrative system, the Bishop of Nicomedia was the curator of about 20 provincial metropolitans including: Thessaloniki, Servia and Kozani, Vidin, Veria (Karaferye), Mesembria, Mythemna, Grevena, Imbros (Gökçeada), Vraila, Lovech (Lofça), et al. See Dimitris A. Stamatopoulos, *Metarrithmisi kai Ekkosmikevsi: pros mia anasynthesi tis Istorias tou Oikoumenikou Patriarcheiou kata ton 19o aiona* [Reform and secularization: towards a reconstruction of the history of the Ecumenical Patriarchate in the nineteenth century] (Athens: Alexandria, 2003), 419.

Patriarch, and Gerasimos, Bishop of Chalcedon, they were the leading figures of the highest orthodox clergy at this time.

His case, however, is interesting because it creates doubts for many
of the certainties that haunt us when we study Eastern Orthodoxy, even
more so when it comes down to "Helleno-Christianism". Helleno-Christianism constituted the cornerstone and the primary methodological tool
in understanding the growth of Greek nationalism in the nineteenth century. This neologism by Zampelios appeared at a very crucial time (1852):[3]
shortly after the historic compromise between the Ecumenical Patriarchate and the Autocephalous Church of Greece (1850)[4] and shortly before
the outbreak of the Crimean War (1853), which was an early field of the
application of irredentist policies.[5] Along with Konstantinos, Paparrigopoulos Zambelios was the intellectual who introduced the incorporation
of the Medieval (Byzantine) Ages into the dominant historiographical
narrative of Greek nationalism, giving the theoretical background of the
Great (Megali) Idea. Before the period of the Crimean War it was a paradox in the intellectual circles of Greece to combine these two contradictory concepts: Hellenism and Christianity. For the first time Zambelios
tried to transcend this historical contradiction by introducing a new term
which reflected the new content of the national identity: the claim of Athens (antiquity) to conquer/liberate Constantinople (Byzantium).

Yet, here emerged a paradox: the integration of Byzantium into the
mainstream modern Greek historiographical narrative, which stressed
Athens' desire to reach Constantinople, coincided with the failure of
this first irredentist version of the Great Idea as well as the adaptation of

---

3 See his introduction in Spyridon Zambelios, *Asmata Dimotika tis Elladas ekdothenta meta meletis
   istorikis peri Mesaionikou Ellinismou* [Demotic songs of Greece published with a historical study of
   medieval Hellenism] (Corfu: Typografeion Ermes, 1852).
4 The Patriarchate of Constantinople recognized the Autocephalous Greek Church in 1850, seventeen
   years after the proclamation of its establishment in 1833. See, among others, Dimitris A. Stamatopoulos, "The Orthodox Church of Greece," in *Eastern Christianity and Nationalism in Nineteenth-
   Century Europe*, ed. Lucian Leustean (New York: Fordham University Press, 2014), 34–64.
5 It is important to understand that when we refer to the "Great Idea," we must acknowledge the irredentist dimension—the obvious geopolitical strife against the Ottoman Empire. Also, we must
   underline the "cultural" competition against Western Colonial Great Powers like France that were
   yearning to assume the role of the civilizer of the Orient. On this matter see Stamatopoulos, *Byzantium after the Nation: The Problem of Continuity in Balkan Historiographies* (Budapest: CEU Press,
   2021).

Greek foreign policy to the demands of the Western Great Powers, Great Britain and France, that safeguarded the territorial integrity of the Ottoman Empire.

This is the reason why Constantinople[6] did not adopt, or rather remained ambivalent towards, the new nationalized concept of Byzantium, something that was paradoxical as well. At a moment when Greek nationalism placed the capital of the empire at the heart of its long-term aims, Constantinople, and more specifically the elite of the Greek Orthodox community, treated this ideological and political shift with reservations, to say the least. What we call Helleno-Ottomanism was in truth a strategy of isolation for the most radical nationalists, who were to be found in Istanbul as well,[7] although many may have wished to interpret it as the Ottoman reflection of the Great Idea. Constantinople displayed this inclination of differentiation long before Joachim III openly distanced himself from the strategy of Greek foreign policy in the 1880s. We cannot examine the matter in further depth at this point because we will direct our study primarily toward the position of the highest-ranking Orthodox clergy. An illustrative example would be the policy of nominating honorary members of the Greek Philological Association, the only association in Istanbul that effectively questioned the ideological hegemony of the Ecumenical Patriarchate. The association never included Paparrigopoulos or Zambelios among its honorary members. Yet, this may have been due to either foolishness, or in any case, to political cautiousness that related to how the Ottoman authorities might react in such an occasion. Nonetheless, the matter is viewed in a different light if we consider who the first honorary member of the association was: the French classicist Girardin, a sworn enemy of the romanticists as well as a scholar that caused the indignant criticism of Paparrigopoulos early in the 1850s as a result of Girardin's hostile views against

---

6   I used the name of Constantinople in a symbolic level, especially when I refer to the Patriarchate or to Constantinople as the "second center of Hellenism," and Istanbul for literalism.

7   Certainly, the Greek Orthodox community was not uniform. It was not only the differentiations and stratification among leading elites of Stavrodromion (Beyoğlu), secular or clerical, from the poor masses of Diplokionion (Beşiktaş). There were also several waves of newcomers from Ottoman provinces and the Greek state that kept coming to the city throughout the nineteenth century to consider, and these were in a perpetual process of assimilation and validation.

Orthodox.[8] That symbolic gesture displayed the association's proposed course of action at a time when its Neo-phanariot founders had not lost control to the radical nationalists.[9]

But beyond the Neo-phanariots, the supremacy of Helleno-Ottomanism was more due to the ability of the Orthodox clergy to adapt and maneuver in a period of reforms that endeavored to modernize the Ottoman state. At this point we will examine three examples, the first being that of Dionysios of Nicomedia, that prove the ability of the Orthodox clergy to reproduce and redefine its ideological and political hegemony through the instrumental utilization of sentiments, identities, and ideological concepts such as nationalism and ecumenism. And we analyze whether this kind of approach entailed the adherence to, or the rejection of, the concepts of Helleno-Christianism. Let us not forget that the problem of interpreting the latter with regards to events in the Greek kingdom is inextricably linked to two matters that the Orthodox clergy of Constantinople could not possibly overlook: the matter of the nation treating religion as an instrument, and the matter of subordinating the Church to the state. The examples that we will discuss are effectively the response of Constantinople to the political stakes of Helleno-Christianism.

INSTRUMENTALIZING SENTIMENTS: ON RUSSIA

The example of Dionysios weeping on demand was obviously not a unique one in the Patriarchate's history. Comparable examples of weeping bishops can be traced all the way back to the early days of the Ottoman conquest.[10] The case of the Bishop of Nicomedia is different because he reused that "aging" routine of soothing the authorities at a moment when the empire was at the threshold of introducing several reforms, whence several new forms of (secular and political) representation were substituting the

---

8 Stamatopoulos, "Hellenism versus Latinism in the Ottoman East: Some Reflections on the Decline of the French Influence in the Greek Literary Society in Istanbul," *Etudes Balkaniques* 43, no. 3 (2007): 79–106.

9 We may chronologically place this shift at the beginning of the 1870s, when the systematic withdrawal of the association's founding members commenced. On the matter see Stamatopoulos, *Metarrithmisi kai Ekkosmikevsi*, 217–219.

10 One of the last heirs of this legacy, according to oral testimonies of modern prelates, was the Ecumenical Patriarch Athinagoras (1948–1972).

old ones. And it is an interesting case because, as we already said, it creates doubts for many of the certainties that we are obsessed with when examining the history of the Ecumenical Patriarchate in the nineteenth century.

The first certainty: the Orthodox clergy of the Ottoman Empire was close to tsarist Orthodox Russia. Dionysios, whose secular name was Demetrios Kotakes, was born in Mesaria of Andros to an aristocratic family of the island, and was a personal friend, or rather a protégé, of the French ambassador to Istanbul Édouard-Antoine de Thouvenel (1855–1860) and of his successor Marquis de Moustier (1861–1866), who both later became ministers of foreign affairs of Napoleon III. So Dionysios represented the Francophile faction in the Patriarchate, which had a long-lasting tradition even after the fall of the "ancient regime" in 1789.[11] In a comparable manner, an "Anglophile" faction of high-ranking clerics emerged as well, especially from 1840–50, when Canning was quite popular in Istanbul, as was his protégé, Stefan Vogoridi. The Russian faction led by Megas Logothetes Nicolaos Aristarches could not easily promote its own agenda, especially after the end of the Crimean War, and was forced into a game of compromises, especially with ex-Francophiles. This ever-changing political and ideological reality of the Patriarchate was illustrated by Pavlos Mousouros in a letter of his to his brother Constantinos, Ambassador of the Ottoman Empire in London (and brother-in-law of Stefan Vogoridi), when he was called upon to face the same "prejudices" on the alleged dependence of the Orthodox clergy on the Russian factor. He ironically spoke of the "brains" of the Foreign Office, who "discover that the emperor of Russia is the head of the whole Greek Church... I will start studying astrology in order to illuminate the course of the stars that have so enlightened the brains of all foreign ministers on earth and on the moon."[12]

---

11   At those times, the end of the eighteenth century, its main representative was Gregorios V, even if this seems strange to some. Gregorios was the protégé of the "Francophile" family of Soutsoi, see Gedeon, *I pnevmatiki kinisis tou Genous kata ton 18o kai 19o aiona* [The spiritual movement of genos/nation during the eighteenth and the nineteenth century] (Athens: 1970), 58–59. Furthermore, one of the six brothers of Dionysios, Leontios, was a deacon of the Ecumenical Patriarch Gregorios V and was arrested along with the Patriarch by the Ottomans after the Greek Revolution started and was executed, cf. D. Paschales, "Silivrias kai eita Nikomideias Dionysios Io. Kotakis" [The Bishop of Silivria and then Nicomedia Dionysios I. Kottakis] *Thrakika* 12 (1939): 86–93.

12   Archive of Constantinos Mousouros (Gennadeios Library, Athens), file 24, no. 12, Pavlos Mousouros to Constantinos Mousouros, Istanbul, December 17, 1850. Also see the same judgment by an ac-

However, from this point of view, the stance of Francophile Dionysios to help the Russian intervention in 1853 by weeping, which in an objective manner would improve the position of the Ecumenical Patriarchate in the Ottoman Empire, it could be considered as an indication of an instinct of political survival which transcended national identities or group and individual interests.[13]

The second certainty: the Orthodox clergy and the Orthodox Levant in general were passive to the emergence of modernism. This is what we must underline in the stance of the Bishop of Nicomedia; the weeping on demand was not a mere display of submission, nor only in compliance with some higher purpose. It was more of a way to understand the political, and the means of imperial political mediation. The conscientious instrumental utilization of sentiments, the "extreme" example of Dionysios, may help us understand the link between utilization and political intermediation as the key element of the Orthodox clergy's functioning within the Ottoman Empire. Weeping on demand is not only a method, nor is it merely a hint about the clarifying differences between means and purposes. It is proof of how strong the tradition of political mediation is within the Patriarchate of Constantinople; if the instrumental utilization of sentiments can contribute towards successful negotiations with the representatives of the state, then it is naturally domineering.

INSTRUMENTALIZING NATIONALISM: ON THE BULGARIAN SCHISM

If the paradigm of the Bishop of Nicomedia is enough to illustrate the framework of church-state relations within an imperial background, then the paradigm of Neophytos, Bishop of Derkoi, can illuminate the problem of Church-Nation relations, also within an imperial background. Neophytos (his secular name was Nikolaos Drymades), unlike Dionysios who as we mentioned was born to an aristocratic family, was a low-

---

claimed observer of Ottoman realities, M. A. Ubicini, *Letters on Turkey: An Account of the Religious, Political, Social, and Commercial Condition of the Ottoman Empire*, vol. 2 (London: 1856), 236–7.

13 Dionysios was a messmate of the royal couple of Greece, Othon and Amalia. But he probably represented a type of cosmopolitan prelate and thought well of the king and queen mostly because they had delegated the Prime Minister's post to a Francophile politician like Ioannis Kolletis, see Stamatopoulos, *Metarrithmisi kai Ekkosmikevsi*, 65.

born man from Drymades of Epirus (thus the surname he used), a township that was in the jurisdiction of the metropolitan of Dryinoupolis. When Joachim, later Bishop of Cyzicus and eventually patriarch known as Joachim II, was pastoring in that Bishopric, Neophytos came to be his protégé. In other papers of mine I have already thoroughly examined the cycle of clerics and laymen that Joachim had created as early as the mid-1840s; given the political support of Ioannis Psycharis, Bey of Chios, and later the financial support of the powerful bankers Georgios Zarifes and Christakes Zografos, Joachim was to be the basis around which a group of high ranking clerics emerged. From that group, personalities such as Joachim III and Neophytos of Derkoi arose.[14]

It is impressive that both of these personalities belonged to the same circle of clerics and were patronized by the same circle of bankers, supporters also of their spiritual father. It is well known that Joachim III projected a kind of "ecumenism" that was prearranged by his predecessor Joachim II; by that we mean a policy that wanted to encompass the pan-Orthodox (i.e., an open stance towards the Russian and Bulgarian sides) with the imperial orientation (a stance in defense of the Ottoman Empire). On the contrary, Neophytos was on the blacklist of the Russian embassy and ambassador Ignatiev considered him as the head of the nation-centric circles of the Greek Orthodox community in Istanbul. In the event of succession to the patriarchal throne in 1863, when he tried to succeed his spiritual father in an attempt of the bankers to keep the Patriarchate under their control, the Porte erased his name from the list of candidates for being an alleged supporter of the Great Idea. Truly, Neophytos in the following years (from 1865 on he held the metropolitan of Derkoi and with the help of Zarifes he permanently settled in Istanbul) rose to be a leading figure among the Patriarchate's hardliners that caused the excommunication of the followers of the Bulgarian Exarchate after the Schism of 1872.

In general, we can easily identify the instrumental treatment of the national issue from the point of view of the ecumenicists of this circle, Joachim II and Joachim III; the former, although he was one of the ex-Patriarchs that signed the Schism against the Bulgarian Exarchate, when

---

14   Stamatopoulos, *Metarrithmisi kai Ekkosmikevsi*, 47–52, 367–370.

he became Patriarch again in 1873, he solved the matter of the Saint Pan-teleimon's monastery in Mount Athos by choosing the head abbot the Russians wanted, while he received the dependency (*metochion*) of Saint Sergios in Moscow. The latter implemented the same policies towards Russia to the extent that the Charilaos Trikoupes Greek government be-came suspicious of him. Even more so given that while he had proclaimed himself as an Ethnarchis (head-of-the-Nation, a nationalist post-interpre-tation of the concept of "millet başı"), he was the first patriarch to accept the termination of some of those "privileges" that are known in the histo-ry of the Ecumenical Patriarchate. Somehow, he was a Russophile and a Turcophile at the same time.

But in the case of Neophytos, it seems that ideas and actions were in correlation, and so were the sentiments. Although one may observe that the writer of an article titled "Finis Ecclesiae," that criticized then patriarch Anthimos VI for his modest plan of solving the Bulgarian is-sue he proposed in autumn 1871, did not react in a similar manner when Joachim II, his spiritual father, approved the Russian suzerainty over the Saint Panteleimon monastery, he cannot but acknowledge his consisten-cy regarding his fight against any kind of Pan-Slavists, hidden or not. Or maybe not?

In a collection of his writings that were published after his death[15] some "details" worthy of attention can be found. It is worth mentioning that what was eventually known was but a fraction of what was in a con-tainer full of sorted documents that Neophytos had prepared to be sent to the Greek Philological Society of Constantinople, as he sensed his near-ing end, along with the instruction for the container to be opened only af-ter fifty years had passed. But his passing came early in 1875 and the con-tainer was passed on to the Patriarchate. His spiritual father, Joachim II, who was the patriarch at the time, declined to deliver the container to the Association. His successor Joachim III, however, a bitter friend of Neo-phytos, approved and eventually delivered the container's documents. Yet almost everyone was certain that the documents published in 1881 were

---

15 Neophytos (Drymades), metropolitan of Derkoi, *Erga tina (meta tis viografias avtou), ekdidome-na ypo V. Diamantopoulou, dapani tou exohotatou Christaki effendi Zografou* [Some works with his biography, published by V. Diamantopoulos at the expense of his excellency Christakes Zografos effendi] (Constantinople: 1881).

only a portion of the initial collection allowed to go public after some selection by the two Joachims.

It is therefore of great interest to note that in this published collection we find two letters of Anthimos, Bishop of Vidin dated 1868.[16] In the first of these, Anthimos expresses his thanks to Neophytos for his mediation in the matter regarding the Patriarchate's decision for him to receive 2,000 kuruş per month, paid from the Church's National fund "until my given difficulties here are solved," Anthimos said.

I was lucky to discover in the archives of the Bulgarian Academy of Sciences, where Anthimos' archive is kept, the letter with which Neophytos announced the subsidy of these 2,000 kuruş (and he did so in the margins of the letter).[17] Anthimos was no random figure; he was the first exarch of the Bulgarian Exarchate. To be precise, the first elected exarch was Ilarion, Bishop of Lovech, yet, in view of his radical ideas the Porte, the Russian embassy and the Bulgarian conservatives under Gavril Krăstovich took care to promptly replace him with Anthimos, who was a target of Tchankov's *Macedonia* for being too moderate in his views against the Patriarchate. It is safe to assume that Neophytos, despite his aggressive rhetoric against the Bulgarians, could understand a little too well the significance of supporting the moderate side that had more chances of effectively communicating with the Patriarchate. On the other hand, none could reject the possibility that the good relations between the two continued in subsequent years and especially in 1871 (shortly before the Schism). On the contrary, if Joachim III, an ecumenicist, chose to leave that letter in the container of the late Neophytos for it to get published, he must have had his reasons. He probably wished to illustrate that it was not only the moderate ecumenicists of the Patriarchate that retained contacts with the other side, but those that propagated the Great Idea within Constantinople did so as well. The utilization of the ethno-centric rhetoric of Neophytos was not meant to be

---

16   Neophytos (Drymades), metropolitan of Derkoi, *Erga tina,* 257–259.

17   Stamatopoulos, "The Splitting of the Orthodox Millet as a Secularizing Process: The Clerical-Lay Assembly of the Bulgarian Exarchate (Istanbul 1871)," in *Griechische Kultur in Südosteuropa in der Neuzeit. Beiträge zum Symposium in memoriam Gunnar Hering* (Wien, 16.–18. Dezember 2004). Herausgegeben von Maria A. Stassinopoulou und Ioannis Zelepos, *Byzantina et Neograeca Vindobonensia Bd. XXVI,* Vienna 2008, 243–270.

used against he who appears to be an enemy of the Nation in the irredentist game that was to be set in the territory of the Ottoman Empire in the following years. It was meant to support the definition of a leading strategy within the Greek Orthodox community that aimed at weakening opposing patriarchs and any popular support that they may have had. Both Neophytos and Joachim III at different occasions formulated and expressed such alternative strategies so that they facilitated, in any case, the social and economic hegemony of the group of bankers; Neophytos did so in 1873 by proclaiming the Patriarch their shared spiritual father again, while Joachim in 1878 did so as the successor of their common spiritual father.

The paradigm of Neophytos will make us think deeper into the problematic relations between nation and religion in the era of the rise of national movements during the eighteenth and nineteenth centuries. Usually the dominant historiographical patterns dealt with this matter by considering that religion became a tool of the nationalists' aspirations in the Balkans, and that it did its part in shaping national identities. Was it not this that Helleno-Christianism was all about? This undoubtedly accurate observation must be supplemented by a thorough investigation into how the problem of the rise of nationalism was dealt with by the religious elites of the Ottoman Empire (Christian, Muslim and Jewish). Specifically, if and how they managed to adapt in the new circumstances and what consequences their attitudes had in the key issue of state and church relations (and in general in secular-state and religious scope) among the newly formed nation-states of Southeastern Europe. The meticulous study of the religious elites' behavior (and when we speak of religious elite, we do not limit ourselves to the study of the clergy but we also study the lay elements that are associated with them) may provide us with the interpretive key to understand why the representatives of religion, and especially those of the Orthodox Church, managed to reproduce and reaffirm their socially strong and politically and ideologically hegemonic position within the framework of the modern bourgeois states. At a moment when the Church managed to reaffirm its scheme of adaptation within the Ottoman imperial framework, which I described in view of the Bishop of Nicomedia, its representatives managed to display an exceptional ability to use and instrumentalize both ecumenical and nationalistic motifs, depending on circumstances, either to isolate political opponents or to reinforce their position within the State.[18]

DEFENDING THE EMPIRE: ON METROPOLITAN-JANISSARY

Manouel Gedeon, Megas Chartophylax of the Patriarchate who provided us with this information on the Bishop of Nicomedia, also speaks of some more interesting things for another bishop of this period: Panaretos, Bishop of Heraclea, who was from Ganochora of Thrace.[19] He reports that when Panaretos died and his body was being prepared to be shrouded they discovered the emblem of the 31st Janissary battalion scarred on his arm (*otuz-bir orta*). Perhaps not even he could have foreseen his own personal development. We know little of his early career. Yet, at the height of the Greek Revolution he became Megas Protosygkelos of the Patriarchate, possibly during the reign of Anthimos III (1822–1824), and immediately after the ascension to the patriarchal throne of his successor Chrysanthos in July 1824 Panaretos was elected as Bishop of Philadelphia.[20] He remained there until 1838 when he was transferred to the Bishopric of Tarnovo.[21] It was there that Bishop Panaretos, known to the locals not only as the "janissary" but also as *pehlivan* (wrestler), collided with the local dignitaries. He was revoked and was replaced in August 1840 by Neophytos Vyzantios. Eight years later he was elected for the metropolitan of Heraclea, where he remained until he died.

Neophytos replaced Panaretos in view of some scandals. The latter, as we said already, had been a janissary and a wrestler (*pehlivan*). In articles of the Bulgarian newspaper *Carigardski Vestnik* (Constantinople News) of 1857 there are accusations against him regarding extortions of monas-

---

18 Let us not think that Neophytos had adopted any form of secularized perception of the relation between church and state because he had a specific view on the relation between church and nation. See his negative criticism for the National Assembly in the years 1858–60, cf. Neophytos (Drymades), metropolitan of Derkoi, *Erga tina,* 19–20.

19 Gedeon, "Kanonismon apopeirai" [Efforts for regulations], *Ecclesiastical Truth* 44 (1920): 246; idem, *Istoria ton tou Christou peniton* [History of the poors of Christ] no. 3, (Athens, 1939) 261–262.

20 Aimilianos Tsakopoulos, "Episkopikoi katalogoi kata tous kodikas ton Ypomnimaton tou Arheiofylakeiou tou Oikoumenikou Patriarcheiou" [Bishop Catalogues according to the Codices of the Archives of the Ecumenical Patriarchate] *Orthodoxia* 31 (1956): 445.

21 Tsakopoulos, "Episkopikoi katalogoi kata tous kodikas ton Ypomnimaton tou Arheiofylakeiou tou Oikoumenikou Patriarcheiou" *Orthodoxia* 32 (1957): 91.

teries and churches, stealing of golden and silver ecclesiastical utensils and ornaments, extortions of abbots that were forced to sell the properties of their monasteries in order to pay their debts to him and more. The above-mentioned accusations, although their factuality must be examined, provided the excuse for Panaretos' fall from grace. In truth, as Ivan Radev comments, his revocation was a victory of the Bulgarian Party that was not yet in the forefront.[22] The Patriarchate was in no position to realize at the time that his authority was being questioned indirectly. In any case, Panaretos was involved in cases of abusing ecclesiastical revenues during his time in Heraclea as well: he was accused by the populace of Galatista in Chalkidiki of embezzling about 500,000 kuruş from the revenues of the monastery of Saint Anastasia of which he was the curator. For a period of 3 years he delivered only 35,000 kuruş to the monastery, which owned massive estates in Moldovlachia.[23]

We cannot help but wonder; did the ex-janissary and pehlivan bishop enter the Ecumenical Patriarchate's institution in order to find a refuge just before the imminent slaughter of his order by sultan Mahmud II (which eventually happened in the summer of 1826) or was he one of many clerics (mainly Bulgarian speaking) that manned the ecclesiastical institution after the Greek elements fell from grace because of the Greek Revolution being at the same time a connecting link with the Bektashi order of Janissaries?[24] The second possibility seems more plausible in view of his overall career within the Patriarchate. This bishop janissary seems to have contributed towards the safekeeping of Ottoman legitimacy, either in a Patriarchate in crisis, or in a metropolitan where the nationalistic sentiments of the Bulgarians had begun to transform into inescapable political imperatives.[25] The adaptable identity of Panaretos corresponded to the

---

22   Ivan Radev, *Istorija na Veliko Târnovo* [History of Veliko Târnovo] (2000), 336.

23   Gedeon, *Istoria ton tou Christou peniton*, 171.

24   Stamatopoulos, "Bulgarian Patriarchs and Bulgarian Neophanariotes: Continuities and Disconti-nuities in the Ecumenical Patriarchate during the Age of Revolution," in *(Mis)understanding the Balkans: Essays in Honour of Raymond Detrez*, ed. Michel De Dobbeleer, and Stijn Vervaet (Ghent: Academia Press, 2013), 45–57.

25   We have to remind here that the bishopric seat of the metropolitans of Philadelphia was Venice. That means (although we do not know if Panaretos resided permanently there) that our bishop pehlivan avoided to see the slaughter of his colleagues in the flesh in the summer of 1826. But someone could but notice that he kept his position even after the extermination of Janissaries which means that his loyalty had not been in doubt or the clerical scheme was hiding effectively his true Bektaşi soul.

protection of an imperial reality that was very hard to relate to any sort of religious or national "purity."

Conclusions

These three cases of clerics that we examined show that we cannot employ a holistic approach when we study the role of the highest-ranking clergy unless we consider three levels of analysis: the management of sentiments, the management of ideologies, and the management of identities, which constitute an indivisible field of social and political mediation that was impossible for the Orthodox clergy to abandon in the name of some Westernizing reformation, even more so in the name of the "nation" that necessarily promoted the dissolution of the empire. Therefore, the issue of Helleno-Christianism becoming the primary ideological and political pattern among the leading clerical elites (for the secular ones the matter is analyzed elsewhere) of the empire comes into question, at least until the period of the Easter Question's crisis. Neither the instrumental utilization of religion by the nation, nor the subjugation of the religious institution to the secular attitude can be accepted with ease. At least this is not the case with this generation of bishops that learned how to weep on demand and not consider that being a pehlivan and being a bishop are utterly incompatible. And here is the most important point: we can create a history of institutions or even a history of ideas far more easily than we can observe the identities that historical beings adopt and repudiate through time.

References

Gedeon, Manuel I. "Kanonismon apopeirai" [Efforts for regulations]. *Ecclesiastical Truth* 44 (1920).

———. *Aposimeiomata Chronografou* [Notes of a chronographer]. Athens: 1932.

———. *Istoria ton tou Christou peniton* [History of the poors of Christ] no. 3. Athens, 1939.

———. *I pnevmatiki kinisis tou Genous kata ton 18o kai 19o aiona* [The spiritual movement of genos/nation during the eighteenth and the nineteenth century] Athens: 1970.

Neophytos (Drymades), metropolitan of Derkoi, *Erga tina (meta tis viografias avtou), ekdidomena ypo V. Diamantopoulou, dapani tou exohotatou Christaki effendi Zografou*

[Some works with his biography, published by V. Diamantopoulos at expense of his excellency Christakes Zografos effendi]. Constantinople: 1881.

Paschales, Dimitrios. "Silivrias kai eita Nikomideias Dionysios Io. Kotakis" [The Bishop of Silivria and then Nicomedia Dionysios I. Kottakis]. *Thrakika* 12 (1939): 86–93.

Stamatopoulos, Dimitris A. *Metarrithmisi kai Ekkosmikevsi: pros mia anasynthesi tis Istorias tou Oikoumenikou Patriarcheiou ston kata ton 190 aiona,* [Reform and secularization: towards a reconstruction of the history of the Ecumenical Patriarchate in the nineteenth century] Athens: Alexandria, 2003.

———. "Hellenism versus Latinism in the Ottoman East: Some Reflections on the Decline of the French Influence in the Greek Literary Society in Istanbul." *Etudes Balkaniques* 43, no. 3 (2007): 79–106.

———. *To Vyzantio meta to Ethnos: to provlima tis synecheias stis Valkanikes Istoriografies* [Byzantium after the nation: the problem of continuity in the Balkan historiographies]. Athens: Alexandria, 2009.

———. "Bulgarian Patriarchs and Bulgarian Neophanariotes: Continuities and Discontinuities in the Ecumenical Patriarchate during the Age of Revolution." In *(Mis)understanding the Balkans: Essays in Honour of Raymond Detrez*, edited by Michel De Dobbeleer, and Stijn Vervaet. Ghent: Academia Press, 2013.

———. "The Orthodox Church of Greece." In *Eastern Christianity and Nationalism in Nineteenth-Century Europe*, edited by Lucian Leustean, 34–64. New York: Fordham University Press, 2014.

———. *Byzantium after the Nation: The Problem of Continuity in Balkan Historiographies.* Budapest: CEU Press, 2021.

Tsakopoulos, Aimilianos. "Episkopikoi katalogoi kata tous kodikas ton Ypomnimaton tou Arheiofylakeiou tou Oikoumenikou Patriarcheiou" [Bishop Catalogues according to the Codices of the Archives of the Ecumenical Patriarchate]. *Orthodoxia* 31 (1956).

Ubicini, M.A. *Letters on Turkey: An Account of the Religious, Political, Social, and Commercial Condition of the Ottoman Empire.* Vol. 2. London: 1856.

Zambelios, Spyridon. *Asmata Dimotika tis Elladas ekdothenta meta meletis istorikis peri Mesaionikou Ellinismou* [Demotic songs of Greece published with a historical study of medieval Hellenism]. Corfu: Typografeion Ermes, 1852.

Fujinami Nobuyoshi

Hellenizing the Empire Through Historiography: Pavlos Karolidis and Greek Historical Writing in the Late Ottoman Empire

It is a widely held assumption that in modern states historiography and nation building went hand in hand. This assumption often accompanies the view that, after the "awakening" of ethnic consciousness of their various subject peoples, it became almost unpractical for multi-ethnic empires to survive. This in turn leads to the idea that only ethnically monolithic nation building was possible. In the Age of Empires of the late nineteenth and early twentieth centuries, however, the relation between historiography and nation building appeared in a much more nuanced light. The dissolution of multi-ethnic empires and the formation of ethnically monolithic nation states in their stead was not regarded necessarily as the only, or sometimes even a desirable, choice by contemporaries. Contrary to the retrospective understandings of later generations, at the turn of the twentieth century a significant number of intellectuals took the multi-ethnic composition of their empires for granted; more often than not they saw the framework of the empire as a useful field of action in which their respective ethnic groups could play a more productive role in the global economy and/or politics. In the Habsburg, Russian, and Qing empires, corresponding to the attempts on the part of their respective governments to build a multiethnic imperial nation, multi-ethnic historiographies on an imperial scale were being constructed. The Ottoman Empire provides us with one such case.[1] And the Ottoman Greeks were no exception.

---

1   On the development of modern Ottoman historiography see, among other studies, Neumann, *Das indirekte Argument*; Herzog, *Geschichte und Ideologie*; Ersanlı, *İktidar ve Tarih*; Kafadar and Ka-

In recent years, Greek experiences in the modern Ottoman Empire have attracted the attention of historians. With as many Greek subjects as in the Hellenic Kingdom, late Ottoman society owed much to its Greek elements who played an indispensable role in the financial, industrial, and economic sectors of the Empire.[2] The Greeks' presence in intellectual affairs was no less impressive: in educational, cultural, philanthropic, and feminist activities in the Ottoman public sphere, Greek projects often appeared much more influential than those of the governmental and/or Muslim-Turkish ones.[3] Moreover, the Ecumenical Patriarchate in Istanbul was not merely one of two centers of the Greek nation, along with the Hellenic government; equipped with its age-old tradition of ecumenism, it functioned as *the* center of all the Orthodox Christian subjects of the Sultan.[4] With these vested interests in the social, economic, and ecclesiastical spheres, the Greek ethnic consciousness within the Ottoman context did not necessarily contradict the Muslim-Turkish predominance in the administration. Many Greek intellectuals, especially after the Tanzimat reforms, dreamed of Hellenizing the Empire from within through their economic and cultural supremacy.[5]

Nevertheless, relatively little is known about the relationship between the Muslim Turks and the Orthodox Greeks in terms of their historiog-

---

rateke, "Late Ottoman and Early Republican Turkish Historical Writing," 559–77 and Akbayrak, *Milletin Tarihinden Ulusun Tarihine.*

2 On Ottoman Greek economic activities see Panayotopoulos, "On the Economic Activities of the Anatolian Greeks," 87–128; Exertzoglou, "The Development of a Greek Ottoman Bourgeoisie"; Kasaba, "Economic Foundations of a Civil Society"; Chatziiosof, "I bel epok tou kefalaiou," 309–49. On the living conditions of Asia Minor Greeks in general see also Augustinos, *The Greeks in Asia Minor*; Anagnostopoulou, *Mikra Asia, 190s aionas-1919*; Stamatopoulos, "From Millets to Minorities in the 19th-Century Ottoman Empire," 253–73.

3 Exertzoglou, *Ethniki taftotita stin Konstantinoupoli ton 190 aiona*; idem, *Oi 'hamenes patrides' pera apo ti nostalgia*; Kanner, *Ftoheia kai filanthropia stin orthodoxi koinotita Konstantinoupolis*; eadem, *Emfyles koinonikes diekdikiseis apo tin Othomaniki Aftokratoria stin Ellada kai tin Tourkia.* On the Greeks' contribution as Ottoman men of letters see Strauss, "The Greek Connection in Nineteenth-Century Ottoman Intellectual History," 47–67.

4 Papadopoullos, "Nouvelle Rome." For its development in modern history see also Kitromilides, "The Legacy of the French Revolution," 229–49; and Stamatopoulos, "Ecumenical Ideology in the Orthodox Millet (19th–20th c.)," 201–47.

5 This way of thinking is called Helleno-Ottomanism in Greek historiography. For the variations of this idea see Skopetea, *To 'Protypo Vasileio' kai i Megali Idea*; Skopetea, "Oi Ellines kai oi ehthroi tous," 9–35; Anagnostopoulou and Kappler, *"Zito Zito o Soultanos/Bin Yaşa Padişahımız,"* 47–78; Anagnostopoulou, "To telos tis aftokratorikis logikis, to telos tis aftokratorikis Konstantinoupolis," 483–503; Stamatopoulos, *Metarrythmisi kai ekkosmikefsi*, 355–70.

raphies as well as their geopolitical visions especially after the Young Turk Revolution of 1908. Ottomanist scholars, always placing emphasis on the Committee of Union and Progress (*İttihat ve Terakki Cemiyeti*) and its members (hereafter the CUP and Unionists, respectively), tend to pay little, if any attention to aspects of the Greek participation in late Ottoman intellectual history. The underlying assumption, widely held in both Turkish and non-Turkish academia, is that the CUP was determined to Turkify everything Ottoman while non-Turks were hostile to everything Ottoman.

In my opinion, however, an in-depth comparative study on the political as well as intellectual orientations of the Empire's various subject peoples, Muslims and non-Muslims alike, is still needed. Such an approach would shed some new light on the history of the latest years of the Ottoman Empire, which was not necessarily conditioned by mutually exclusive ethno-nationalistic currents alone. Recent studies question the hitherto dominant ethno-nationalistic readings of late Ottoman history. While many scholars have begun to doubt the validity of the so-called "Turkification" theory,[6] the Ottomanist state of mind of non-Turkish intellectuals is now also being reexamined.[7]

As one of the most ethnically and religiously diverse empires in the world, a rereading of the Ottoman case would, I hope, provide us with a fresh point of reference in analyzing and comparing the structures of various multi-ethnic empires in terms of their many subject peoples' intellectual as well as political orientations at the turn of the twentieth century.

From this perspective, I would like in the present chapter to examine the case of Ottoman Greek historical writing by analyzing the words and deeds of a historian-cum-politician, Pavlos Karolidis (Παῦλος Καρολίδης, 1849–1930). I place his ideas within the context of the Second Ottoman Constitutional politics leading up to the Balkan Wars and then to the Asia Minor Catastrophe. For this purpose, I utilize two kinds of primary

---

6   Kayalı, *Arabs and Young Turks*, 2–4, 82–96; Toprak, "Bir Hayal Ürünü: İttihatçıların 'Türkleştirme Politikası'," 14–22. On the Ottomanist aspects of Turkish nationalism see also Arai, *Turkish Nationalism in the Young Turk Era*.

7   For the Greek case, see, among other studies, Noutsos, "The Role of the Greek Community," 77–88; and Kechriotis, "Greek-Orthodox, Ottoman Greeks or just Greeks?" 51–71. For the Arab and Armenian cases, see, among others, Herzog, "'Abd al-Ḥamīd az-Zahrāwī und das Problem des Osmanismus," and Koptaş, "Armenian Political Thinking in the Second Constitutional Period."

sources: Karolidis's books written in Greek between the 1890s and 1930s for Greek readers, and his speeches in Turkish delivered before Ottoman audiences in the years between 1908 and 1912.

KAROLIDIS IN OTTOMAN POLITICS

Pavlos Karolidis was born in 1849 in Cappadocia in Ottoman Anatolia as a Turcophone Orthodox Christian. He first attended Greek schools in Istanbul and Izmir, and then continued his studies abroad at the universities of Athens, Munich, Strasbourg, and Tübingen. After his return to the Empire, Karolidis held teaching posts in Izmir and Istanbul. Eventually, in 1893, he was nominated to the chair of professor of history at the University of Athens, as successor to Constantine Paparrigopoulos, "the father of modern Greek historiography." After 1898 he collaborated in Neoklis Kazazis's journal *Hellenism* and espoused a vision of anti-Slavic Greek nationalism. In 1908, after the Young Turk Revolution had broken out and the new constitutional regime had been proclaimed, Karolidis began to involve himself in Ottoman politics. He was elected from Izmir to the newly reopened Ottoman Chamber of Deputies (*Meclis-i Mebusan*), enjoying the support of the Theotokis government of the Hellenic Kingdom with which he had close connections.[8] Besides his duties as deputy, Karolidis became one of the founding members of the Ottoman Historical Society (*Tarih-i Osmani Encümeni*). He contributed to the Society with a translation of Kritovoulos, a Greek chronicler of Mehmet the Conqueror.[9]

Constant political upheavals together with a delicate intellectual environment awaited Karolidis when he set out for the Ottoman political arena. The terrible defeat of the 1897 Ottoman-Greek War on the one hand, and the intensification of the Macedonian Question (especially after 1903) on the other, had put the Hellenic Kingdom into a very dif-

---

8   A biographical sketch of Karolidis is provided in Kechriotis, "A Cappadocian in Athens, an Athenian in Smyrna, and a Parliamentarian in Istanbul," 297–309. For his early life and his participation in the local politics of Izmir just after the Revolution, see also Kechriotis, "Celebration and Contestation," 157–83.

9   Kritovulos, *Tarih-i Sultan Mehmet Han Sani*. See also Strauss, "The *Millet*s and the Ottoman Language," 243–47.

ficult position vis-à-vis the powerful Ottoman state as well as the aggressive Bulgarian nationalists. The situation was no less confusing after 1908. While in the Ottoman Empire the Young Turk Revolution dramatically changed the style of governance from Hamidian autocracy to a constitutional monarchy, the Goudi Coup of 1909 eventually invited Eleftherios Venizelos, a Cretan, to the seat of power in the Hellenic Kingdom, resulting in a fundamental reshuffling of the political scene on both shores of the Aegean. Simultaneously, there occurred a change in the power structure within the Ottoman Orthodox community. With new ideologies and new actors who had entered the scene after 1908, Ottoman Greeks were anything but a monolithic entity. Replacing the Joachimist–anti-Joachimist controversy of the Hamidian era, the Greek Political League (*Rum Meşrutiyet Klübü* / *Ελληνικός Συνταγματικός Πολιτικός Σύνδεσμος*), a political party organized primarily by the Greeks of Macedonia with a support of the secularist middle class as well as the Hellenic diplomatic service, divided the Orthodox community into two opposing camps.[10]

The League soon became antagonistic to the CUP. It pursued a policy of Greco-Bulgarian rapprochement in the autumn of 1910, seeing the future of Hellenism in fighting against the "chauvinistic" Unionists and the "Turkish yoke." However, a number of elite Ottoman Greeks, especially Istanbulite notables, as well those from Asia Minor and the Aegean islands, opposed this new policy. They found the League's behavior too aggressive and even detrimental to the welfare of Hellenism. Indeed, many Greeks rejected rapprochement with the Bulgarians because, given the schism with the Bulgarian Exarchate since 1872, such a rapprochement represented not only a political error but also a religious sin. In other words, many Greeks thought that to ally themselves with the Bulgarians would prove far more dangerous than to cooperate with the Turks.

---

10 The League itself was controlled by the behind-the-scenes headquarters, the Society of Constantinople (*Οργάνωσις Κωνσταντινουπόλεως*), a veteran organization of the Macedonian Struggle. On this society and its ideological tenets see Panayotopoulos, "The 'Great Idea' and the Vision of Eastern Federation," 331–65 and Veremis, "The Hellenic Kingdom and the Ottoman Greeks," 181–91. Even if the Society espoused a vision of a multi-ethnic federation of the East, the way it actually behaved in day-to-day Ottoman politics and how it was regarded by other Ottoman actors must be studied in its own right. I have the impression that in Greek academia the "civic" aspects of its leaders' thoughts are overemphasized.

In addition, at least according to Karolidis, the League's judgments of the Unionists in particular and the Ottoman political scene in general were prejudiced and one-sided. He judged that the anti-Unionist politicians with whom the League collaborated were not only split among themselves but no less fanatic and chauvinistic than the Unionists.[11] Indeed, there was little that suggests sincerity on the part of the anti-Unionists when they offered an alliance to some non-Muslim factions as late as the end of 1911. They had demonstrated no more understanding to the non-Muslims' claims than the Unionists had during the previous four years of constitutional rule and showed favor to non-Muslims only after the dissolution of the Chamber of Deputies became inevitable, a tactical move with the sole aim of opposing their own rival, the CUP.[12]

Neither the Unionists nor the Greeks were acting in a political vacuum. Ideological divergence alone did not determine the course of Ottoman politics. After all, there were many other participants in the Ottoman political arena who had different orientations and priorities, such as the "Old Turks," the military, the Porte bureaucracy, the Neo-Phanariotes, the Galata bankers, the Joachimists and anti-Joachimists, socialists, provincial notables, and many other ethnic groups such as the Bulgarians, Armenians, Kurds, Arabs and so on.[13] In such an environment it was imperative for any participants in the theatre of Ottoman politics to give priority to one of their many demands over the others and to discover who could be their ally in satisfying it. The conflict between the League and Karolidis stemmed more from the difference in their judgments of the political situation than their intrinsic ideological standpoints.

For whatever reasons, the League eventually lost its faith in the CUP and began to identify with the foreign policy of the Venizelist Hellenic state, whereas many Greek politicians of the Ottoman Orthodox community, including Karolidis, saw the CUP as the sole responsible decision-making power in the Empire and opposed the policy of the League. In so

---

11 Karolidis, *Logoi kai Ypomnimata*, 329, 371–85. I would like to express my sincere gratitude to the late Vangelis Kechriotis, who kindly provided me with a copy of this book.

12 For a more detailed discussion see Fujinami, *The Ottomans and Constitutionalism*, chapter 5 (in Japanese).

13 For an overall description of Ottoman constitutional politics see Ahmad, *The Young Turks*, and Akşin, *Jön Türkler ve İttihat ve Terakki*. The Greeks' role within it is the theme of Boura, "The Greek Millet in Turkish Politics," 193–206, and Kerimoğlu, *İttihat-Terakki ve Rumlar*.

doing, these anti-League Greek politicians had, behind and beyond tactical preferences, constructed a vision of Hellenizing the Ottoman Empire in collaboration with a Muslim power holder, in this case the CUP, an idea that went back to the Tanzimat Helleno-Ottomanism and the ecumenical vision of the Joachimists during the Hamidian era. At the same time, their vision was influenced by certain new elements, namely the constitutionalist logic of the Ottoman public sphere after the Revolution. Karolidis was one of the most ardent advocates of this vision of Hellenizing the Empire.

THE VISION OF EMPIRE UNDER OTTOMAN CONSTITUTIONALISM

Describing the Ottoman state in its historical sequence and the Greeks' place within it, Karolidis emphasized that the Ottoman Empire had been an Islamic theocratic state.[14] This was not necessarily intended as a criticism or a slight. In fact, Karolidis repeatedly corrected the Young Turk as well as Western assumptions that the Ottoman Empire had been a Turkish state. According to Karolidis, the Ottoman Empire was never an ethnically oriented state. It was above all a patriarchal and patrimonial state of the Ottoman dynasty. It was also an Islamic state under Muslim, not Turkish, domination.[15] Karolidis thought it essential to defend the religious characters of both the imperial Ottoman state and the Orthodox community for the sake of Hellenism, hence his definition of the Empire as a theocratic state.

Remarkably, because Karolidis advocated this vision in an age of secular constitutionalism when the slogan of "liberty, equality, justice, and fraternity," regardless of one's race and creed, became catchwords.[16] Against the mainstream Ottoman public opinion, Karolidis insisted that the prerogative of the Sultan does not contradict the principle of national sovereignty (*hakimiyet-i milliye*); on the contrary, it was only the Sultan-Caliph who could defend sovereignty on behalf of the Ottoman nation. Accord-

14 Karolidis, *Istoria tou IXX aionos met'eikonon,* vol. 2, 43.
15 Karolidis, *Synhronos Istoria ton Ellinon kai ton loipon laon tis Anatolis apo 1821 mehri 1921,* vol. 4, 279–80; idem, *Istoria tis Ellados apo tis ypo ton Othomanon aloseos tis Konstantinoupoleos (1453) mehri tis vasileias Georgiou tou A,* 218–19.
16 Demirci, "1908 Parlamentosunda Meşrutiyetin Değerleri ve İlkeleri," 83–104.

ing to Karolidis, the Ottoman Sultan, as the Caliph of Muslims all over
the world, had to be given no fewer powers than those of the "smallest rulers of Europe."[17]

Similarly, the Ecumenical Patriarch, as the "Ethnarch" (ἐϑνάρχης /
milletbaşı) of all the Orthodox flock, should be given full lay as well as ecclesiastical authority. The Ottoman imperial system must be safeguarded
by a cordial relationship between the two despots, the Sultan-Caliph and
the Ecumenical Patriarch, both of whom should be beyond any constitutional restrictions. In this context, Karolidis harshly condemned the
National Regulations (Γενικοί Κανονισμοί / Rum Patrikliği Nizamatı) of
1862, the pseudo-constitutional texts for the administration of the Orthodox community drafted under the strong influence of the Sublime
Porte, which bestowed power to the lay elites, in particular to certain
Galata bankers.[18] Karolidis criticized these Regulations because:

> They created within the Church a constitutional monarchy with the
> Synod and National Council as executive power (without responsibil-
> ity!) and the Patriarch could govern only with these two bodies. This,
> opposite to the tradition and History of the Church, totally secular-
> ized the Church, radically turned over the basis of ecclesiastical pol-
> ity, and annihilated the authority of the office as well as the personal
> power and activity of the Patriarch.[19]

From the viewpoint of Karolidis, the Reform Edict (Islahat Fermanı) of
1856 as well as the National Regulations of 1862 were the fruit of the Porte's
ill-fated attempt to secularize the Church and the state. This resulted in
the abolition of "all the national autonomy" of the Greeks and transferred
power "to ignorant notables or to Çorbacıs [as the Patriarch Joachim III
had called them] of the Constantinopolitan quarters and to the corrupt

---

17   *Takvim-i Vekayi*, 246: 8. (Meclis-i Mebusan Zabıt Ceridesi Devre 1, Sene-i İçtimaiye 1, İçtima 89)
      (hereafter *TV* and *MMZC*, respectively); *TV*, 250: 8. (MMZC Devre 1, Sene-i İçtimaiye 1, İçtima
      92); MMZC Devre 1, Sene-i İçtimaiye 3, İçtima 41: 1154; İçtima 44: 1213.
18   On these Regulations and their implementation see Stamatopoulos, *Metarrythmisi kai ekkosmikef-
      si*. For the economic as well as political activities of the Galata bankers, especially Georgios Zarifis,
      see Exertzoglou, *Prosarmostikotita kai politiki omogeneiakon kefalaion*, and Hulkiender, *Bir Galata
      Bankerinin Portresi*.
19   Karolidis, *Logoi kai Ypomnimata*, 185–86.

youngsters of Galata and Pera," namely, the Galata bankers.[20] Karolidis's denunciation extended to the Tanzimat reformers, especially Ali and Fuat Pashas, because of their secularist tendencies. It was these Westernizing Pashas as well as the influential Galata bankers who undermined the ancient religious constitutions of both the Empire and the Church.[21] Taking this judgment into account it becomes easy to understand the reason why in his historical writing Karolidis made as little reference as possible to the role and influence of Galata bankers in the affairs of the Orthodox community, even if he knew well that banking was one of the most active and productive sectors among the Greeks in modern Ottoman history.[22]

But what made Karolidis so antagonistic towards secularist elements within the Empire? Without doubt one of the reasons is to be found in his fundamental ideology. Karolidis was no friend of secular democracy. He saw Orthodoxy as being at the core of Greek identity. Therefore, to secularize the Orthodox Christians appeared to be nothing less than a demolition of the very basis of their Greekness. Accordingly, Karolidis looked for a monarchy supported and legitimized by Orthodox Christianity both for the Hellenic and Ottoman Greeks. He did not hesitate to criticize the secularizing policies that had been implemented in the early years of the Hellenic Kingdom.[23]

In the particular context of the Second Ottoman Constitutional politics, two urgent concerns were added to Karolidis's anti-secularist reasoning. First, he was driven to stress the religious character of the original constitution of the Empire in order to safeguard the religious identity of the Orthodox community in the eyes of the Muslim Turkish public. To put it more precisely, Karolidis tried to defend the interests of Greeks from the secular logic of Ottoman constitutionalism. This is especially apparent when the so-called "religious privileges" (*imtiyazat-ı mezhebiye*) of non-Muslim communities became the bone of contention. Non-Muslims had tried to safeguard their communal rights such as their autonomy in the areas of marriage, justice, education, and so on. In the Second Constitution-

20 Karolidis, *Synhronos Istoria ton Ellinon*, vol. 5, 44–45.
21 Karolidis, *Istoria tis Ellados*, 781; idem, *Synhronos Istoria ton Ellinon*, vol. 5, 26–27, 33–36, 39–46.
22 Karolidis, *Synhronos Istoria ton Ellinon*, vol. 6, 182.
23 Karolidis, *Synhronos Istoria ton Ellinon*, vol. 4, 44–46, 54–55, 109–18. His monarchist approach to understanding history is also found in Karolidis, *I Elliniki Vasileia os Megali Idea*.

al period, these privileges became the target of Muslim criticisms, as being contrary to the principle of equality among all the citizens of the state regardless of one's race and creed, whereas the non-Muslims considered them as sine qua non for their very existence under the "theocratic" rule of the Muslim majority.[24] In this context, underlining the prerogative of the Sultan-Caliph, by whom these privileges had supposedly been given, seemed to offer an effective counter-argument in support of the privileges.

The second reason for Karolidis's anti-secularism derived from his hostility towards Bulgarians. As a staunch anti-Slavist, he found it logical to defend the unity of all the Sultan's Orthodox subjects by asserting the "historical rights" of the Ecumenical Patriarchate, sanctioned traditionally by the successive Ottoman Caliphs for centuries, thus rebuffing the claims of the Bulgarians to have a national church of their own. In an era of secular Balkan nationalisms, Karolidis tried his best to underplay the secular ethnic consciousness of the Balkan peoples while emphasizing the significance of their common religious bonds with the Greeks.[25] Here his Helleno-centric attitude was obvious. When it came to the rights of the Ecumenical Patriarchate, Karolidis did not hesitate to ignore the ethnicities of Orthodox Christian peoples other than the Greeks.[26]

The path left for Karolidis was indeed a narrow one in the light of the civic logic of Ottoman constitutionalism. To deny any ethnic rights other than the Greek one among the Orthodox Christians inevitably invited the criticism of the Muslims, as well as the non-Greek Christians. In fact, Karolidis once proclaimed, in conformity with the civic constitutionalist discourse of the unity of various elements (*ittihad-ı anasır*), that the Ottoman nation was comprised of many constitutive elements and therefore their ethnic and religious identities should be respected.[27] Apparently, for Karolidis, to emphasize the multi-ethnic character of the Ottoman nation was one thing; to ignore the multi-ethnic character of the Orthodox com-

---

24 Fujinami, "Privileged but Equal," 33–59. On the development of the privilege question see also Exertzoglou, "To 'pronomiako' zitima," 65–84, and Kechriotis, "The Modernization of the Empire and the Community 'Privileges,'" 53–70.

25 Fujinami, *The Ottomans and Constitutionalism*, chapter 4. An earlier English version is available in Fujinami, "'Church Law' and Ottoman-Greeks in the Second Constitutional Politics, 1910," 107–32.

26 *TV*, 117: 9–10. (MMZC Devre 1, Sene-i İçtimaiye 1, İçtima 22); MMZC Devre 1, Sene-i İçtimaiye 2, İçtima 51: 564–65.

27 *TV*, 290: 11–12. (MMZC Devre 1, Sene-i İçtimaiye 1, İçtima 115).

munity was another. In both cases what was at stake was the Greeks' interests. In the former case he urged the Turks to pay respect to the Greeks' rights by reminding them of the multi-ethnic composition of the Empire, while in the latter he opposed the Bulgarian claims by ignoring the existence of various ethnic elements within the Orthodox community. Yet the simple fact that both arguments were made in the same political arena, namely the Ottoman public sphere, eventually made clear the contradiction inherent in the Greeks' double-standard tactics.

With these two concerns in his mind, Karolidis seemed determined not to alienate the CUP. Given his alliance with the latter, Karolidis had to make some compromises with the CUP's secular Ottomanist tendencies. This is not to say that he was prepared to renounce the religious privileges or to seek the favor of the CUP at the expense of the Greeks or the Ecumenical Patriarchate. He simply saw it as wise and reasonable to achieve his goals—specifically, to retain the privileges as well as the unity of the Orthodox community—by cooperation with the CUP against their common enemy, the Bulgarians. Karolidis believed that the Unionists would offer a rational solution to the privilege question if the Greeks sincerely cooperated with them.[28] In any case, Karolidis was confident that he had done his best to the benefit of both the Ottoman and Hellenic peoples. In his own words:

> I performed my duty both to the Hellenic and the Ottoman states with a true mind, always declaring the truth and having the impregnable principle that in the Ottoman chamber I never said anything that I could not say in the Hellenic one while in the Ottoman chamber I dared to say all I wanted to say in the Hellenic one.[29]

IMPERIUM IN IMPERIO: ECUMENISM WITHIN OTTOMAN BORDERS

The spatial aspects of Karolidis's historiographical vision also merit some investigation. His imagined geography of the Greek East stretched not only beyond the territory of the Hellenic Kingdom but beyond the ju-

---

28 Karolidis, *Logoi kai Ypomnimata*, 333–35.
29 Karolidis, *Logoi kai Ypomnimata*, 146–47.

risdiction of the Ecumenical Patriarchate. This is not to say that he over-looked the significance of the geographical range of each ecclesiastical au-thority. In the Greek East, besides the Ecumenical Patriarchate in Istanbul and the Greek Church in Athens, there were the autocephalous Patriarch-ates of Antioche, Jerusalem and Alexandria as well as the Archbishop-ric of Cyprus. Being aware of this fact, Karolidis was willing to present the jurisdiction of the Ecumenical Patriarchate as wide as possible, since in his view the rights of the Greeks had been inseparably connected to the privileges of the Great Church.[30] Nonetheless, the unity of the Greek world always mattered more to him than the ecclesiastical hierarchy with-in the Orthodoxy. Although religiously oriented, in this respect Karolid-is was definitely a Greek nationalist. This directed his attention to a series of non-Orthodox states. The conquest of Alexander the Great was one of the most important events in the historical expansion of the Greek East as an integral domain. Alexander's legacy had been inherited throughout history under the Hellenistic Kingdoms, the Romans, the Byzantines, and finally, the Ottomans.[31] Although non-Orthodox, Alexander and the Ottomans occupied special places in Karolidis's writings because the his-torical integrity of Hellenism owed much to their dominations.

The manner in which Karolidis evaluated the role the Ottomans played in the history of Hellenism seems ambivalent. On the one hand, in accordance with the dominant narrative of Greek nationalism, Karolid-is enumerated the negative aspects of Turkish rule that put an end to the Greek rule of Byzantium and replaced it with "Asiatic" despotism. On the other hand, he did not ignore the positive elements the Ottoman Turks of-fered to Hellenism, the best known aspect of which was the reunification of the Greek population as well as of the four Eastern Patriarchates un-der the single Ottoman flag.[32] In addition, Karolidis argued that the Ot-toman Empire had contributed to the benefit of the Greeks, even if un-consciously, by strengthening the prerogative of the Ecumenical Patriarch and thus making the Great Church a "state within a state," under which

30 Karolidis, *Synhronos Istoria ton Ellinon,* vol. 4, 47–54, 72–109.
31 Karolidis, *Istoria tou IXX aionos met'eikonon,* vol. 2, 130–32, 140–41; Karolidis, *Peri tis ethnikis ka-tagogis ton orthodoxon hristianon Syrias kai Palaistinis, passim.*
32 Karolidis, *Peri tis ethnikis katagogis ton orthodoxon hristianon Syrias kai Palaistinis,* 29–32, 382; Karolidis, *Istoria tis Ellados,* 305–06.

the Greeks' identity could be preserved to his own days.[33] The religious privileges had functioned as the core element of this regime, according to Karolidis and many other Ottoman Greek intellectuals. Acknowledging this fact, Karolidis gradually began to put more emphasis on the positive side of the Ottoman rule.

Arguably, the threat of Panslavism as well as the secularizing logic of Western modernity urged Karolidis to emphasize this aspect of his ideology. After all, after the Crimean War with a Russia motivated by Panslavism it was difficult for the Orthodox Greeks to find a more suitable ally than the Muslim Turks against the Slavic as well as the West European threat, both of which negated the Greeks' special role in the East.[34] On the contrary, under Ottoman rule the "Greek" Ecumenical Patriarchate had supposedly functioned as the legitimate organ for all the Orthodox Christian subjects of the Sultan. Additionally, in the context of the Macedonian Question, many Greeks found reasons enough to cooperate with the Muslim Turks against their common enemy, the Bulgarians.[35] This idea pushed Karolidis to explore the positive aspects of Ottoman rule.

It goes without saying that the Greek War of Independence constituted the climax of Karolidis's historiography. In spite of his religious world view, Karolidis never turned his back on Greek nationalism. He frequently expressed his belief that the Greeks should not forget the *Megali Idea* and urged his fellow citizens to pursue it.[36] Nevertheless, he interpreted it as a peaceful penetration of the Greek elements in social and economic fields all over the Ottoman imperial domain, making full use of their vested interests as well as their legitimate ecclesiastical tradition, without alienating the mass of Muslim Turks.[37]

It is interesting to note that, in presenting his own version of *Megali Idea*, Karolidis's geopolitical imagination was conditioned by no other consideration than the actual Ottoman border of his time. Although he was aware that the geopolitical range of ancient Hellenism was not at all

---

33 Karolidis, *Istoria tou IXX aionos met'eikonon*, vol. 2, 36–43; Karolidis, *Logoi kai Ypomnimata*, 380–81.
34 Karolidis, *Logoi kai Ypomnimata*, 390–92.
35 Karolidis, "I Anatoliki Romylia kai o Ellinismos," 5 (1902): 743–44; 6 (1903): 42–43.
36 Karolidis, *Anamniseis Skandinavikai*, 176–81.
37 Karolidis, *Istoria tou Ellinikou Ethnous tomos ektos,* 295. For a similar attitude among the Hellenic politicians see also Karolidis, *Synhronos Istoria ton Ellinon*, vol. 2, 315–17.

limited to that of today's Greek peoples,[38] and that the cities of South Russia, Romania, and Italy played a crucial role in the Greeks' economic and ideological developments at the turn of the nineteenth century,[39] he rarely, if ever mentioned the Greek centers outside of the Ottoman frontier in his own time, such as Odessa, Bucharest, and Batum when he reminded his readers of their national agenda of the *Megali Idea*. This means that in practice Karolidis was talking about the autochthonous character of Greeks only in those areas under Hellenic as well as Ottoman sovereignty in his own time.

Here, two regions require special attention: Palestine and Macedonia. Both had confronted the threat of "Panslavism" since the middle of the nineteenth century. Palestine became an international issue within the framework of the Eastern Question, and many Greeks saw the Russian presence there as a threat to the unity of Orthodoxy.[40] In this context, Karolidis had to refute the Russian and native Arab claims that the Greeks were alien to Syria and Palestine. In defending the "*ethnic* origins of the Orthodox Christians" in Syria, Palestine, Mesopotamia and Egypt, he argued that all the Christian inhabitants there were actually Greeks, regardless of their *racial* origin, mother tongue, and self-consciousness. He knew that neither the Orthodox Arabs of Syria or Palestine spoke Greek, nor did they consider themselves to be Greek. In order to include them as members of the Greek nation, Karolidis found religion the most convenient criterion. In his view, Orthodox Christians were Greeks because—as the very basis of the Christian identity was their religious bond to the Great Church—they were inevitably under the strong influence of the Greek language and culture, and that made them ethnically Greek.[41] In other words, the religious bond made them ethnically Greek, whether they recognized it or not.

The same holds true for Macedonia. Karolidis insisted that there were only Greeks in Macedonia. Local non-Greek speaking Christians were be-

---

38 See, for example, Karolidis, *Anamniseis Skandinavikai*, 177–78; Karolidis, *Synhronos Istoria ton Ellinon*, vol. 2, 273.

39 Karolidis, *Istoria tou IXX aionos met'eikonon*, vol. 2, 109–14.

40 Stavrou, "Russian Policy in Constantinople and Mount Athos in the Nineteenth Century," 225–49. See also Vovchenko, "Creating Arab Nationalism?" 901–18.

41 Karolidis, *Peri tis ethnikis katagogis ton orthodoxon hristianon Syrias kai Palaistinis*, 11–33, 385–89.

ing forcibly compelled by the Bulgarian authorities and bandits to think of themselves as Bulgarians just because they spoke the Bulgarian vernacular. In actuality, according to Karolidis, as long as they had retained their identity as Orthodox Christians, they were Greeks, just like the Turcophone Orthodox Christians of Asia Minor who considered themselves Greeks, regardless of their mother tongue. Interestingly, Karolidis introduced his own case as the best example of this.[42] In his own words:

> Race is one thing; nation is another. We should distinguish *race* and *nationalité* from each other... While I have Greek ancestors, for certain reasons my fathers and grandfathers began to speak and use the Turkish language. The same could be said to those Greeks living in Macedonia. The Vlahs there, they are actually Greeks.[43]

Karolidis's definition of race ($\varphi \upsilon \lambda \acute{\eta}$ / *cins*) and nation ($\acute{\varepsilon} \vartheta \nu o \varsigma$ / *millet*) was intriguing. The former concerned only physical origins and did not necessarily determine one's ethnicity; the latter was a product of historical construction made up through common belonging or consciousness. Neither language nor blood could define one's ethnicity; in contrast, religion did make ethnicities, at least in the specific circumstances of the Greek East under the Islamic Ottoman state, where religion had always been the most important denominator of its subject peoples.[44]

In this way, Karolidis presented an image of an imperial domain, now under the Ottoman sovereignty, which had been distinguished by the continuous existence of Greeks endowed with their strong religious feeling as a binding element, in spite of the local population's various vernacular mother tongues. The Ottoman framework thus gave a concrete shape to his imagined geopolitical range of Hellenism. From this perspective he was able to view Ottoman Islam favorably and include the

---

42   *TV*, 117: 9–10. (MMZC Devre 1, Sene-i İçtimaiye 1, İçtima 22). See also Karolidis, *Peri tis ethnikis katagogis ton orthodoxon hristianon Syrias kai Palaistinis*, 39–40; Karolidis, "I Anatoliki Romylia kai o Ellinismos," 6: 56–58.

43   MMZC Devre 1, Sene-i İçtimaiye 2, İçtima 51: 564. The words *race* and *nationalité* in the second sentence were originally given in French.

44   For his definition of race and nation see Karolidis, *Istoria tou IXX aionos met'eikonon*, vol. 2, 148–55; idem, *Peri tis ethnikis katagogis ton orthodoxon hristianon Syrias kai Palaistinis*, 34–42. See also Skopetea, "Oi Ellines kai oi ehthroi tous," 12–13.

Greek experiences under Ottoman rule in the context of the history of the Greek nation with more subtlety than most of his Hellenic colleagues did. And this made it possible for Karolidis to view history with a kind of cultural relativist approach. He stated that one should pay suitable respect to Islamic ideology when studying the Muslim peoples of the East.[45] Moreover, Karolidis argued that the Turks introduced their own tradition of state building to the Greek East during the long decline of Byzantium.[46] Muslim Turks remained almost the only nation that was not Hellenized after their conquest of mainland Greece.[47] Karolidis referred not only to the Greeks but also to the Turks as an integral element of the history of the East, and described the Muslim Turk rulers such as the Seljuk monarchs in a fairly positive manner.[48] This is why Karolidis criticized the historiographical approaches of Ranke who ignored the contribution of Asiatic peoples in the history of Hellenism as well as Europe.[49] From these arguments it became apparent that Karolidis's ideal vision of the East was a kind of dual monarchy of a Hellenized Empire: the Greek nation, as the leader of the Orthodox Christians, with the help of the Hellenic state, and the Ottoman Turks under the legitimate guidance of the Sultan-Caliph, should be the co-rulers of the East. What mattered was to construct an indigenous imperial domain within which the Greeks could enjoy their historical rights free from the Slavic and Western threats.

In light of these ideas it is not at all surprising that Karolidis considered the existence and integrity of the Ottoman Empire as invaluable for the future of Hellenism. Karolidis often expressed his conviction that the Hellenic state should not expand its territory at the expense of the Ottomans. This is what he had in mind when he declared that:

the Greeks look at Istanbul with good feelings. The Greeks want to see the Ottoman Empire performs its duties. We want the empower-

---

45 Karolidis, *Eisagogi eis tin Katholiki i Pagkosmia Istoria*, 209–21.
46 "Karolidi Efendi'nin Beyanatı," *İkdam*, November 24, 1908, 3.
47 Karolidis, *Istoria tou IXX aionos met'eikonon*, vol. 2, 62–63.
48 Karolidis, *Enheiridion Vyzantinis Istorias*, 224–26, 256–90; Karolidis, *O aftokrator Romanos o Diogenis*. See also Skopetea, "Oi Ellines kai oi ehthroi tous," 13.
49 Karolidis, *Eisagogi eis tin Katholiki i Pagkosmia Istoria*, 167–79.

ment of the Ottoman governance. Only in this way could the Greeks put their fundamental historical mission into effect.[50]

Or, in other words,

We the Greeks want the constitutional government to continue in the Ottoman state and this land to progress for the sake of our own national interest... Our sole wish is the territorial integrity of the Ottoman Empire. Friendship between the Turks and the Greeks should be manifest in the Chamber of Deputies.[51]

Therefore, Karolidis was critical of the hawkish faction within the Hellenic state as well as the abusive attitudes Hellenic diplomats adopted on Ottoman soil.[52] In fact, the significance of the Ottoman Empire was not confined to the Orthodox Greeks only. In order for many indigenous peoples of the East to remain independent in an age of Western imperialism, the Ottoman framework was so useful that they would have prayed God to create it had there not been an imperial domain such as the Ottomans'.[53] This resulted in the Greeks' wish to cooperate with the Turks. Indeed, according to Karolidis, this collaboration had already been realized throughout the nineteenth century.

During the reign of Abdülaziz (1861–76), the highest freedom was given in the Ottoman Empire to all the *mission civilizatrice* deriving from Greece and the Greek element... Constantinople then turned out to be the great center of the civilizing Greek element... Economically Turkey became a Greek state with all economic life and public works performed by Greeks and through Greek capital. Greek and unprejudiced foreign critics thought that the Hellenization of the great Ottoman state was only a question of time.[54]

---

50 MMZC Devre 1, Sene-i İçtimaiye 3, İçtima 13: 328.
51 "Karolidi Efendi'nin Beyanatı."
52 MMZC Devre 1, Sene-i İçtimaiye 2, İçtima 92: 1729. See also Karolidis, *Logoi kai Ypomnimata*, 44–45, 237–40; idem, *Synhronos Istoria ton Ellinon*, vol. 2, 263–70, 276, 284; Karolidis, *Istoria tou Ellinikou Ethnous tomos ektos*, Part 2, 64–70, 75–81, 88–92, 119.
53 *TV*, 290: 11. (MMZC Devre 1, Sene-i İçtimaiye 1, İçtima 115).
54 Karolidis, *Istoria tou Ellinikou Ethnous tomos ektos*, Part 2, 393.

This is how Karolidis described the Greek experience in the Tanzimat period. And the Greeks had continued to prosper both under the Hamidian autocracy and after the Young Turk Revolution.

> The government of Abdülhamid II [1876–1909], despite all its dissatisfaction concerning the events that happened in Crete, never changed its tolerant policy toward its Greek subjects and their Church. From a general viewpoint it is possible to say that under Abdülhamid II, as under Abdülaziz I, the power and prosperity of the Greeks of the Ottoman Empire had come to the highest bloom... The Revolution of 1908 did not change this situation for the time being. It was cheered by the entire Greek nation with enthusiasm brought about by the Revolution, and there emerged a great hope for an immediate transformation of the Turkish state to a Greek one as well as the resurrection of Byzantium.[55]

This thought had, at least according to Karolidis, wide popularity among his fellow Ottoman Greeks.

> From among the frequently repeated frictions between Greece and Turkey there emerged and gradually increased an idea of rapprochement towards Turkey, for strengthening the place and influence of the Greek element in the great empire, ethically helped by free Greece, in order for the Turkish state to become a Helleno-Turkish state.[56]

However, this vision of Hellenizing the Empire was doomed to failure by the Balkan Wars.

THE BALKAN WARS AND AFTER

Karolidis's career as an imperial historian ended with the fall of the Empire. He left the Ottoman territory after the outbreak of the Balkan Wars of 1912–13 of which he was a fervent opponent. To attack the Ottoman

---

55 Karolidis, *Istoria tou Ellinikou Ethnous tomos ektos*, Part 2, 115.
56 Karolidis, *Istoria tou Ellinikou Ethnous tomos ektos*, Part 2, 393.

refuge through an alliance with the Slavs was, in his eyes, a nightmare. Karolidis held the "Old Turks" as well as the League responsible for this calamity.

In the first place it was the Old Turks, not the Young Turks, who created the preconditions of the war. In July 1912, the Unionists fell from power due to the intervention of the Old Turks. The anti-Unionists, with whom the League had collaborated during the 1912 general election, welcomed this intervention. With the Libyan War already in progress since September 1911, this crisis offered an invaluable chance for the Balkan alliance to attack the Ottomans. What was the Balkan alliance then? According to Karolidis it was nothing but a deceptive trap on the part of the Slavs to both betray the Greeks and expel the Turks. He criticized the Venizelist Hellenic government and the League for their disastrous decision to ally themselves with the Slavs.[57] It was the reason why Karolidis published his speeches and memoranda in a lengthy volume. He tried to convince his Greek readers that the League had made a wrong choice. By contrast, he had made his best endeavor to defend the interest of Hellenism, by performing his duty as an Ottoman deputy in collaboration with the Unionists.

Karolidis's sympathy towards the Turks and hatred towards the Slavs persisted. Recognizing the reality of the multi-ethnic and multi-religious Ottoman East, Karolidis continued to see the Turks as potential allies of the Greeks and struggled against the Venizelists who had promoted the policy of aggression towards the Ottomans. Remarkably, this belief did not change even after the demise of the Empire and the Asia Minor Catastrophe. Karolidis expressed his suspicion of the Balkan federation project despite its popularity among Balkan intellectuals in the late 1920s. Karolidis had no confidence in such a project in which the Slavs would participate as core members. On the contrary, Karolidis repeatedly reminded his readers about the lost chances of Hellenizing the Empire while arguing for the need to cooperate with the newly born secularist Turkish Republic. It seems that Karolidis still dreamed of the *Megali Idea* as a cultural and economic undertaking.[58]

---

57 Karolidis, *Logoi kai Ypomnimata*, 242–97; idem *Istoria tou Ellinikou Ethnous tomos ektos*, Part 2, 131–36, 157.

58 Karolidis, *Istoria tou Ellinikou Ethnous tomos ektos*, Part 2, 131, 390–96, 399–401, 407–10, 416.

Unfortunately, the years that followed the Balkan Wars left little room for such a vision to be realized. Neither the possibilities of coexistence between the Greeks and the Turks nor the religion-based administration could outlive the Empire in the turbulent years of the Balkan Wars, World War One, and the Asia Minor Catastrophe. Nevertheless, Karolidis's vision is of no small value when we analyze the Greeks' and the Ottomans' world views at the turn of the twentieth century. Karolidis was representative of the vision of a Hellenized yet multi-ethnic and multi-religious Empire of the East, as an indigenous regional order of its own.

CONCLUSION

Pavlos Karolidis was an extraordinary figure. He was at one and the same time Greek and Ottoman, historian and politician. His vision of the Greek East reflected a patriarchal and religious version of Helleno-Ottomanism in an age of secular constitutionalism. Espousing religion as the basis of imperial polity, this vision was conditioned geopolitically by the actual expansion of the area now under Ottoman sovereignty.

His pro-CUP and anti-League activity might not find a comfortable place in today's Greek historiography which tends to be critical to the Unionists and to praise the League's self-proclaimed project of Balkan federation. However, he was definitely not alone. We can find many similarities between his historiographical as well as geographical view and the ideas of many of his compatriots, especially in underlining the significance of Byzantium and Orthodoxy in the history of Hellenism, while supporting the anti-Slavic and anti-European indigenous regional order with its dual universal center of the Sultan-Caliph and the Ecumenical Patriarch.

In a sense, Karolidis synthesized the Greek historiographies on both shores of the Aegean, namely of both the Ottoman and the Hellenic backgrounds. On the one hand, he inherited Paparrigopoulos's rediscovery of Byzantium as mediaeval Hellenism, which constituted a milestone in the development of modern Greek historiography.[59] On the other hand, in his emphasis on the value of Orthodoxy he had much more in common

---

59   Kitromilides, "On the Intellectual Content of Greek Nationalism," 25–33.

with his Ottoman Greek colleagues, who considered the Ecumenical Patriarchate as *the* guardian of their historical continuity. They took the role of the Great Church for granted when it came to the Greeks' rights and privileges.[60]

As is demonstrated by the ideas of Karolidis, historical writing, at least until the eve of World War One, did not necessarily exclude, from a political as well as an ideological standpoint, the existence and role of one's partner nation(s). In the particular case of the Greeks, the Turks were seen as potential allies. It must be pointed out, however, that the Turks' and Greeks' perceptions of their own pasts were asymmetrical even if they shared the same historical geography. The Muslim Turks, when they rediscovered their legacy from Byzantium, did not feel any obligation to share it with the Greeks; it was simply what fell to their lot through the conquest of Constantinople.[61] The Greeks had to comply with the reality of Ottoman rule, no matter how their ecumenical vision tempted them to imagine a Helleno-centric world order of their own. Therefore, just as Karolidis did in his historical writings, the Greek intellectuals could only vacillate between two poles: to attack the "Turkish yoke," or to evaluate the Ottoman imperium and the Greeks' roles within it as their own positive experiences.

As Stamatopoulos has articulated, Byzantium provided the intellectuals of the Balkans and the Near East with an important point of reference when they ventured to construct their own versions of imagined historical geography.[62] In this context, it will be of great value if we analyze modern Ottoman history and historiography in a truly multi-ethnic and multi-religious manner, through a comparative approach that takes into account the multiple viewpoints of its various subject peoples, Muslims and non-Muslims alike. In the case of the Greeks, for example, their historiographical endeavors can be understood properly only when situated within the background and context of both the Ottoman and Hellenic intellectu-

60   See, for example, the historical writings of Karolidis's contemporary Ottoman Greeks as examined in the following works: Hamoudopoulou-Konstantinidou, *Smyrni-Konstantinoupoli-Athina, 1870–1908*, 375–99; Kechriotis, "On the Margins of National Historiography," 124–42.

61   Ursinus, "Byzantine History in late Ottoman Turkish Historiography," 211–22; Ursinus, "From Süleyman Pasha to Mehmet Fuat Köprülü," 305–14.

62   Stamatopoulos, *To Vyzantio meta to ethnos.* See also Vovchenko, "Modernizing Orthodoxy," 295–317 for how the Russians used Byzantium in their historical writings.

al milieus. Karolidis was one such figure who tackled the problem of historiographical reinterpretation of the Ottoman imperial domain for the sake of Hellenism. The Balkan Wars, however, put an end to that project by destroying any possibility of Hellenizing the Empire without alienating the Turks. After the subsequent years of war, both Kemalist Turkey and Venizelist Greece abandoned the hitherto valid multi-ethnic and multi-religious style of nation-building and pursued their respective plans of building an ethnically monolithic nation state. Accordingly, historical writings in both states were henceforth strongly expected to serve their respective projects of ethnically monolithic national history; hence Karolidis's subsequent oblivion in the context of Ottoman as well as Greek intellectual histories.

REFERENCES

Ahmad, Feroz. *The Young Turks: The Committee of Union and Progress in Turkish Politics, 1908–1914*. Oxford: Clarendon Press, 1969.

Akbayrak, Hasan. *Milletin Tarihinden Ulusun Tarihine: İkinci Meşrutiyet'ten Cumhuriyet'e Ulus-Devlet İnşa Sürecinde Kurumsal Tarih Çalışmaları* [From Millet's history to Ulus's history: organizational historiographical works in the nation-state construction process from the second constitutional period to the republic]. Istanbul: Kitabevi, 2009.

Akşin, Sina. *Jön Türkler ve İttihat ve Terakki* [Young Turks and the Union and progress]. Istanbul: Remzi, 1987.

Anagnostopoulou, Sia. "To telos tis aftokratorikis logikis, to telos tis aftokratorikis Konstantinoupolis: i megali peripeteia" [The end of imperial logic, the end of imperial Constantinople: the great venture]. In *Mnimi Penelopis Stathi: Meletes Istorias kai Philologias* [In memory of Penelope Stathi: studies in history and literature]. Edited by Kostas Lappas et al., 483–503. Iraklio: Panepistimiakes Ekdosis Kritis, 2010.

———. *Mikra Asia, 19os aionas–1919. Oi Ellinorthodoxes koinotites: Apo to millet ton Romion sto Elliniko ethnos* [Asia Minor, from the nineteenth century to 1919: Greek Orthodox societies from the Rum Milleti to the Hellenic nation]. Athens: Ellinika Grammata, 1998.

Anagnostopoulou, Sia, and Matthias Kappler. "Zito Zito o Soultanos/Bin Yaşa Padişahımız: The Millet-i Rum Singing the Praises of the Sultan in the Framework of Helleno-Ottomanism." *Archivum Ottomanicum* 23 (2005/2006): 47–78.

Arai, Masami. *Turkish Nationalism in the Young Turk Era*. Leiden: E.J. Brill, 1992.

Augustinos, Gerasimos. *The Greeks in Asia Minor: Confession, Community, and Ethnicity in the Nineteenth Century*. Kent, OH: Kent State University Press, 1992.

Boura, Catherine. "The Greek Millet in Turkish Politics: Greeks in the Ottoman Parliament (1908–1918)." In *Ottoman Greeks in the Age of Nationalism: Politics, Economy, and Society in the Nineteenth Century*. Edited by Dimitri Gondicas and Charles Issawi, 193–206. Princeton: The Darwin Press, 1999.

Chatziiosif, Christos. "I bel epok tou kefalaiou" [The belle époque of capital]. In *Istoria tis Elladas tou 200u aiona: Oi Aparhes 1900–1922* [History of twentieth century Greece: the beginning, 1900–1922], edited by Christos Chatziiosif, vol. A., part 1, 309–49. Athens: Vibliorama, 1999.

Demirci, H. Aliyar. "1908 Parlamentosunda Meşrutiyetin Değerleri ve İlkeleri" [Constitutional values and principles in the 1908 Parliament]. *Doğu-Batı* 45 (2008): 83–104.

Ersanlı, Büşra. *İktidar ve Tarih: Türkiye'de "Resmî Tarih" Tezinin Oluşumu (1929–1937)* [Power and history: the formation of "official historiography" thesis in Turkey]. Istanbul: İletişim, 2003.

Exertzoglou, Haris. "The Development of a Greek Ottoman Bourgeoisie: Investment Patterns in the Ottoman Empire, 1850–1914." In *Ottoman Greeks in the Age of Nationalism: Politics, Economy, and Society in the Nineteenth Century*, edited by Dimitri Gondicas and Charles Issawi, 89–114. Princeton: The Darwin Press, 1999.

———. "To 'pronomiako' zitima" [The "privilege" question]. *Ta Historica* 16 (1992): 65–84.

———. *Ethniki taftotita stin Konstantinoupoli ton 190 aiona: O Ellinikos Filologikos Syllogos Konstantinoupoleos, 1861–1912* [Ethnic identity in nineteenth century Constantinople: the Hellenic Philological Society of Constantinople, 1861–1912]. Athens: Nefeli, 1996.

———. *Oi 'hamenes patrides' pera apo ti nostalgia: mia koinoniki-politismiki istoria ton Romion tis Othomanikis Aftokratorias, mesa 190u–arhes 200u aiona* ["Lost motherlands" beyond nostalgia: a sociocultural history of the Greeks of the Ottoman Empire, from the middle of the nineteenth to the beginning of the twentieth century]. Athens: Nefeli, 2010.

———. *Prosarmostikotita kai politiki omogeneiakon kefalaion. Ellines trapezites stin Konstantinoupoli: to katastima 'Zarifis-Zafeiropoulos', 1871–1881* [Adaptability and policy of Greek expatriate capital. Greek bankers in Constantinople: The Zarifis-Zafeiropoulos Branch, 1871–1881]. Athens: Idryma Erefnas kai Paideias tis Emporikis Trapezas Elladas, 1989.

Fujinami, Nobuyoshi. "Privileged but Equal: The Privilege Question in the Context of Ottoman Constitutionalism." In *Balkan Nationalism(s) and the Ottoman Empire*. Vol. III: *The Young Turk Revolution and Ethnic Groups*, edited by Dimitris Stamatopoulos, 33–59. Istanbul: Isis, 2015,

———. *The Ottomans and Constitutionalism: Politics, Religion, and Communities in the Young Turk Revolution*. Nagoya: The University of Nagoya Press, 2011 (in Japanese).

———. "'Church Law' and Ottoman-Greeks in the Second Constitutional Politics, 1910." *Études Balkaniques* 43, no.1 (2007): 107–32.

Hamoudopoulou-Konstantinidou, Virginia D. *Smyrni-Konstantinoupoli-Athina, 1870–1908. Minas D. Hamoudopoulos, 1843–1908, Megas Ritor tis Megalis tou Hristou Ekklisias, Dimosiografos-Istorikos-Geografos-Politikos Foreas tis Ellinorthodoxou Paradosis* [Izmir-Istanbul-Athens, 1870–1908: Minas D. Hamoudopoulos, 1843–1908, the great orator of the great Christian church, demographer, historian, geographer, and political conveyor of the Greek Orthodox tradition]. Athens: Armos, 2008.

Herzog, Christoph. "'Abd al-Ḥamīd az-Zahrāwī und das Problem des Osmanismus, 1908–1916." Magisterarbeit, Albert-Ludwigs-Universität zu Freiburg i. Br., n.d.

———. Geschichte und Ideologie: Mehmed Murad und Celal Nuri über die historischen Ursachen des osmanischen Niedergangs. Berlin: Klaus Schwarz Verlag, 1996.

Hulkiender, Murat. Bir Galata Bankerinin Portresi: George Zarifi (1806–1884) [Portrait of a Galata banker: George Zarifi (1806–1884)]. Istanbul: Osmanlı Bankası Arşiv ve Araştırma Merkezi, 2003.

İkdam [Ottoman newspaper]. "Karolidi Efendi'nin Beyanatı" [Comments of Karolidi Efendi]. November 24, 1908.

Kanner, Efi. Emfyles koinonikes diekdikiseis apo tin Othomaniki Aftokratoria stin Ellada kai tin Tourkia: O kosmos mias ellinidas hristianis daskalas [Social demands of gender from the Ottoman Empire to Greece and Turkey: the world of a Greek Christian teacher]. Athens: Papazissis, 2012.

———. Ftoheia kai filanthropia stin orthodoxi koinotita Konstantinoupolis, 1753–1912 [Poverty and philanthropy in the Orthodox community of Istanbul]. Athens: Katarati, 2004.

Kafadar, Cemal, and Hakan T. Karateke, "Late Ottoman and Early Republican Turkish Historical Writing." In The Oxford History of Historical Writing. Volume 4: 1800–1945, edited by Stuart Macintyre, Juan Maiguashca, and Attila Pók, 559–77. Oxford: Oxford University Press, 2011.

Karolidis, Pavlos. "I Anatoliki Romylia kai o Ellinismos: Thraki kai Makedonia" [Eastern Rumelia and Hellenism: Thrace and Macedonia]. Hellenismos 5 (1902): 730–45; 6 (1903): 42–61.

———. Anamniseis Skandinavikai: meta mikron simeioseon peri tou en Stokholmi kai Hristiania to 1889 synelthontos VIII diethnous synedriou ton asianologon [Scandinavian memories: with small notes on the Eighth International Conference of Asialogues held in Stockholm and Christiania in 1889]. Athens: ek tou Typografeio ton Adelfon Perri, 1890.

———. Istoria tis Ellados apo tis ypo ton Othomanon aloseos tis Konstantinoupoleos (1453) mehri tis vasileias Georgiou tou A [History of Greece from the conquest of Constantinople by the Ottomans (1453) to the reign of Georgios I]. Athens: Eleftheroudakis, 1925.

———. Istoria tou IXX aionos met'eikonon [The history of the nineteenth century with images], tomos B [vol. 2], (1821) 1830–1856. Athens: Ekdotis Georgios Kasdonis, 1892.

———. Eisagogi eis tin Katholiki i Pagkosmia Istoria [Introduction to universal and world history]. Athens: Ekdoseis adelfon Perri, 1894.

———. O aftokrator Romanos o Diogenis [Emperor Romanos Diogenes]. Athens: Syllogos pros Diadosin Ofelimon Vivlion, 1906.

———. Enheiridion Vyzantinis Istorias meta ton kyriotaton kefalaion tis loipis mesaionikis istorias pros hrisin ton foititon tis filologias [Companion to Byzantine history with the principal chapters on other medieval history, for the use of students of philology]. Athens: Nik. Tzokas, 1906.

———. Peri tis ethnikis katagogis ton orthodoxon hristianon Syrias kai Palaistinis [On the national origin of the Orthodox Christians of Syria and Palestine]. Athens: 1909.

———. *Logoi kai Ypomnimata. Logoi Apaggelthentes en ti Othomaniki Vouli kai Ypomnimata pemfthenta apo Konstantinoupoleos pros ton epi ton Exoterikon Ypourgon Georgion Valtatzin kai pros ton Proedron tis Kyverniseos k. E. Venizelon* [Speeches and memoranda: speeches delivered in the Ottoman Parliament and memoranda sent from Constantinople to the Minister of Foreign Affairs Mr. Georgios Valtatzis and Prime Minister Mr. E. Venizelos]. Athens: ek tou Typografeiou P. A. Petrakou, 1913.

———. *I Elliniki Vasileia os Megali Idea* [The Greek monarchy as Megali Idea]. Athens: ek tou Typografeiou Paraskeva Leoni, 1916.

———. *Synhronos Istoria ton Ellinon kai ton loipon laon tis Anatolis apo 1821 mehri 1921* [Contemporary history of the Greeks and other peoples of the Orient from 1821 to 1921]. Vols. 1–7. Athens: ek tou Typografeiou Alex. Vitsikounaki, 1922–29.

———. *Istoria tou Ellinikou Ethnous tomos ektos: apo tis teleftaias periodou tou Agonos tou 1821 mehri tou 1930* [History of the Greek nation volume six: from the last period of the struggle of 1821 until 1930]. Athens: Eleftheroudakis, 1932.

Kasaba, Reşat. "Economic Foundations of a Civil Society: Greeks in the Trade of Western Anatolia, 1840–1876." In *Ottoman Greeks in the Age of Nationalism: Politics, Economy, and Society in the Nineteenth Century*, edited by Dimitri Gondicas and Charles Issawi, 77–87. Princeton: The Darwin Press, 1999.

Kayalı, Hasan. *Arabs and Young Turks: Ottomanism, Arabism and Islamism in the Ottoman Empire, 1908–1918*. Berkeley: University of California Press, 1997.

Kechriotis, Vangelis. "A Cappadocian in Athens, an Athenian in Smyrna, and a Parliamentarian in Istanbul: The Multiple Personae and Loyalties of Pavlos Carolidis." In *Living in the Ottoman Realm: Empire and Identity, 13th to 20th Centuries*, edited by Christine Isom-Verhaaren and Kent F. Schull, 297–309. Bloomington: Indiana University Press, 2016.

———. "Celebration and Contestation: The People of Izmir Welcome the Second Constitutional Era in 1908." In *Mnimi Penelopis Stathi: Meletes Istorias kai Philologias* [In memory of Penelope Stathi: studies in history and literature], edited by Kostas Lappas et al., 157–83. Iraklio: Panepistimiakes Ekdosis Kritis, 2010.

———. "Greek-Orthodox, Ottoman Greeks or just Greeks? Theories of Coexistence in the Aftermath of the Young Turk Revolution." *Études Balkaniques* 41, no. 1 (2005): 51–71.

———. "On the Margins of National Historiography: The Greek İttihatçı Emmanouil Emmanouilidis—Opportunist or Ottoman Patriot?" In *Untold Histories of the Middle East: Recovering Voices from the 19th and 20th Centuries*, edited by Amy Singer et al., 124–42 London: Routledge, 2011.

———. "The Modernization of the Empire and the Community 'Privileges': Greek Orthodox Responses to the Young Turk Policies." In *The State and the Subaltern: Modernization, Society and the State in Turkey and Iran*, edited by Touraj Atabaki, 53–70. London: I. B. Tauris, 2007.

Kerimoğlu, Hasan Taner. *İttihat-Terakki ve Rumlar 1908–1914* [The Union and progress and the Greeks, 1908–1914]. Istanbul: Libra, 2009.

Kitromilides, Paschalis M. "On the Intellectual Content of Greek Nationalism: Paparrigopoulos, Byzantium and the Great Idea." In *Byzantium and the Modern Greek Identity*, edited by David Ricks and Paul Magdalino, 25–33. Aldershot: Ashgate, 1998.

———. "The Legacy of the French Revolution: Orthodoxy and Nationalism." In *Cam-*

bridge History of Christianity. Vol. 5, *Eastern Christianity*, edited by Michael Angold, 229–49. Cambridge: Cambridge University Press, 2006.

Koptaş, Murat. "Armenian Political Thinking in the Second Constitutional Period: The Case of Krikor Zohrab." Master's thesis, Bogaziçi University, 2005.

Kritovulos, Michael. *Tarih-i Sultan Mehmet Han Sani* [History of the Sultan Mehmet II]. Translated by Pavlos Karolidis. Istanbul: Ahmet İhsan ve Şürekası Matbaacılık Osmanlı Şirketi, 1328.

Meclis-i Mebusan Zabıt Ceridesi [Proceedings of the Ottoman Chamber of Deputies].

Neumann, Christoph K. *Das indirekte Argument: ein Plädoyer für die Tanzīmāt vermittels der Historie: die geschichtliche Bedeutung von Aḥmed Cevdet Paşas Ta'rīḫ*. Münster: Lit, 1994.

Noutsos, Panagiotis. "The Role of the Greek Community in the Genesis and Development of the Socialist Movement in the Ottoman Empire: 1876–1925." In *Socialism and Nationalism in the Ottoman Empire 1876–1923*, edited by Mete Tunçay and Erik J. Zürcher, 77–88. London: British Academic Press, 1994.

Panayotopoulos, A. J. "The 'Great Idea' and the Vision of Eastern Federation: A Propos of the Views of I. Dragoumis and A. Souliotis-Nicolaïdis." *Balkan Studies* 21, no. 2 (1980): 331–65.

Panayotopoulos, Alkis J. "On the Economic Activities of the Anatolian Greeks, Mid-19th Century to Early 20th." *Deltio Kentrou Mikrasiatikon Spoudon* 4 (1983): 87–128.

Papadopoullos, Theodore H. "Nouvelle Rome: aspects de l'œcuménisme orthodoxe post-byzantin." In *Atti del I Seminario Internationale de Studi Storici "Da Roma alla Terza Roma," April 21–23, 1981*. Roma, 1981.

Skopetea, Elli. "Oi Ellines kai oi ehthroi tous: i katastasi tou ethnous stis arhes tou 20ou aiona" [The Greeks and their enemies: the situation of the nation in the early 20th century]. In *Istoria tis Elladas tou 20ou aiona: Oi Aparhes 1900–1922* [History of twentieth century Greece: the beginning, 1900–1922], edited by Christos Chatziiosif, vol. A, part 1, 9–35. Athens: Vibliorama, 1999.

———. *To 'Protypo Vasileio' kai i Megali Idea: opseis tou ethnikou provlimatos stin Ellada, 1830–1880* [The "ideal kingdom" and the Megali Idea: aspects of the national problem in Greece]. Athens: Polytypo, 1988.

Stamatopoulos, Dimitris. "Ecumenical Ideology in the Orthodox Millet (19th–20th c.)." In *Economy and Society on Both Shores of the Aegean*, edited by Lorans Tanatar Baruh and Vangelis Kechriotis, 201–47. Athens: Alpha Bank Historical Archives, 2010.

———. *Metarrythmisi kai ekkosmikefsi: pros mia anasynthesi tis istorias tou Oikoumenikou Patriarheiou ton 19o aiona* [Reform and secularization: towards a reconstruction of the history of the Ecumenical Patriarchate in the nineteenth century]. Athens: Alexandreia, 2003.

———. "From Millets to Minorities in the 19th-Century Ottoman Empire: An Ambiguous Modernization." In *Citizenship in Historical Perspective*, edited by S. G. Ellis, G. Hálfadanarson and A.K. Isaacs, 253–73. Pisa: Edizioni Plus–Pisa University Press, 2006.

———. *To Vyzantio meta to ethnos: To provlima tis syneheias stis balkanikes istoriografies* [Byzantium after the nation: the problem of continuity in Balkan historiographies]. Athens: Alexandreia, 2009.

———. *Byzantium after the Nation: The Problem of Continuity in Balkan Historiographies.* Budapest: CEU Press, 2021.

Stavrou, Theofanis G. "Russian Policy in Constantinople and Mount Athos in the Nineteenth Century." In *The Byzantine Legacy in Eastern Europe*, edited by Lowell Clucas, 225–49. Boulder: East European Monographs (distributed by Columbia University Press), 1988.

Strauss, Johann. "The Greek Connection in Nineteenth-Century Ottoman Intellectual History." In *Greece and the Balkans: Identities, Perceptions and Cultural Encounters since the Enlightenment*, edited by Dimitris Tziovas, 47–67. Aldershot: Ashgate, 2003.

———. "The Millets and the Ottoman Language: The Contribution of Ottoman Greeks to Ottoman Letters (19th–20th Centuries)." *Die Welt des Islams* 35, no. 2 (1995): 189–249.

Takvim-i Vekayi [Official paper of the Ottoman Empire].

Toprak, Zafer. "Bir Hayal Ürünü: İttihatçıların 'Türkleştirme Politikası'" [An imaginary product: the "Turkification policy" of the Unionists]. *Toplumsal Tarih* 146 (2006): 14–22.

Ursinus, Michael. "Byzantine History in late Ottoman Turkish Historiography." *Byzantine and Modern Greek Studies* 10 (1986): 211–22.

———. "From Süleyman Pasha to Mehmet Fuat Köprülü: Roman and Byzantine History in Late Ottoman Historiography." *Byzantine and Modern Greek Studies* 12 (1988): 305–14.

Veremis, Thanos. "The Hellenic Kingdom and the Ottoman Greeks: The Experiment of the 'Society of Constantinople.'" In *Ottoman Greeks in the Age of Nationalism: Politics, Economy, and Society in the Nineteenth Century*, edited by Dimitri Gondicas and Charles Issawi, 181–91. Princeton: The Darwin Press, 1999.

Vovchenko, Denis. "Modernizing Orthodoxy: Russia and the Christian East (1856–1914)." *Journal of the History of Ideas* 73, no. 2 (2012): 295–317.

———. "Creating Arab Nationalism? Russia and Greece in Ottoman Syria and Palestine (1840–1909)." *Middle Eastern Studies* 49, no. 6 (2013): 901–18.

Ariadni Moutafidou

International Crisis and Empire:
Muslim and Jewish Solidarity with the Ottoman
Imperial Ideal in the Greek-Ottoman War of 1897

The Greek-Ottoman War of 1897 shifted the focus of Europe to the Near East. Although the Balkans were not the first priority as a target of the imperialist policies of the Great Powers at the end of the nineteenth century, because of the transition from European to world policy and the enlargement of the Great Powers' field of action, they were still highly important due to the immense economic interests in the region. For the Ottoman Empire, this was the first confrontational war since the beginning of Abdülhamid's reign in the 1870s, a conflict that the sultan had been eager to avoid. The crisis challenged the Hamidian state to defend the Ottoman territory effectively, after the introduction of military reforms according to the European model, and to pursue and promote the rights of the Empire in the international arena. For the non-Christian populations of the Ottoman Empire, the crisis functioned to unify and solidify the imperial ideal. The imperial reaction to the Southeastern European nationalisms drew the non-Christian populations closer together around the imperial central power. It was motivated not only by loyalty to the dynasty, even under an autocratic regime, but also by the need to preserve a safe Ottoman homeland. Abroad, whether in the small national states of Southeastern Europe, or in the multinational empires of Austria-Hungary and Russia or in the colonial empires of the Great Powers, the reactions of solidarity and the public display of support for the Ottoman cause, especially by the Muslim populations, were a clear sign of resistance to Christian sovereignty. On an official level, the Hamidian bureaucracy and the ruling elite ensured, organized and promoted the public displays of loyalty and unlimited support for the Muslim populations within the Empire. They pursued a course of action that would allow them to consolidate the Hamidian regime and later on, push for their rights and demands regarding the desirable benefits of swift Ottoman victory against the preponderance of European Powers in the diplomatic field. The Ottoman imperial state and its ruling elite were actors in the power game of the Great Powers, since they were accepted and considered themselves to be part of the European system and its interstate arena.

During his reign, Abdülhamid II succeeded in reinstating the absolute authority of the sultanate, establishing a centralized state bureaucracy that he oversaw closely. Throughout the Hamidian era, the sultan, his government, and the entire Hamidian bureaucracy used unprecedented means to reinforce the legitimacy of the imperial power within the Ottoman Empire and abroad. Absolutism and Panislamism formed the pillars of the Hamidian regime. The modern state, as it is perceived today, was shaped within the Ottoman Empire only after the Tanzimat reforms in 1839. It has been argued that the Ottoman state enjoyed a better administration and was stronger after the reforms of the mid-nineteenth century than it was at the end of the eighteenth century. The modern autocratic government of Abdülhamid II secured his absolute authority through the control of state power never known before. Even so, there were limits to his power and authority, and Abdülhamid had to deal with the ruling elite and the Empire's diverse populations. The palace and the Hamidian state apparatus controlled the rest of the executive government and all the populations of the Empire, and all facets of life in the center and the provinces. Serious efforts were made to establish a secular foundation for the state ideology through the use of traditional religious motives, Islamic vocabulary and Islamic ideological tools to create new forms of association. Abdülhamid II used his title as caliph to build some degree of unity and solidarity among Ottoman Muslims within the Empire and to solidify the support of overseas Muslims, while at the same time creating distraction and harassment for the European imperial powers. The Ottoman Caliphate as an institution was widely accepted by Muslims within and outside the empire at least until the end of the Ottoman state. The Hamidian regime used all available means (press, telegraph, telegrams, etc.) to mobilize the center and the periphery, to create new patterns and to form the prototypes of heroes and patriots within the Empire, but also to defend its positions and image abroad and to promote Ottoman demands in the international scene. In Europe, the Hamidian regime pursued the narrative of "we are like you." Reciprocity was the principle of legitimacy. In the international field, the Ottomans had to reestablish their legal rights as a member of the European concert, as it had been acknowledged officially after the Crimean War in the peace treaty of Paris in 1856.[1]

The present study will investigate the reactions, mobilization and solidarity of Muslim and Jewish communities in regard to the Ottoman imperial ideal, and will explore the functioning of control mechanisms and the strategies of power legitimation of the Hamidian regime in a crisis situation at the end of the nineteenth century, namely the Greek-Ottoman War of 1897.

Solidarity and Mobilization

The Greek-Ottoman War of 1897 belongs to the history of the Eastern question, and specifically of the Cretan question, the intensification of which was one of the major causes for the outbreak of the war. The conflict of 1897 is a typical case of "peripheral imperialism," meaning the peripheral party provoked action in order to achieve intervention at the center. Before the First World War, the small nation states disposed of a broader field of action due to the existing intertwining of alliances and the larger opportunities for exerting pressure on the Great Powers than they would have from the interwar period and beyond. Although for different reasons, neither the Greek government and King, nor the sultan wished the outbreak of the war. In addition to the economic difficulties the Ottoman Empire had to deal with (the International Financial Control was already imposed on it), Abdülhamid feared that the outbreak of war would provoke a general uprising in Macedonia and carry along with it all the states of Southeastern Europe. European diplomats in Istanbul

---

1 Deringil, *The Well-Protected Domains*; Findley, *Bureaucratic Reform in the Ottoman Empire: The Sublime Porte 1789–1922*, 224–290; Shaw and Shaw, *History of the Ottoman Empire and Modern Turkey*, 206–218; Karpat, *The Politicization of Islam*; Kayali, *Arabs and Young Turks*, 30–38; Hoyle and Williams, "Perceptions of Hamidian Legacies: An Institutional Analysis of the Legacy of the Hamidian Caliphate," 147–162.

also reported the sultan's fears of victorious generals endangering his personal safety and threatening his absolute power. However, Abdülhamid had to deal with the strong pressure of public opinion, the council of ministers and a strong war party. The war ended within a month with an overwhelming Ottoman victory and was too short for the Balkan national states to escalate the conflict into a major conflagration.[2]

The crisis itself led to the confrontation with the other, namely with the Christians within the Empire and abroad, and was actually on its own a factor of solidification. The war intensified tensions not only between Muslims and Greeks, but between Muslim and Christian populations throughout the Ottoman Empire,[3] and promoted the solidarity and mobilization of Muslim and Jewish communities for the imperial cause.[4] Muslim and Jewish refugees from Crete[5] sought refuge in the large cities such as Istanbul and Salonica (Thessaloniki) which contributed to the sentiments of rage and fear of the non-Christian populations, further pressuring the sultan to undertake aggressive action against the Hellenic Kingdom, and thereby intensified the prevailing panic. In an analogous way the Christian refugees from Crete, who sought refuge mainly in Athens, strongly influenced Greek public opinion, exerting pressure on the Hellenic government that was initially reluctant to get involved in Crete, but finally had to give way and send the Greek fleet to the island. From the very beginning of the Cretan crisis and shortly after the outbreak of the war, a general agitation was observed among the Muslim population of the Ottoman Empire. The activities of the Greek irregular units in the Ottoman territory,[6] the advance or the expected or even rumored mobi-

---

2   Moutafidou, *Beitrag zur Konflikt- und Allianzforschung vor dem Ersten Weltkrieg. Die Politik Österreich-Ungarns gegenüber dem osmanisch-griechischen Krieg von 1897*, 13–17, 33–34. See also Papadopoulos, *England and the Near East, 1896–1898*, 139, 145.

3   Passim, Haus-, Hof- und Staatsarchiv Wien (henceforth: HHStA Vienna), Politisches Archiv (henceforth: PA) XVI, box 83 and 84. On the period before the outbreak of the war, see: Lévy, "Salonique et la guerre gréco-turque de 1897: Le fragile équilibre d'une ville ottomane," 72–75; Cohen, "Between Civic and Islamic Ottomanism: Jewish Imperial Citizenship in the Hamidian Era," 244–247.

4   Lévy, "Salonique," 54–57, 87–90; Cohen, "Between Civic and Islamic Ottomanism," 244–247.

5   Shaw and Shaw, *History of the Ottoman Empire*, 206–207; Cohen, "Between Civic and Islamic Ottomanism," 244–247; Pierron, *Juifs et Chrétiens de la Grèce moderne. Histoire des relations intercommunautaires de 1821 à 1945*, 42–45.

6   On the activities of the irregular bands and the uprising of the Greek populations of the Ottoman Empire as reported by the representatives of Austria-Hungary, see Moutafidou, *Beitrag*, 39–41. On

lization of the Greek army, and the dreaded prospect of the arrival of the Greek fleet in the large Ottoman ports (especially Salonica) caused a fear of excesses and therefore panic among the local populations in Izmir, Salonica, Ioannina, Manastir, Kavala, and other areas, that was easily transformed into anti-Christian wrath. In Ioannina, the Muslim population left the city en masse or fled to the fortress for protection. In Salonica, it was rumored that the vali had sent his family from the city for reasons of safety, a precautionary measure that heightened the general reigning panic. In Izmir, the initial turbulent public demonstrations of Greek patriotism enraged the Muslim crowd, but further upheavals were prevented after the joint intervention of the vali and the Greek consul. It was reported that in Izmir the constant agitation derived mainly from the *muhacir*, refugees from Bulgaria, Bosnia, and elsewhere, regions that had passed over to Christian dominion.[7] The *muhacir* manifested anti-Christian feelings and developed gradually a proto-social radicalism, due to their feelings of humiliation and the enmity that they had experienced from the Balkan Christians. In Scutari, on the eve of the war, troubles between the Catholic and Muslim communities, due to Catholic provocation, threatened to lead to further escalation, and this was prevented only by the intervention of the vali.[8] Violent confrontations were reported all over the Ottoman Empire from Scutari to Ankara and Izmir. In Salonica an episode of violence by the Muslim and Jewish crowd towards a convoy of Greek prisoners of war (among whom were Red Cross nurses) passing through the city, was widely reported by the local and international press and European representatives.[9] Fearing reprisals, the Israelites of Greece[10] addressed a letter to the Jewish community of the city. For Charles Allatini, son of the philanthropist Dr. Moïse Allatini, such persons were just

---

7   Jankó to Gołuchowski, Izmir, April 21, 1897, HHStA Vienna, PA XVI, box 83.
8   Lévy, "Salonique," 73–74; Cohen, "Between Civic and Islamic Ottomanism," 244.
9   Plessen to Hohenlohe, rep. no. 180, 1 enclosure, Athens, May 17, 1897, Politisches Archiv des deutschen Auswärtigen Amtes, Berlin (henceforth: PAAA Berlin), R12265.
10   On the Greek reactions to the Jewish population of Thessaly in 1897, see: Pierron, *Juifs et Chrétiens*, 48–52. Compare also with the differentiation made between the Greek Royal Army that was given strict orders against excesses and the Greek irregulars serving on a volunteer basis: Rozen, *The Last Ottoman Century and Beyond*, 135.

the Greek irregular bands and their activities in 1896–1897, see John S. Koliopoulos, *Brigands with a Cause: Brigandage and Irredentism in Modern Greece, 1821–1912*, 215–223.

"Jewish scamps."[11] The notables of the Jewish community of Salonica distanced themselves from the attitude of the mob, whose violent actions, as was pointed out by the representative of the *Alliance Israélite Universelle*, could "only fill with indignation all Christian and Jewish people who respected themselves."[12]

The Jewish communities were massively mobilized for the imperial cause in all the large cities such as Salonica, Istanbul, and Alexandria. Committees were created for the collection of money that was handed over to the Ottoman authorities for the needs of the war. The money derived mainly from two sources: the wealthiest members of the community, as in the case of the Allatini and Modiano families of Salonica—charity was one of the fundamental elements of legitimation of the elite of a city—and women's charity organizations such as Charity and Relief Society that served as models for similar Muslim women's organizations. Jewish voluntarism was only marginal (pharmacists and physicians serving in military hospitals, etc.).[13] It has been argued that during the crisis the Jewish elites showed their willingness to work within a framework of Islamic Ottomanism, in response to the Hamidian regime's mobilization of Islam.[14] Indeed, whether within the framework of civic or Islamic forms of imperial identification, the fact of the matter remained that the reasons for Jewish solidarity to the Ottoman cause were mainly the security that the community, in general terms, enjoyed within the Ottoman dominion in contrast to their experiences in European countries, and the fear of European anti-Semitism both in Central and Western, as well as in Eastern and Southeastern Europe. These fears increased, especially in the 1890's, with the arrival of Jewish fugitives who had escaped the pogroms in Russia and the Balkans. Additionally, the conflict and the developments in Macedonia made them fear a fragmentation of the broader geographic space that would damage the scope of their commercial enterprises.[15]

---

11 Officially, Charles Allatini pointed out to the English consul in Salonica that among a numerous Jewish population there were inevitably certain bad citizens. Molho, *Oi Evraioi tis Thessalonikis, 1856–1919. Mia idiaiteri koinotita*, 49–50.

12 Lévy, "Salonique," 70–72; Cohen, "Between Civic and Islamic Ottomanism," 244.

13 Lévy, "Salonique," 54–59, 87–91; Cohen, "Between Civic and Islamic Ottomanism," 244–247; Anastassiadou, *Salonique, 1830–1912. Une ville ottomane à l'âge des Réformes*, 407.

14 Cohen, "Between Civic and Islamic Ottomanism," 237–255.

15 Rozen, *The Last Ottoman Century*, 134–135, n. 11, 150–151; Lévy, "Salonique," 54–57, 87–89;

The Muslim community was mobilized mainly through the women's charity committees of the Red Crescent that were established with great success, especially during war periods, and which solemnly declared their active support of the imperial cause. The committees were established by well-to-do women of Muslim high society in all the big cities of the Empire, but also abroad. The sultan welcomed their work and devotion, but dissolved these committees after the end of each crisis, since the creation of new elites could become a potential threat to his absolute power.[16] Absolutism and Panislamism constituted the basis of the Hamidian regime.

VOLUNTARISM

Ottoman voluntarism within the Ottoman Empire was directed and organized by the Hamidian provincial administration in order to counteract Muslim national movements and to allow public manifestation of Muslim devotion towards the sultan, as was the case with the South Albanians. The latter action, at the initiative of the vali of Kosovo, marked the endeavors of the Ottoman state machinery to promote Albanian Muslim loyalty as a counter-weight to the Albanian autonomist movement that had developed after the congress of Berlin. The vali of Kosovo came to an understanding with the Albanian chiefs of Prizren, Kalkandelen and other districts and persuaded them to send volunteers to the war. In recognition of his services in that matter, the sultan conferred on the vali of Kosovo first class of the Order of Osmanieh. Indeed, the Albanian chiefs of Kalkandelen and other districts of the vilayet of Kosovo supplied 10,000 volunteers who were accepted officially by the vali. They were formed into separate companies, and were commanded by the chiefs of the clans to which they belonged.[17] These South Albanian vol-

Cohen, "Between Civic and Islamic Ottomanism," 247–249. Compare also with the reactions of the Israelites of Salonica in 1912 as reported by J. Cohen, the rector of the boys' school of the *Alliance Israélite Universelle;* M. Allatini, on the "Ottoman homeland," considered as their "most secure and firm basis," in Molho, *Oi Evraioi tis Thessalonikis,* 242–243.

16   Lévy, "Salonique," 89–90.

17   Saurma to Hohenlohe, rep. No. 112, 1 enclosure, PAAA Berlin, R12255. See also Moutafidou, "Kosovo-Albaner als Freiwillige im osmanisch-griechischen Krieg von 1897," 287–290. On Albanian nationalism in the nineteenth century, see Clayer, *Aux origins du nationalisme albanais. La naissance d'une nation majoritairement musulmane en Europe*; Gawrych, *The Crescent and the Eagle: Ottoman Rule, Islam and the Albanians, 1874–1913.* Especially on Kosovo see Malcolm, *Kosovo—*

unteers were responsible for acts of violence and were unwanted and generally feared by both Muslim and non-Muslim populations, not only at the front and in the occupied regions of Thessaly and Epirus, but in all big cities and regions of the Ottoman Empire that lay in their path to and from the front.[18] The Hamidian bureaucracy used the press in order to promote the motif of an Albanian volunteer, a fourteen-year-old boy, who presented himself to the volunteer committee of Prizren and begged with tears in his eyes to fight for the sultan and who was rewarded for his loyalty by being accepted to serve as a personal guard of Abdülhamid. The sultan sent a telegraph with a special *Irade* ordering that the boy should be attached to his person with the rank of a sergeant. It was solemnly proclaimed by the press that even children were offering their services on behalf of "faith and country."[19]

A similar motif of devotion to the sultan by a Vlach volunteer hero and his ensuing reward was also promoted in the Ottoman press. Goltz, the organizer of the Ottoman military in the 1880's, reports of about 1,000 Catholic Vlachs from South Pindos whose volunteer services were not accepted by the Porte.[20] According to the Austrian-Hungarian envoy in Volos, an insignificant number of Vlach volunteers fought on the side of the Ottomans.[21]

Volunteers from abroad derived mainly from the Muslim communities of the former Ottoman provinces now incorporated in Christian national states (Thessaly, Greece)[22] or under European occupation (Bosnia, Austria-Hungary). Voluntarism in both cases was meant as an act of resistance to Christian sovereignty. It is characteristic that especially the Bosnian volunteers did not return to Bosnia after the end of the war,

---

A Short History; Clayer, "Kosova: The Building Process of a Territory from the Nineteenth to the Twenty-First Century," 79–92.

18 Moutafidou, *Beitrag*, 134–136. On the problems they caused on their way to and from the front, see also: Lévy, "Salonique," 38–39. Compare also Goltz, *Der Thessalische Krieg und die Türkische Armee*, 222–225; Gonzaga, *O ellinotourkikos polemos tou 1897 en Thessalia*, 60.

19 Saurma to Hohenlohe, rep. no. 112, 1 enclosure, PAAA Berlin, R12255.

20 Goltz, *Der Thessalische Krieg*, 224.

21 Marichich to Gołuchowski, rep. no. 57, Volos, July 4, 1897, HHStA, PA XVI, box 85. On the participation of Greek Vlach units fighting on the side of the Greeks, see e.g.: Sarantis, *To horio Perivoli Grevenon. Symvoli stin istoria tou armatolikiou tis Pindou*, 119ff.

22 Goltz, *Der Thessalische Krieg*, 23–24. Goltz claimed that in North Thessaly, with a majority Greek population, there was a Muslim community of about 40,000 people who provided the volunteers.

but joined the Bosnian revolutionary movement in Istanbul that was directed against Austria-Hungary and which had been established by Bosnian palace employees who were in contact with emigrants and Muslims in Bosnia. According to the doyen and ambassador of Austria-Hungary in the Ottoman capital, the movement was not supported by the official Ottoman state. The Italian press used the opportunity to denounce Austro-Hungarian sovereignty while promoting the unofficial irredentist aspirations of the Italians. The Italian newspapers were eager to present Bosnian voluntarism as a clear sign of the harsh and unbearable Austro-Hungarian rule in Bosnia-Herzegovina. They argued that the Bosnian volunteers preferred to leave their belongings and assets at home and live humbly in Turkey, rather than go back to Bosnia under Austrian-Hungarian occupation.[23]

Zionist voluntarism, even though extremely limited, reflected the endeavors of Theodor Herzl to promote his plans for the creation of a home in Palestine for all Jewish people recognized by the Ottoman state.[24] Herzl tried to support the Ottoman cause with collections of money and volunteer services. When the war broke out, Herzl was in Vienna and was preoccupied with preparations for the First Zionist Congress in Basel, Switzerland, with the help of the academic association Kadima (a name meaning "forward," or "to the East,"—in other words, to Palestine). Herzl's endeavors to collect money for the Ottoman wounded, to organize a mission of distinguished physicians of the General Hospital (*Allgemeines Krankenhaus*) in Vienna to the Ottoman General Staff, and afterwards to the front, were unsuccessful. Apart from his personal contribution no money was raised, while the mission of the General Hospital physicians could not be financed because of the high compensation demanded. In order to rescue himself from the importunities of the Ottoman ambassador of Vienna who was eager to receive the promised help,

---

23 Müller to Gołuchowski, rep. no. 43, 1 enclosure, Rome, August 2, 1897, HHStA Vienna, PA XII, box 168; Welsersheimb to Calice, tel. no. 843, Vienna, August 18, 1897, HHStA Vienna, PA XII, box 168; Calice to Gołuchowski, rep. no. 43E, Buyukdere, October 21, 1897, HHStA Vienna, PA XII, box 168. See also Moutafidou, *Beitrag*, 245–247.

24 On the official policy of the Ottoman state to Zionism and on Jewish immigration to Palestine at that time see Deringil, "Jewish immigration to the Ottoman Empire at the Time of the First Zionist Congresses: A Comment," 141–149. For the year 1897 up to the First Zionist Congress held in Basel from August 29–31, 1897, see Friedman, *Germany, Turkey and Zionism, 1897–1918*, 48–59.

Herzl persuaded five Zionist physicians belonging to Kadima[25] to offer their voluntary services at the Thessalian front under the aegis of the Red Crescent.[26] Even though the Sephardic Jews in Vienna held public prayers for the Ottoman state and later on sent their congratulations to the victorious Ottoman army,[27] there was clearly no general support for Herzl's pro-Ottoman actions, as was expected. Not only the Ottoman Jewish leaders,[28] but also, in this specific case, the Jewish community of Vienna distanced themselves from the Zionist movement. Only the Sephardic Jewish communities of Bulgaria, where Yosef Marco Barukh had considerable impact, were receptive to Zionism. Barukh was also an impressive exception to the rule with respect to Jewish solidarity to the Ottoman cause during the crisis. Barukh, "the classical political agitator," "a professional revolutionary par excellence,"[29] joined the Italian volunteers who fought along with the Greeks in Crete and later on at the Thessalian war front under the leadership of Ricciotti Garibaldi.[30] It has been argued that Barukh considered the Jews' fight for national restoration as a struggle for the honour of the Orient in general. Therefore, his enlisting with the Italian Garibaldians on the side of the Greeks was rather for reasons of tactical pragmatism. Although fighting for the Greeks, Barukh argued, he was actually struggling as a Jew, as a "Zionist." In 1898 he published in *Il Correo Israelitico* a series of articles on his experiences from the Greco-Ottoman War as a 'Jewish Garibaldian.'[31]

---

25 They were Philipp Schwarz, Albert Donreich, Metall, Schalit, and the Unitarian Gottlieb Stern. See: Rosenhek, *Festschrift zur Feier des 100. Semesters der akademischen Verbindung Kadimah, 1883–1933*, 90–93.

26 Rosenhek, *Festschrift*, 90–93. See also Moutafidou, "Alvanoi, Vosnoi, Evraioi Sionistes, ethelontes sto plevro ton Othomanon ston polemo tou 1897," 106–108.

27 Cohen, "Between Civic and Islamic Ottomanism," 245.

28 Cohen, "Between Civic and Islamic Ottomanism," 244.

29 Rozen, *The Last Ottoman Century*, 213, 214. Barukh "preached a halt to fundraising for the settling of Erez Yisrael and, at the same time, the taking up of arms to wrest it from the crumbling Ottoman Empire." He was therefore deeply disillusioned when he was informed that Herzl sought a meeting with the sultan.

30 Rozen, *The Last Ottoman Century*, 213–219. On the Italian volunteers in the Greek-Ottoman War of 1897, see Moutafidou, "Italian state politics and the disruptive factor of volunteer groups," 27–44; Liakos, "1897: Socialistes, garivaldinoi kai polemos" 163–177; Pécout, "Amitié littéraire et amitié politique méditerranéennes. Philhellènes français et italiens de la fin du XIXe siècle," 207–218.

31 Daccarett, "1890s Zionism Reconsidered: Joseph Marco Baruch," 328–329.

CELEBRATIONS AND NEGOTIATIONS

The victory over Greece was celebrated all over the Muslim world, a result of the active Panislamic policy of Abdülhamid in the previous years.[32] Massive demonstrations were directed against Greeks, Christians, and Europeans in Egypt, as well as in India, where millions of Muslims and Hindus celebrated the Ottoman victories, as reflected primarily by their strong opposition to British occupation. In Egypt, the Khedive Abba Hilmi Pasha and a strong Muslim party under the leadership of Muhtar Pasha adopted a rigid pro-Ottoman attitude in their endeavors to strictly apply the Ottoman decree on the expulsion of Greek subjects within fourteen days,[33] although in previous years, rivalry and tensions were reported[34] between the Egyptian leadership and the sultan. This pro-Ottoman attitude brought tension and a strong reaction from the British administration, since the decree could seriously damage the Egyptian and European economic interests.[35] As Lord Cromer put it, the Ottoman victories over Greece gave a serious encouragement to a small but powerful Muslim party that was opposed to British occupation.[36]

Moreover, the massive demonstrations of millions of Muslims, as well as Hindus,[37] that took place in India and their reactions and pro-Ottoman expressions of sympathy disturbed England, particularly in a period when the problems at the Northwestern frontiers were becoming acute. However, despite their investigations the British did not find any indications of an Ottoman conspiracy against British sovereignty in India as they had suspected. They concluded that Ottoman propaganda in India had a defensive rather than an aggressive character

---

32 Lewis, *The Emergence of Modern Turkey*, 334–337; Özcan, *Pan-Islamism: Indian Muslims, the Ottomans and Britain, 1877–1924*, 40–126; Hoyle and Williams, "Perceptions of Hamidian Legacies: An Institutional Analysis of the Legacy of the Hamidian Caliphate," 147–162.

33 Heidler to Gołuchowski, rep. no. 16, very confidential, Cairo, April 23, 1897, HHStA Vienna, PA XVI, box 83; Heidler to Gołuchowski, rep. no. 17, confidential, Cairo, April 28 and 30, 1897, HHStA Vienna, PA XVI, box 83. See Moutafidou, *Beitrag*, 42–45.

34 Deringil, *The Well-Protected Domains*, 144ff.

35 Moutafidou, *Beitrag*, 43–45.

36 Papadopoulos, *England and the Near East, 1896–1898*, 157–158.

37 Rémy to Gołuchowski, rep. no. 2 pol., 1 enclosure, Bombay, May 31, 1897, HHStA Vienna, PA XVI, box 84; Rémy to Gołuchowski, rep. no. 3 res, 1 enclosure, Bombay, June 2, 1897, HHStA Vienna, PA XVI, box 85. See Moutafidou, *Beitrag*, 130.

aimed at the strengthening and the consolidation of the spiritual position of the sultan.[38]

The echo of the Ottoman victory was so overwhelming and its impact so powerful that in 1899 the American Secretary of State, John Hay, asked for and indeed obtained the intervention of Abdülhamid in the Philippines, so that the Sulu Muslims of the islands did not join the revolutionaries, but recognized American sovereignty and put themselves willingly under the control of the American army.[39]

Due to the Ottoman victories, the prestige of the sultan as a Muslim leader was re-established all over the world, as was his image as a Triumphant Conqueror.[40] According to the words of a "Turkish gentleman" at the court of Istanbul, it was all due to "this rotten victory over Greece" that was still the country of Alexander the Great and the land of the wise for the uneducated Muslim.[41] These developments had an impact on the Young Turk movement that for a time underwent a temporary setback.[42] However, the German ambassador reported to Berlin that because of the unwarlike character of the sultan, a number of pashas with large followings had established a war party and the sultan was in danger of removal. Chancellor Hohenlohe went so far as to ask Murav'ev directly whether it would be advisable to give the sultan the necessary time to get rid of the members of the war party by the usual means. The Russian foreign minister answered that the Young Turk movement was no danger to the sultan.[43]

During the peace negotiations, resistance to the European demands was organized by the Hamidian bureaucracy in order to support the

38 Moutafidou, *Beitrag*, 130; Papadopoulos, *England and the Near East, 1896–1898*, 158–160, 160; Özcan, *Pan-Islamism*, 101–107. In India "very few Muslims knew or indeed cared to know the extent or the strength of the State of Greece. All they knew was that the Caliph's army defeated and destroyed Christian forces in Europe itself." Özcan, *Pan-Islamism*, 102.

39 Karpat, *The Politicization of Islam*, 234–235; Moskin, *American Statecraft: The History of the U.S. Foreign Service*, 204f.

40 See also Calice to Gołuchowski, rep. no. 19C, Istanbul, May 6, 1897, HHStA Vienna, PA XII, box 167.

41 Papadopoulos, *England and the Near East, 1896–1898*, 160.

42 Hanioğlu, *The Young-Turks in Opposition*, 95–100; Lévy, "Salonique," 159–160. Compare also with the uncovering in 1897 of a Young Turk conspiracy in Istanbul and the banishment of the seventy-eight conspirators to Fezzan in Libya; see also: Kayali, *Arabs and Young Turks*, 47; Clayer, *Aux origins du nationalisme albanais*, 335; Georgon, "Selanik musulmane et deunmé," 108.

43 Saurma to the Foreign Office, tel. no. 343, Pera, June 10, 1897, PAAA Berlin, R12271; Hohenlohe to Radolin (concept of Holstein), tel. no. 170, Berlin, June 11, 1897, PAAA Berlin, R12271. See Moutafidou, *Beitrag*, 130–131.

Ottoman cause and, specifically, to achieve the return of Thessaly. They used all available means and resources for the promotion of Ottoman demands in the media. The usual mobilization mechanisms came into operation. In addition to massive demonstrations in the capital and the big cities, resistance was also organized in all the provinces. The palace gave directives to the provincial governors, and consequently the notables edited and sent signed telegrams in the name of the Turkish people begging Abdülhamid to preserve Islamic dignity and not yield to European demands. The argument that Thessaly had been reconquered with the blood of the sons of the country was put forward and heatedly debated in educated circles in the capital and in the big cities. The news of massive demonstrations and the hundreds of telegrams from all over the provinces were relayed to the press in the interior and abroad in support of the argument that the sultan could in no way yield to the demands of the Great Powers since this would severely endanger his position because of public pressure.[44] Besides, as pointed out by the Ottoman ambassador in London to Lord Salisbury, while Great Britain insisted on the withdrawal of the Ottoman army from occupied Thessaly and its return to Greece, London did not consider doing the same in Egypt.[45] For the Hamidian regime, reciprocity was the essence of legitimacy.

In an analogous way, a major consequence of the Vlach petitions was orchestrated by the Hamidian regime in occupied Thessaly. The new Greek-Ottoman border of 1881 made difficulties for the nomadic life of the Vlachs and the whole directed action of petitions seemed to have taken advantage of the new circumstances. Telegrams with thousands of signatures of self-defined Vlachs from occupied Thessaly were sent to all European capitals requesting the return of the province to Ottoman sovereignty. The Greek Vlachs reacted strongly and denounced this orchestrated action to the Greek government and asked for protection. The Austro-Hungarian government, accused of being involved in that action, ordered an investigation in order to flush out the instigators and organizers. They came to the conclusion that the people signed under duress or for payment, and that

---

44 Moutafidou, *Beitrag*, 129–131.
45 Trauttenberg to Gołuchowski, Copenhagen, confidential letter, July 15, 1897, HHStA Vienna, PA XVI, box 86.

this so-called Vlach movement was directed by the Ottomans with the ultimate goal of the return of Thessaly to the Ottoman Empire.[46]

Though Ottoman victories considerably strengthened the position of the sultan, their influence also had limits. The official documentation of the Greek-Ottoman War of 1897 by the Jewish community of Istanbul, a product and a reflection of the Hamidian spirit, presented both the manifestation of the glory of the Ottoman victory, and concealed its unwanted limitations.[47] Minna Rozen argued that the Jewish ruling elite of Istanbul perceived the state environment they lived in as a world of safety, in which a victorious and powerful sultan would protect them from all evil. All manifestations of power and splendor were to be described in detail, whereas what was disputable should be made light of, embellished or passed over in silence.[48] The Greek-Ottoman War of 1897 was described accurately, since it was the perfect Ottoman victory of a triumphant Sublime Porte. The only minor detail that was omitted regarded "the small strategic regulation of the Thessalian border"—that is to say, the return of occupied Thessaly to Greece.[49] The known factor of the Christian population, liberated from Muslim rule and not returned to Muslim sovereignty, was still generally valid in the diplomatic scene.[50] Christian Europe was now the one to impose its will even after a victorious Ottoman outcome.

EPILOGUE: IN THE AFTERMATH OF WAR

On September 28, 1897, as the peace negotiations were slowly approaching an end and the Cretan question was still unsettled, a petition was sent

---

46 On the Vlach petitions, the reactions of the Great Powers, the Greek Vlachs and Greece, the Austrian-Hungarian investigations and the involvement of Romania, see Moutafidou, *Beitrag*, 136–140. On the Vlachs, see Veremis and Koliopoulos, *Ellas. I synchroni synecheia. Apo to 1821 mehri simera*, 105–107; Gounaris, "Vlachs and 'Their Own' History," 75–84; Gounaris and Koukoudis, "Apo tin Pindo sti Rodopi. Anazitontas tis engatastaseis kai tin taftotita ton Vlachon," 91–137.

47 The reign of Abdülhamid was the only one to be officially documented by the Jewish community of Istanbul. The documents were meant purely for internal use, not for public perusal. See Rozen, "The Hamidian Era Through the Jewish Looking-glass: A Study of the Istanbul Rabbinical Court Records," *Turcica* 37 (2005): 113–154.

48 Rozen, "The Hamidian Era."

49 Rozen, "The Hamidian Era," 121–122, 144–145.

50 Compare: Calice to Gołuchowski, Buyukdere, June 10, 1897, rep. no. 25B, 5 enclosures, HHStA, PA XVI, box 85. See also Moutafidou, *Beitrag*, 129.

by the mayor and the notables of Chania in the name of the Muslim people of Crete to the German foreign minister, who transmitted it immediately to all European capitals. The telegram pointed to the dimensions of the misery of the civilian non-combatant populations and to the work of Islamic philanthropy and the limitations it labored under, and thus pleaded for a speedy settlement of the Cretan crisis.

[Content] Tel. of the inhabitants of Crete. Prayer for help.
Tel. Chania, 27 September, 1897, 9:20
Arrival: 28 September, 1897, 12:30
Our situation is becoming unbearable. The winter approaches; we are more than 20,000 families without anything at all and living only on one hundred grams of flour that the Muslim charity is offering to us daily. Our Christian compatriots continue to burn our olive trees and the island soon will be cleared; at the same time and despite the rope around our throats that suffocates us they take the few herds that are remaining to us. The sowing season begins in October. If by then we do not return home, how shall we manage the sowing? To this point, public charity has spent more than one million francs and no guarantee exists that support will continue for a month. We too are creatures of God and in the name of humanity please hear our last cry to put an end to our desperate situation.

On behalf of the Muslims of Crete:
The mufti sherif Mayor of Chania Badrizade Bey.

The notables of Chania: Housseni Neym Begyzade, I. E. Bedri Bey Zade Ahmed, Nessimi Lielmizade, Zeki Sourourzade, Imbrahim Softazade, Nessib Chefik Effendi Zade.[51]

On a basic level, the document reflects, or rather sketches, the reality of the intolerable difficulties faced by civilian populations and refugees during crisis situations, revolts, revolutions and wars. An analogous pic-

---

51   Tel. of the mufti sherif mayor of Canea and the notables of Canea to the German foreign minister, Canea, September 27, 1897, PAAA Berlin, R12294. Translated from the French original by the author of the present study.

ture is depicted in the official steps taken by the Greek Foreign Office to draw the attention of the Great Powers to the desperate situation of the Greek refugees who came from Crete, Epirus and Thessaly after the Ottoman invasion and occupation of the Thessalian, which was the granary of the country, by the Ottoman troops.[52] As for the Muslim populations, following the position taken by the palace and the Hamidian bureaucracy, the local state representatives composed and addressed a telegram to Christian Europe giving expression to the desires of the Muslim refugees in Crete. In this case, too, the petitions were used by the central government as a strategic means of pressure and as a strong negotiating tool in the diplomatic field to drive forward Ottoman goals and demands for the settlement of the Cretan affair. The state machinery used all available modern means for the defense and promotion of Ottoman policy. The Ottoman elite wished to push forward the strategy of reciprocity, and to promote to the outer world the idea that "we are like you."

On another level, the representatives of the Muslim population of Crete addressed their petition explicitly to the German foreign minister. From the very beginning of the crisis, Berlin publicly displayed a provocative policy of Ottoman solidarity. Germany claimed the moral high ground as a defender of the Ottoman Empire in the political, economic and military sphere, and as a protector of the Muslim populations, thus breaking with its traditional role and with an imperial tradition of centuries. Setting aside official interstate policy and exchange, it is characteristic of the way ordinary Ottoman people seem to have perceived in this early stage the protective role of Germany in the person of the German Kaiser. It was widely reported by the press and by European representatives that in two Greek coffee houses in Salonica the pictures of the Kaiser had been defaced. The landlord and a number of customers who participated in this action were arrested immediately and the café was shut down by the police. The two porters who reported the defacement of the picture of Kaiser William II to the authorities were rewarded with gifts of money by the German consulate.[53] This rather insignificant episode could

---

52 Moutafidou, *Beitrag*, 111.
53 Marschall to Saurma, tel. no. 414, Berlin, May 12, 1897, Bundesarchiv Berlin (Federal Archiv Berlin, henceforth: BA Berlin), R901/33737; Plessen to Hohenlohe, rep. no. 146, 1 enclosure, Athens, April 23, 1897, BA Berlin, R901/33737.

be indicative of the way that the new German course and the new image of the German Empire and the Kaiser transgressed the broader Christian and Muslim masses, shaping new concepts of the enemy and the friend, and also of the way they were reflected in the tensions between the Ottoman Empire's religious communities. It should be remarked that the Sublime Porte superbly exploited the unlimited support of the German government in order to realize the Ottoman strategic military and political negotiation goals, although the Ottomans gave a clear preference to Russia, the powerful support of which was indisputably needed and built a major and undoubted priority for the Ottoman Empire.[54]

When Russia put forward the candidacy of a Christian governor in Crete in the person of Prince George of Greece,[55] Kaiser William warned of the risks from Muslim public opinion should the victorious sultan give away the "fruits of his victory."[56] But Germany was not in a position to win this fight and soon withdrew from the Concert of Europe. So did Austria-Hungary, which could by no means allow such a dangerous precedent to be set on the diplomatic scene, endangering its own existence as a multinational empire. It was not until another uprising took place in Crete that a final settlement was reached. In September 1898, a Muslim uprising in Chania led to the loss of the lives of several hundred Christians, fourteen British soldiers and the British Vice-Consul. The German emperor attempted to persuade the Tsar to adopt a pro-Ottoman attitude in order to save the sultan's position vis-à-vis his army and as Caliph vis-à-vis the whole Muslim world, and to take into consideration the possible Panislamic implications that could be exploited against or as a counterweight to the common British rival.

> "Remember," he wrote to Tsar Nicholas, "what you and I agreed upon at Peterhof—never to forget that the Mahometans were a tremendous card in our game in case you or I were suddenly confronted by a war

---

54 Moutafidou, *Beitrag*, 81–154; Moutafidou, Ariadni, "Der osmanisch-griechische Waffenstillstand von 1897," 73–79.

55 On diplomatic developments with respect to the Cretan crisis, see Driault and Lhéritier, *Histoire diplomatique de la Grèce de 1821 à nos jours*, 438–468; Langer, *The Diplomacy of Imperialism, 1890–1902*, vol. 1, 355–384, especially 377–379; Papadopoulos, *England and the Near East, 1896–1898*, 195–223.

56 Papadopoulos, *England and the Near East, 1896–1898*, 206–207.

with a certain meddlesome Power. ... If you quietly go on following the lead of the other Power in Crete as has been done till now, the effect will be deplorable upon your own Mahometan subjects and on Turkey, and you lose a most precious à tout out of your play." "Turkey is very much alive and not a dying man. Beware of the Musulmans if you touch their National honor or their Caliph."[57]

But the German empire was on its own in this estimation of the situation. Under the threat of coercive measures, the sultan was forced to yield, maintaining only a nominal sovereignty over the island. The appointment of Prince George of Greece, in November 1898, as High Commissioner of Crete was generally considered the first step to the union of the island with Greece. Just as Muslims were allowed to emigrate to Ottoman territory after the final peace agreement of 1897,[58] the final settlement of the Cretan question was followed by the departure of Muslim refugees to Anatolia.[59]

In the Greek-Ottoman War of 1897, the response to the threatening danger of the vehemence of Southeastern European nationalisms forged solidarity between non-Christian communities to the Ottoman imperial ideal within the empire and took, specifically in the case of Muslim populations, the shape of a clear reaction to Christian European rule and colonial imperialism abroad. The Great Powers were unanimously unwilling to allow the peace of Europe to be threatened in any way. Determined to preserve the status quo, the European powers defined decisively the limits of both the Greek defeat and of the Ottoman victory. The intense pressure put on the sultan by public opinion, the war party and the council of ministers, aimed for the adoption of a harder negotiating line towards the Great Powers, though, without sucess. All the same, the Ottoman Empire came out strengthened from that conflict, since the Ottoman victories raised Abdülhamid's prestige not only within the Empire but throughout

---

57 As cited in Papadopoulos, *England and the Near East, 1896–1898*, 222. In his visit to Syria in the year 1898, the Kaiser declared himself the friend of the three hundred million Muslims all over the world. Özcan, *Pan-Islamism*, 61–62.

58 Article 7, Traité de Paix Définitif, HHStA Vienna, PA XVI, box 87. Compare also with article 7 of the preliminary peace treaty: Article 7, Préliminaires de Paix Définitif, HHStA Vienna, PA XVI, box 87.

59 Shaw and Shaw, *History of the Ottoman Empire and Modern Turkey*, 206–207.

the Muslim world, and in Europe as well. The Cretan crisis and the Otto-man victory of 1897 showed Europe that the Ottoman Empire was capa-ble of resisting and defending itself, and that there was no immediate or imminent danger of rolling up the Eastern question. For the next decade the Near East was put on ice and played a clearly secondary role in Euro-pean international politics.

REFERENCES

Anastassiadou, Meropi. *Salonique, 1830–1912. Une ville ottomane à l'âge des Réformes*. Leiden and New York: Brill, 1997.

Clayer, Nathalie. *Aux origins du nationalisme albanais. La naissance d'une nation majori-tairement musulmane en Europe*. Paris: Karthala, 2007.

———. "Kosova: The Building Process of a Territory from the Nineteenth to the Twenty-First Century." In *Ottoman Legacies in the Contemporary Mediterranean: The Balkans and the Middle East Compared*, edited by Eyal Ginio and Karl Kaser, 79–92. Jerusalem: The European Forum of the Hebrew University of Jerusalem, 2013.

Cohen, Julia Phillips. "Between Civic and Islamic Ottomanism: Jewish Imperial Citizen-ship in the Hamidian Era." *International Journal of Middle East Studies* 44 (2012): 59–81.

Daccarett, Paula. "1890s Zionism Reconsidered: Joseph Marco Baruch." *Jewish History* 19, no. 3–4 (2005): 315–345.

Deringil, Selim. *The Well-Protected Domains*. London: I. B. Tauris, 2004.

———. "Jewish Immigration to the Ottoman Empire at the Time of the First Zionist Congresses: A Comment." In *The Last Ottoman Century and Beyond*. Vol. 2 of *Pro-ceedings of the International Conference on "The Jewish Communities in the Balkans and Turkey in the 19th and 20th Centuries through the End of World War II,"* edited by Min-na Rozen, 141–149. Tel Aviv: The Chair for the History and Culture of the Jews of Sa-lonica and Greece, The Goldstein-Goren Diaspora Research Center, 2002.

Driault, Edouard, and Michel Lhéritier. *Histoire diplomatique de la Grèce de 1821 à nos jours*. Vol. 4. Paris: Les Presses Universitaires de France, 1926.

Findley, Carter V. *Bureaucratic Reform in the Ottoman Empire: The Sublime Porte 1789–1922*. Princeton N.J.: Princeton University Press, 1980.

Friedman, Isaiah. *Germany, Turkey and Zionism, 1897–1918*. Oxford: Clarendon Press, 1977.

Gawrych, George W. *The Crescent and the Eagle: Ottoman Rule, Islam and the Albanians, 1874–1913*. London: I. B. Tauris, 2006.

Georgon, François. "Selanik musulmane et deunmé." In *Salonique, 1850–1918. La 'ville des Juifs' et le reveil des Balkans*, edited by Gilles Veinstein, 105–118. Paris: Editions Autre-ment, 1992.

Goltz, Colmar Freiherr von der. *Der Thessalische Krieg und die Türkische Armee. Eine kriegsgeschichtliche Studie*. Berlin: Ernst Siegfried Mittler und Sohn, 1898.

Gonzaga, Maurizio Ferrante. *O ellinotourkikos polemos tou 1897 en Thessalia* [The Greek-Ottoman War of 1897 in Thessaly]. Translated from the Italian by Eugenios Rizos Ragkavis. Athens: Ypourgeio Stratiotikon, 1906.

Gounaris, Basil C. "Vlachs and 'Their Own' History." *Etudes balkaniques* 5 (1997): 3–4.

Gounaris, Basil C., and Asteris I. Koukoudis. "Apo tin Pindo sti Rodopi. Anazitontas tis engatastaseis kai tin taftotita ton Vlachon" [From Pindos to Rodopi: in search of Vlach settlements and identity]. *Istor* 10 (1997): 91–137.

Hanioğlu, Şükrü M. *The Young-Turks in Opposition*. New York and Oxford: Oxford University Press, 1995.

Hoyle, Justin, and Paul Williams. "Perceptions of Hamidian Legacies: An Institutional Analysis of the Legacy of the Hamidian Caliphate." In *Ottoman Legacies in the Contemporary Mediterranean: The Balkans and the Middle East Compared*, edited by Eyal Ginio and Karl Kaser, 147–162. Jerusalem: The European Forum of the Hebrew University of Jerusalem, 2013.

Karpat, Kemal H. *The Politicization of Islam: Reconstructing Identity, State, Faith, and Community in the Late Ottoman State*. New York: Oxford University Press, 2001.

Kayali, Hasan. *Arabs and Young Turks: Ottomanism, Arabism, and Islamism in the Ottoman Empire, 1908–1918*. Berkeley: University of California Press, 1997.

Koliopoulos, John S. *Brigands with a Cause: Brigandage and Irredentism in Modern Greece, 1821–1912*. Oxford: Oxford University Press, 1987.

Langer, William Leonard. *The Diplomacy of Imperialism, 1890–1902*. Vol. 1. New York and London: Alfred A. Knopf, 1935.

Lévy, Noémi. "Salonique et la guerre gréco-turque de 1897: Le fragile équilibre d'une ville ottomane." University of Paris I, 2002.

Lewis, Bernhard. *The Emergence of Modern Turkey*. London and New York: Oxford University Press, 1961.

Liakos, Antonis. "1897: Socialistes, garivaldinoi kai polemos" [1897: socialists, Garibaldians and war] In *O polemos tou 1897. Diimero me tin efkairia ton 100 chronon (4 kai 5 Dekemvriou 1997)* [The War of 1897: two-day conference on the occasion of the 100th anniversary, December 4–5, 1997]. Athens: Etaireia Spoudon Neoellinikou Politismou kai Genikis Paideias, 1999.

Malcolm, Noel. *Kosovo—A Short History*. New York: New York University Press, 1998.

Molho, Rena. *Oi Evraioi tis Thessalonikis, 1856–1919. Mia idiaiteri koinotita* [The Jews of Thessaloniki: a unique community]. Athens: Themelio, 2001.

Moskin, J. Robert. *American Statecraft: The History of the U.S. Foreign Service*. New York: St. Martin's Press, 2013.

Moutafidou, Ariadni. "Alvanoi, Vosnoi, Evraioi Sionistes, ethelontes sto plevro ton Othomanon ston polemo tou 1897" [Albanians, Bosnians and Jewish Zionists in the Greek-Ottoman War of 1897: volunteers on the side of the Ottomans]. *Thessaliko Imerologio* 44 (2004): 102–108.

———. *Beitrag zur Konflikt- und Allianzforschung vor dem Ersten Weltkrieg. Die Politik Österreich-Ungarns gegenüber dem osmanisch-griechischen Krieg von 1897*. Hamburg: Dr. Kovač, 2003.

———. "Der osmanisch-griechische Waffenstillstand von 1897." *Südost-Forschungen* 52 (1993): 73–79.

———. "Kosovo-Albaner als Freiwillige im osmanisch-griechischen Krieg von 1897." *Biblos* (National Library, Vienna) 48 (1999): 287–290.

———. "'Restless Elements and the Worse Imaginable Riffraff': Italian Philhellenism and the Uncontrolled Dynamics of Volunteer Groups." In *Ausdrucksformen des europäischen und internationalen Philhellenismus vom 17.–19. Jahrhundert*, edited by Evangelos Konstantinou, 211–217. Frankfurt a.M.: Lang, 2007.

Özcan, Azmi. *Pan-Islamism: Indian Muslims, the Ottomans and Britain, 1877–1924.* Leiden and New York: Brill, 1997.

Papadopoulos, George S. *England and the Near East, 1896–1898.* Thessaloniki: Institute for Balkan Studies, 1969.

Pécout, Gilles. "Amitié littéraire et amitié politique méditerranéennes. Philhellènes français et italiens de la fin du XIXe siècle." *Philhellénismes et transferts culturels dans l'Europe du XIXe siècle, Revue germanique internationale 1–2*, special issue, edited by Michel Espagne and Gilles Pécout (2005): 207–218.

Pierron, Bernard. *Juifs et Chrétiens de la Grèce moderne. Histoire des relations intercommunautaires de 1821 à 1945.* Paris: Editions l'Harmattan, 1996.

Rosenhek, Ludwig, ed. *Festschrift zur Feier des 100. Semesters der akademischen Verbindung Kadimah, 1883–1933.* Vienna: Glanz, 1933.

Rozen, Minna. "The Hamidian Era Through the Jewish Looking-glass: A Study of the Istanbul Rabbinical Court Records." *Turcica* 37 (2005): 113–154.

———. *The Last Ottoman Century and Beyond.* Vol. 1 of *The Jews in Turkey and the Balkans 1808–1945.* Tel Aviv: The Goldstein-Goren Diaspora Research Center, The Chair for the History and Culture of the Jews of Salonica and Greece, 2005.

Sarantis, Theodoros K. P. *To horio Perivoli Grevenon. Symvoli stin istoria tou armatolikiou tis Pindou* [The village Perilovi in Grevena: a contribution to the history of the armatolic of Pindos]. Athens: G. Tsiveriotis, 1977.

Shaw, Stanford J., and Ezel Kural Shaw. *History of the Ottoman Empire and Modern Turkey.* Vol. 2. Cambridge and London: Cambridge University Press, 1977.

Veremis, Thanos, and Yiannis Koliopoulos. *Ellas. I synchroni synecheia. Apo to 1821 mehri simera* [Hellas. The modern sequel: from 1821 up to the present day]. 4th ed. Athens, Kastaniotis, 2006.

Part II

The Balkan Empires

Bogdan Trifunović

Dreaming of an Empire: Discourse Analysis of Serbian Poetry at the Beginning of the 20th Century

My choice of poetry as a source for revealing dominant Serbian collective memory discourses before 1918 was based on its hermetical
character in regard to the national idea and patriotism. The great changes
that took place after 1875 across the Balkans—the uprising in Herzegovina, the wars of 1876 and 1878, the creation of San Stefano Bulgaria, the
Congress of Berlin, and the Austro-Hungarian occupation of Bosnia and
Herzegovina in 1878—had a dramatic psychological effect on the Serbs
and showed that their pre-1876 ideals were based on nationalist overesti-
mations. This had a marked effect on their literature, in which a more realistic genre emerged, marking the replacement and the subsequent downfall of the until-then dominant Romanticism.[1]

The change in prose writing from national to social themes was swift
and significant, but poetry did not follow in its footsteps. The influence
of the most important representatives of Serbian poetic romanticism—
Petar II Petrović Njegoš (1813–1851), Đura Jakšić (1832–1878), and Jovan
Jovanović Zmaj (1833–1904)—lasted until well after 1878, and so at the
beginning of the twentieth century, the so-called patriotic poetry came
to be regarded as rather anachronistic and of lesser value when compared
to modern and realistic poetic styles.[2] Patriotic poetry still managed to
garner a wide reception and remain publicly influential nevertheless,
keeping persistently to its traditions as it poetically addressed the elements of the national idea. Romanticism in Serbian poetry became more

---

1   Pavić, "Mladi Vojislav," 49.
2   Pavić, "Mladi Vojislav," 50.

than just a passing trend, occupying a special place in people's hearts and spirits for much longer than was the case with other literary movements like Realism. In 1914, an anthology of Zmaj's patriotic poetry was published in Sremski Karlovci (then part of Austria-Hungary), with the aim of conveying to the widest range of the Serbian nation "patriotic, noble feelings" about the Serbian name, its ideals and hopes for the future, in the moment of "national gathering and consolidation." It was thought that the poetry of Zmaj would be the best tool for such task, because it was regarded as an "artistic patriotic poetry" with roots in the people's oral traditions.[3]

If there is a relative continuity in patriotic poetic expression before and after 1878, it is possible to recognize dominant images and symbols based on their presence and persistence in national culture and memory. These poetic images stem both from older epic-poetry traditions and from the ideology of the modern Serbian state; but the latter should not be seen as static category of ideology based on myths from the past and simply transferred to contemporary times.[4] Rather, it should be addressed through the discourse of cultural memory characterized by a fixed point of view which does not change with the passing of time but is very present in contemporary culture (in the words of Jan Assmann such memory is "contemporized past").[5] This, at first glance somewhat paradoxical phenomenon can be recognized in the life and work of Vojislav Ilić (1860–1894), whose history-inspired poetry was influenced by contemporary developments in politics and culture.[6] Ilić published under the inspiration of patriotic themes mostly after 1885 and Serbia's lost war with Bulgaria, which provoked a resurrection of patriotism in Serbia, similarly as Sedan did in France after 1871. As the events of 1878 and the decisions of the Congress of Berlin closed Serbia's "destined" path toward Bosnia, an al-

---

3   Nedeljković, "Rodoljubive pesme Zmaja Jovana Jovanovića," 3–5.
4   Such dynamism in poetic images is observable in the case of the nineteenth century poetry which was themed around Stefan Dušan and his empire, which could not have been influenced by the epic poetry of earlier times, because this epic poetry above all cherished the myth of Vidovdan, hajduk traditions and the cults of Prince Lazar and Marko Kraljević. See Trifunović, "Memory of Old Serbia and the Shaping of Serbian Identity," 26–67.
5   Assmann and Czaplicka, "Collective Memory and Cultural Identity," 129.
6   Skerlić, "Vojislav J. Ilić," 228.

ternative space to the south, in Macedonia,[7] was put forward as more visible and desirable, particularly after 1885.

As "one condition for defining the range of every national culture is the necessity of understanding its borders,"[8] it is important, in order to be able to comprehend the range of the notion of the "Serbian Empire," to investigate more closely the spread or the range of the Serbian cultural space. The latter had been already defined in the poetry of Petar II Petrović Njegoš, the prince-bishop and ruler of Montenegro, in his most famous work, *Gorski vijenac* (The mountain wreath, 1847). The range is very specific in this epic poem and is based on Serbian medieval mythology and epic poetry traditions. It is not framed by geographical references or borders, as one might expect, but rather with figures of memory from oral epic poetry and medieval traditions of knighthood. It starts with the name of Stefan Dušan, and therefore includes in its cultural range the whole of his empire. Then follow the names of a dozen or so figures (Stefan Nemanja, Prince Lazar Hrebeljanović, Miloš Obilić, etc.), some historical and some mythological, including the extent of the lands they ruled individually: Macedonia, Kosovo, the Albania of Gjergj Kastrioti (Skanderbeg), Dalmatia, Raška, Montenegro, Bosnia and Herzegovina.[9] It is evident from the work of Njegoš that the Serbian cultural range placed a heavy emphasis on the medieval empire. This corresponds with the ideas of Ilija Garašanin (1812–1874), the Serbian prime minister who in 1844 made a plan (*Načertanije*), the first Serbian political program, based on the concept of the Polish Prince Adam Jerzy Czartoryski (1770–1861), for the future unification of all Serbs living in the Ottoman and Habsburg Empires. According to Dušan T. Bataković, Njegoš was familiar with the *Načertanije*,[10] so we can assume that "The Mountain Wreath" was influenced from that side also. This is further indicated by the fact that the range proposed by the Montenegrin prince-bishop corresponds with the political program formulated by Garašanin.

---

7 Unless otherwise noted, the term "Macedonia" here specifically designates the broad geographical region in the Balkans defined by the valley of the Vardar River, the so-called "Vardar Macedonia." See Dragi, "The Name Macedonia in the Ottoman Period," 105–36.

8 Sujecka, "Prostranstvo," 238.

9 Stijović, "Tri posvete kao tri bisera."

10 Bataković, "Ilija Garašanin's *Načertanije*."

Poetry and the Context of Remembrance of an Empire

Milica V. Mišković (1876–1967) was the daughter of the teacher, writer, and state official Dimitrije Mita Petrović, whose other children included the painter Nadežda Petrović (1873–1915) and the writer Rastko Petrović (1898–1949). Although a member of an artistically productive and inspiring family, Milica expressed herself in literature only after she was married, publishing her first poems at the turn of the century. Her poetry is not regarded as original or with high pretensions, but more as a product of the time and the patriotic fervor in which she was raised and lived. In 1910 she published her first and only collection of patriotic and love poems, simply titled *Poems*[11], before the outbreak of the First Balkan War and after the annexation of Bosnia and Herzegovina by Austria-Hungary in 1908.[12] In this book, which could be viewed as a poetic contribution to the national cause by an individual outside public life,[13] the author followed the dominant canon of patriotic poetry, which held that writers should be behind the threshold of homeland, writing about the glory of the Serbian nation. The book starts with a pair of poems, "Serbian Poem" (*Srpska pesma*) and "Speak, Poem!" (*Reci pesmo*), viewed by critics as an apotheosis of patriotic poetry. There followed a stream of poems describing the centuries of the Turkish yoke, but also of the miseries of South Slavs living in Austria-Hungary. These poems have a projected patriotic style seen already in the poetry of other writers from that time, and these texts are clearly engaged in addressing several sites of memory: Kosovo, Emperor Stefan Dušan, the Empire, and the Vardar and Danube rivers. The nature of her motifs appears plainly in her first three poems, where she addresses her compatriots with the poem dedicated to the "whole nation" (*svome rodu*),[14] while the poem "Oh Will it Be?" (*O da li će biti?*) goes so far as to foresee the age of warfare as a bright future for the Serbian nation that will bring freedom and better days, identified in the poem with the symbol of sunshine: "Will the Sun shine, and when will it come / The age of clash!".[15]

---

11 Mišković, *Pesme.*
12 Nedeljković, "K'o voda s odnetim cvetom."
13 Nedeljković, "K'o voda s odnetim cvetom."
14 Mišković, *Pesme*, 6.
15 "Da l' će sinut sunce, i kad li će doći/ Doba okršaja!" Mišković, *Pesme*, 9.

"From Kosovo" (*Sa Kosova*) heads a series of poems dedicated to specific localities or historical figures which enables us to map the image of history that had inspired her. Although the first of these poems has in its title Kosovo as a geographical determinant, Kosovo in the poem is actually more of a mythical symbol than a precise toponym. Mišković's Kosovo is the source of a "national groan" which started with the battle of Kosovo Field in 1389, already epitomized as a myth rather than a historical event, and lasts until today, calling for the relief of sorrow and thus losing its particular geography and borders.[16] While the author had introduced the Danube as a northern geographical border and simultaneously as a symbol for identification of all Serbs, its antipodes is "the south," mentioned three times in the poems.[17] In "Fly, Poem!" (*Leti pesmo!*) she uses the adjective "floral" to describe the south, but immediately contrasts this positive image of the south by speaking of it also as a land of tears, of sad brothers who have to fight with swords against the harsh conditions of life. The Danube is the place—the family house of Mišković was in Belgrade—from where the author sends greetings to her brothers in the south, thus poetically transferring a message of unified Serb-hood in the north (Serbia Proper) to the south, to the region of Kosovo and Vardar Macedonia, which at that time was called "Old Serbia," in memory of the old Serbian medieval state which had had its centre in Kosovo and Vardar Macedonia.[18]

While Mišković uses the Danube as a symbol of modern Serbia, a symbol of liberation, freedom, stability and might,[19] its opposite is the Vardar River (in the poem "Vardar"). The Vardar exists in her poetry as a river which flows through the lands of "horrible cries" (*što teče zemljom strašnog plača*) or in the gloomy south calling for liberation from centuries-long slavery.[20] In "I'd Like to be There" (*Tamo bih*) the Vardar is not specifically mentioned, but it is clear which river's "weeping waves" (*plaču vali*) are "where bright memory awakes Serbian heart" (*Kuda svetli spomen srpsko srce budi*), a river which—significantly—flows somewhere in

16 Mišković, *Pesme*, 9.
17 For instance, on page 12.
18 Trifunović, "Memory of Old Serbia," 9–11.
19 Mišković, *Pesme*, 22.
20 Mišković, *Pesme*, 13.

the south.[21] The Vardar has thus a very important place as a site of memory in Mišković's poetry. It is simultaneously an important border line, a geographic entity that defines the region of Serbia and its cultural spread, and more importantly an imagined space from historical times, filled with the glory of the Middle Ages and all those places like Skopje, or figures like Stefan Dušan, incorporated in the Serbian collective memory of the past. Her poem "Saint George's Day" (*Đurđev-danu*) defines these borders as framed by four rivers: the Danube, Drina, Vardar, and Struma.[22] These were also roughly the borders of the major part of the empire of Stefan Dušan in the mid-fourteenth century.

Stefan Dušan is one of a few names cited by Mišković, alongside Miloš Obilić,[23] who symbolized the spirit of knighthood, and the imagined defenders of Kosovo. In the poem "Hello Brothers!" (*Zdravo braćo!*), which is dedicated to the Serbian knights and calls for the mobilization of modern warriors, the image of Dušan was used as a unifying figure, reconciling past grandeur and Serbia's modern pretensions: "In a line will stand a friend with his friend, / With the flag of Dušan."[24] We can trace the transformation of Dušan's image from a purely historical figure to a mythological one, symbolized in this case by the sites of memory (such as flags or monuments), who is always ready to do battle and to stand up against the forces of destiny, according to the universal myths of Savior and Hero.[25] And this national hero, the mythical ruler who will gather his people once more, is simply Dušan; not the Emperor, nor the Mighty. The symbolism is so strong in this case that arguably a common name starts to crystallize national identity-meaning; it itself becomes the site of memory. The other aspect of this image of Stefan Dušan is its connection with the mightiness of his empire and of him as a ruler. This is plainly shown in the poem "Gloomy Sky" (*Sumorno nebo*), which talks about the gloomy days of Serbianhood, now overshadowed by Dušan's glory.[26] Thus we can conclude that the im-

---

21 Mišković, *Pesme*, 18.

22 Mišković, *Pesme*, 19.

23 A mythological figure sometimes nicknamed *Kobilović* (born of a mare) who allegedly killed Sultan Murad I in the Battle of Kosovo. The traditions of Obilić are shared by many nations in the Balkans—Serbs, Albanians, Vlachs, to name just a few.

24 "U red staće s drugom drug, / Sa zastavom Dušanovom." Mišković, *Pesme*, 15.

25 Žirarde, *Politički mitovi i mitologije,* 91.

26 Mišković, *Pesme*, 17.

age of Stefan Dušan in this book is conceived as a twofold site of memory: the first is the image of a mighty ruler unifying the nation around him for the conclusive battle and the nation's Savior; the other site of memory is his name in and of itself, which symbolizes much more than just a person behind that name.

The historical facts about Stefan Dušan and the empire he forged, and the re-interpretation and reception of the image of Dušan in modern Serbia, are quite different things. The image of the emperor and the functioning of the memory of empire in nineteenth-century politics, society, and arts in Serbia acquired all the characteristics of a Golden Age myth, but also more specifically the myth of the military prowess of the Serbs and their predestined rule over the central part of the Balkan Peninsula, which became an essential part of modern Serbian mythology and, subsequently, ideology.

Nevertheless, the dominant image of Emperor Stefan Dušan throughout the centuries after the eventual Ottoman conquest of Serbia in 1459 was that of a mighty ruler who built the strongest state in the Balkans, and one of the strongest in Europe at that time. This image existed throughout the centuries of Ottoman domination as a collective memory and a consolation for foreign rule.[27] This discourse gained strength particularly after the Principality of Serbia gained independence in the nineteenth century, parallel to plans for the reunification of all Serbs into one state and the reestablishment of the Serbian empire, meaning Dušan's empire.[28]

THE MEMORY OF OLD EMPIRE

Vladislav Petković Dis (1880–1917) was an impressionist poet, a member of the movement known in Serbia as "moderna" (modern style), as opposed to the traditional classicism of the poets and writers dominating contemporary Serbian art and culture at the end of the nineteenth and the early twentieth century. His first book, *Utopljene duše* (Drowned souls), appeared in 1911, marking a significant event in the history of Serbian literature, with some of the most beautiful, lyrical verses ever written in the Serbian lan-

---

27 Žirarde, *Politički mitovi i mitologije,* 9.
28 Stojančević, *Istorija srpskog naroda,* 404.

guage. My analysis will focus on Dis's second book, titled *Mi čekamo cara* (We are waiting for an emperor) and published in 1913, just after the Balkan Wars ended. Almost unanimously, literary critics agree that this book marks a swift turn in the sensibility of Dis's poetry.[29] This turn was evidenced in the book's title, which suggests that it is a collection of patriotic poems inspired by recent wars against the Ottomans and Bulgarians—a sort of lyrical war diary. Dis had published *We Are Waiting for an Emperor* with personal funds, while the second edition in 1914 had financial support from the court office of Crown Prince Aleksandar, to whom the preface of both editions contains a dedication. As Dis was rejected at the time of the mobilization in 1912 because of poor health, his inspiration regarding the war derived from conversations with soldiers and wounded men as well as the general national euphoria after the declaration of war against the "Turks" and the swift military victories in Macedonia.

Dis's poetic motifs in 1912 and 1913 are similar to those of other poets of that time such as Jovan Dučić (1871–1943), Veljko Petrović (1884–1967), Aleksa Šantić (1868–1924), and Milan Rakić (1876–1938), as appears in their poems: *Vardar* (The Vardar) and *Car* (The Emperor) by Dučić; *Zapis cara Dušana* (The inscription of Emperor Dušan) and *Povratak* (The return) by Petrović; *Jutro na Kosovu* (Morning in Kosovo) by Šantić; *Na Gazimestanu* (At Gazimestan) by Rakić, as well as in poems by others. The historical context provides a key to understanding Dis's book as a whole. This context suggests that Dis's poetry in 1913 was written with the changed national and cultural circumstances in mind, specifically the idea that all national resources, physical and mental, should be mobilized for the national cause of liberation of the Serbian lands under Ottoman rule and the unification of all Serbs in one state—a reborn empire of Stefan Dušan. This is why Dis writes about waiting for some new emperor as a great hope and salvation, which corresponded with the actual popular sentiment in Serbia and also with the tendencies of official Belgrade. It was probably for this reason that Dis used the title of the first poem in the collection as the title of the whole book.

The poems in this book contain many stereotypes which were widely used in the patriotic literature of that time, and critics regard them as

---

29   Ranković, *Osobenosti Disove poezije*, 271.

being of a lesser value compared with those poems which were written during the First World War, when Dis personally experienced the horror of modern warfare and exile.[30] We will investigate the topographical and chronological aspects of these poems as well their deeper ideology in an effort to analyze the mnemonical function of their symbols as the places of memory, namely Emperor Stefan Dušan and his empire, Macedonia, Vardar, and Kosovo.

The first part of the book, titled "Grand Days" (*Veliki dani*), starts with the poem "We Are Waiting for an Emperor." This poem should be understood as a prologue for the rest of the collection, while the other poems (sixteen in total) chronologically follow certain events in war. The chronology of the poem "We Are Waiting for an Emperor" is marked by the events following the First Balkan War (from the mobilization in early autumn 1912 until August 1913). The topographic and spatial aspect of the poem is clearly defined in a number of verses, as Dis names places and regions: "We embrace Serbs from Kosovo and Skopje, / Veles, Prilep, Bitola and Debar";[31] "But when we conquered the Adriatic coast."[32] So it is obvious that Dis refers to and includes Kosovo and the cities in Macedonia west from the Vardar River. It is interesting that Kosovo exists in this poem as a single entity, but this is not the case with Macedonia, which is represented only through the mention of some of its cities, of which Skopje and Prilep have a significant place in the collective memory of the Serbs.[33] The importance of Kosovo is emphasized once more in the verse "God's day saw again the land of tears again,"[34] which is the reflection of the Kosovo myth as a tragic and crucial point in Serbian history.

Parallel to these real geographic reference points in the poem, Dis adds another spatial layer, of more imagined and mental character, at least for Serbian readers. This layer contains an image of empire: "From combat to combat, / We have found the lands of old empire."[35] This image of an empire derives from the "ruins of glory, wells of moans" (*razvaline stare,*

---

30 Delić, "Vladislav Petković Dis kao pjesnik promjene senzibiliteta," 87.
31 "Zagrlismo Srbe s Kosova i Skoplja, / Velesa, Prilepa, Bitolja i Debra."
32 "Al kad osvojismo obalu Jadrana." Petković, *Mi čekamo cara*, 7, 8.
33 Kostić, *Naši novi gradovi na jugu*, 12–19, 34–40.
34 "Dan božji opet zemlju plača vide." Petković, *Mi čekamo cara*, 8.
35 "Iz borbe u borbu, sa pobedom svuda, / Mi smo našli zemlje stare carevine."

izvore jauka),[36] which are symbolic places from medieval times, now in ruins, and from the imagined sorrow in which the Serbs lived in the Ottoman Empire. As there was only one "old" empire, that established by Stefan Dušan in 1346, we can see how the poet poeticized Dušan's empire and its revival. In the poem's final verses he explicitly says: "We are awaiting the emperor beside the sea, / That we may be able peacefully to lie down in the grave."[37] This "emperor" could have referred to the contemporary Serbian King Petar Karadjordjević (1903–21), who was nicknamed "The Liberator" after the wars 1912–13 or, in a more metaphysical sense, any Serbian ruler who would bear the standard of Stefan Dušan in an effort to re-establish the Serbian empire. Although Aleksandar Jovanović, literary critic, has thought that the whole poem is not about an emperor in the likeness of Stefan Dušan or any other medieval ruler but that it is rather an allegory of Jesus Christ and his second return (the Apocalypse),[38] this is not a view I share. Jovanović thinks that the whole tone of the poem, and the rest of the book, with the dead and graves as central motifs, supports this hypothesis and allows a different reading of the book.[39] If we take into consideration what we previously said about the sites of memory, the fact that Dis used the words "Grand days" for the first part of the book and his reflections on the war actions of 1912 and 1913, I believe that emperor here is not Christ, but the imagined symbol of a ruler who is able militarily to obtain and defend the freedom and unity of the Serbs in their empire, stretching from the Danube in the North, to the Bitola and Adriatic in the South. At the same time, that emperor has a deeper spiritual role, assuming the prerogatives of a divine being, able to provide peace and tranquility to believers at the moment of their death. The condition of this collective and, at the same time, individual peace is the reemergence of an empire under one ruler for all Serbs, embodied in the collective memory of the Emperor Stefan Dušan.

---

36 Petković, *Mi čekamo cara*, 7.
37 "Mi čekamo cara kraj pučine sive, / Da bi mogli mirno tada u grob leći." Petković, *Mi čekamo cara*, 7–8.
38 Jovanović, "Disova rodoljubiva poezija," 348–49.
39 Jovanović, "Disova rodoljubiva poezija," 348–49.

The Notion of Space and Time of an Empire

Setting aside these images of the reborn empire and the emperor, Dis's notion of history is actually quite complex. In *Prva pesma sreće* (The first poem of happiness) he depicts the Ottoman rule in "Old Serbia" as "five centuries, black as five ravens,"[40] or as centuries filled with "dungeon and darkness," "shame," and "graves."[41] The notion of shame arising from the lost battle of 1389, as well as from the Turkish rule over the territories in the south (Kosovo and Macedonia), was common to that whole generation of poets. It was at the core of an idea that such an unbearable situation must be resolved through long overdue vengeance. Not by chance were the wars of 1912–13 steered by such a notion, which corresponded with the belief that war would bring a long awaited vengeance for the defeat of Kosovo.[42] But Dis's view about the past is also a voice of collective memory which was common in older epic poetry, where the Kosovo myth connected the great defeat on the battlefield with, at the same time, a glorious sacrifice for a higher cause, the heavenly kingdom. So Dis also uses this motif, dreaming about the "old times" that will be resurrected again after five centuries. We may attribute the epithet "the Golden Age" to these old times. As Dis saw it, the period 500 years before his time was a heroic one, before the Turks, defeats and slavery, when people were accustomed to using weapons to defend freedom. Moreover, for Dis this new time was born after "races" had clashed, meaning Serbo-Christian versus Turko-Muslim, when the "people have created a new time."[43]

This antagonism between heroic and non-heroic times can be observed in the constellation of "heroic" versus "non-heroic" characters, as well as the continuum between heroic and non-heroic times.[44] This model could be used in analyzing the poets here, particularly Dis. Dis felt a contrast between a supposed contemporary weakness, influenced by his poor health and physical underdevelopment, on the one hand, and the mightiness of the past, embodied in the figures of past rulers, knights and warriors, on

---

40   "Pet vekova, crni kao pet gavranova."
41   Petković Dis, *Mi čekamo cara*, 11.
42   Vitošević, *Srpsko pesništvo 1901–1914*, 206, 207, 211.
43   "Videh kako narod stvara novo vreme." Petković, *Mi čekamo cara*, 12.
44   Simeonov, "Mitât za geroicheskata smârt," 111.

the other. At the same time this feeling of mightiness was sparked in the fantasy of a mighty empire, transmitted to the present times through rich epic poetry and mythology.[45] With this approach the whole sense of the interchangeability of time and space in regard to Old Serbia can be seen as a comparison, or even collision, between Old Serbia and Modern Serbia, between the Middle Ages and the modern period. The "heroic range" concept is founded in folklore and mythology, so the mythological reflex acts with tremendous power, especially for the images of the other. In the case of Serbian patriotic poetry and the sites of memory in relation to Old Serbia, the conflict with the Bulgarians proved to be a rich source of inspiration. The same could also be said on the Bulgarian side[46] for Ivan Vazov and his poetic and prose works. In fact, Vazov's novel *Pod igoto* (Under the yoke, 1894) introduced the sense that only in the "enemy range" (an unfriendly territory) is a heroic death possible.[47]

The notion of the Serbian range of space and time is obvious in the poem "The First Poem of Happiness." This poem also incorporates a spatial aspect, through the river Vardar ("How the Vardar today flows through Serbia")[48] and the city of Ohrid, ("How the Serbian night falls over Ohrid").[49] It is interesting to note the fluidity of space and time in Dis's poetry, related to some recognizable sites with high positions in the collective memory of the Serbian nation of his time. Not just the space is fluid, however, because just as he identifies in the flow of a river an analogy with the spread of national boundaries, he also sees time through a national looking glass, so that it can be a "Serbian night" which falls over the Serbian Ohrid. Here we can recognize elements of the symbolic time-space continuum, defined by geographical terms and historical figures as

---

45 In the Bulgarian context, a similar discourse existed in the poetry of Ivan Vazov, who published *The Epic of the Forgotten* (Bulgarian: *Епопея на забравените*, 1881–1884) to commemorate the Bulgarian fight for freedom against the Ottoman Empire, and at the same time to criticize the moral decline of the Bulgarian nation after the Liberation, by comparison to the heroic figures and events of the recent past. See Gancheva, "Liricheskiat obraz na predcite od srednovekovieto u Ivan Vazov," 65.
46 "The time and space argument, which is present in history, is the reason why Ottoman Macedonia may be at the same time a land inherited from its ancestors, a Western-Bulgarian state that saved medieval Bulgarian statehood from disaster, the Serbian Tsardom of Tsar Dušan, and also the Tsardom of Samuil, the first Macedonian state." See Sujecka, "The Semantics of the Balkans," 356.
47 Simeonov, *Mitât za geroicheskata smârt*, 111, 113.
48 "Kako Vardar danas kroz Srbiju teče."
49 "Kako nad Ohridom pada srpsko veče." Petković, *Mi čekamo cara*, 12.

the sites of memory, similarly as it was for the Bulgarians (defined with the three seas surrounding Bulgarian lands, together with the figure of the medieval Bulgarian emperor Simeon).[50] The significance of time as an aspect important for understanding sites of memory like the medieval Serbian empire[51] is also emphasized in the poem *Zvona na jutrenje* (Bells for morning Mass) which describes how in "the time" (actually "days") to come, two-headed eagles (the emblem of the medieval Nemanjić dynasty of Stefan Dušan) will pass over all Serb graves, to awake sleeping spirits and the "late" Empire.[52] Here, time is cyclical in character, as is the notion of space. All Ottoman Slavic communities developed such an understanding of temporal and spatial contexts of history, which facilitates the hope and possibility to be able "to return to the space that had been lost as a result of the [Ottoman] invasion."[53]

The poem *Pod zvezdom sreće* (Under the lucky star) brings together a number of places and figures, in the process creating a very complex system of images of Serbian history, together with the imagined national destiny. In this poem old graves call for a war, together with the "thought of pledge" (*zavetna miso*), God's will, the spirit of the great emperor and pleas from the Vardar and Kosovo. In fact, what the poet has made is a symbolic representation of two constitutional geographical elements of Old Serbia—Macedonia and Kosovo—through the symbols of the Vardar and the Field of Kosovo. Obviously, the poet combines universal Biblical elements, like the notion of God's will, with highly significant Serbian elements, like Kosovo, and to a lesser degree the Vardar (shared also in the Bulgarian historical traditions) in creating this system of memory or mental map. A very important element of this mental map is the "great emperor" (*veliki car*), who is at the same time both a national and universal element, for the image of a great ruler from the past is a widely recognized symbol of a Golden Age myth.[54] There is no doubt that this ruler, the great emperor, in the Serbian context could only be Stefan Dušan and

50　Sujecka, "Za semantika na moreto v bulgarski kulturen hronotop," 101.
51　Jolanta Sujecka sees in this attitude the sacralization of the whole time and space that encompassed the battles with the Turks. See Sujecka, "The Semantics of the Balkans," 353.
52　Petković, *Mi čekamo cara*, 18.
53　Sujecka, "The Semantics of the Balkans," 353.
54　Žirarde, *Politički mitovi i mitologije*, 115.

his legacy. In the fourth stanza of the poem, the memory of old empire is revived again, when Dis uses sites like Kumanovo, Bitola, the Prilep of Marko Kraljević and Gračanica in Kosovo, as being important for understanding the extent of the new, reborn empire.[55] One condition for defining the range of every national culture is the necessity of understanding its borders.[56] In this case, the important geographical and spiritual places of Serb culture define these borders. In the poem *Mnogih neće biti* (Many shall not be) this notion of the range of national culture is marked by the sites (of memory) of the very recent battles in the First Balkan War against the Turks, namely Kumanovo, Merdare, Prilep, and Bitola, signifying the "fulfilled oath from the field of Kosovo."[57]

Confronting Perspectives on the Shared Memory

The last element to be analyzed in this system of framing a unified space for the national range are the Bulgarians, who are treated as "others," and thus will be helpful in better understanding and defining "us." In the second to last stanza of the poem "Many Shall Not Be," Dis's memory space is defined through the Battle of Bregalnica (June–July 1913), which marked the defeat of the Bulgarian troops by the Serbian army in the struggle for Vardar Macedonia after the collapse of the Ottoman forces in 1912.[58] Dis had paired this recent site of memory with one more ancient, the Battle of Velbužd, fought in 1330 between the armies of the Bulgarian and Serbian kings, again over the possession of the lands of Vardar Macedonia. The poem suggests that the almost seven centuries in between these two events serve somehow to connect rather than disconnect the sites of memory, in this case the two battles, which are able to cohabit the same space when the intended mission is to explain the past as an affirmative justification for the national cause. This justification is based on the image of the history of Macedonia as a Serbian land taken from Byzantium, defended

---

55 Petković Dis, *Mi čekamo cara*, 25.
56 Sujecka, "Range," 238–239.
57 "Ko dovršen zavet sa Kosova Polja." Petković Dis, *Mi čekamo cara*, 37. This verse Dis repeated in almost the same form in the very next poem, on page 39.
58 In the same year as Dis, 1913, Jovan Dučić published his poem *Bregalnica*, which depicts Bregalnica as the symbolic path to be followed by the nation.

in 1330 against the Bulgarians, temporarily possessed by the Turks, regained by means of force in 1912, and finally defended again in 1913 from the "poisonous hatred of vicious Bulgarians."[59]

Such a poetical vision of Serbian history (and of the history of Vardar Macedonia) from the fourteenth century onward, served to affirm that the righteous nation proved its path and historical rights over the territory, that it has been reinstated into the national domain.[60] Thus, recent events in political and military history, like the Battle of Bregalnica, which was fought more or less during the time when Dis was writing his book, became national site of memory thanks to its connection with another contextually similar event, the Battle of Velbužd, which was already long ago an established symbol of national pride and glory.[61] In this context even a national defeat, like the Battle of Slivnica after 1885 was seen as the anti-memory, if viewed as a separate event in the Balkans' history, it could be used for proving the aforementioned concept, as Dis had plainly showed in the poem *11 avgust 1913 godine* (11th August of the year 1913): "Through the roar of cannons and the smoke of rifles / The old empire has arisen at last. / You have achieved everything. Now there are no Turks, / no Slivnica, nor the anger of Bulgarians."[62] So, Slivnica had been erased from the collective memory of the Serbian nation with the event of Bregalnica and the subsequent fulfillment of the ultimate aim and imagined destiny of national history: the re-establishment of the old empire, symbolized in the victories over its eternal enemies, the Turks and Bulgarians, and in repossession of the Serbian lands once part of Stefan Dušan's empire. The significance of the collective memory in treating major historical events was shown in the catchphrase, very popular during the Second Balkan War in 1913: "For Kosovo-Kumanovo, for Slivnica-Bregalnica" (*Za Kosovo-Kumanovo, za Slivnicu-Bregalnicu*). This way the imagined sources of national frustration, like historic defeats, would be reconciled and healed with new victories, despite the fact they were fought in different regions, periods of time and historical contexts, and finally between different adversaries.

---

59 "Od otrovne mržnje podmuklih Bugara." Petković, *Mi čekamo cara*, 38.

60 Sujecka, "The Semantics of the Balkans," 353.

61 Gancheva, "Liricheskiat obraz na predcite od srednovekovieto u Ivan Vazov," 68.

62 "Kroz topovsku riku i dim od pušaka / Podigla se najzad carevina stara. / Vi ste postigli sve. Sad nema Turaka, / Nema ni Slivnice, ni besa Bugara." Petković, *Mi čekamo cara*, 39.

Contrary to this discourse emerges the Battle of Belasica (1014) in the context of Bulgarian memory. In nineteenth-century texts prior to 1878, the event at Belasica did not appear, because it was regarded as a shameful defeat for the emerging national identity and glory. It only emerged in the patriotic poetry of Ivan Vazov and Konstantin Velichkov at the end of the nineteenth century and the beginning of the twentieth century, as a synonym for national defeat and tragedy, contrasted to the victory at the Šipka Pass in the "war of national liberation" fought in 1877–78.[63]

CONCLUSIONS

Medieval images seemed to be quite adaptable for the contemporary purposes of projecting the unity of the nation and the imagined glory of the country and its people.[64] This practice of linking the medieval perspective of time with the modern tendencies was common practice in the nineteenth-century Balkans.[65] But as Holm Sundhaussen has suggested, the application of modern terms, perceptions, emotions and judgments to past events, places and figures played (and still play) a dangerous role in the political and cultural processes in the Balkans, as they can influence the reception of the past and, subsequently, collective memory and identity: "The major problems are collective and topographic names, as well as present terms applied in the past... Just the mere use of those words evokes associations which are too often in antagonism with the reconstructed past and relate to the subjective referential system. Historical terms always stand in the context of time."[66]

The poems from the turn of the century present political ideals from the past, like emperor and empire, and symbolize the political desires of the contemporary Kingdom of Serbia for the unification of Serbdom and the re-creation of some new empire. This symbolism, when translated into the category of "sites of memory" through the aforementioned symbolic and functional images of Emperor Stefan Dušan, could be used for purposes defined as "being for the national cause." The figure of Emperor Ste-

---

63 Sujecka, "Prostranstvo," 240–41.
64 Gancheva, "Liricheskiat obraz na predcite od srednovekovieto u Ivan Vazov", 67–68.
65 Sujecka, "The Semantics of the Balkans," 353.
66 Zundhausen, *Stare tabue zamenjuju novi.*

fan as a site of memory also incorporates the image of a national hero, a mythical ruler who will gather his people to him once more. The other sites of memory are at the core of the collective remembrance of Old Serbia and the medieval empire, including Kosovo, the Vardar, Skopje, Prizren and so on. Taken together they form the symbolism essential for national identity since the eighteenth century, and in the late nineteenth century they subsequently became incorporated into the political ideology which sought to justify expansion to the south. That is why the "south," as an element of remembrance, features so prominently as site of memory in the poetry we have analyzed. This trend is observable from the earlier poets, like Vojislav Ilić, through the patriotic poetry of Milica Mišković, up to the poetry of Vladislav Petković Dis. Analyzed poetry show differences in the style or symbolism used, but it is evident that there was a strong pattern in poetical image of an empire that derived from the Serbian collective memory of that time.

References

Assmann, Jan, and John Czaplicka. "Collective Memory and Cultural Identity." *New German Critique* no. 65 (Spring–Summer 1995): 125–33.

Bataković, Dušan T. "Ilija Garašanin's *Načertanije*." Projekat Rastko-History. Accessed November 23, 2013. http://www.rastko.rs/istorija/batakovic/batakovic-nacertanije_eng.html.

Delić, Jovan. "Vladislav Petković Dis kao pjesnik promjene senzibiliteta" [Vladislav Petković Dis as a poet of changing sensibility]. In *Disova poezija: zbornik radova* [Dis's poetry: collection of works], edited by N. Petković, 53–108. Belgrade-Čačak: Institute for Literature and Arts-Public Library Čačak, 2002.

G'orgiev, Dragi. "The Name Macedonia in the Ottoman Period (14th–19th Century)." In *Macedonia: Land, Region, Borderland*. Vol. 2 of *Colloquia Balkanica*, edited by Jolanta Sujecka, 105–36. Warsaw: Wydawnictwo DiG, Wydział "Artes Liberales" UW, 2013.

Gancheva, Bistra. "Liricheskiat obraz na predcite od srednovekovieto u Ivan Vazov" [The lyrical image of the ancestors from the medieval period in Ivan Vazov's works]. In *Predci i predtechi–Mitove i utopii na Balkanite* [Ancestors and predecessors: myths and utopias in the Balkans], edited by Ilia Konev et al, 65–69. Blagoevgrad: SWU "Neofit Rilski," 1997.

Jovanović, Aleksandar. "Disova rodoljubiva poezija" [Dis's patriotic poetry]. In *Disova poezija: zbornik radova* [Dis's poetry: collection of works], edited by N. Petković, 339–59. Belgrade-Čačak: Institute for Literature and Arts-Public Library Čačak, 2002.

Kostić, Kosta N. *Naši novi gradovi na jugu* [Our new cities in the south]. Belgrade: Serbian Literary Guild, 1922.

Mišković, Milica V. *Pesme* [Poems]. Belgrade: New Printing Company Davidović, 1910.

Nedeljković, Milan, ed. *Rodoljubive pesme Zmaja Jovana Jovanovića* [The patriotic poems of Zmaj Jovan Jovanović]. Sremski Karlovci: Zmaj, 1914.

Nedeljković, Olivera. *K'o voda s odnetim cvetom* [Like the water with the gone flower]. Accessed November 23, 2013. http://www.cacak-dis.rs/dokumenti/digitalizacija/Milica-Miskovic.pdf.

Pavić, Milorad. "Mladi Vojislav" [Young Vojislav]. In *Vojislav Ilić*, edited by M. Pavić, 27–96. Belgrade: Institute for Textbooks, 1966.

Petković, Vladislav Dis. *Mi čekamo cara* [We are waiting for an emperor]. Belgrade: s. n., 1913.

Ranković, Milan. *Osobenosti Disove poezije* [The characteristics of Dis's poetry]. Belgrade: Narodna knjiga, 1976.

Simeonov, Roman. "Mitât za geroicheskata smârt—prostranstveni izmereniя na romanata povestvovatelna logika" [The myth of heroic death—spatial dimensions in the novel's narrative logic]. In *Predci i predtechi–Mitove i utopii na Balkanite* [Ancestors and predecessors: myths and utopias in the Balkans], edited by Ilia Konev et al, 110–20. Blagoevgrad: SWU "Neofit Rilski", 1997.

Skerlić, Jovan. "Vojislav J. Ilić." In *Vojislav Ilić*, edited by M. Pavić, 206–65. Belgrade: Institute for Textbooks, 1966.

Stijović, Svetozar. "Tri posvete kao tri bisera: srpstvo u pesničkom delu Petra Drugog Petrovića Njegoša" [Three dedications as three pearls: Serbianhood in the poetic works of Petar II Petrović Njegoš]. *Istorijske sveske*, broj 12, 1998. Accessed November 23, 2013. http://www.srpsko-nasledje.co.rs/sr-l/1998/12/article-13.html.

Stojančević, Vladimir, ed. *Istorija srpskog naroda* [History of the Serbian nation]. Vol. 2. Belgrade: Serbian Literary Guild, 2000.

Sujecka, Jolanta. "The Semantics of the Balkans." In *Interpretations: European Research Project for Poetics and Hermeneutics*. Vol. 2, *Memory and Art*, edited by K. Kulavkova, 349–59. Skopje: Macedonian Academy of Sciences and Arts, 2008.

Sujecka, Jolanta. "Za semantika na moreto v bulgarski kulturen hronotop" [What is the meaning of "sea" in the Bulgarian cultural space-time continuum]. In *Bregăt–moreto–Evropa: sbornik s materiali ot Meždunarodnata naučna konferencija "Bregăt, moreto i Evropa. Modeli na interkulturna komunikacija"* [Littoral–sea–Europe: collection of materials from the International Scientific Conference "Littoral, sea and Europe. Models of intercultural communication"], edited by Mila Santova, Iva Stanoeva, and Miglena Ivanova, 99–104. Sofia: Akad. Izdat. "Prof. Marin Drinov", 2006.

Sujecka, Jolanta. "Prostranstvo: Bъlgarskoto nacionalno prostranstvo" [Range: the Bulgarian national range]. In *Koncepti na blgarskata kultura* [Concepts of Bulgarian culture], edited by Dechka Chavdarova et al., 238–46. Shumen: Shumen University, 2010.

Trifunović, Bogdan. *Memory of Old Serbia and the Shaping of Serbian Identity*. Vol. 3 of *Colloquia Balkanica*. Warsaw: Wydawnictwo DiG, Wydział "Artes Liberales" UW, 2015.

Vitošević, Dragiša. *Srpsko pesništvo 1901–1914: razdoblje, razvoj, obeležja* [Serbian poetry, 1901–1914: period, development, characteristics]. Vol. 2. Belgrade: Vuk Karadžić, 1975.

Žirarde, R. [R. Girardet]. *Politički mitovi i mitologije* [Political myths and mythology]. Zemun-Belgrade: Biblioteka XX veka-Plato, 2000.

Zundhausen, Holm. "Stare tabue zamenjuju novi" [Old taboos changed to new ones]. Accessed May 13, 2015. http://www.danas.rs/vesti/feljton/stare_tabue_zamenjuju_novi.24.html?news_id=143049.

Nikolay Aretov

An Attractive Enemy: The Conquest of Constantinople in Bulgarian Imagery

Situated on the periphery of the peninsula, Constantinople has been undoubtedly at the very center of the historical process and cultural life of the Balkans for more than a millennium. The capital of Byzantium and of the Ottoman Empire held a key position in Bulgarian mental geography and historical imagery since the establishment of the first Bulgarian state until at least the early twentieth century. During this time the city was the capital of two or even three Empires (and later of a Republic), and presented as the main enemy, as hostile and evil, by Bulgarian nationalism. And indeed, history is full of wars between Bulgarians and the rulers of Constantinople—Byzantines, Crusaders of the Latin Empire, and later, Turks.

The Ottoman conquest of Constantinople in 1453 was a critical event in the history of the Balkans, and left a profound imprint on the Bulgarians' notions of their past and their self-image. Behind the seemingly unambiguous evaluation of this event—a defeat of Christendom that has a connection with the previous fall of the Bulgarian Kingdom—the observer can discover a more complicated and nuanced picture. This paper identifies some particularities:

A) The capture of an important city is a widespread mythical plot presented in many mythical structures, including the Bible. One might try reconstructing an archetype to trace its realization in different texts and to analyze them as a specific structure with interconnected elements. The Ottoman invasion in the Balkans generated such a structure comprising different texts (written and oral) that mirrored each other, following the Biblical archetype. So narrations about the Fall of Tarnovo (that happened earlier, in 1393) evidently followed the model of the Fall of Constantinople, which happened later. One should also bear in mind the opposition between two types of events by which the Ottoman conquest was represented—one was the siege of a city (Constantinople, Tarnovo), the other was the clash on the battlefield (the Battle of Kosovo, 1389).

B) The city was unsuccessfully attacked by the Bulgarians several times in the past; they still think themselves through the lens of these wars.

C) After the Ottoman conquest of Constantinople, the question of its legacy had to be tackled. This event generated, or at least stimulated, the emerging idea of The Third Rome, intensively applied by Russian imperial politics that extended beyond the Bulgarian image of the city.

D) Byzantines (Greeks) and Ottomans (Turks) are the traditional enemies in Bulgarian national mythology. Their conflict and their interrelations as a whole generate different reactions and multiple plots. Sometimes they were even presented as perfidious allies against the Bulgarians. Similar plots are not lacking in Greek national mythology either.

E) In the nineteenth century, when the foundations of Bulgarian nationalism were being laid, Constantinople (Istanbul) was probably the city with the largest Bulgarian population, and the stage for many of the important events in Bulgarian society. In a sense, for Bulgarians at that time this city was "ours."

F) Istanbul was an important target for the Bulgarian army during the First Balkan War (1912–1913). The Bulgarian invasion was stopped at the Battle of Çatalca (November 1812) 40 kilometers from Istanbul.

G) Istanbul became a preferred tourist destination for Bulgarians after the fall of the Berlin wall—it was relatively nearby, affordable, and exotic at the same time. It was even a profitable location for so called "suitcase trade"[1] practiced by many Bulgarians in the early 1990s. The short span of time between the so-called "Revival Process" (the forceful assimilation of Bulgaria's Turkish minority between 1985 and 1989) and the explosion of tourist (and trade) trips to Istanbul in the early 1990s caused the greatest shift in the Bulgarian image of this city; for many people influenced by nationalist propaganda visiting Istanbul and the Turkish Mediterranean resorts generated a grave psychological problem.

This paper offers a brief review of the main types of Bulgarian texts from the nineteenth and early twentieth centuries dealing with the fall of Constantinople, comparing them with certain Byzantine sources, as well as with some Greek and other interpretations of this event, and focuses in particular on one not-so-popular dramatic work, written in verse by Svetoslav Milarov in the early 1870s. Here the ambivalent attitude of a part of Bulgarian society to the Ottoman conquest of Constantinople is more clearly visible.

* * *

The conquest of Constantinople is a well-documented event, presented in Greek sources—Doukas, George Sphrantzes (also Phrantzes or Phrantza, Greek: Γεώργιος Σφραντζής or Φραντζής, 1401–c. 1478), Laonikos Chalkokondyles, Kritoboulos of Imbros (Michael Critobulus, Μιχαήλ Κριτόβουλος), Leonard of Chios—and in Ottoman and other chronicles, letters, memoires and documents, including those by Konstantin Mihailović (a Serbian who served as a janissary), Patriarch Gennadius Scholarius and Cardinal Isidore of Kiev. Various contemporary texts from elsewhere in Europe refer to this remarkable event; particularly important among them is the diary of the Venetian physician Nicolo Barbaro.

---

1   In suitcase trade goods which are allowed for customs-free and tax free import are purchased in one country and brought across the border into another country in small packages such as luggage or bags. The goods are then sold in domestic market.

Influential historians and writers like Dimitrie Cantemir, Voltaire, Edward Gibbon, Joseph von Hammer-Purgstall, and Alphonse de Lamartine also dealt with it more recently. Curiously, the image of Sultan Mehmed II in *belles lettres* linked him not so much with this remarkable historic event but with his legendary love affair with a Christian woman (Irene), fratricides, with his relations with the Italian painter Gentile Bellini, and so on.

The fall of the most important Christian city desperately needed explanation. One Orthodox perspective, applied by contemporaries and more recent writers, stressed the newly established Catholic-Orthodox Union. Alternatively, there were Catholic writers, Pope Nicholas I among them, who claimed that it was the rejection of the Union that caused the disaster.

Greek folklore also presented the event. Scholars have perceived an evolution in the published texts and a shift from an emphasis on Christianity to nationalism, and from initial fatalism to optimism.[2] The earlier focus was on the lament of the fallen Constantinople, and especially Hagia Sophia, and the tears that appeared in the eyes of Our Lady on the icon. Earlier variants were addressed to Our Lady: "With the passing of years and in time she will be yours again." In more recent variations the pronoun was different—the temple will be "ours" (meaning belonging to the Greeks), and not "yours" (to the Virgin Mary and the saints). Michael Herzfeld supposed that the real sense of the last verse was: "And still, whatever the times may bring, it is *still* yours!"[3] The same song was arranged for mixed choir by Manolis Kalomiris, who, faithful to Greek ideals, included it in his opera "Constantine Paleologos," whose libretto was written by Nikos Kazantzakis.

However, Steven Runciman, in his 1965 study of the event, bearing in mind the Western focus on Greek Antiquity and its influence, claimed that the fall of Constantinople was not so important an event for Greek national mythology as one might have supposed.

European images of the Fall of Constantinople were mixed. Side by side with dominating tragic representations and a demonization of the invaders one can detect different perspectives towards Turks, determined by

2   Herzfeld, *Ours Once More: Folklore, Ideology, and the Making of Modern Greece*, 129–139ff.
3   Herzfeld, *Ours Once More*, 134. Earlier publications with "our" in Cl. Fauriel, *Chants populaire de la Grèce moderne*, 340. Cf. Manousos, *Tragoudia ethnika*, 179.

internal motives. Some German *Fastnachtspiele* (theater plays staged during the Carnival) such as *Das Turken Fastnachtspiel* and *Ein Lied von dem Turken* (A song of the Turk) by Hans Rosenplut that appeared as early as 1453, contained positive images of a mighty and generous Sultan, whose subjects lived happily and did not pay taxes.[4] Later, some enlightenment writers also praised the sultans in their texts.

Russian images of Ottoman enemies were predominantly negative, of course, and according to the Tsar's plans, Constantinople should be Christian, even Russian. Quite the opposite were some representations by allies of the Turks. A popular song from the time of the Crimean War (1853–1856) expressed a will to defend the city from a potential new invasion:

> We don't want to fight but by jingo if we do...
> We've got the ships; we've got the men, and got the money too!
> We've fought the Bear before... and while we're Britons true,
> The Russians shall not have Constantinople...
> "Macdermott's War Song"[5]

* * *

Constantinople has always been a very special place for Bulgarians. In general, it was something alien, but in some situations, it could be "our own" in a sense, or at least something desired. It was simultaneously a home of evil (even of demons) and a place where richness and refined pleasures could be discovered. Such is often, if not always, the perspective of all the 'barbarians' and foreigners, whether they are newcomers or the local population from the surrounding villages.

Constantinople was considered "alien" when King Simeon the Bulgarian came from the north in the late ninth and early tenth centuries, or during the Balkan wars in the twentieth century, and even later on when the Ottomans came from the southeast. In the early twentieth century, one could find traces of the idea that Simeon refused to capture the city because he did not want history to present him as an ungrateful

---

4   Burçoğlu, "Slikata za Turchinot vo Evropa, vo minaloto i denes: kritichesko patuvaњe," 119–20.
5   Macdermott's War Song (1878), written and composed by G. W. Hunt, http://www.cyberussr.com /hcunn/q-jingo.html.

barbarian. Such marginal ideas revealing the ambivalent attitude of Bulgarians towards the city of Constantine were articulated by influential writers including Petko Todorov and Nikolay Raynov.[6]

* * *

The "History of the Capture of the Glorious Imperial City (King's city, in Bulgarian), Called the City of Constantine and New Rome, Conquered by Mehmed II, Eighth Turkish Sultan, in the year A.D. 1453"[7] was the most widespread pre-modern text about this important event translated into Bulgarian. The author and the time of composition are unknown. The text circulated in other Slavic languages and in Romanian too. There are reasons to see behind it something like an *Urtext* and to try to trace a specific mythical pattern that was adapted in different cultures. This did not mean that common topics in different accounts about the same event were results of its direct influence. This could be the effect of other sources and influences—for example of Greek chronicles, or even of texts about other cities. There existed different texts of the same type, Biblical and apocryphal, for example the "Narration of Jeremiah Concerning the Capture of Jerusalem," translated into Bulgarian in the tenth century.[8] An unsuccessful siege of Constantinople was also mentioned in the anonymous "Bulgarian Chronicle," preserved in copies from the sixteenth century.[9]

The "History of the Capture of the Glorious Imperial City" was faithful to the overall picture created by Byzantine authors. At the same time some elements that are common to most narrations about the capture of great cities and form the archetype, the very mythos of such narrations can be traced in the text. The author put a traumatic focus on the reasons for the tragedy, his explanation focused on the quarrels, envy, lawlessness and avarice among Christians. Strangely enough, the Sultan himself pronounced the deserved explanation. When he saw the enormous wealth of the city, he exclaimed:

---

6   Todorov, *Sabrani proizvedeniya*; Raynov, *Izbrani proizvedeniya*. See also Hranova, *Istoriografiya i literatura. Za sotsialnoto konstruirane na istoricheski ponyatiya i Golemi razkazi v balgarskata kultura. XIX–XX vek.*

7   Text in Petkanova, ed., *Narodnoto chetivo prez XVI–XVIII v.* All quotations below are from this edition.

8   Text in Petkanova, ed., *Starobálgarska Literatura. Enčiklopedičen Rečnik*, 334.

9   Bozhilov, ed., *Stara balgarska literatura*, vol. 3, 334.

Oh, you insane people! Where is your progressive sense [напредничав разум]? With such a treasure and with such wealth you could not only stop but even beat everybody in this world. With your greediness you destroyed the Kingdom of your ancestors.[10]

The clash between real and false faith was a topic to be expected in such a context. And it was presented in the narration—the defenders of the city were fighting and dying for their faith, and for their Orthodox Church. Nevertheless, this aspect of the text was not so much highlighted in the nineteenth and twentieth centuries in Bulgarian versions. It is most obvious in the history textbooks reviewed by Lilova.[11]

The situation was complicated. The author of the first Bulgarian history—the monk Paisius of Hilendar (eighteenth century)—did not mention the event in his manuscript, possibly because he did not see it as an important part of the past of the "Slav-Bulgarian" people he was dealing with. The second most famous early Bulgarian history writer, the monk Spyridon, dedicated a special chapter to the event in his "Short History Concerning the Bulgarian Slav People" (1792, also a manuscript). By contrast, the Franciscan monk Blasius Kleiner, probably from Transylvania, ended the first part of his "History of Bulgaria" (eighteenth century) with the fall of the Byzantium, where it was presented as an important part of Bulgarian history. This perspective was only partially adopted by Bulgarian historians of the nineteenth and twentieth centuries.

The fall of Constantinople was also featured in Bulgarian folk songs and legends. St. Stoykova identified one peculiar model that was very distant from historic events and from records in the chronicles.[12] In some texts, the invaders even appeared to be Bulgarians. Nevertheless, some of the elements were similar and one can trace their links with the myth— the predictions, God's intervention, the death of the King, the prophecy of the future revival of the Kingdom, etc.

* * *

10 *Padanieto na Tsarigrad.* Drama v pet deystviya ot S. N. Milarov. *Napredak*, No. 4 and 5, 1883.
11 Lilova, "Balgarskiyat razkaz za padaneto pod osmanska vlast: istoricheski kanon bez mesianistichen mit," 255–275.
12 Stoïcova, "La chanson de la chute de Constantinople dans le folklore bulgare," 478.

There is one Bulgarian literary work dedicated to the event that was, and still is, less popular—the drama in verse titled "The Fall of the King's City" by Svetoslav Milarov. It was written from 1871–72 in an Istanbul prison; parts of it were published in the newspaper *Napredak* (Progress) in 1874, but the full text not until 1883,[13] after the establishment of the new Bulgarian state. Contemporaries and critics never expressed high regard for this ambitious attempt by an ambitious author. The process of writing the play was well documented in its relatively long Afterward and in Milarov's excellent "Memoirs from the King's City Prisons."[14] The Afterward reveals his pretention for authentic presentation of the historic events and his source, the "Histoire de la Turquie"[15] by Alphonse de Lamartine. After finishing his work the author came across another source, "one a popular Russian book (*О разорении и взятии Царь-града*, Москва, 1882 [About the destroying and capture of the King's City, Moscow, 1882])"[16] that confirmed his historical picture.

Lamartine's work, published in eight volumes in 1854–1855 was actually a compilation created by the famous (but bankrupt) poet, mainly for commercial motives. In just a few years he managed to publish several extensive historic works: *Histoire de la Restauration, 1852; Histoire des Constituants, 1853; Histoire de la Russie, 1855*. Later, every month readers received a part of his *Cours familiers de littérature* (1856–1869). Milarov followed the narration of Lamartine and other authors, but he also added his own plot that connected historic events with the private life of real or fictional characters.

One confession of Milarov is extremely interesting in the context of the place that Constantinople had in the Bulgarian imagination and to what extent it was "alien" or "our own":

---

13 *Napredak*, IX, No. 2 and 4, 13 and July 27, 1874; *The Fall of Constantinople: A Drama in 5 acts* by S. N. Milarov (Sredec, State printing house, 1888). Cf. Priturka kam Periodichesko spisanie, No. 4 i 5 [Supplement to the periodical [Napredak (Progres), No. 4 and 5] 1883.

14 Milarov, *Memoirs from the Prisons of Constantinople*.

15 Extracts of Lamartine's History were published at that time (1877–1891) in Turkish translation. Cf. Zaimova, "La modernité balkanique de l'historien Lamartine," *Études balkaniques*, 1 (2005): 101–109. Slaveykov has also referred to Lamartine but did not mention the precise source. Cf. for example: "Edin pogled kam minaloto" (1887), P. S. Slaveykov. *Sachineniya* [Selected Works] (Sofia: Balgârski pisatel, 1979), vol. 3, 289 and 444; see also 329.

16 Milarov, *Nebesniyat prevrat*, 125. In this edition is also published the full text of the author's Afterward to the drama, "The Fall of the King's City."

I wanted to glorify, to carve the memory of the most beautiful place in the world, of my native city, of the King's city. I love this city in the way someone loves a girl.[17]

Indeed, Constantinople was presented as "our own" in the text; the author took the viewpoint of the inhabitants, and going against the dominant trend of Bulgarian literature of the time, he portrayed the Byzantines as heroes. Paradoxically enough, this did not imply an anti-Ottoman tendency. Howsoever, the author himself and the editor of *Napredak* claimed that the newspaper was banned because of the phrase "The name of this dragon (ламя сура) was Mohamed..." (1:1). It referred to Sultan Mehmed and was pronounced by Isidore of Kiev (ex-Metropolitan of Moscow), a character in the play who is portrayed negatively.

Broadly speaking, the play followed the way the chronicles presented the historic events and the appreciation in their importance. There were fewer, if any, miracles, and the causes of the fall of the city were not the focus of the author's attention. The invaders were more numerous and stronger, the defenders were not united, and the allies were insufficient, and being Catholics were not particularly trustworthy, etc.[18] All this is directly said in the text, but it is relegated to the background.

One important reference was the appearance on the stage of the "Ghost of Byzantine Kingdom" and the "Ghost of Leonidas." They reveal themselves to Emperor Constantine, but it was not clear if this is a dream or a real appearance. Leonidas is easy to identify, though the name is used as if it was generally known; one might guess that this was Leonidas I King of Sparta, the hero of the Battle of Thermopylae (480 BC), glorified by Herodotus (Histories, XII, 225), Simonides of Ceos ("O Stranger, send the news home to the people of Sparta that here we are laid to rest: the commands they gave us have been obeyed.") and so on. This leads to

---

17   [Аз исках да възвелича, да издялам спомена – за най-прекрасния предел на света, за своя роден град, за Цариград. Аз обичам този град, както някой би обичал една девойка.] Milarov, *Nebesniyat prevrat*, 130. Milarov passed his life without finding a spouse or even a true love.

18   Milarov's relations with Catholicism were complicated. He graduated from a French school. His father was among the men that were advocating an independent Bulgarian Church, but later he embraced the Union with Catholicism and even became an officer in the United Bulgarian Union Church. See Sapunov, *Dnevnik po sagrazhdaneto na parvata balgarska tsarkva v Tsarigrad,* 189–192.

at least two conclusions regarding the author's ideas. The first one is that Byzantium was seen as direct inheritor of Ancient (and pagan) Greece—this was the thesis of so called "Philhellenism," Laonikos Chalkokondyles being among its late advocates. The second was the analogy between the Turks (Ottomans) and the Persians, familiar from other medieval and early modern Bulgarian texts that were connected with the Alexander romance. One could also speculate on the probable place of all this in Bulgarian imagery and its ideas about "own" and alien.

Milarov was educated in literature at the French college in Bebek and at high school in Zagreb, knew something about theatrical performances and was presumably aware that it was not so easy to present spectacular battles on stage. So the events the war were presented through the narrations of the characters, though the main plot had to do with love: a beautiful and virtuous noble girl—Eudoxia, daughter of Notaras ("first dignitary and Byzantine admiral")—was in love from a distance with Constantine (the "last Byzantine Emperor"); on the other hand, other men were also in love with her—the "roguish monk Gennadius," the Italian knight Giovanni Giustiniani, and even Sultan Mehmed. Two characters in the play bear the name of Gennadius—the "roguish monk" and the Ecumenical "Patriarch of Constantinople."

Different narrations about the love affairs of Mehmed with Christian women circulated in European literature. Among them, one linked him with Maria Gattilusio (widow of Alexander, a brother of Emperor David of Trebizond), who was called the most beautiful woman of her day and who disappeared into the sultan's harem. Her son Alexios became a page, but seems to have been beheaded not long afterwards. Some of these stories of affairs ended with the death of the woman, but all of them differ from Milarov's variation.

The story of Eudoxia was not recorded by Lamartine, but the other elements of the plot were, and they have their roots in the chronicles where the Sultan also caused the death of Notaras and his sons and even had sexual aspirations for one of the boys. This episode fits too perfectly to the European image of "The Turk," and so it too was possibly "imagined"; Edward Gibbon claimed that some similar fate befell the son of the historian Sphrantzes.[19]

---

19 Cf. Gibbon, E., *Zalez i unadâk na Rumskata imperia,* 398 and 620 (notes).

Lamartine's Mehmed treated the wife of the Byzantine dignitary politely and respectfully:

Le lendemain de son éntrée trionphante, il [Mohamet II] sortit à cheval du palais, parcourut la ville avec un petit nombre de cavaliers, et alla render visite à la princesse, femme du grand-duc Notaras, qu'une infirmité grave retenait dans son lit. Il s'entretint respectueusement avec cette princesse, qui lui présenta ses fils.[20]

The sentimental line, most probably invented or at least more fully elaborated by Milarov and charged with clear ideological implications was the most specific element of his work. The mythical structure that underlined it was well known. According to it Byzantium, like Bulgaria in many other texts, was portrayed as a beautiful young woman, the object of aspirations on the part of different foreigners. Byzantium as an innocent virgin was quite atypical for Bulgarian imagery, and not only for Bulgarians! The opposing ideological poles personified by these suitors were multiple. Apart from the Orthodox Byzantines and infidel Turks, there were Catholics, personified in the knight Giustiniani and the Roman Cardinal Isidore, openly hated by large part of the people. According to Milarov's version almost all of them, except the Emperor—Giustiniani, Gennadius, Notaras—appear to be traitors or at least collaborationists.

Eudoxia, like other mythical characters in her situation, turned out to be not so defenseless; she alone, without the assistance of any man, managed to extort an oath from the Sultan and then to kill herself. The core of the mythical motif was in the final scene—the dialogue between the powerful Turk and the beautiful Christian girl. She turns out to be rather cunning, declaring:

> Oh, you are really noble!
> I say this openly.
> So listen to me, King, and swear
> With words strong and hard

---

20 de Lamartine, Alphonse, *Histoire de la Turquie*, 257.

That in your vast state
Christ will be as free
As Mohamed; and then take me:
Then let this body be yours.[21]

The oath was pronounced and the Sultan got the body of the maiden, who on the instant "took a small knife and stabbed herself."[22] Apart from the heroic aspect of this act, it explained the destiny of the historic Notaras, who was at first accepted by the Sultan but later executed.

* * *

Bulgarian texts presenting the Ottoman capture of Constantinople were part of a textual network that had common sources, a common mythical basis and even a common archetype. The links between the different representations were complex and not always direct. The role of external, non-Balkan imagery was also important. Milarov's variation was not the most popular but is still representative and reveals some tensions between nationalist imagery and other perspectives toward history.

The attitude of nationalism towards the Ottoman invaders should by now be clear. More complicated and even ambivalent was the attitude towards Constantinople—the traditional object of fears, hate, desire, aspirations, and so on. Therefore, the image of the city and the interpretations of historic events differ, or sometimes even contradict nationalist ideas. Constantinople appears to be not only Byzantine, the Virgin Mary's, Ottoman, but also, in a sense, "ours"—that is, Bulgarian, through the claims of national mythology.

---

21 Наистина, ти си благороден!
    Казвам ти го със начин свободен.
    И чуй, царю ето – закълни се
    пред мен тука с дума твърда и здрава,
    че в твойта пространна държава
    Христос равна свобода ще има
    с Мохамеда, и тогаз – земи ме:
    Това тяло нек се падне тебе.
22 *Padanieto na Tsarigrad.* Drama v pet deystviya ot S. N. Milarov. *Napredak*, No. 5, 1883.

References

Bozhilov, I., ed. *Stara balgarska literatura* [Old Bulgarian literature]. Vol. 3. Sofia: Balgârski pisatel, 1983.
Burçoğlu, Nedret Kuran. "Slikata za Turchinot vo Evropa, vo minaloto i denes: kritichesko patuvaнje" [The image of the Turk in Europe, past and present: critical journey]. In *Balkanska slika na svetot. Prireduvach Katitsa Kulavkova* [The Balkan image of the world], edited by K. Kulavkova, 117–134. Skopje: Macedonian Academy of Sciences and Arts, 2006.
de Lamartine, Alphonse. *Histoire de la Turquie.* Vol. 3. Paris: Librairie du Constitutionnel, 1854.
Fauriel, C. *Chants populaire de la Grèce moderne.* Vol. 1. Paris: Chez Firmin Didot, père and filles, 1824.
Gibbon, E. *Zalez i unadâk na Rumskata imperia* [The history of the decline and fall of the Roman Empire]. Vol. 4, edited by A. Daskalov. Sofia: Лик, 2003.
Herzfeld, Michael. *Ours Once More: Folklore, Ideology, and the Making of Modern Greece.* Austin: University of Texas Press, 1982.
Hranova, A. *Istoriografiya i literatura. Za sotsialnoto konstruirane na istoricheski ponyatiya i Golemi razkazi v balgarskata kultura. XIX–XX vek* [Historiography and literature: about the social constructing of historic notions and the grand narrative in Bulgarian culture, nineteenth–twentieth centuries]. Vol. 1. Sofia: Prosveta, 2011.
История во кратце о болгарском народе словенском. Сочинися и исписа в лето 1792 йеросхимонах Спиридон. Стъкми за издание В. Златарски. София, 1900. [Istoriya vo krattse o bolgarskom narode slovenskom. Sochinisya i ispisa v leto 1792 yeroshimonah Spiridon. Stakmi za izdanie V. Zlatarski. Sofiya, 1900.]
Lilova, D. "Balgarskiyat razkaz za padaneto pod osmanska vlast: istoricheski kanon bez mesianistichen mit" [The Bulgarian narration about the Ottoman conquest: historical canon without messianic myth]. *Kritika i humanizam* 1 (2006): 255–275.
Manousos, Antonios. *Tragoudia ethnika* [National songs]. Corfu: Typografeion Ermis; Reprint Athens: Rizos, 1909.
Milarov, S. N. *Nebesniyat prevrat. Politicheski dnevnik, pisma, statii, kroezhi* [Celestial take-over: political diary, letters, articles, plans]. Edited by P. Velichkov. Sofia: Fakel, 2003.
———. *Padanieto na Tsarigrad.* Drama v pet deystviya ot S. N. Milarov. Sredets. Darzhavna pechatnitsa, 1883. [The Fall of Constantinople. Drama in 5 acts by S. N. Milarov. Sredec, State printing house, 1888. Supplement to Periodical magazine *Napredak* (Progres), No. 4 and 5, 1883.]
———. *Spomeni ot tsarigradskite tamnitsi* [Memoirs from the prisons of Constantinople]. Edited by I. Todorov. Sofia: GAL-IKO, 1994.
Petkanova, D., ed. *Narodnoto chetivo prez XVI–XVIII v.* [Popular literature from the sixteenth and seventeenth century]. Sofia: Balgârski pisatel, 1990.
———, ed. *Starobâlgarska Literatura. Enčiklopedičen Rečnik* [Old Bulgarian literature. Encyclopedic dictionary]. Sofia: Petar Beron, 1992.
Raynov, N. *Izbrani proizvedeniya* [Selected works]. Vol. 1. Sofia: Balgârski pisatel, 1969.
Runciman, S. *The Fall of Constantinople.* Cambridge: Cambridge University Press, 1964.

Slaveykov, P. S. *Sachineniya* [Selected works]. Vol. 3. Sofia: Balgârski pisatel, 1979.

Sapunov, N. *Dnevnik po sagrazhdaneto na parvata balgarska tsarkva v Tsarigrad* [Diary concerning the building of the first Bulgarian church in Istanbul]. Edited by Hr. Temelski. Veliko Tarnovo: PIK, 1999.

Stoïcova, S. "La chanson de la chute de Constantinople dans le folklore bulgare." *Balkan Studies: A Biannual publication of the Institute for Balkan Studies* 25, no. 2 (1984): 475–483.

Todorov, P. *Sabrani proizvedeniya* [Selected works]. Vol. 1. Sofia: Balgârski pisatel, 1957.

Zaimova, R. "La modernité balkanique de l'historien Lamartine." *Études balkaniques*, no. 1 (2005): 101–109.

Naoum Kaytchev

"Turkish Illyrians" or Bulgarians/Serbs? Ottoman South Slavs Within the Croatian and Bulgarian National Models (1830s–1840s)

In January 1843, a central Habsburg decision imposed a ban on the use of the very terms "Illyria" and "Illyrian" for journalistic, political, educational and all public purposes. As a result, the established Zagreb weekly *Danica ilirska* and the newspaper *Ilirske narodne novine* were forced to change their titles and to abandon any use of the words that were central to the national model they were advancing. The repression was mild and strictly literary. When the publisher Ljudevit Gaj endeavored to issue his new political journal *Branislav* from abroad, from the Serbian capital Belgrade, its pages were full of protest against "Hungarian censorship" in Croatia, but were at pains to show continuing loyalty to the existing Austrian imperial order. After all, Illyrianism was one of the smaller regionalisms-cum-nationalisms that were protected, if not encouraged, by the imperial centers.[1] One of the examples cited of the brutal suppression was the seizure of copies of the first volume of Dragutin Seljan's geographic work, as well as the ban and the unhappy fate of its second volume, destined to languish in manuscript form.[2]

This initial setback to the Illyrianist movement is well known. Less known is the content of Dragutin Seljan's proscribed work and its ideological message. In fact, the second unpublished volume is a geography of Bosnia, Serbia and Bulgaria, or, in the words of the author, of the "lands inhabited by the Illyro-Slav people" in "Turkish Europe."[3] The manu-

---

1 Cf. Berger and Miller, "Introduction: Building Nations in and with Empires: A Reassessment," 23.
2 *Branislav* 1 (1844): 1–3, 11–15, 37.
3 NSK Zagreb [Manuscript Collection of the National and University Library in Zagreb], R

script represents the intersection of scholarly geography with the Illyrian-ist national construction, or, more precisely, the attempt to project the Il-lyrian ideologeme[4] over some concrete spatial reality.

The very principle of the book—abandoning the division along exist-ing state borders in favor of the geographical Illyrian lands—might ex-plain why the work was easily targeted by the Habsburg censorship. Dra-gutin Seljan was a young priest and an established member of the inner Illyrianist circle. Born in 1810, and just one year younger than Gaj, he early devoted himself to a cleric career and became an influential educa-tor at the Zagreb *convictorium*, a boarding establishment of the Catho-lic schools in the town. He joined ranks with young priests like the poet Pavao Štoos and embraced the new principles of Illyrianism. Moreover, he was personally at the heart of the emerging new cultural movement: he became a close personal admirer of Gaj and distinguished himself in his Illyrianist activities as an organizer of Zagreb youth. For example, in early

---

3013, Dragutin Seljan, *Zemljopis pokrainah Bosne, Serbie, Bugarske iliti ogledalo zemlje na ko-joj pribiva narod ilirsko-slavjanski sa opisanjem berdah, potokah, gradovah i znatnih městah po-lag sadanjeg stališa s kratkim dogodopisnim dodatkom*. The first volume was published originally as: Dragutin Seljan, *Zemljopis pokrainah ilirskih iliti ogledalo zemlje, na kojoj pribiva narod ilir-sko-slavjanski sa opisanjem berdah, potokah, gradovah i znatniih městah polag sadanjeg stališa, s kratkim dogodopisnim dodatkom i priloženim krajobrazom iliti mapom*. [Geography of the Illyr-ian provinces or mirror of the land inhabited by the Illyrian-Slav people with a description of mountains, rivers, towns and more important places in their present state, with a short histori-cal addition and an attached map], Vol. 1, *Pokrajine austriansko-ilirske* [Austrian-Illyrian prov-inces] (Zagreb: Tisak Ljudevita Gaja, 1843). Recently Seljan's work was republished in a new edition that included the first volume and only the initial chapter on Bosnia from the second volume: Dragutin Seljan, *Zemljopis pokrainah ilirskih iliti ogledalo zemlje* [Geography of the Il-lyrian provinces or mirror of the land] (Zagreb: Dom i Svijet, 2005); this edition is accompa-nied with introductions by Vladimir Stipetić and Mirko Kratofil. Thus the core of the second volume is still available only in manuscript form. The references below from the first volume are from the original 1843 edition.

4   The Illyrian ideologeme has been defined as a "historically determined conceptual or semantic complex of intertextual nature with a high performative potential which thematizes and discur-sively produces the common origin, linguistic unity, territorial magnitude and exceptional qual-ities of 'Illyrians', variously identified within the ethnic complex of Slavdom" (Blažević, *Illyrism before Illyrism*, 33, 346). Cf. Blažević, "Inderemi-Nation: Narrative Identity and Symbolic Poli-tics in the Early Modern Illyrism," 205–206. In the 1830s–1840s a new wave of Croatian intellec-tuals upgraded the earlier ideologeme by combining it with the tradititonal legal-historical proto-nationalism of the Croatian estates and the novel premises of the Herderian linguistic-cultural concept of the nation, adopted among the Slavs by Jan Kollar and other Czecho-Slovak cultural leaders. Thus a new Illyrianist (supra)national ideological complex was forged. Kaytchev, *Iliria ot Varna do Vilah: Hărvatskoto natsionalno văzrazhdane, sărbite i bălgarite (do 1848)*.

July 1841 he orchestrated a celebration in Zagreb to welcome Gaj after his extensive trip through Dalmatia.[5]

Even more important was his literary work and input in the elaboration and dissemination of Illyrianist ideas. While contributing to *Danica ilirska*, in 1840 he issued his first book dealing with the progress of Illyrian literature which was one of the first systematic accounts of the activities of Gaj and his followers. More originally, the last chapter of the book—under the typical emotive title *Description of Great Illyria*—in fact offered some novel means for the spread of the Illyrianist national complex. Heretofore erected grand spatial dimensions of Illyria tended to be more of an emotional poetic nature like the famous lyre of Gaj angled on Villach, Varna and Scutari (Shkodra)[6] or his giant lying over half of Europe and gripping the Black Sea with one hand and the Baltic Sea with the other.[7] Unlike most of his other fellow revivalists, Seljan went beyond the favored avenues of literature, history and theatre—he preferred to develop and propagate Illyrianism using the language of scholarly geography.[8] In the following years he continued to develop this approach, aiming to create a voluminous geographical work that would advance the new national construction. In two years he completed the first volume treating the "Austro-Illyrian" territories and produced it in Gaj's printing office in the late autumn of 1842.[9] That volume is considered as the first-ever geography published in the Croatian language. Despite the January 1843 ban on Illyrian terminology, Seljan proceeded with his work at an unabated pace; by 1845 he had almost completed it. The second part dwelled extensively on regions under direct or indirect Ottoman rule: Bosnia (pp. 3–44 in the manuscript), Serbia (pp. 45–104), Bulgaria (pp. 105–144), Albania (pp. 145–185) and Montenegro (pp. 187–194). Predictably, the work emphasized the "Illyro-Slav" nature of the portrayed territories. It even went one step further—these outlined

---

5   Seljan and Vakanović, "5.VII.1841"; Horvat, *Ljudevit Gaj: Njegov život, njegovo doba*, 182.

6   Gaj, Ljudevit, "II proglas,"113.

7   Gaj, Ljudevit, "Naš narod," 112.

8   Seljan, *Početak, naprědak i vrědnost literature ilirske. S kratkim geografičko-statističkim opisom Ilirskih děržavah*, 68–88.

9   Seljan, *Zemljopis pokrainah ilirskih*. Although 1843 is the year printed on the title page (hence its official 1843 entry in all bibliographies) the sources prove that copies of the book were in circulation from the end of October 1842. In 1843 the publication of a book with such a title would have been impossible. Novak, *Početak, naprědak i vrědnost literature ilirske. S kratkim geografičko-statističkim opisom Ilirskih děržavah*, 300–301.

regions were portrayed in wider Pan-European perspective as particularly fit for attainment of the ultimate goal, the sovereign state: "The Slavs could settle their own free, proud and independent motherland in no other place so easily as in Turkish Europe."[10] Yet the immediate prescription to this end was hardly expected: Serbian-Bulgarian political and ethnic-linguistic unification should be accompanied by alliance with Turkey. The Slavs were viewed as the true nucleus of the European Turkey. If the Sublime Porte wished to prosper, it should give a constitution to the Slavs:

> Let the state be not only Turkish but also Slav and Greek. Every branch should have profit from this and should support the throne perpetually, every faith should enjoy full liberty, Hatti-Sherif of Gülhane should become true reality in which every Moslem and Christian should be entitled not only to civic but also to political equality.[11]

Was this support for a reformed imperial Ottoman model based on some vague trialist "Turkoslavist" or "Turko-Slavic-Greek" principles characteristic of the Illyrian movement or did it only derive from its most enthusiastic and emblematic geographer? One often overlooked aspect of the Illyrian ideological complex is its imagined "Turkish Illyrian" or Bulgarian dimension. Previous studies on the movement have tended to ignore this part of its ideology or in the best of cases only cited some key Illyrianist statements uniting all South Slavs, including Bulgarians, into the imagined Illyrian nationality. The Bulgarians were the most far away and obscure members of the common Illyrian people.[12] In what follows we will try to outline how exactly the South Slavs of the Ottoman Empire were incorporated into the Illyrianist national discourse and what their relative importance in it was. Was the chief intellectual construct and official aim of the movement, "Great Illyria," seen as leading to an imagined empire or a nation-state? Drawing on major studies on nationalism we would counterpose the Illyrianist to the Bulgarian national concept and

---

10 NSK Zagreb, R 3013, 132.
11 NSK Zagreb, R 3013, 135–137.
12 Cf. the otherwise commendable classic research on the subject: Despalatović, *Ljudevit Gaj and the Illyrian Movement*, 87–90; Šidak, *Hrvatski narodni preporod. Ilirski pokret*, 122, 133; Stančić, "Hrvatski narodni preporod 1790–1848," 24; idem, *Hrvatska nacija i nacionalizam u 19 i 20 stoljeću*, 172.

their relation in turn to different imperial models including the Ottoman one. This study makes use of Anthony Smith's concept of *mythomoteurs*[13] and the related postmodernist term *topi*, applied especially to the Croatian case by Zrinka Blažević.[14] The Bulgarian, and especially Illyrian, case might illustrate the strengths and limits of postmodernist theories of the nation as imagined community or narration.[15]

* * *

Gaj, the literary-ideological leader of the movement, was convinced at the early stages of the formulation of his national narrative, at least from 1832–1833, that the Bulgarians were a South Slavic "tribe" belonging to the Illyrian community. The Croatian historian Nikša Stančić presumes that Gaj in those years was following the authority of the language-based classifications of the earlier Pavel Šafařík and that he considered the Bulgarians as a part of the Serbian people.[16] Gaj's image of the Bulgarians, however, was not entirely bookish. Judging by his remarks he was in personal contact with a number of Bulgarians in the decisive years when he constructed his national concept. In 1831 in Pest he read to certain "valued Bulgarians" the patriotic poem "Statue of the Homeland" (*Kip domovine*) composed by his compatriot Pavao Štoos and was touched by their emotional reaction, breaking in tears when the verses were read to them. This poem had an important influence on the Croatian self-image in the early 1830s and was accordingly published by Gaj in one of the initial issues of the first Croatian journal, *Danicza horvatzka, slavonzka y dalmatinzka* (its name subsequently altered to *Danica horvatska, slavonska i dalmatinska* and then to *Danica ilirska*).[17]

---

13   Smith, *The Ethnic Origin of Nations*, 15–16, 58–68. While the original term denotes the complex of symbols, memories, values and myths that generally embraces the entire identity narration on the past of a given ethnic community, making a "constitutive myth of the ethnic polity," I use "mythomoteur" mainly to designate certain key defining elements of that narration; it could rest on real historical experiences as well as on fictional legendary developments in the past.

14   Blažević, *Ilirizam prije ilirizma*, 88–91.

15   Cf. Smith, "Gastronomy or Geology? The Role of Nationalism in the Reconstruction of Nations," 3–23.

16   Stančić, *Gajeva "Još Horvatska ni propala" iz 1832–1833. Ideologija Ljudevita Gaja u pripremom razdoblju hrvatskog narodnog preporoda*, 138.

17   Štoos, "Kip domovine vu početku leta 1831," 245–250.

In his famous article "Our People," of August 1835 Gaj presented in concise and condensed form the outlines of the reformulated Illyrian ideological complex. Though the elaborated image was strictly cultural, its potential political application would have produced not a nation-state but rather an empire of great magnitude: it turned out that "Our people" were all the Slavs, consisting of two branches (*grane*) that in their own turn were divided each in two and thus formed all-in-all four major sub-branches (*koljena*): Illyrian, Russian, Czech and Polish. The Illyrianists were forced to concede that the imagined Pan-Slav entity so central to their beliefs was divided into different units on several levels not unlike the contemporary Habsburg imperial conglomerate that included vast numbers of Croats and various other Slavs. Closest to his readers, and occupying first place in the classification, was the Illyrian sub-branch, which sought to integrate a range of assorted elements: Slovenes (Vinds), Croats, Slavonians, Dalmatians, Bosnians, Montenegrins, Serbs and Bulgarians. Reflecting the already prevalent regionalism and the fluid ethnic composition of the South Slav regions, Gaj employed territorial labels to denote the different Illyrian components. These ideas were further developed by subsequent authors, yet the concept they shared remained far from the one-dimensional uniformity of the nation-state; the Illyrianist construction was multi-layered and hierarchic, and more in tune with the empire models.

According to this systematization, the Illyrian sub-branch included three major "tribes" living largely under the Ottomans: Bosnians, Serbs and Bulgarians. The Bulgarians were firmly included in the Illyrian family as an element separate from the Serbs.[18] Gaj and his circle devoted substantial attention to the Bulgarians as principle Illyrians living under the Ottoman writ. Numerous articles in the Illyrianist press, starting from 1837, presented them as a sympathetic, peaceful, earth-loving people, but far from any substantial literary or economic accomplishments.[19] This description explicitly raised the figure of the "undeveloped" section of the imagined self-community: while the Illyrian community was composed of several component parts with varying cultural level, the Bulgarians were at the very bottom. This uneven structure might imply a prospective, compli-

---

18 Gaj, "Naš narod," 112–116.
19 "Bulgarske žeteljke" [Bulgarian women], *Danica ilirska* 3:32–33 (August 5–12, 1837):130–131, 136.

cated, constitution not dissimilar to the well-known imperial composite state under the Habsburgs. However, the Illyrianists, at least on the level of ideas, were very far from standard imperialist models that postulated subjugation or control over the well-defined peripheral segments of the overall entity.[20] On the contrary, they fancied the future elevation of their Ottoman-dominated brethren to the level of the other more developed Illyrian Slavs. From 1842 onwards they joyfully recorded the substantial literary and cultural advancement of the Bulgarian component of the imagined self-community. The periodical *Danica* offered a number of articles on the emerging Bulgarian literary life. For example, it welcomed the publishing of one of the first Bulgarian geography textbooks, translated from Russian by Ivan Bogorov. Especially enthusiastic was the reception of the first Bulgarian magazine, *Lyuboslovie*, published by Konstantin Fotinov in Smirna in 1844–1846, and of the first newspaper, *Bălgarski orel* (Bulgarian eagle), edited in Leipzig in 1846–1847 by the same Ivan Bogorov.[21]

Another important Illyrianist engagement with the imperial was the continuing self-definition in relation to the Ottoman polity. Bulgarians were generally presented as an ethnic and cultural entity outside of the existing official state structures. If Ottomans were involved, then the attitude toward them was largely negative. Especially influential in this respect was the poem "Echo from the Balkan (Mountain)," or "The Tears of the Bulgarian, Bosnian and Herzegovinian Christians," by Ognjeslav Utješenović Ostrožinski, an Eastern Orthodox "Illyrian" from the Habsburg Croatian Military Frontier. It was conspicuous for several decades in Croatian public discourse, symbolizing the misfortunes of their brethren suffering under the Turkish yoke. Signing himself as the "whining Bulgarian" (*bugareći Bugarin*) coming "from the springs of river Maritsa in the Balkan," the author implied that the term Bulgarian generally meant a co-national suffering under Turkish rule. Seen from free Christian Zagreb, all Illyrians under the Turks—be they in Bulgaria, Bos-

---

20 This model is outlined in different ways by various authors including Lieven, *Empire: The Russian Empire and its Rivals*, 4–6; Doyle, *Empires*, 30–45; Howe, *Empire: A Very Short Introduction*, 9–30.

21 "Sveslavjanske věsti" [All-Slav news], *Danica ilirska* 9:18 (April 30, 1842), 9:43 (October 22, 1842); "Slavjanska tiskarnica u Carigradu" [Slavic printing house in Constantinople], *Danica horvatska, slavonska i dalmatinska* 11:49 (December 6, 1845); *Danica horvatska, slavonska i dalmatinska* 12:21 (May 23, 1846); 12:23 (June 6, 1846).

nia, Herzegovina or in other unknown lands—could be classed as Bulgarians.[22] In the 1840s the Illyrianists continued to present the Bulgarians as brethren suffering under the infidel yoke.[23]

The attitude to the Ottoman Empire itself was to a certain extent ambivalent. *Ilirske narodne novine*, the official newspaper edited by Gaj, was generally affirmative of Constantinople, publishing many stories on the modernizing pro-European policy of Sultan Mahmud II. The attentive reader could learn of undertakings to improve roads and water canals and to reform army and police along the Western models. The progress extended into the educational field as well: a medical institute was opened in Istanbul and various other establishments in the provinces. Some of them introduced French as the teaching language. The sultan or his viziers adopted a number of European attitudes. They were influenced by the Western diplomatic protocol; some of them attended and enjoyed the balls arranged by various ambassadors. Even more surprisingly, *Ilirske narodne novine* reported on certain Ottoman actions that eroded the deep-rooted stereotypes towards them as enemies of Christendom: Mahmud II inspected the construction of an Orthodox cathedral, he allowed the erection of five new Catholic churches in Constantinople, and authorized entry of Christians into mosques. On a Black Sea trip he proclaimed the equality of all his subjects regardless of their faith. In fact, these articles were for the most part reprinted from the Austrian press; being influenced by the official Habsburg attitudes they reflected Viennese rather than Zagreb views on the neighboring empire.

The literary weekly *Danica ilirska*, on the other hand, put forward a completely opposite image of the Ottoman empire. The Tanzimat reforms were not even mentioned; whereas numerous fictional descriptions of conflicts between the South Slav Christians and the Balkan Turks were offered instead. Most of the Turkish-related articles shared the spirit of the abovementioned ballad "Echo from the Balkan." Nor should we for-

---

22 Utješenović Ostrožinski, Ognjeslav, "Jeka od Balkana ili suze bugarskih, hercegovačkih i bosanskih hristianah" [Echo from the Balkan Mountain] or [The tears of the Bulgarian, Bosnian and Herzegovinian Christians], 37–38.

23 "Bugarska i Bugari" [Bulgaria and Bulgarians], *Danica horvatska, slavonska i dalmatinska* 10:5 (February 4, 1843); "Něšto o Bugarih" [Something on Bulgarians], *Danica horvatska, slavonska i dalmatinska* 10:11 (March 16, 1843).

get to mention significant parts of the poem "Croatian Homeland" by Antun Mihanović, published on March 14, 1835 in *Danica*. It did not point to any named state or nation, but since the designated romantic battlefield was "beyond the river Una," in other words in Bosnia, it was clear who really was dubbed as *dushman* (the oppressing enemy):

> Magla, što li, Unu skriva?
> Ni l' to našiu jauk turobni?
> Tko li moleć smert doziva?
> Il' slobodni, il' su robni?
>
> "Rat je, bratjo, rat junaci,
> Pušku hvataj, sablju paši,
> Sedlaj konjče, hajd pešjaci,
> Slava budi, gdi su naši!"
>
> Buči bura, magla projde, –
> Puca zora, tmina běži, –
> Tuga mine, radost dojde, –
> Zdravo slobost, – dušman leži![24]

This poem presently serves as the Croatian national anthem, though the above cited verses are not included in the official text.

---

24 Is it fog that hides the Una?
Isn't that our people's dreary scream?
Who is it who prays for death?
Is it the free, or is it slaves?

"'Tis war, O brothers, war, O heroes,
Snatch your rifle, take a saber,
Saddle your horses, let's go, footmen,
May glory be, there where ours are!"

The *Bora* [wind] roars, the fog is gone,–
Dawn breaks, and the darkness flees,–
Sorrow fades, and joy arrives,–
Hail freedom, – the *dushman* fallen lies!

The Illyrianists canonized the seventeenth-century Croatian epic *Osman* by Ivan Gundulić. It was not by chance that they chose to republish firstly the episode of the old man Ljubdrag and his daughter Sunčanica, which recreated a poetic picture of the South Slav space and its people suffering under "harsh slavery."[25] A number of similar literary items in *Danica* reaffirmed the standard discourse on the Turks as "infidels from the East" that had conquered the Christian lands of South East Europe; the new masters had ruled by force over these lands for centuries and caused their civilizational backwardness and separation from the Christian West. Illyrian texts with their typical negative stereotyped images of the Turks as "the Conqueror," "the Religious enemy," "the Violator," and "the Primitive," were in line with other key contemporary literary works concerned with the Turkish theme. The travelogue *View on Bosnia* (1842) by Matija Mažuranić presented Ottoman Bosnia as an exotic space, the break with European civilization started directly from the other bank of the Una and Sava rivers; the drama *Juran and Sofija or the Turks under Sisak* (1838) by Ivan Kukuljević Sakcinski celebrated the victory over the Ottomans in 1593 and thus continued the well-established *mythomoteur* of Croatia and Croatians as "the bulwark of Christendom" (*antemurale Christianitatis*); while the epic *The Death of Smail-Aga Čengić* (1845) by Ivan Mažuranić reached new heights in the demonization of the Turks in Croatian culture, hyperbolizing Turkish violence and maximizing the motives of religious hatred. The articles in *Danica* together with these dominant Illyrianist literary works constituted a single narrative determining Croatian perception and imagining of the Ottomans. These works had a far more powerful effect than the scattered and soon forgotten stories of the modernizing pro-European policy of Sultan Mahmud II.[26] The Illyrianist attitude clearly shared some of the basic tenets of what is now termed Orientalism, though it differed from it in some aspects. While the classic Orientalist discourse stemmed from the deep-rooted sense of superiori-

---

25 Gundulić, Ivan. "Sunčanica kći Ljubdragova" [Sunčanica–daughter of Ljubdrag], *Danica ilirska* 2:34–37 (August 20–September 10, 1836): 133–134, 137–139, 141–143, 145–146.
26 The last paragraphs draw from the research and conclusions of Dukić, "Dvije ilirske Turske: Imagološki pogled na Novine i Danicu od 1835. do 1839," 233–249. On Croatia as "bulwark of Christendom" see Žanić, "The Symbolic Identity of Croatia in the Triangle Crossroads-Bulwark-Bridge," 35–45.

ty generated by Western imperial cultures, the Illyrianist narration originated from a community subordinated to real empires, Habsburg and
Ottoman. Although the new Zagreb (supra)national ideological complex
espoused some imperial features—encompassing vast territories and populations, acknowledging their diversity, consisting of many layers and subjected to clear hierarchic order, it had neither an actual empire behind it
nor a shaped sense of self-confident prepotency. Hence, the Turkish Empire was not a feminine Orient that could be easily embraced and possessed but rather a strong masculine force that required an ultimate mobilization of civilized forces to deal with it. Though inherently corrupt and
backward, the Ottoman state still had enough power to oppress the Illyrian brethren.[27]

It was precisely in this context that Dragutin Seljan put together his
volume on the "Illyrian-Slav" lands of Turkey-in-Europe. The genre of
scholarly geography in which he wrote precluded him from taking openly emotional attitudes towards the Ottomans. He relayed mostly impar-
tial information on the Ottomans' administrative divisions and their rule
of the different regions. Only at certain isolated moments did the author
express dissatisfaction with the existing political status quo. Thus he explained the high proportion of Turkish foreign names in Bulgarian topography as the result of the long foreign rule that managed to export the Ottoman official designations and to impose them on the wider European
world. The original Slavic appellations were preserved just for internal use
by the common people subjected for centuries to an alien rule; hence the
foreign scholarly community remained largely ignorant as to the real geographic names in the province.[28] In Seljan's opinion the Serbs and Bulgarians were not as fanatic in their Eastern Orthodoxy as the Greeks were,
therefore their ties to Russia were not so strong. He further criticized the
leading figures of the Orthodox hierarchy—the Constantinople patriarch and his local bishops—for holding services only in Greek and thus
diminishing Slavonic culture. The whole Eastern Orthodox clergy, from
the patriarch through bishops to the parish priests, sinned in their materi-

---

27　On Orientalism and Empire see Said's original texts: Said, *Orientalism* 13–15; Said, *Culture and Im-
　　perialism*, IX-XXX; 1–14; cf. also: Todorova, *Imagining the Balkans*, 7–19.
28　NSK Zagreb, R 3013, 107.

al exploitation of the common Bulgarian folk.[29] Yet despite these isolated criticisms, as noted earlier, Seljan's text explicitly advocated a certain trialist "Turkoslavist" or "Turko-Slavic-Greek" reordering of the Ottoman Empire that implied not a revolutionary liberation or Slav re-conquest, but a reform and a respect of both the Ottoman-Muslim and Greek positions.

In this respect, Seljan was not espousing the mainstream Illyrianist ideological model—here he was decisively influenced by his sources. Since he had no opportunity to travel and conduct personal research on the spot, the end result was to a great extent a compilation of a number of other texts processed through his Illyrianist lenses. Despite deploring the educated Europe's preference to explore Chinese, Indian and other far-flung territories, Seljan himself still resorted mostly to French and German sources in order to recreate and describe "our beautiful Turkish-Illyrian lands."[30] Chief among them, especially on Bulgarian issues, was the freshly published work by the French Slavist Cyprien Robert, who from February 1842 onward published a series of extensive texts in the influential journal, *Revue des Deux Mondes*. They were issued separately in early 1844 in two volumes under the title *Les Slaves de Turquie*. Achieving instant success among the South and Western Slav intellectual élites as well as among observers and specialists on the Slavs, the book was immediately translated into German and issued in two separate editions.[31] Although the publication contained extensive geographical and ethnographical descriptions of European Turkey, it was overtly political in predicting future developments and providing specific prescriptions for the French policy towards the "Greek-Slav peninsula."

Robert painted an appealing, if somewhat simplified, picture of the 2.5 million Serbs plus 4.5 million Bulgarians constituting the dominant core of the peninsula and being "the continental guardians" of the Bosphorus. Tied to them were one million "Mirdits" and "Skipetars" (Albanians), "whose interest would push them to join the coalition." Meanwhile the

---

29 NSK Zagreb, R 3013, 11. Seljan explicitly cited the work of his Ukrainian-Russian contemporary Venelin, *On the Birth of the New Bulgarian Literature*, as his source for this claims.
30 NSK Zagreb, R 3013, 196.
31 Robert, Cyprien, *Die Slawen der Türkei, nämlich Serbier, Montenegriner, Bosniaken, Albanesen und Bulgaren*; idem, *Die Slawen der Türkei, oder die Montenegriner, Serbier, Bosniaken, Albanesen und Bulgaren, ihre Kräfte und Mittel, ihr Streben und ihr politischer Fortschritt.*

three million Greeks were "the maritime guardians" of Constantinople.[32] The Turks in Europe, numbering about a million, were insufficient to ensure the preservation of Ottoman power in its current form. The author considered that continued French support for the centralized Ottoman Empire could lead only to its delivery into the hands of Russia, Austria and England, initially as its protectors from Greek-Slav insurgents and ultimately as its masters. Therefore, France should rely on and support the real powers of the Balkans—the Greeks and the Slavs. Unlike the Illyrianists or the Slavophiles, Robert stressed the cultural proximity of these two "races" who shared common mores, institutions and history. Indeed, the very title of his text, as it appeared initially in the *Revue des Deux Mondes,* was "The Greek-Slav World." In addition, the Greeks, Serbs and Bulgarians had a very rational interest in being united in order to achieve their aims, especially in front of the Ottoman policy of *divide et impera* (divide and rule). However, the best option for any Bulgaro-Serb union was not to break away from the Empire on the Bosphorus since it would be easily exposed to harsher Russian and Austrian rule. Should the sultan provide the Slavs with sufficient guarantee of their rights and autonomy, they would do better to support him, because the reformed or confederated Ottoman Empire would ensure them more independence than Russian or Austrian domination. French interests on this issue overlapped with that of the Slavs and Ottomans. Therefore, it would be in the long-term interest of Paris to support the decentralization and confederation of the Ottoman Empire. In Europe this reformed empire would consist of several units representing the interests of its three major constituents: the Serbo-Bulgarians, the Greeks, and the Turks.[33]

The Illyrianist geographer was seduced by Cyprien Robert's vision of the unity, vastness and potential prominence of the Turkish Slavs; the ap-

---

32 Cyprien Robert, *Les Slaves de Turquie: Serbes, Monténégrins, Bosniaques, Albanais et Bulgares, leurs ressources, leurs tendances et leurs progrès politiques*, Paris: Passard & Jules Labitte, 1844, t. I, p. 7, 19–25, t. II, p. 337–342.

33 Cyprien Robert, "Le monde gréco-slave: État actuel, mœurs publiques et privées des peuples de la péninsule," 383, 389–393; idem, "Le monde gréco-slave: L'union bulgaro-serbe. Affaires de Serbie," 271–275; *Les Slaves de Turquie: Serbes, Monténégrins, Bosniaques, Albanais et Bulgares, leurs ressources, leurs tendances et leurs progrès politiques* t. I, 7, 19–25, t. II, 337–342. On Cyprien Robert see Sekeruš, "Siprijen Rober i južni sloveni," 7–49; idem, *Cyprien Robert: un slavisant français du XIXe siècle*; Kuk, "Cyprien Robert, slavisant angevin et la grande émigration polonaise," 505–515.

peal was further aggrandized by the reputation of the journal *Revue des Deux Mondes*, so closely related to the center of the French cultural life that the articles on the Slavs secured a chair for their author in the Collège de France. On a number of times Seljan underpinned his narration with explicit references to the authority of the "celebrated French traveler," whose work he came to through the German translation of Marko Fedorović (Tedorović).[34] *Les Slaves de Turquie* employed the term Illyrians very marginally but it did not reject it either, and that was another important reason for its success in Illyrianist circles. Swayed by the appeal and authority of the French Slavist, Seljan reproduced many of that author's political visions and developed them even further by presenting a clearer picture of a reorganized Turkish-Slav-Greek Empire.

Seljan offered another innovative proposal that had more chances for acceptance and incorporation into the Illyrian ideological complex than the dream of a reorganized trialist Ottoman Empire: he incorporated Albania into the ideal of a "Great Illyria." Originally Ljudevit Gaj had not included the Albanian regions in his desired homeland. As noted earlier, even his famous Illyrian lyre ended at the border town of Scutari, an important symbol comparable with such far away points as Villach and Varna. Later, however, a particularly positive image of the Albanians was created by the Illyrianists. While long texts narrated Skanderbeg's struggles, with the thinly veiled aim of stirring emotions against the foreign Ottoman conquerors, a special journal article on the Albanians presented them as a brave people, master of the space between Scutari (Shkodra) and Arta, and, more importantly, as independent and distinct from Slavs, Turks or Greeks.[35] However, Seljan developed some alternative notions on this distant population. Already in his first book in 1840 he included Northern and Central Albania in the Illyrian space and listed the towns of Scutari and Berat among other Illyrian urban centers stretched from Varna to the east to Trieste to the west. Seljan presented the populace of these Albanian regions as quite mixed—apart from the Skipetars more than half of the inhabitants were of Illyrian-Slav origin:

---

34 NSK Zagreb, R 3013, 106, 109, 140, 174.
35 "Arbanasi" [The Albanians], *Danica ilirska* 5:52 (28.XII.1839); "Juraj Skenderbeg i Amurat" [George Skanderbeg and Murad], *Danica ilirska* 5:45–49 (9.XI.–7.XII.1839); "Juraj Skenderbeg i Muamed" [George Skanderbeg and Mehmed], *Danica ilirska* 6:2–10 (11.I.–7.III.1840).

In general one could say that the language of the people both in *Ar-banaska* [Albania] and Macedonia is a Slav-Illyrian dialect. The Turks call the Skipetars *Arnauts*, who though an individual people (*vlastiti narod*), because of trade are in alliance with the Illyrian people; they speak Illyrian and do not object to calling themselves Slavs.[36]

This assimilationist view was an important ideological turn in the imperialist direction. Imagining ethnically different Albanian lands as part of the projected Great Illyria, Seljan unconsciously turned the latter into a nascent but full-fledged empire. Had his cultural construction one day become reality, it would have encompassed a region with marked ethnic and cultural differences, destined to be a special periphery to the core regions (in fact, this was never fulfilled, if we do not count the inclusion of Kosovo in somewhat different polities, namely Serbia/Kingdom of Serbs, Croats and Slovenes /Yugoslavia).

Despite his differences with the earlier Illyrianist tradition, Seljan was reinforced in his thinking during the next few years. His admired Paris authority, Robert, also presented Albanians as a mixture of Skipetars and Slavs, the former being allegedly prone to the overwhelming influence of the latter.[37] In public advertisement for his geographical volume he not only included Albania but gave it a special preference. While the other regions were grouped mostly in pairs—so that not only Istria and Dalmatia or Thrace and Macedonia but also Bosnia and Bulgaria were supposed to share a chapter between themselves—Albania was the only Illyrian land that formed by itself a separate section.[38] Ultimately most of the regions received a similar treatment and Albania was covered on equal basis with lands such as Bosnia or (Northern) Bulgaria (in the surviving manuscript the chapter on Montenegro remained unfinished while those on Thrace and Macedonia were never written).

His scholarly pretensions notwithstanding, Seljan persistently applied the notions of the Illyrianist ideological complex even if that entailed changes in the accepted geographical divisions: he insisted on the upper-

36 Seljan, *Početak, naprědak,* 70, 79–80, 83.
37 Robert, *Les Slaves de Turquie,* vol. 2, 361–362.
38 HDA [Croatian State Archive] Zagreb, f. 711 (ob. Drašković), kut. 100, Dragutin Seljan, Književni oglas, June 20, 1842.

most importance of ethnic composition as the ultimate determinant of the boundaries of the regions under investigation. For example, he was unable to claim the whole of Syria because of its German-speaking majority, so he included only the two southern districts of Maribor and Celje with their clear Slav majority.[39] Similarly he left out "Lower Albania (Epirus)," for it was populated, according to his data, not by Slavs but just by Albanians and Greeks. His Illyrian Albania embraced territories from Bar in the north to Valona in the south, incorporating the easternmost parts of Kosovo (Peć and Djakovo) and Macedonia (Ohrid and Struga). Seljan continued to consider the majority of the inhabitants there as co-Illyrians. Finding support for his arguments not only in Robert's work, but also in a newly published book by Joseph Müller, Seljan affirmed that although the diverse Albanian population spoke different dialects, the chief common language was Slavonic-Illyrian. While the Skipetars seemed to be in the minority, the Serbs inhabited the northwestern and eastern portions of Albania, whereas Bulgarians dominated in the districts around Resen and Ohrid, mixing north of the latter town with Skipetars.[40]

Thus Seljan's narrative persisted in directing the Illyrian ideological complex towards the imperial model. The Illyrianist edifice was already too overambitious and complicated by including vast South Slav regions with quite different historical and cultural traditions. By upholding the Illyrianness of Albania, Seljan provided an intellectual construction with a clear periphery that should somehow be ruled over by the core regions. However, any future control, domination or integration of the ethnically different "Skipetarian" society would have been pregnant with difficulties.

Seljan's Illyrianist imagination increasingly expanded. He was no longer content to confine his narrative within South-East Europe and proceeded to write a small section on "Illyrians in the Kingdom of Naples." To the various previously described groups was now added a completely new type of co-national community, that of overseas Illyrians. The projected Illyrian Empire could even dream of establishing its own overseas dependency. Ironically, Albanians again provided the foundation for this

---

39 Seljan, *Zemljopis,* 8.
40 NSK Zagreb, R 3013, p. 145–148, 173–174. The work Seljan referred to was Joseph Müller, *Albanien, Rumelien und die Österreichisch-montenegrische Gränze* (Prague: J.G. Calve, 1844).

next conceivable imperialist stage, for they were the majority of the Illyrian settlers in South Italy.[41]

While Seljan was penning his ideas in 1845, the Illyrian national ideological complex was already under attack from different quarters. Open Hungarian coercion and its partial success through Vienna were only the surface of the problem. The virulent "Croatian-Hungarian" party viciously attacked Illyrianism in its heartland around Zagreb and forced the latter to emphasize its Croat origins at the expense of wider South Slav dimension.[42] Equally importantly, the Illyrianists were failing to convince Serbian intellectuals and power-holders of the virtues of their model.[43] As a result of Hungarian-Habsburg censorship Seljan's work languished in manuscript form, which hampered the dissemination of his ideas on Slavic Albania.

In the short period until its downfall in 1848–49 Illyrianism did evolve somewhat towards the incorporation of Albania. The symbolic song "The Homeland of the Slav" included it in the list of Slavonic countries.[44] Similarly Ivan Kukuljević Sakcinski, an important Illyrianist ideologue and political leader, embraced Albania in his essential poem *Slavjanke* that directly and extensively defined the Slav community versus various foreign Others ranging from Hellenes and Romans through "Osmanlis" and Italians to Hungarians and Germans.[45] Nevertheless, the appropriations of Albania were rare and still not part of the core Illyrianist discourse; towards the end of the Illyrianist journey in 1849 the mental mapping of Great Illyria into an imagined empire was more of a tendency than an accomplished pattern.

---

41   NSK Zagreb, R 3013, p. 185–186.

42   Kaytchev, *Iliria ot Varna do Vilah*, 167–168. On the pro-Hungarian party see: Kolak Bošnjak "Horvatsko-vugerska stranka 1841–1848" [Croatian-Hungarian party 1841–1848] (PhD diss., University of Zagreb, 2012).

43   Mamuzić, "Ilirizam i Srbi," 1–91.

44   "Domovina Slavjanina" [The homeland of the Slav], *Danica horvatska, slavonska i dalmatinska* 13:6 (February 6, 1847): 21.

45   Ivan Kukuljević Sakcinski, *Slavjanke*, 6. Later Kukuljević Sakcinski abandoned his Slavising stance on the Albanians. On his national concept during the Illyrianist period see Kristian Novak, "Po rodu, po karvi i po jeziku: Nacionalni identitet u političkim i publicističkim tekstovima Ivana Kukuljevića Sakcinskog" [By Kin, by Blood and by Language: National Identity in Ivan Kukuljević Sakcinski's Political and Publicist Texts], 147–174. On Kukuljević's manuscript play about George Skanderbeg see Ahmeti, "Jedan nedovoljno poznati rukopis I. Kukuljevića Sakcinskog o Skenderbegu," 163–178.

If the Albanians were endowing the Illyrianist edifice with its quali-
tative definite imperialist character, it was the Bulgarians who, with their
numbers and territorial enormity, were providing most of its building
blocks. Seljan proclaimed that their alliance with the proud and politically advanced Serbs would produce a great and powerful entity that indus-
trially would soon compete with France and Russia.[46] If this union alone
could rival such imposing empires, what would be the potential of the
imagined unified Illyria? It was indeed the numerous co-nationals in Turkey—Bulgarians and Serbs—which provided Illyrianists with the main
impetus for their large-scale projects.

* * *

To what extent were "the Bulgaro-Illyrians" influenced by the national
thinking coming from Zagreb intellectuals?

The Bulgarian national model from its nascent stage, beginning with
the work of the monk Paisii of Hilendar (1762), despite acknowledging
the common Slavic roots, immediately emancipated itself from the other
Slav communities. Paisii's *Slavonic-Bulgarian History* not only recreated
the glorious past of the medieval Bulgarian Empire as a source for contemporary pride, but also clearly separated his prospective audience from
their only immediate Slav neighbors, the Serbs. A special chapter on the
Serbian kings aimed to demonstrate the inferiority of their ancient polity
which did not deserve to be an example for his readers. Among other arguments Paisii outlined that all "languages (peoples) on earth know the
Bulgarians and all histories witness and write on them" whereas "Latin
and Greek histories offer no evidence on the Serbs."[47]

Thus intellectuals from both sides of the Balkan range did not hesitate on the naming and the general scheme of their national narration—
the Bulgarian name of the past and future state was undisputed.[48] The big

---

46 NSK Zagreb, R 3013, p. 133. Here Seljan once again was decisively influenced by Cyprien Robert.
47 Hilendarski, *Slavonic-Bulgarian History*, 45–50.
48 A useful English language summary of the numerous historiographical visions on the Bulgarian re-
    vival period is offered in Daskalov, *The Making of a Nation in the Balkans: Historiography of the Bul-
    garian Revival*. It is characteristic that this book does not note any post-Paisii doubt on the national
    name, or any inclination or hesitation towards submerging the Bulgarians into the wider Slav com-
    munity. Illyrianism is not even mentioned.

debates were on specific *mythomoteurs* or *topi* of the national narration: on the origin of the community, the foundation of its state, the position and contribution of given important rulers, the precise territorial scope, as well as on the role of different contested key regions like Macedonia. Despite some uncertainties over the particulars of the boundaries embraced, the general geographical frame of the nation was beyond doubt—the regions to the west of Niš were clearly part of the Slav-Serbian and definitely non-Bulgarian world.

In this context it is hardly surprising that the emerging Bulgarian intellectual elite remained distant from or unaware of the version of the national identity imagined and proclaimed by the Illyrianists. During the 1830s–1840s several Bulgarian geography textbooks were published; two of them were compiled or translated by the above-mentioned Ivan Bogorov, but in neither of them could one find any special appreciation of Illyrianist or Croat ideas. His main textbook, adhering to its Russian original, strictly followed the contemporary political nomenclature, and the Croatian regions were divided between the Hungarian kingdom and the Austrian empire. In sections on Hungary, no Croat or any Slavic population was mentioned, even in the specific region of "Civil Croatia." According to Bogorov and his sources, Illyria denoted only an ordinary Austrian province embracing a space somewhat larger than the twenty-first century Slovenian republic: it included as its important towns not only Laibach (Ljubljana), but also Trieste and Klagenfurt. "Military Croatia" was included as a direct Austrian province, not belonging to the Hungarian kingdom, let alone to its region of Civil Croatia.[49]

The term Illyria was briefly mentioned in another 1843 textbook translated from Greek. Here it was an ancient name that stood for vague parts of European Turkey: Albania and possibly Dalmatia, Bosnia and Turkish Croatia.[50] This conservative reading of Illyria as a former Roman province was the closest Bulgarians could get to the Illyrianist geography.

Most books pointed to the similarity of the different Slavonic languages, but never noted any existing Illyrian tongue or dialect. Thus Neofit Bozveli, the future leader of the Bulgarian ecclesiastical and national

---

49 Bogorov, *Vseobshta geografiya za dětsata*, 49–50, 191–194.
50 Radulov, *Stihiyni urotsi zemleopisaniya*, 24–32.

emancipation, pointed out in 1835 that "the Slavonic language is the main and mother tongue to the 'Moscovian,' 'Lechian' [Polish], Bohemian, Serbian, Bulgarian, Bosnian, Dalmatian, Raguzian and Croatian." Later textbooks, however, omitted reference to the last four languages and thus Serbian was left as the only other Slavic language in the proximity.[51]

Bulgarian intellectuals did not come to know the Zagreb Illyrianist editions directly. Even those that were interested in general Slavic constructions imported them from Russian or Czech sources but not from Croatia. Thus the Illyrianist interpretations did not succeed in reaching the Bulgarian public. One case is very characteristic for the failed ideological transfer. Pavel Šafařík in his influential 1842 book made an important concession to Illyrianism by uniting Serbian, Croatian and Slovenian dialects in a common Illyrian language unit. Extracts of his findings were published in Russia, and from there in Bulgaria. Yet after the first translation in St. Petersburg, his Illyrian designation was subsequently changed abruptly into a Serbian one. Due to the Russian intermediation all non-Bulgarian South Slavs—"Serbian-Illyrians" (Štokavian speakers), "Croats" (Čakavian speakers), and "Korutans" (Slovenes and Kajkavian speakers)—were presented to the Bulgarian readership as Serbians.[52]

Thus when in 1850 a Bulgarian pro-Austroslav journal *Mirozrenie* was finally published in Vienna, it concluded with resignation that Bulgarians were ignorant of the other South and Western Slavs, with the exception of the portion of the Serbs that was living in the Ottoman Empire proper. By contrast, the Austrian Slavs knew more about the Bulgarians than vice versa.[53]

In general, Bulgarian national ideology shied away from any attempts to include substantial ethnically or linguistically foreign populations, and this approach was applied, among others, to Albanians. The modern Herderian ideas of language nationalism combined with the historical

---

51 Neofit Hilendarski (Bozveli), *Kratkoe politicheskoe zemleopisanie za obuchenie na bolgarskoto mladenchestvo*, 7; Bogorov, *Vseobshta geografiya za dětsata*, 107.

52 Šafařík, *Slowanský národopis*, 47–73, 148–150; Savel'ev-Rostislavich, *Slavyanskiy sbornik*, 5–15; *Lyuboslovie*, 2:14 (February 1846): 22–24.

53 *Mirozrenie*, 1:3 (Nov. 1850):48. On this periodical and its editor see Danova, *Ivan Dobrovski v perspektivata na bălgarskiya XIX vek*, 160–208, 517–548; Danova, "Ivan Dobrovski à Vienne. Contribution à l'histoire de *Vienne* en tant que centre politique et culturel des peuples balkaniques au XIXe siècle," 3–45.

capital of medieval Bulgaria provided "awakeners" with enough ammunition for their task among the huge Slavic masses inhabiting vast geographical territory in Bulgaria (ancient Lower Moesia), Thrace and Macedonia. The immediate task of the Bulgarian nation-builders was not toward imperial appropriations but the other way around. They strove to achieve separation and emancipation from the larger composite *Rum millet* community and from the domination of the Greek name and the culture associated with it. Some imperial traces in the Bulgarian national model might be found in the use of the historical resources associated with the medieval Bulgarian Empire; yet the main argument after the 1820s was prevailingly modern and connected with the authority of contemporary European science. The emphasis on language and ethnicity opened large avenues to Bulgarian national development.

From the viewpoint of its creators, the Illyrianist national complex was not dissimilar to the Bulgarian one, it also rested on perceived linguistic and ethnic commonality. To the extent that the ideal of Great Illyria had any political equivalent—for such an independent polity was definitely not feasible at the time—it was imagined as a nearly homogeneous nation-state rather than a composite empire. Nevertheless, the advanced Illyrianist model was much closer to the imperial formula. As already noted, the self-proclaimed nation was an all-Slav one; it would lead to the creation of a giant super union larger than the already existing Russian empire. However, though publicly declared, even in Gaj's time this was too abstract a construction. Immediate allegiance was owed to the Illyrian community that already encompassed a wide enough geographical space. Should such an entity become a basis for an autonomous polity, regardless of its composition, it was bound to dominate over southeast Europe and be a match for all neighboring empires. Indeed, in terms of real politics, such a state would take the place of the Ottoman Empire on the European continent. Potentially, it might become even more vital and powerful because it would be entirely European and based on modern "civilized" values.

Regardless of proclaimed ethnic and linguistic proximity, in reality Illyrianists embraced in their vision divergent populations which could hardly adopt their ideal. The tendency to ascribe Albanians into the Illyrian-Slav community additionally manifested the highly illusory and imperial leanings of Illyrianism. Despite the best intentions of its intellectual creators to build a monoethnic or national state, Great Illyria in practice was bound to be an entity with imperial features.

The Illyrianist attitude to the Bulgarians as main co-nationals living under Ottoman writ was more than sympathetic, but up to 1849 it was entirely romantic—neither were direct connections established nor any practical efforts undertaken to attract them to the Illyrianist cause. Crucially significant for the entire endeavor was the well-documented failure to draw the Orthodox Serbian Slavs into the common fold. That community was already well on the way to the creation of its own Serbian national identity, and its leaders, not only in the Serbian principality but also in the Austrian empire, preferred to reject approaches from Zagreb and to proceed with their own Serbian national concept. Despite the strong emotions it inspired, Illyrianism eventually failed to take root, not only among the Bulgarians, Serbs and future Slovenes, but also with the Catholic inhabitants of Croatia, Dalmatia and Slavonia. Regardless of the enthusiastic activity of the dedicated revivalists-creators of the Illyrian nation, and notwithstanding the appeal and the initial success of the "imagined community of Illyrians," it foundered and ultimately served as a basis not of an Illyrian but of a rather different Croatian nation.

REFERENCES

Unpublished sources

HDA [Croatian State Archive] Zagreb, f. 711 (ob. Drašković), kut. 100, Dragutin Seljan, Književni oglas. June 20, 1842.
NSK Zagreb [Manuscript Collection of the National and University Library in Zagreb], R 3013, Dragutin Seljan, *Zemljopis pokrainah Bosne, Serbie, Bugarske iliti ogledalo zemlje na kojoj pribiva narod ilirsko-slavjanski sa opisanjem berdah, potokah, gradovah i znatnih městah polag sadanjeg stališa s kratkim dogodopisnim dodatkom.*

Published sources and secondary works

Ahmeti, Musa. "Jedan nedovoljno poznati rukopis I. Kukuljevića Sakcinskog o Skenderbegu" [An insufficiently known manuscript of I. Kukuljević Sakcinski on Skanderbeg]. *Zbornik Odsjeka za povijesne znanosti Zavoda za povijesni i društvene znanosti HAZU* 17, (2000): 163–178.

Berger, Stefan, and Alexei Miller. "Introduction: Building Nations in and with Empires—a Reassessment." In *Nationalizing Empires*, edited by Stefan Berger and Alexei Miller, 1–30. Budapest: Central European University Press, 2015.

Blažević, Zrinka. "Inderemi-Nation: Narrative Identity and Symbolic Politics in Early Modern Illyrism." In *Whose Love of Which Country: Composite States, National Histories and Patriotic Discourses in Early Modern East Central Europe*, edited by Balázs Trencsényi and Márton Zászkaliczky, 203–223. Leiden: Brill, 2010.

———. *Ilirizam prije ilirizma* [Illyrism before Illyrism]. Zagreb: Golden Marketing–Tehnička knjiga, 2008.

Bogorov, Ivan. *Vseobshta geografiya za dětsata* [A general geography for children]. Belgrade: Typography of the Principality of Serbia, 1843.

Danova, Nadia. *"Ivan Dobrovski à Vienne. Contribution à l'histoire de Vienne en tant que centre politique et culturel des peuples balkaniques au XIXe siècle." Etudes balkaniques* 39, no. 2 (2003): 3–45.

———. *Ivan Dobrovski v perspektivata na bălgarskiya XIX vek* [Ivan Dobrovski in the perspective of the Bulgarian nineteenth century]. Sofia: Valentin Trayanov, 2008.

Daskalov, Roumen. *The Making of a Nation in the Balkans: Historiography of the Bulgarian Revival*. Budapest: Central European University Press, 2004.

Despalatović, Elinor Murray. *Ljudevit Gaj and the Illyrian Movement*. Boulder: East European Quarterly, 1975.

Doyle, Michael. *Empires*. Ithaca: Cornwell University Press, 1986.

Dukić, Davor. "Dvije ilirske Turske: Imagološki pogled na Novine i Danicu od 1835. do 1839" [Two Illyrianist Turkeys: imagological view on Novine and Danica from 1835 to 1839]. *Kolo* 16, no. 2 (2006): 233–249.

Gaj, Ljudevit. "II proglas" [Second proclamation]. In *Programski spisi hrvatskog narodnog preporoda* [Programmatic writings of the Croatian national revival], edited by Miroslav Šicel, 113–116. Zagreb: Matica Hrvatska, 1997.

———. "Naš narod" [Our people]. In *Polemike u hrvatskoj književnosti* [Polemics in the Croatian literature], edited by Ivan Krtalić. Vol. 1, *Pet slova rogatih* [Five "horned" words], 112–116. Zagreb: Mladost, 1982.

Gundulić, Ivan. "Sunčanica kći Ljubdragova" [Sunčanica—daughter of Ljubdrag]. *Danica ilirska* 2, no. 34–37 (August 20–September 10, 1836): 133–134, 137–139, 141–143, 145–146.

Hilendarski, Paisiy. *Istoriya slavěnobolgarskaya* [Slavonic-Bulgarian history]. Sofia: Bulgarian Academy of Sciences, 1914.

Horvat, Josip. *Ljudevit Gaj: Njegov život, njegovo doba* [Ljudevit Gaj: his life, his times]. Zagreb: Sveučilišna naklada Liber, 1975.

Howe, Stephen. *Empire: A Very Short Introduction*. Oxford: Oxford University Press, 2002.

Kaytchev, Naoum. *Iliria ot Varna do Vilah: Hărvatskoto natsionalno văzrazhdane, sărbite i bălgarite (do 1848)* [Illyria from Varna to Villach: Croatian national revival, Serbs and Bulgarians (until 1848)]. Sofia: Paradigma, 2015.

Kolak Bošnjak, Arijana. "Horvatsko-vugerska stranka 1841–1848" [Croatian-Hungarian party 1841–1848]. PhD diss., University of Zagreb, 2012.

Kuk, Leszeck. "Cyprien Robert, slavisant angevin et la grande émigration polonaise." *Annales de Bretagne et des pays de l'Ouest* 99, vol. 4 (1992).

Kukuljević Sakcinski, Ivan. *Slavjanke.* Zagreb: F. Župan, 1848.

Lieven, Dominic. *Empire: The Russian Empire and its Rivals.* New Haven: Yale University Press, 2001.

Mamuzić, Ilija. "Ilirizam i Srbi" [Illyrism and the Serbs]. *Rad JAZU* 247, 1933: 1–91.

Mihanović, Antun. "Horvatska domovina" [Croatian homeland]. *Danicza horvatzka, slavonzka y dalmatinzka* 1, no. 10 (14.III.1835): 37.

Müller, Joseph. *Albanien, Rumelien und die Österreichisch-montenegrische Gränze.* Prague: J.G. Calve, 1844.

Neofit Hilendarski (Bozveli). *Kratkoe politicheskoe zemleopisanie za obuchenie na bolgarskoto mladenchestvo* [A short political geography for the education of Bulgarian youth]. Kragujevac: Typography of the Principality of Serbia, 1835.

Novak, Kristian. "Po rodu, po karvi i po jeziku: Nacionalni identitet u političkim i publicističkim tekstovima Ivana Kukuljevića Sakcinskog" [By kin, by blood and by language: national identity in Ivan Kukuljević Sakcinski's political and publicist texts], *Povjesni prilozi* 34 (2008): 147–174.

Novak, Viktor. *Magnum tempus. Ilirizam i katoličko sveštenstvo. Ideje i ličnosti. (1830–1849)* [Magnum tempus: Illyrism and the Catholic clergy, ideas and personalities (1830–1849)]. Belgrade: Nova knjiga, 1987.

Paisiy Hilendarski. *Istoriya slavěnobolgarskaya* [Slavonic-Bulgarian history]. Sofia: Bulgarian Academy of Sciences, 1914.

Radulov, Sava. *Stihiyni urotsi zemleopisaniya* [Elementary courses of geography]. Smirna: Damianov, 1843.

Robert, Cyprien. *Die Slawen der Türkei, nämlich Serbier, Montenegriner, Bosniaken, Albanesen und Bulgaren.* 2 vols. Stuttgart: Franckh, 1844.

———. *Die Slawen der Türkei, oder die Montenegriner, Serbier, Bosniaken, Albanesen und Bulgaren, ihre Kräfte und Mittel, ihr Streben und ihr politischer Fortschritt.* Translated from French by Marko Fodorovitsch. 2 vols. Dresden–Leipzig: Arnoldische Buchhandlung, 1844.

———. "Le monde gréco-slave: État actuel, mœurs publiques et privées des peuples de la péninsule." *Revue des Deux Mondes,* Paris, 39 (February 1, 1842) : 380–430.

———. "Le monde gréco-slave: L'union bulgaro-serbe. Affaires de Serbie." *Revue des Deux Mondes,* Paris, 3 nouvelle série, (July 1, 1843): 271–312.

———. *Les Slaves de Turquie: Serbes, Monténégrins, Bosniaques, Albanais et Bulgares, leurs ressources, leurs tendances et leurs progrès politiques.* 2 vols. Paris: Passard & Jules Labitte, 1844.

Šafařík, Pavel. *Slowanský národopis* [Slavic ethnography]. Prague, 1842.

Said, Edward. *Culture and Imperialism.* London: Vintage Books, 1994.

———. *Orientalism.* New ed. London: Penguin, 1995.

Savel'ev-Rostislavich, Nikolay. *Slavyanskiy sbornik* [Slavonic collection]. St. Petersburg: Konrad Vingeber, 1845.

Sekeruš, Pavle. "Siprijen Rober i južni sloveni" [Cyprien Robert and the south Slavs]. *Zbornik Matice srpske za slavistiku* 41 (1991): 7–49.

———. *Cyprien Robert: un slavisant français du XIXe siècle.* Novi Sad: Filozofski fakultet, 2009.

Seljan, Dragutin. *Zemljopis pokrainah ilirskih iliti ogledalo zemlje, na kojoj pribiva narod ilirsko-slavjanski sa opisanjem berdah, potokah, gradovah i znatniih městah polag sadan-jeg stališa, s kratkim dogodopisnim dodatkom i priloženim krajobrazom iliti mapom* [Geography of the Illyrian provinces or mirror of the land inhabited by the Illyrian-Slav people with description of mountains, rivers, towns and more important places in their present state, with a short historical addition and an attached map.] Vol. 1 of *Pokrajine austriansko-ilirske* [Austrian-Illyrian provinces]. Zagreb: Tisak Ljudevita Gaja, 1843. Reprint.

———. *Zemljopis pokrainah ilirskih iliti ogledalo zemlje* [Geography of the Illyrian provinces or mirror of the land]. Zagreb: Dom i Svijet, 2005.

———. *Početak, naprědak i vrědnost literature ilirske. S kratkim geografičko-statističkim opisom Ilirskih državah* [The beginning, progress and value of the Illyrian literature: with a short geographical-statistic description of the Illyrian states]. Zagreb: Tisak Ljudevita Gaja, 1840.

Šidak, Jaroslav. *Hrvatski narodni preporod. Ilirski pokret* [The Croatian national revival: the Illyrian movement]. Zagreb: Školska knjiga, 1988.

Šrepel, Milivoj. "Iz ostavine Antuna Vakanovića" [From the papers of Antun Vakanović]. *Građa za povijest književnosti hrvatske* 2 (1899): 241–293.

Smith, Anthony. "Gastronomy or Geology? The Role of Nationalism in the Reconstruction of Nations." *Nations and Nationalism* 1, no. 1 (1995): 3–23.

———. *The Ethnic Origin of Nations*. Oxford: Blackwell, 1986.

Stančić, Nikša. "Hrvatski narodni preporod 1790–1848." [The Croatian national revival 1790–1848. In *Hrvatski narodni preporod 1790–1848. Hrvatska u vrijeme Ilirskog pokreta* [The Croatian national revival 1790–1848: Croatia during the times of the Illyrian movement], edited by Nikša Stančić, 1–30. Zagreb: Povijesni muzej Hrvatske, 1985.

———. *Gajeva "Još Horvatska ni propala" iz 1832–1833. Ideologija Ljudevita Gaja u pripremom razdoblju hrvatskog narodnog preporoda* [Gaj's "Croatia has not yet fallen" from 1832–1833: Ljudevit Gaj's ideology in the preparatory period of the Croatian national revival]. Zagreb: Globus, Zavod za hrvatsku povijest Filozofskog fakulteta, 1989.

———. *Hrvatska nacija i nacionalizam u 19 i 20 stoljeću* [The Croatian nation and nationalism in the nineteenth and twentieth centuries]. Zagreb: Barbat, 2002.

Štoos, Pavao. "Kip domovine vu početku leta 1831" [Statue of the homeland in the beginning of the year 1831]. In *Hrvatski narodni preporod* [The Croatian national revival], edited by Jakša Ravlić. Vol. 1, 245–250. Zagreb: Matica Hrvatska, 1965.

Todorova, Maria. *Imagining the Balkans*. New York: Oxford University Press, 1997.

Utješenović Ostrožinski, Ognjeslav. "Jeka od Balkana ili suze bugarskih, hercegovačkih i bosanskih hristianah" [Echo from the Balkan Mountain] or [The tears of the Bulgarian, Bosnian and Herzegovinian Christians], *Danica ilirska* 9, no. 10 (March 5, 1842): 37–38.

Venelin, Yuriy. *O zarodyishe novoy bolgarskoy literatury* [On the birth of the new Bulgarian literature]. Moscow: Tipografiya N. Stepanova, 1838.

Žanić, Ivo. "The Symbolic Identity of Croatia in the Triangle Crossroads-Bulwark-Bridge." In *Myths and Boundaries in South-Eastern Europe*, edited by Pål Kolstø, 35–76. London: Hurst & Co., 2005.

Part III

Eastern Slavic Empires

Magdalena Żakowska

Russia in Serbian and Bulgarian National Mythologies Until the First World War

> Kat' Rusiya nyama vtora
> tŭĭ mogŭshta na sveta.
> Tya e nashata opora,
> tya e nash`ta visota[1]
>
> P. R. SLAVEĬKOV,
> *Vyarata i nadezhdata na bŭlgarina kŭm Rusiya*[2] (1877)

This chapter will analyze how indigenous Balkan and Russian imperial motifs influenced Serbian and Bulgarian national discourses from the second part of the nineteenth century until the First World War. It will focus especially on how the Russian Slavophil and Pan-Slav ideologies affected Balkan national myths, such as the Bulgarian myths about Dyado Ivan and Rayna, and the Serbian myth about the Battle of Blackbird's Field (Kosovo Polje). It will explain how these myths, rather than being based on reality, tended instead to create it, and how they influenced Serbian and Bulgarian domestic politics and foreign affairs, identity and national sympathies.

The term "national myths" will be defined here as a set of simplified interpretations of national history, based on an idea of on-going confrontation between one nation, perceived as both virtuous hero and victim, and other nations, perceived as incarnations of evil.[3] Such motives can be found in mythical schemata all over the world, but are especially potent

---

1   "There is no country in the world so powerful as Russia. She is our rock, she is our hope" (free transl. MŻ).
2   "Bulgarian faith and hope in Russia."
3   Mandic, "Myths and Bombs: War, State Popularity and the Collapse of National Mythology," 26.

during wars and social conflicts.[4] Serbia and Bulgaria on the eve of the twentieth century were no exceptions to this rule. Their national myths in that period were composed of the idea of martyrdom, experienced as due to the Turks, of the memory of glorious uprisings against Ottoman rule, and of on-going threats to their Slavonic Orthodox identity, coming from Muslims but also from the West.

It needs emphasizing that the image of Russia, as reflected both in the Bulgarian and Serb national myths on the eve of the twentieth century, was predominantly positive. The national discourse about her in that period referred to the image of a country which had been formed hundreds of years earlier, at least in the sixteenth century, and had not evolved meaningfully thereafter. It was the image of "Russia-the-Liberator": the state was seen as a mighty empire and the Russians as Orthodox Slavonic brothers. Yet the main purpose of the present chapter is to discover why and in which way the Serbian and Bulgarian discourses about Russia differed from each other in the period in question. Therefore, these discourses will be analyzed first of all through the prism of their ambiguity between "pro-Russian" and "pro-European" outlooks.

What was the historical background that influenced the nineteenth-century image of Russia in the Balkan region? In the fifteenth century, the Russian monarchs began to consolidate the former lands of Kievan Rus', which had been mostly conquered by the Golden Horde, and in the sixteenth century they began to fight—more and more effectively—against the mighty Ottoman Empire ruling over the former Byzantium and other Orthodox Christian monarchies on the Balkan Peninsula. According to the idea of Russia-the-Third-Rome,[5] Russia became the political and moral successor of the Eastern Roman Empire and her destiny was to provide spiritual and political guidance over the Byzantine inheritance.[6]

In the nineteenth century, this rhetoric was reinforced by Slavophile and Pan-Slavic ideas. The Slavophil movement was a concept that postulated Russia's future development would be based not on Western European values but on indigenous Slavic history and culture. The Slavophiles considered Western Europe, which had embraced the Roman Catholic

---

4   Gerth and Mills, eds., *From Max Weber: Essays in Sociology*, 335.
5   The concept of Russia-the-Third-Rome was formulated by Philoteus of Pskov in 1510.
6   Bazylow, *Historia Rosji*, 67.

and Protestant faiths, as morally bankrupt, and regarded Western political and economic institutions (e.g., constitutional government and capitalism) as outgrowths of a deficient society. The Russian people, who, by contrast, shared a common Orthodox faith and church, were supposed to be united in a Christian community based on natural, harmonious, human relationships. Therefore—according to the Slavophiles—Russia was destined to revitalize the West by replacing European rationalism, materialism, and individualism with the aforementioned spiritual values.[7]

In the 1860s the Slavophil principles were adapted in Russia by extreme nationalists, the Pan-Slavs.[8] One of the most influential adherents of this movement, Nikolay Y. Danilevsky, stated that the Slavic world, unified and reinforced by the Orthodox faith, could constitute an alternative to the spiritual nullity of Western Christianity and to the political dominance of Western Europe.[9] He and other Pan-Slavs believed that Russia's historic mission was to gain supremacy over the whole continent, and that to achieve this goal she should liberate all the Slavs and other Orthodox people living under the rule of the Turks, Hungarians, and Austrians, and unite them in a Slav confederation, dominated by the Russian Empire.[10] Indeed, Russia fought four wars against the Ottoman Empire in the nineteenth century, successfully supporting the indepen-

---

7   Walicki, *Rosyjska filozofia i myśl społeczna od Oświecenia do marksizmu*, 141–150.

8   The term "Pan-Slavism," first used by a Slovak, Ján Herkel, in a work *Elementa universalis lingue slavicae e vivis dialectis eruta et sanis logicae principiis suffulta* (1826), has been generally used to "denote the historic tendency of the Slavic peoples to manifest in any tangible way, whether cultural or political, their consciousness of ethnic kinship" (Petrovich, *The Emergence of Russian Panslavism 1856–1870*, 3). William Leatherbarrow states that "the Crimean campaign... increased awareness among educated Russians of the plight of the southern Slav nations under Turkish occupation. This allowed classical Slavophilism to develop further emphasis on Slavic solidarity and facilitated its eventual evolution into Pan-Slavism and the belief in Russia's mission to liberate and unite the Slavs in a process that would bring the 'light from the East' to illuminate and revive a moribund West." (Leatherbarrow, "Conservatism in the age of Alexander I and Nicholas I," 112–113).

9   Dimitris Stamatopoulos, "From the Vyzantism of K. Leont'ev to the Vysantinism of I. I. Sokolov: The Byzantine Orthodox East as a Motif of the Russian Orientalism," 342–346.

10 Especially after 1867 various Russian Pan-Slavs affirmed that "the Ottoman and Habsburg empires were in the last stages of dissolution and... sooner or later Russia would be forced to fill the political vacuum left by their demise." Nicholas Iakovlevich Danilevskii (1822–85) in his book *Russia and Europe: A View of the Slavic with the Germano-Roman World* (1869) formulated precise plans for a Slavic union as a federation of the following eight units: the Russian Empire, the Czech-Moravian-Slovak Kingdom, the Kingdom of the Serbs-Croats-Slovenes, the Bulgarian Kingdom, the Rumanian Kingdom, the Hellenic Kingdom, the Magyar Kingdom, the District of Constantinople; Petrovich, *The Emergence of Russian Panslavism*, 268–70.

dence movements of the Greeks, Montenegrins, Romanians, Serbs, and Bulgarians.[11]

The Russian cultural influence on contemporary Balkan peoples should also be underscored. Russia was, for the nineteenth-century Serbs and Bulgarians, "a source of inspiration and an example by virtue of its own cultural attainments," as well as "a mediator insofar as it was via its culture and language that a number of [Balkan] intellectuals gained access to Western European and North American systems of ideas and artistic achievements," as Ludmila Kostova states.[12]

Although the Russian government never officially supported Pan-Slavic ideology, its adherents had an enormous impact on Russian politics and public opinion in the second half of the nineteenth century.[13] In particular, the Bulgarian War (1877–1878) was accompanied by strong Pan-Slavic feelings in Russian society. An expressive impression of the public opinion of this time was given by Leo Tolstoy in *Anna Karenina* (1878):

> The massacre of men who were fellow-Christians, and of the same Slavonic race, excited sympathy for the sufferers and indignation against the oppressors. And the heroism of the Serbians and Montenegrins struggling for a great cause begot in the whole people a longing to help their brothers not in word but in deed.[14]

For a second time, strong—although not as strong as in the 1870s—brotherly emotions towards the Balkan Slavs emerged in Russian society in 1908, after Austria-Hungary annexed Bosnia-Herzegovina. Although it happened without political objection from the Russian government, this move was perceived in Russian public opinion as a betrayal of a Serbian ally,[15] and—what is also important—as a warning. On the one hand, it

---

11 Stamatopoulos, "From the Vyzantism of K. Leont'ev to the Vysantinism of I. I. Sokolov," 426–434.

12 Kostova, "Getting to Know the Big Bad West?" 108–109.

13 Furthermore, on the eve of the First World War in Russia there was a widespread social network of Pan-Slavs which included both government and non-government members, as well as those in economic and academic circles (Zlatar, "The Structure and Extent of the Pan-Slav Network in Imperial Russia 1910–1915: A Preliminary Survey," 115).

14 Tolstoy, *Anna Karenina*, part 8, chap. 1, accessed August 1, 2012, http://literature.org/authors /tolstoy-leo/anna-karenina/part-o8/chapter-o1.html.

15 The Bosnian Crisis began after Austria-Hungary annexed Bosnia and Herzegovina in October 1908—the territories occupied and administered by Austria-Hungary since the Treaty of Berlin

was a warning against emerging German expansion. On the other hand, it was a warning against the internal threat connected with Russia's own cultural insecurity, "the feeling that they were living on the edge of a backward, semi-Asian society and that everything modern and progressive came to it from the West."[16]

The other factor that influenced the attitude of Balkan people toward Russia was their inferiority complex towards Western Europe. In Maria Todorova's opinion, both the Western European and the pro-European indigenous Balkan discourse about the Balkan region had much in common with the "oriental," "colonial discourse," in the meaning given by Edward W. Said. Said argues that Western people have made use, consciously or unconsciously, of an orientalist discourse, according to which the West is considered as the main point of reference on issues concerning the universal patterns of civilization and "all human values," while the East is seen as the personification of all that is associated with a lack of culture and backwardness. The West is rational, masterful, masculine, and creative, while the East is unpredictable, affectionate, feminine, and passive.[17]

According to Todorova, Balkanism—a Western European discourse about the Balkans—differed from Orientalism in some important points. Firstly, the region was not perceived as totally alien, but as Europe's "incomplete self."[18] Secondly, the Balkan culture was seen as a masculine one: as "suspended between 'machismo' and imagined 'feminine frailties' such as impulsive spontaneity, hyper-emotionality, moody unpredictability and unreliability."[19] Yet, the mentioned image of the Balkans was still negative, just like the Western image of the Orient.

The Western Europeans tended to see this region according to the criteria of "Europeanness," measured through a lens of concepts that were

---

(1878). The great powers of France, Britain, Russia, and Italy, as well as the Ottoman Empire and Serbia, viewed these events as violations of the Treaty of Berlin. As a result, a flurry of diplomatic protests and discussions began. The crisis eventually ended in April 1909. The great powers agreed to the amendments of the Treaty of Berlin and accepted the new status quo. Nevertheless, the crisis destroyed relations between Austria-Hungary on the one hand and Russia and the Kingdom of Serbia on the other, which indirectly contributed to the outbreak of the World War.

16 Orlando Figes, *A People's Tragedy: A History of the Russian Revolution 1891–1924*, 247.

17 Said, "Nationalism, Colonialism and Literature: Yeats and Colonization," 7.

18 Todorova, *Imagining the Balkans*, 18.

19 Curticapean, "Bai Ganio and Other Men's Journeys to Europe: The Boundaries of Balkanism in Bulgarian EU-Accession Discourses," 23–25.

formulated during the Age of Enlightenment, such as "rationality" and "progress." The masculinity of the Balkans was considered different and in fact inferior to Western masculinity because it was supposed to be lacking such enlightened male qualities as reason or rationality. Progress in "civilizing" the Balkans was estimated by the degree to which the Balkan states had assimilated the technological output as well as the development of economic and political systems that had been elaborated in the West. According to the above mentioned criteria, the people of that region were still considered "barbarians."[20]

The majority of the Balkan intelligentsia, especially the liberal part, shared this kind of negative opinion about the Balkan region. The representatives emphasized the necessity of modernizing the newly established states along European patterns. They underscored the extreme importance of fighting illiteracy and traditional peasant thoughts, as well as of supporting the underdeveloped industry and agriculture. They considered this an especially pressing problem because the basic political, social, and economic reforms aimed at Europeanizing the Balkans were not completed until the turn of the twentieth century.[21]

Political realities also played an important role in creating the image of the Balkans in this period. After the unification of Italy and Germany in 1870 and 1871, Western Europeans preferred to consider all nations without their own countries as too immature to create them, and the establishment of new states as a way to damage the European balance of power. This way of thinking led, in turn, to the newly established countries in the Balkans being seen as, at most, semi-independent actors of international relations, and therefore as being unable to maintain an autonomous existence without the "parental" care of the great powers. It was deemed self-evident that it was the European powers that should decide about establishing new countries in the Balkans and choose monarchs for these states. This kind of thinking was reflected, for instance, in semi-official statements of European politicians like the German Chancellor Otto von Bismack, who said that European governments should make the "sheep thieves" understand that they did not want to be troubled by their rivalries and caprices.[22]

---

20 Malia, *Russia under Western Eyes*, 3–14.
21 Sundhausen, *Geschichte Serbiens. 19.-21. Jahrhundert*, 162–168.
22 Brunnbauer, "'Europa' und der 'Balkan': Fremd- und Selbstzuschreibungen," 5.

Additionally, the monarchs of that region, even those of Balkan origin, usually did not trust their own citizens. Milan Obrenović, King of Serbia, wrote in the 1880s to his friend Alexander of Battenberg, Prince of Bulgaria, "Don't count on your Bulgarians... They are Slavs and this fact speaks for itself. My Serbs are not better and we have to accomplish our duty exactly against their will."[23] The European superiority complex towards the Balkan region was mirrored in Western European satirical discourse as well. The Balkan territories were presented either as European *enfants terribles*: small, weak, and easy to beat, but at the same time barbarian and aggressive like capricious children, or as inanimate nature— like sticky mud, or like a kettle boiling the "European war."[24]

Indeed, the majority of political events in the Balkans caused much anxiety throughout Europe. The period in question saw several outbreaks of military conflicts, as well as of Balkan nationalism, growing under the flags of Pan-Hellenism,[25] Illyrism,[26] Great Serbia,[27] or Great Bulgaria.[28] What is more, events such as the Bosnian crisis from 1908 to 1909, when

---

23 Corti, *Leben und Liebe Alexanders von Battenberg*, 209.

24 Żakowska, "The Bear and His Protégés—Life in the Balkan Kettle According to the German-Language Caricatures of the Belle Époque," in *Competing Eyes: Visual Encounters with Alterity in Central and Eastern Europe*," 308–309.

25 The modern idea of Pan-Hellenism—a union of all Greeks in a single political body—emerged in the 1820s, resulting in the Greek War of Independence (1821–1829) against the Ottoman Empire, and became a potent movement in Greece shortly prior to, and during, the First World War. Marriott, *The Eastern Question: An Historical Study in European Diplomacy*, 8–9; Crawley, "The Near East and the Ottoman Empire, 1798–1830," 545–49.

26 Illyrism was a cultural and political movement that emerged in the nineteenth century among the South Slavs of the Austro-Hungarian Empire, especially the Croats. The adherents of Illyrism wanted to unify all the South Slavs culturally, with a common Slavonic language, and politically, within an independent Slavonic state. Wachtel, *Making a Nation, Breaking a Nation: Literature and Cultural Politics in Yugoslavia*, 26; Banac, *The National Question in Yugoslavia: Origins, History, Politics*, 76–7.

27 The term "Great Serbia" applies to the Serbian national ideology and movement, originally formulated in 1844. Its main aim was to unite all Serbs, or all historically Serb-ruled or Serb-populated lands, into one state, including the territories of modern day Croatia, Bosnia and Herzegovina, Montenegro, Macedonia, Albania, Bulgaria, Hungary, and Romania; Marriott, *The Eastern Question*, 16–17.

28 The modern idea of Great Bulgaria refers to nineteenth-century Bulgarian territorial aspirations, based on historical arguments (Bulgarian conquests in the ninth–beginning tenth century) but also on what the Bulgarian nationalists of the nineteenth century understood as "Bulgarian ethnicity," related especially with the language. Great Bulgaria of the Treaty of San Stefano was to include, besides the territory of the Principality of Bulgaria from 1878, the territories of East Rumelia, Macedonia, and Thrace. Richard J. Crampton, *A Concise History of Bulgaria*, 84–85; Marriott, *The Eastern Question*, 355–356.

Serbia dared to make a diplomatic intervention against the annexation of Bosnia-Herzegovina by Austria-Hungary, proved that Balkan countries ultimately tended to revolt against the status quo established by the great powers.

The ambiguous relations between Russia and Europe should be also considered among the factors that influenced the image of Russia in the Balkan region in this period. On the one hand, Russia had never come closer to the ideal of Europeanness than at that time.[29] According to Martin Malia, this situation was connected with the Russian defeat in the Crimean War and the peace established between Turkey and Russia in 1856. It was also related to the social reforms carried out in Russia by Alexander II (1855–1881), such as the abolition of serfdom (1861), the introduction of a unified, independent court system with the institution of jury trial and professional advocates, and the institution of provincial- and district-elected self-governments (*zemstvos*) (1864). These reforms initiated the process of building a civil society in Russia, especially of the intelligentsia—a group that began to lead the discourse on the role of Russia in Europe. These changes were perceived as a sign of the gradual Europeanization of Russia.

On the other hand, the images of Russia and Europe were still functioning as complementary entities in that period. In the literary and philosophical discourse in the West, but also in Russia, there were prevailing images of the latter as an Other, an imagined space that is strange, dangerous, and psychopathic. A popular way of describing the relations of the Western Europeans with the Tsarist State was as a collision between Europe and Asia. Russia was treated as an example of a world gone awry and the source of threats, caused by militarism and Asiatic despotism hidden under the appearance of Europeanness.[30]

During the Napoleonic Wars, hundreds of thousands of recruits from Central and Eastern Europe marched through Russia, and those who came back brought the memory of the inhumanities they experienced in the East. The Russian army was treated in Western Europe as a liberator from French occupation. Nevertheless, the memory of the Cossacks' cruelties which had been committed on Russian, German, or French territo-

29 Malia, *Russia under Western Eyes: From the Bronze Horseman to the Lenin Mausoleum*, 211–217.
30 Crudopf, "Russland-Stereotypen in der deutschen Medienberichterstattung," 28.

ries, remained in the historical consciousness of the Central and Western Europeans.[31]

From the end of the Napoleonic era until the beginning of the First World War—apart from during the Crimean War (1853–1856)—there was peace between the European countries and Russia. Nevertheless, the major European powers actively competed with Russia for spheres of influence in the Middle and Far East and worried about its political and territorial demands. Additionally, Russian internal politics was raising anxiety among the European public. The social perturbations in the Tsarist State after the fiasco of the reforms of Alexander II evoked fear of the country's unpredictability. The conservatives warned against the menace posed by the Russian revolutionists. The social democrats and the liberals pitied the inhabitants of the Tsarist State, who lived like slaves. In nationalist discourse, the Russians were denied the right to be treated as equal to Western European nations. The Tsarist state even became an object of the German ideology of *Drang nach Osten*.[32]

Summing up, in the period in question, both Russia and the Balkan countries tended to be seen by the Europeans as the regions most striving to "catch up with Europe." The inhabitants of these countries also perceived Europe as the most important reference point: both as an unattainable ideal as well as a threat to their national identity. The mutual perception of the Balkan countries and Russia was, on the contrary, built on the conviction of the reciprocal and far-reaching historical and cultur-

---

31 Cf. the considerations of Alan Forrest: "More than a third of the Grand Armée was not French. It contained the soldiers all across the empire, regions that France had occupied and colonized. The reactions of the soldiers reflect the collective prejudices of the European continent;" "[For] the French troops in Russia... the nations of Asia inspired an exaggerated fear. They did not fight with the same rules, the same sense of honor, or the same weapons... Of the different groups in the Russian army Cossacks enjoyed a particular reputation for sadism and cruelty... Their very appearance inspired fear, especially during the French retreat from Moscow, where they were employed to great effect in harrying the army's rear guard and attacking weak links in the main marching column." Forrest, "The French at War. Representations of the Enemy in *War and Peace*," 59–73. The image of a "Cossack" and the name itself—as a synonym of a Russian man or Russian soldier—was popularized in the first half of the nineteenth century throughout the whole of Europe. Initially it had a neutral or even positive meaning, but by the second half of the nineteenth century it was used only in a negative context. The term and its variations (such as "Cossack politics") gained enormous popularity not only in satirical magazines but also in daily newspapers. Żakowska, "Niedźwiedź i zegarmistrz. U źródeł metafory 'rosyjskiego niedźwiedzia' w Szwajcarii w drugiej połowie XIX w.," 173–174.
32 German for "yearning for the East," "thrust toward the East," "push eastward," or "drive toward the East."

al bonds between the Balkan countries and Russia, and that Russia's destiny was to obtain a leading position—politically and culturally—in the Balkan region.

The Russian Messiah Crying upon Heavenly Serbia

In Serbian culture, Russia was traditionally perceived as an Orthodox brother, an "eternal ally," and a future liberator.[33] These Russophile images were especially widespread among the Serbian folk and the conservative part of the Serbian intelligentsia.[34] Nevertheless, the specificity of the Serbian attitude towards Russia consisted especially of strong mystical connotations of Russia's image. One vision that was highly influential was the idea of Russia-the-Savior—the image of a Russian Messiah. This meant the Serbian myth about Russia had much in common with Serbian quasi-sacralized beliefs about their own national specificity.

The Serbian national identity at that time was based on the ancient— launched in the fourteenth century, and constantly reinforced—Kosovo myth which consists of a legendary vision of the Battle of Blackbird's Field[35] in 1389 and its consequences. The battle took place between the army led by Serbian Prince Lazar Hrebeljanović[36] and the invading army of the Ottoman Empire,[37] and ended with the death of both commanders, Prince Lazar and Sultan Murad I. The most likely outcome of the battle was that it was a draw. What is more, it did not have any short-term negative results for Serbian statehood.[38] Nevertheless, as all Serbian historians state, "in the Serbian 'collective memory' the battle is remembered as a fateful defeat which led to the loss of independence and the 'five century-long Turkish yoke.'"[39]

---

33 Mitani, "From Serbia with Love: Verbal Representation of Russia in Serbian Society," 354–355.
34 Ian D. Armour, "Killing Nationalism with Liberalism? Austria–Hungary and the Serbian Constitution of 1869," 356.
35 Also known as the Battle of Kosovo or Kosovo Field.
36 His army consisted predominantly of Serbian Christian forces. Bosnians, Bulgarians, Albanians, and Vlachs as well as some Hungarians are also believed to have participated in the battle on the Serbian side.
37 The Turkish army also included Serbian, Albanian, and other Christian vassals and mercenaries.
38 Serbia survived for another seventy years before finally capitulating to the Ottoman Empire in 1459.
39 Dejan Djokic, "Whose Myth? Which Nation? The Serbian Kosovo Myth Revisited," 215–233.

According to the Kosovo myth, the battle was a symbol of national tragedy, but also of Serbian heroism and the hope of resurrection. Serbian heroism was exemplified there through two main motives. First, by the motive of Prince Lazar, who rejected the "earthly kingdom" in favor of the nobler ideals of victimhood and sacrifice, the "kingdom in heaven." As Dejan Djokić says:

> According to legend, on the eve of the battle the Holy Prophet Elijah offered Prince Lazar a choice between an empire in heaven and an empire on earth. Lazar's choice—a heavenly empire—would mean defeat by the Ottomans but it would secure a kingdom in heaven for the Serbian nation. The sacrifice that Lazar and his knights made at Kosovo turned a military defeat into a moral victory.[40]

In other words, Lazar died so that his people could live. Therefore, the Kosovo myth implies a direct analogy between Lazar and Jesus.[41] Second, Serbian heroism was exemplified in the aforementioned myth through the motif of Miloš Obilić, the brave and faithful knight, who allegedly killed the Sultan, thus avenging Prince Lazar's death.[42]

It seems, therefore, that the Serbian myth about Russia was significantly influenced by the Kosovo myth in the period we are considering: the image of Russia was predominantly perceived through the lens of the significant component of that myth—the cult of self-sacrifice and death.[43] In the following considerations the Serbian discourse concerning figures and plots connected to Russia and the narratives on the Kosovo myth will be traced starting from that time.

Most of all, these figures and plots were based on narratives about Russian heroes who sacrificed their lives while defending or fighting for the independence of Serbia. The image of the Russian Orthodox ally was especially connected with Russian reactions to the Serbian anti-Turk uprisings in the nineteenth century. From 1875–1878, about 3,000 Russian volunteers, including 700 officers, rushed to the Principality of Serbia, making

---

40   Djokic, "Whose Myth? Which Nation?," 218–219.
41   Djokic, "Whose Myth? Which Nation?," 215–233.
42   Judah, *The Serbs: History, Myth and the Destruction of Yugoslavia*, 30–40.
43   Masek, "Milos Crnjanski's Homecoming to a Migrating National Family," 216.

selfless sacrifices to help the Serbs fight the Ottoman Empire. Many of them became commanders of the large Serbian military formations, and many died and were revered in Serbia as national heroes. [44]

In particular, Count Nikolay Rayevsky (1840–1876) became such a personage. He volunteered to go to Serbia, willingly joined the army of Russian General Mikhail Chernyaev, and as a commandant of a detachment of the Serbian army showed great courage in the victorious battles of Šumatovac and Aleksinac. Yet the decisive fact that started the impulse to create a legend about him was his death in the lost Battle of Adrovac at the age of 36. This meant that the Serbs could make of Rayevsky not only a heroic warrior, but also a young man sacrificing his life for a beloved country. It should be pointed out that Serbs have been drawn to the idea of some scholars that Leo Tolstoy made Rayevsky a model for Count Alexei Vronsky—the tragic lover of Anna Karenina[45]—which made the figure of Rayevsky appear even more tragic. He came across as a noble man with a broken heart, longing for death in a battle. Serbian myth thus associated him with a great number of their own Serbian heroes who, like Prince Lazar in the Battle of Kosovo, chose the heavenly kingdom and death in the field of glory.

Pera Todorovic, one of the first modern Serbian journalists, dramatically described in his *Diary of a Volunteer* the battle of Adrovac and the death of another Russian volunteer:

> We saw Russians taking... poor Kirillov from the battlefield... We kissed his gory forehead... An old Russian man standing next to me kissed Kirillov and said: "Good-bye, old friend... You served an honourable Christian mission."[46]

It is worth mentioning that on the place where Rayevsky was killed, the bishop of Niš, with the help of the Serbian Queen Natalya, built a Russian church with frescos commemorating the hero (1903).

---

44 Kurjak, Popović-Obradović and Šuković, *Russia, Serbia, Montenegro.*

45 Anna Karenina, the heroine of Leo Tolstoy's novel of the same name, is an aristocratic married woman who has an affair with an army officer, Count Alexei Vronsky. After leaving her husband and going to live with her lover, Anna falls into social disgrace. She soon becomes extremely jealous, suspecting Vronsky of infidelity. Eventually she commits suicide.

46 Kapor, *Puteshestviye po biografii,* accessed August 1, 2012, http://www.senica.ru/forum /index. php?showtopic=359&st=80.

The Russian diplomat Ivan Yastrebov (1839–1894) is another example of a Serbian national hero whose life and death was interpreted through the prism of the myth of self-sacrifice. Yastrebov was the Russian consul in Shkodra and Prizren (1879–1886) and an ethnologist, one of the most prominent researchers of Old Serbia (Kosovo) and Albania in the second half of the nineteenth century.[47] Nevertheless he became famous first and foremost as the incarnation of the Serbian *hajduk*, a kind of Balkan "noble robber."[48] His often illegal acts against the Ottoman authorities in favor of Serbian people discriminated against in Kosovo made him similar to such figures as Milos Obilić—the man who allegedly killed Sultan Murad I in the Battle of Blackbird's Field and therefore became the first "avenger of Kosovo." Yastrebov's death in Thessaloniki also became the subject of legends. The Russian consul died suddenly in mysterious circumstances after visiting the Turkish authorities. This fact was strongly emphasized by the Serbs because it enabled them to make Yastrebov not only a noble robber but also a Slavic Orthodox martyr.[49]

---

47 The monument of Ivan Yastrebov was built in Prizren churchyard near the monument of Serbian national hero, Emperor Stefan Dusan, in the 1980s (and destroyed by Albanians in 1999).

48 *Hajduk* (probably from the Turkish word *haiduk* or *hayduk* meaning bandit)—a term commonly referring to outlaws, highwaymen or freedom fighters in the Balkans and Central and Eastern Europe. In Balkan folkloric tradition, the hajduk was the romanticized figure of a hero who steals from, and leads his fighters into battle against, the Ottoman or Habsburg authorities; Aleksandar Petrović, *The Role of Banditry in the Creation of National States in the Central Balkans during the 19th Century. A Case Study: Serbia*, accessed October 1, 2015, http://www.rastko.org.rs/istorija/xix/apetrovic-banditry_eng.html.

49 Soon after his death Ivan Yastrebov became a hero of Serbian popular folk songs (Sukhorukov, "Russkiy konsul – v serbskoy pesne," accessed August 1, 2012, http://serbska.org/serbia/author/admin /page/2763/?nggpage=2). He was also commemorated in a novel *Russian Consul* of Vuk Drašković (1988). The novel includes numerous reflections on Yastrebov's life and deeds which resemble hagiographic notes (Cf. "V kontse proshlogo veka... etot tsarskiy diplomat otnyud' ne diplomaticheskimi metodami, no chisto po-gaydutski zashchishchal pravoslavnoye naseleniye na serbskom Kosove ot tiranii polumesyatsa. O podvigakh yego slagalis' legendy: rasskazyvali, chto ni islamskiye sabli, ni ruzh'ya ne mogut prichinit' yemu ni maleyshego vreda. Sluchalos', chto vsya odezhda moguchego russkogo borodacha byvala izreshechena pulyami, na tele zhe neizmenno ne ostavalos' ni yedinoy tsarapiny. Buduchi narodom epicheskogo dukha, serby legko smeshivayut real'nost' i fantaziyu. U geroyev nashikh yunatskikh pesen po tri serdtsa, oni zhivut po trista let, ikh koni krylaty, a sabli imeyut glaza. Net nichego udivitel'nogo, chto russkiy konsul Yastrebov byl shchedro nadelen vsemi kharakternymi chertami fol'klornykh geroyev. Takim on ostalsya v pamyati serbov. Yastrebov rodilsya 27 yanvarya. U serbov eto den' svyatogo Savvy, nashego velichayshego svyatitelya. Kogda zhe u russkogo konsula v Prizrene Yastrebova RODILSYA SYN, on dal yemu imya Rastko. U russkikh takogo imeni net. No tak zvali svyatogo Savvudo yego postrizheniya v monakhi. YA ne somnevayus', chto Yastrebov prekrasno soznaval sud'bonosnost' daty svoyego rozhdeniya. Ne sluchayno on zaveshchal vse, chto imel, serbam" *Русский консул,* 56).

The Russian Tsars, especially those who fought wars against Turkey, were also revered as caring, selfless protectors of Serbia. Nevertheless, it should be stressed that the strongest empathy among them was gained by Tsar Nicholas II (1894–1917), as he joined the Great War (1914), fighting on the side of Serbia, and three years later was murdered with all his family by communists. In other words, the life and death of the last Russian Tsar stirred deep sympathy among Serbian people largely because it could be interpreted as another variation of the self-sacrifice motive. This was precisely the interpretation of the fate of the last of the Romanovs given by Nikolaj Velimirović (1880–1956), the bishop of Žiča and Ohrid and a future saint of the Orthodox Church.[50] During the First World War he stated in one of his works that:

> The Holy Emperor Nicholas did not hesitate to go to Calvary together with his family and his nation, for the sake of the Serbian people with whom he shared the Orthodox faith. He deliberately chose the heavenly instead of earthly kingdom, as once our pious Prince Lazar did.[51]

Apart from this, the myth about Russia was also used by the representatives of the Serbian conservative movement to strengthen the belief in Serbia's natural place in the "East" rather than in Europe.[52] This can be observed in Serbian literature from the turn of the twentieth century, which was highly influenced by the ideas of Russian Slavophile and Populist ideologies.

These ideas were presented in (among others) the famous novel *Hajduk Stanko* (1896) by Janko Veselinović (1862–1905). The book describes the first Serbian Uprising against the Turks at the beginning of the nineteenth century and can be considered as a "patriotic primer" that glorifies patriotism and the moral values of the Serbian people. However, the novel also had additional political contexts. It targeted the despotic, cor-

50 Nikolaj Velimirović was canonized under the name Saint Nicholas of Serbia in 2003.
51 "Imperator Nikolay II – strastoterpets i muchenik" [Emperor Nicholas II–a passion bearer and martyr], accessed July 1, 2013, http://ruskline.ru/news_rl/2010/06/09/imperator_ nikolaj_ii_ strastoterpec_i_muchenik/.
52 "Russia: Mythical Ally," *Helsinki Bulletin* 76 (2011): 1–5, accessed August 1, 2012, www.helsinki. org.rs/doc/HB-No76.pdf.

rupt, and inefficient policies of the contemporary governments of Milan (1868–1889) and Alexander Obrenović (1889–1903). In Veselinović's novel, salvation for Serbia was seen in the return to traditional folk values. At the center of this philosophy was the idealization of Orthodoxy, autocracy, and nationality—ideas taken from the official Russian state ideology of the nineteenth century. Old Serbia was supposed to represent, just like the old Russia of Russian Slavophiles, an original type of social development. It was personified by the Orthodox—implying "pure" Christian— faith, by mutual confidence between the monarch and his people and by *zadruga*, the extended patriarchal family.[53]

It is important to appreciate that the Slavophil ideology was also adapted by the Populists (*Narodniks*)—the Russian revolutionists acting outside and against the Russian political system. The *Narodniki*, being the adherents of a communist ideology, sought to establish a just society based on indigenous folk institutions, notably the system of communal land tenure known as the *mir*. Although they initially aimed to awaken the masses through peaceful methods, the combination of peasant indifference and government persecution drove them in the mid-1870s to a more radical program and radical, terrorist methods. The Populists became known not only in Russian society; their ideology and activity became famous throughout Europe, including the Balkans. What is more, it was especially in the Balkan region, and first of all probably in Serbia, where the Narodniks found their most eager, determined followers.[54]

It should also be mentioned how the Russophile narratives interacted in nineteenth-century Serbia with the pro-Western discourse. Serbian liberals, constitutionalists and pro-Austrians, including the last two monarchs from the Obrenović dynasty, tended to express more-or-less intense anti-Russian feelings.[55] Milan Obrenović said:

> Most of my problems were caused by the fact that the majority of my people had been hypnotized by Russia so deeply that even in economic issues they expected salvation from this country, while I saw very

---

53 Zieliński, *Serbska powieść historyczna. Studia nad źródłami, ideami i kierunkami rozwoju.*

54 Walicki, *Rosyjska filozofia i myśl społeczna od Oświecenia do marksizmu*, 328–391; Dedijer, *The Road to Sarajevo*, 52, 226–227.

55 Armour, "Killing Nationalism with Liberalism?" 356.

clearly that Serbia both politically and economically depended on Central Europe.[56]

King Milan often accused Russia of treachery, as well as of attempts to manipulate the Balkan countries for the sake of her own purposes. After the Russo-Turkish War of 1828–1829, Serbia achieved autonomy within Turkey, and after the Russo-Turkish War of 1877–1878, formal independence from the Ottoman Empire. Milan was still dissatisfied that in 1878 Austria-Hungary was allowed by the great powers to occupy Bosnia-Herzegovina, a region perceived by the Serbs as their own ethnic territory. Additionally, he was convinced that it was in the Serbian interest to modernize Serbia through European science, technology, and cultural examples, as well as through political and economic cooperation with the Austro-Hungarian Empire.[57]

As a result, a clear division could be observed on the Serbian political stage in the second half of the nineteenth century. The political scene was divided into liberals, who tended to be pro-Austrian and anti-Russian, and conservatives, who tended to be anti-Western and Russophile.

Eventually, however, the anti-Russian option was defeated despite efforts to impose it by Serbian monarchs. This happened mostly because the Serbian "modernizers" of that time managed to discredit their own ideas. The foreign and internal policy of the last Obrenovici turned out to be totally ineffective. Serbian rulers not only did not make any essential progress in modernizing Serbian society, but also became entirely dependent on political and economic support from Austria-Hungary, and led Serbia to defeat in a war with Bulgaria (1885–1886). What is more, they gained a reputation for being depraved and despotic monarchs. Therefore, King Milan was eventually forced to abdicate the throne and his son, Alexander, was assassinated, together with his wife, by ardent Serbian patriots.[58]

---

56   Georgevitch, *Das Ende der Obrenovitsch. Beiträge zur Geschichte Serbiens 1897–1900*, 93, accessed August 4, 2012, http://www26.us.archive.org/stream/dasendederobrenooorgoog /dasendederobrenooorgoog_djvu.txt.

57   Kovačević, *Srbiyâ i Rusiyâ 1878–1889. Od Berlinskog kongresa do abdikaciye Kraylja Milana*, 370.

58   Sundhausen, *Geschichte Serbiens*, 162–168, 204–205.

RUSSIA AS LIBERATOR

The fundamental variations in Bulgarian myths about Russia centered around two narratives: that of Dyado Ivan (Grandpa Ivan), and that of Rayna, a Bulgarian princess.[59]

The myth about Dyado Ivan, in comparison to the myth of Rayna, is older, more widespread, and of genuine Bulgarian origin. In it appears the image of Russia as a mighty Orthodox Christian protector and a liberator, took various forms: of a Russian King, a Russian General, a Russian soldier, and so on.[60] The term Dyado Ivan supposedly went back to the second half of the fifteenth and the sixteenth centuries and was previously associated with the Russian monarchs Ivan III (1462–1505) and Ivan IV the Terrible (1533–1584),[61] who became famous because of their successful wars against the Golden Horde and its successors.[62]

This myth was repeatedly disseminated into Bulgarian culture, but the man who undoubtedly contributed the most to popularizing it was Ivan Vazov (1850–1921).[63] In his works he presented Russia as an external, transcendental power that intervenes in the history of mankind to save the Bulgarian nation. For instance, this motive plays an important role in his novel *Under the Yoke* (1894). The author described the excitement felt within Bulgarian society before the April uprising against the Turks (1876) and the tragic end of the insurgence. In one scene the main character, Boycho Ognianoff, questions a schoolgirl in front of an audience:

---

59 Aretov, "Forging the Myth about Russia: Rayna, Bulgarian Princess," 69.

60 Aretov, "Forging the Myth about Russia: Rayna, Bulgarian Princess," 69.

61 Trifonov, "Istorichesko obyasnenie na vyarata v 'Dyado Ivan' (Rusiya) u bŭlgarskiya narod," accessed August 1, 2012, http://liternet.bg/publish17/iu_trifonov/izbrani/istorichesko.htm.

62 Especially after the 1550s when Ivan the Terrible conquered the Tatar states of Kazan' (1552) and Astrakhan' (1556), which was presented by the official propaganda as a triumph of militant Orthodoxy over the infidels. Moreover, these annexations contributed to the legitimization of Ivan's assumption of the title of tsar, because the khanates were seen in the Muscovite political tradition as tsardoms. These conquests escalated the tension between Muscovy and the powerful Ottoman Empire and its vassal Crimea. These countries concluded a union against Muscovy and jointly attacked Astrakhan' in 1569. Nevertheless, the campaign failed. In 1571 the Crimean khan devastated Moscow, but Ivan's commanders inflicted a defeat on him at the Battle of Molodi in 1572; Alexander Filjushkin, *Ivan the Terrible: A Military History*, 125–127; Sergey Bogatyrev, "Ivan IV (1533–1584)," 255–256.

63 Ivan Vasov was an outstanding nineteenth-century Bulgarian poet and writer. Aretov, "Forging the myth," 69. Peleva and Spassova-Dikova; "Figuring the Motherland and Staging the Party Father in Bulgarian Literature," 177–178.

"Subka, can you tell me what Tsar it was that freed the Bulgarians from the Greek yoke?" "The Bulgarians were freed from the Turkish yoke by..." the child began erroneously. "No, no, Subka," cried her father. "You're to tell us by what Tsar they were freed from the Greek yoke. We all know what Tsar is to free us from the Turkish yoke." ... Subka cried eagerly: "The Bulgarians were freed from the Greek yoke by Tsar Asen, but they will be freed from the Turkish yoke by Tsar Alexander of Russia."[64]

The Russian Tsar Alexander II, who fought the Russo-Turkish War of 1877–1878 and was the main proponent of establishing an independent Bulgaria, became undoubtedly the most representative incarnation of Dyado Ivan in the period in question. Russia itself and Russian soldiers were also used in that discourse as typical themes. In several poems, Vasov played on the linguistic similarity between the words *Rusiya* (Russia) and *Mesiya* (Messiah) (*Russia*, 1876), interpreted the Russo-Turkish War as a struggle between the Ottoman Empire and God (*Plevna has Surrendered*, 1877), and compared the Russian monarch to Jesus, and the act of liberation to the resurrection of Lazar (*Nikolay Nikolaevich*, 1877).[65]

Similar themes can be found notably in Todor Vlaykov's novella *The Russians Have Come to us at Last*, which was published in the second volume of his book *Experience* (1939).[66] The work describes, among others, a cheerful march of the Russian army through a Bulgarian village in 1877:

A crowd of people in the market just light up with joy. Cossacks are seen here and there, each surrounded by men, women, and children who give them something, recount something. Cossacks try to comprehend and answer in Russian. After each word both Cossacks and the people surrounding them are saying: "bratushka, bratushka!" ... I am hanging around, looking into the brave Cossacks' faces, trying to guess the mean-

64 Vasov, *Under the Yoke*, accessed August 1, 2012, http://www.ebooksread.com/authors-eng/ivan-minchov-vazov/under-the-yoke-a-romance-of-bulgarian-liberty-hci/page-7-under-the-yoke-a-romance-of-bulgarian-liberty-hci.shtml.
65 Drzewiecka, "Rosja" [Russia], 257; Chavdarova, "Mif Rossii i stereotip russkogo v bolgarskoy kul'ture po sravneniyu s pol'skim stereotipom," 201–203.
66 Vlaykov, "Nay-posle rusite idvat i u nas," accessed July 1, 2013, http://pravoslavie.domainbg.com/rus/15/vlajkov_bratushki.htm.

ing of what they are saying, which is not very understandable, but full of kindness. I can't stand still... And on the street there is such a huge crowd of people like during Easter! All of them... drunk with joy...[67]

The Bulgarian authorities also strove to worthily commemorate Russian deeds during this period. In 1879 it was decided to build a cathedral in Sofia in honor of the Russian soldiers who died during the last war. The church, eventually founded in 1912, was the biggest cathedral on the Balkan Peninsula and one of the largest Eastern Orthodox cathedrals in the world.[68] The building soon became the most representative symbol of modern independent Bulgaria. What is also significant, the church was dedicated to Saint Alexander Nevsky, patron of the Russian Empire.[69] Moreover, in 1907 an equestrian statue of Alexander II, the "Tsar Liberator," was erected in the center of the Bulgarian capital.[70]

These Russophilic attitudes were also reflected in the Bulgarian historical perspectives of that period. For instance, Bulgarian historian and philologist Yurdan Trifonov published an article in 1908 about the origins of the term "Dyado Ivan," which was largely taken up with a description of the military achievements of Tsars Ivan III and Ivan the Terrible. The author stated there that while these monarchs were "terrible [i.e. fearful] for Muslims and Catholics" they were "great and attractive for [the Bulgarians'] ancestors" who believed that they would "break the head of the snake... that was wrapped around the body of Orthodox Christianity and was sucking its blood."[71]

In contrast to the themes around Dyado Ivan, the second Bulgarian narrative about Russia—Rayna—was popularized in the mid-nineteenth century and was not of Bulgarian, but of Russian, origin. Two features of note are, first, that the motif became popular thanks to the novel *Ray-*

67 Włajkow, "Rosjanie wreszcie przybyli do nas," 151.
68 As of 1989 the biggest cathedral located on the Balkan Peninsula is the Cathedral of Saint Sava in Belgrade.
69 Interestingly, the name of the cathedral was briefly changed to the Saint Cyril and Methodius Cathedral between 1916 and 1920 (since Bulgaria and Russia belonged to opposing alliances in WWI), but then the original name was restored.
70 Neuburger, *The Orient Within: Muslim Minorities and the Negotiation of Nationhood of Modern Bulgaria*, 35.
71 Trifonov, "Istorichesko obyasnenie."

na, Bulgarian Princess (1843) by the Russian writer Alexander Veltman (1800–1870), and second, that its ideology mirrored the views of Russian Slavophiles.[72]

At the center of the story is Rayna, supposedly the daughter of the Bulgarian King Peter (929–969). The plot of *Rayna* has as background the conflicts between Bulgaria and Byzantium, and between Bulgaria and Kievan Rus'. The evil character of the novel, Count Samuel, wants to get the crown of the Bulgarian Empire. He murders King Peter and tries to force his daughter Rayna to marry him. Moreover, he seeks an ally in the hostile Byzantine Empire.[73] Svyatoslav, Prince of Kiev, a heroic and noble warrior, appears to be the last hope and savior of Bulgaria. Svyatoslav is urged to attack Bulgaria by the Byzantine Emperor, but on arrival, he realizes that the Bulgarians are in fact brothers of the Russians and he takes their side in the conflict.[74] Rayna and Svyatoslav fall in love with each other. The Kievan prince defeats Samuel and his Byzantine allies, transfers the authority over Bulgaria to Boris, the son of the murdered King Peter, and goes back to Kiev with Rayna. Unfortunately, they are assaulted by Pechenegs, who were persuaded to attack the prince by Count Samuel. The bandits demand that Svyatoslav gives the princess to them. To save the life of her beloved, Rayna decides to sacrifice herself. She states: "If I die, no one loses anything, but if Svyatoslav dies, then Bulgaria is also destroyed." She secretly places herself in the hands of her enemies and shortly afterwards commits suicide. Prince Svyatoslav also dies in battle with the Pechenegs, while trying to save Rayna.[75]

Based on the above myths, several conclusions can be drawn concerning the specificity of Bulgarian national mythology. First, Bulgaria, as seen on the basis of these myths, was an innocent and passive victim of evil powers—most of all Turkey and Byzantium—and a place where these powers could be rejected only with foreign (Russian) aid.[76] In that sense, these plots are not unique in Bulgarian national mythology. The narrative

---

72 Aretov, "Forging the Myth," 70.
73 Aretov, "Forging the Myth," 71.
74 Aretov, "Forging the Myth," 73–74.
75 Aleksandr F. Veltman, "Rayna, korolevna Bolgarskaya," http://ruslit.com.ua/russian_classic /veltman_af/rayna_korolevna_bolgarskaya.3192.
76 Aretov, "Forging the Myth," 74.

of Bulgarian victimhood is deeply rooted and has even become the prevailing one in the country.[77]

Second, Russia, as seen in these myths, had only one, invariable image, that remained popular and unchanged during the decades in question. This was the image of Russia as the protector and liberator. Russia appeared in Bulgarian history only and unvaryingly in this role. The political tensions and hostilities in Russo-Bulgarian relations were treated as a non-existent problem, with no need for consideration.

The attempt to create an idealized picture of Russia is perfectly transparent in, for instance, the plot of *Rayna*, which in truth contains many historical misrepresentations. The real Svyatoslav invaded and conquered Bulgaria out of quite pragmatic motives. King Peter died in a monastery, a year after abdicating the throne. The historic sources do not confirm that King Peter had a daughter named Rayna. Count Samuel, who eventually became Bulgarian Emperor, was considered a powerful, successful and heroic ruler and was revered as a Bulgarian national hero. The myth of Rayna had much in common with the ideological image of Russia presented by Slavophiles and Pan-Slavs. According to their ideology, the politics of the Russian Empire resembled the politics of the mythical Kievan monarch—a man presented as an unselfish, brave and honest prince, on whose face there was "no enmity or malice," who "had no slaves," and "didn't want to conquer foreign lands like a robber,"[78] and who therefore succeeded in creating an empire.

According to Nikolay Aretov, several factors need to be taken into consideration while analyzing the phenomenon of Bulgarian national mythology, and the most important seems to be the influence of the current political situation: "The willingness to improve relationships with the neighboring country... implies that hostile relations with the antecedents of this country should be dissembled: both victories and traumatic events."[79] It is important to pinpoint that the Bulgarian stereotype of Russia and the Bulgarian self-image was created, to a great extent, precisely on the Russians' own self-stereotype and the Russian stereotype concerning the Bulgarian people. Among the other reasons for the spread of

77   Aretow, "Przemilczane zwycięstwa", 405.
78   Veltman, "Rayna, korolevna Bolgarskaya."
79   Aretow, "Przemilczane zwycięstwa," 402.

the self-victimizing mythical plots by Bulgarian intellectuals, there was the need to mobilize society against external (and internal) foes, and to justify Bulgarian political demands on the neighboring countries.

Third, these myths coexisted with Bulgarians' positive attitude towards events and figures that directly or indirectly symbolized antagonism towards Russia and Russianness. For instance, Prince Alexander of Battenberg (1879–1886), the first monarch of the restored country, was the personal enemy of Tsar Alexander III and was forced to abdicate the throne because of Russian interference. Nevertheless, his remains were buried in a national mausoleum in Sofia (1897) and he was revered in Bulgaria as a national hero.[80]

It is important to make clear that the mythical image of Russia was not the only positive reference point for the Bulgarian people. The other one was "Europe," as manifest by West and Central European countries. According to Ludmila Kostova, "a sense of the difference between Russia and Europe" played "a dominant role in Bulgarian identity":

A considerable amount of Bulgarian writing produced in the late nineteenth and early twentieth centuries [was] informed by a nostalgic longing for a "Europe" of the mind, perceived in terms of civilizational superiority, [while] Bulgaria and its Balkan neighbours [were] represented as sites of symbolic lack: for various reasons they [were] unable to efface the signs of their Oriental(ised) past and to adopt a genuine "European" identity.[81]

---

80 Oroschakoff, *Die Battenberg Affäre. Leben und Abenteuer des Gavriil Oroscharoff oder eine russische-europäische Geschichte*, 9, 264–265; Gürdev, "Za knyaz Batenberg 110 godini sled smŭrtta mu," accessed July 1, 2013, http://www.liternet.bg/publish4/bgyrdev/istoria/abatenberg.htm. Russo-Bulgarian relations in the "long nineteenth century" often had little to do with the Slavophile or Pan-Slavic ideal. Modern Bulgaria was created in 1878 as a Principality under the nominal suzerainty of the Sultan and real control of the Russians. The first monarch of the re-emerged country was Alexander of Battenberg (1879–1886), who proclaimed unification between Bulgaria and Eastern Rumelia, won a war with Serbia (1885), became a Bulgarian national hero and finally had to abdicate under Russian pressure. The next Bulgarian monarch, Ferdinand of Saxe-Coburg and Gotha (1887–1918), became an important influence in international affairs, not only in the Balkans. In 1908 he used the occasion of the eve of the Austro-Hungarian annexation of Bosnia-Herzegovina to proclaim the full independence of Bulgaria from the Ottoman Empire, and in 1912 he spearheaded the formation of the Balkan League that pursued the partitioning of European Turkey. His ideas on foreign affairs were based on close relations with Russia but also with Triple Alliance countries.

81 Kostova, "Getting to Know," 108–109.

Interestingly, a year before *Hajduk Stanko* was published, the above-mentioned patriotic and traditionally-oriented Serbian novel, the Bulgarian author Aleko Konstantinov (1863–1897) wrote his famous self-ironical stories about Bai Ganio. The stories, initially published in 1895, described the adventures of "a contemporary Bulgarian" trader of rose oil who travelled through Europe to sell his products. Bai Ganio was dirty and smelly, greedy and superficial, yet vital and proud of himself, as well as of his Bulgarian nationality. Through his figure, Bulgarians could see themselves reflected in the European mirror as a "barbaric" and "backward" people of "low culture." Yet the stories, full of humor, could and did function as therapy through laughter.[82] They reflected not only the Bulgarians' Eastern identity, but also their belief in the need to catch up with Europe.

Who are We? On Brothers and Savages

In conclusion, we can say that the mythical image of Russia corresponded with the self-images of the Bulgarians and Serbians in the given period. It seems that the Tsarist Empire (as opposed to Western Europe) was perceived by them as a complementary being. While comparing themselves with an eastern "Slavonic brother," the Balkan people could pretend to be innocent victims in front of the mighty liberator, and while comparing themselves to Europeans, they were forced to perceive themselves as savages who needed to be civilized by enlightened nations. It could be supposed that the first option was more attractive for the South Slavs. The self-identification as victims was considered less humiliating than as "sheep thieves," "backward peasants," or "robbers," as the South Slavs were usually spoken of by Western Europeans.[83]

The European and Russian mythical images created by the South Slavs were based on contrast. The narratives about Europe were generally written in ordinary language, whereas those about Russia employed mystical phrases. The former narratives were based on positivistic discourse about modern life, the latter on a kind of romantic fairy-tale. The pro-European

---

82   Curticapean, "Bai Ganio and Other Men's Journeys to Europe: The Boundaries of Balkanism in Bulgarian EU-Accession Discourses," 31–35.

83   Kaplan, *Balkan Ghost: A Journey Through History*, xiv; Brunnbauer, "'Europa' und der 'Balkan': Fremd- und Selbstzuschreibungen," 5.

narratives were created by adherents of gradualist modernization, the pro-Russian ones by both conservatives and revolutionaries.[84] For the people of the Balkans, including the Serbs and Bulgarians, Russia seemed to embody a glorious history, while Europe stood for a dull, ambivalent future.

Serbian cultural and political Russophile discourse was at the same time an anti-occidental discourse. Russia was perceived, just like Serbia, as a country that was an antithesis of corrupt modern Europe and a guardian of real European values. Catastrophic and messianic motifs, focused on religious-cultural themes (e.g. the vision of the "Russian Christ") were prevalent and accompanied by socialist and populist ideas of the Russian revolutionary movement. Serbian Russophiles simultaneously awaited Russian aid (they perceived Russia as Serbia's defender, or even as a Messiah) and experienced a kind of spiritual brotherhood with the Tsarist Empire. For instance, the Serbian poet Jovan Jovanović (1833–1904) stated that "of all the Slav peoples, the Russians have contributed most and the Serbs are those from whom most is expected."[85] The Serbian stereotype of Russia was built both on elements of the Russian self-stereotype and on the most important part of the Serbian self-stereotype. Therefore, the Serbian self-stereotype and the Serbian stereotype of Russia were similar to each other. The concept that played the major role in Serbian national identity, the self-victimization motif, served as a compensatory factor: it offered a way of overcoming feelings of national disgrace and of justifying the need for sacred vengeance on Serbia's enemies. One might say that the fact that the Serbs interpreted Russian messianism from the point of view of Serbian national mythology gave the Serbian national discourse additional compensatory value.

The Bulgarian myth of Russia seemed to be less focused on mystical issues than on political and military ones.[86] The relations between both nations and countries were seen in a simpler way. According to the myth, Russia was a mighty liberator and protector, and Bulgaria a victim praying for help. However, Bulgarian cultural and political Russophile discourse was not incompatible with the occidental discourse. This discourse was more flexible and adaptable to the geopolitical configuration than the

---

84 Armour, "Killing Nationalism with Liberalism?" 356; Dedijer, *The Road to Sarajevo*, 52, 226–227.
85 Ivan Čolović, *The Politics of Symbol in Serbia: Essays in Political Anthropology*, 93.
86 Chavdarova, "Mif Rossii i stereotip russkogo," 204.

Serbian one. Russia was perceived there, just like in Bulgaria, as a country spiritually connected with Europe, but still only on the road to Europeanization, as measured by the contemporary level of civilizational and technical progress. The ideas of Europe, "catching up with Europe," and "returning to Europe," were at least as important as those of awaiting support from the Russian liberator.

References

Aretov, Nikolay. "Forging the Myth about Russia: Rayna, Bulgarian Princess." In *Semantyka Rosji na Bałkanach*, edited by Jolanta Sujecka, 69–89. Warsaw: DiG, 2011.

Aretow, Nikołaj. "Przemilczane zwycięstwa" [Omitted victories]. In *Przemilczenia w relacjach międzykulturowych*, edited by Joanna Goszczyńska and Grażyna Szwat-Gyłybowa, 395–406. Warsaw: Slawistyczny Ośrodek Wydawniczy, 2008.

Armour, Ian D. "Killing Nationalism with Liberalism? Austria–Hungary and the Serbian Constitution of 1869." *Diplomacy & Statecraft* 21 (2010): 343–367.

Banac, Ivo. *The National Question in Yugoslavia: Origins, History, Politics*. Ithaca and London: Cornell University Press, 1993.

Bazylow, Ludwik. *Historia Rosji* [The history of Russia]. Wrocław, Warsaw, Kraków: Zakład Naukowy im. Ossolińskich, 2005.

Bogatyrev, Sergey. "Ivan IV (1533–1584)." In *From Early Rus' to 1689*, edited by Maureen Perrie. Vol. 1 of *The Cambridge History of Russia*, edited by Maureen Perrie, Dominic Lieven, and Ronald Suny, 240–263. Cambridge: Cambridge University Press, 2006.

Brunnbauer, Ulf. "'Europa' und der 'Balkan': Fremd- und Selbstzuschreibungen." *Einführung in die Geschichte Südosteuropas*, 1–15. Accessed December 31, 2016, http://www.kas.de/upload/freundeskreis/Studienreisen2008 /Europa_Balkan.pdf.

Chavdarova, Dechka. "Mif Rossii i stereotip russkogo v bolgarskoy kul'ture po sravneniyu s pol'skim stereotipom" [The myth of Russia and the stereotype of the Russian in Bulgarian culture in comparison to the Polish stereotype]. In *Polacy w oczach Rosjan-Rosjanie w oczach Polaków*, edited by Roman Bobryk and Jerzy Faryno, 200–211. Warsaw: Slawistyczny Ośrodek Wydawniczy, 2000.

Čolović, Ivan. *The Politics of Symbol in Serbia: Essays in Political Anthropology*. London: Hurst & Company, 2002.

Corti, Egon Cäsar Conte. *Leben und Liebe Alexanders von Battenberg*. Graz: Verlag Anton Pustet, 1950.

Crampton, Richard J. *A Concise History of Bulgaria*. Cambridge: Cambridge University Press, 1997.

Crawley, Charles W. "The Near East and the Ottoman Empire, 1798–1830." In *War and Peace in an Age of Upheaval, 1793–1830,* edited by Charles W. Crawley. 525–551. Vol. 9 of *The New Cambridge Modern History*, advisory committee George Norman Clark,

James R. M. Butler, John Patrick Tuer Bury, and Ernest Alfred Benians. Cambridge: Cambridge University Press, 1965.

Crudopf, Wenke. "Russland-Stereotypen in der deutschen Medienberichterstattung." *Arbeitspapiere des Osteuropa-Instituts der Freien Universität Berlin* 29 (2000): 6–51.

Curticapean, Alina."Bai Ganio and Other Men's Journeys to Europe: The Boundaries of Balkanism in Bulgarian EU-Accession Discourses." *Perspectives* 16, no. 1 (2008): 23–56.

Danilevsky, Nikolay. *Rossiya i Yevropa. Vzglyad na kul'turnyye i politicheskiye otnosheniya Slavyanskogo mira k Germano-Romanskomu.* St. Petersburg: Tip. brat'yev Panteleyevykh, 1895.

Dedijer, Vladimir. *The Road to Sarajevo.* New York: Simon and Schuster, 1966.

Djokic, Dejan. "Whose Myth? Which Nation? The Serbian Kosovo Myth Revisited." In *Uses and Abuses of the Middle Ages: 19th–21st Century*, edited by János M. Bak, Jörg Jarnut, Pierre Monnet, and Bernd Schneidmüller, 215–234. Munich: Wilhelm Fink, 2009.

Drašković, Vuk. *Russkiy konsul.* Moskva: Molodaya gvardiya, 1992.

Drzewiecka, Ewelina. "Rosja" [Russia]. In *Leksykon tradycji bułgarskiej*, edited by Grażyna Szwat-Gyłybowa, 257–260. Warszawa: Slawistyczny Ośrodek Wydawniczy, 2011.

Figes, Orlando. *A People's Tragedy: A History of the Russian Revolution 1891–1924.* London: Penguin Books, 1996.

Filjushkin, Alexander. *Ivan the Terrible: A Military History.* London: Frontline Books, 2008.

Forrest, Alan. "The French at War. Representations of the Enemy in *War and Peace.*" In *Tolstoy on War. Narrative Art and Historical Truth in "War and Peace,"* edited by Rick McPeak and Donna Tussing Orwin, 59–73. Ithaca, NY: Cornell University Press, 2012.

Georgevitch, Vladan. *Das Ende der Obrenovitsch. Beiträge zur Geschichte Serbiens 1897–1900.* Leipzig: Verlag von S. Hirzel, 1905. Accessed August 4, 2012. http://www26.us.archive.org/stream/dasendederobrenooorgoog/dasendederobrenooorgoog_djvu.txt.

Gerth, Hans Heinrich, and Charles Wright Mills. *From Max Weber: Essays in Sociology.* London and New York: Routledge, 1991.

Gŭrdev, Borislav. "Zaknyaz Batenberg 110 godini sled smŭrtta mu" [Dedicated to the Prince of Battenberg on the 110th anniversary of his death]. Accessed July 1, 2013. http://www.liternet.bg/publish4/bgyrdev/istoria/abatenberg.htm.

"Imperator Nikolay II-strastoterpets i muchenik" [Emperor Nicholas II—a passion bearer and martyr]. Accessed July 1, 2013. http://ruskline.ru/news_rl/2010/06/09/imperator_nikolaj_ii_strastoterpec_i_muchenik/.

Judah, Tim. *The Serbs: History, Myth and the Destruction of Yugoslavia.* New Haven and London: Yale University Press, 1997.

Kaplan, Robert. *Balkan Ghosts: A Journey Through History.* New York: St. Martin Press, 1993.

Kapor, Momo. *Puteshestviye po biografii* [A journey through biography]. Chapter: "Serbiya – poslednyaya lyubov' Vronskogo" [Serbia—the last love of Vronsky] (2006). Accessed August 1, 2012. http://www.senica.ru/forum /index.php?showtopic=359&st=80.

Kostova, Ludmilla. "Getting to Know the Big Bad West? Images of Western Europe in Bulgarian Travel Writing of the Communist Era (1945–1985)." In *Balkan Departures:*

Travel Writing from South-Eastern Europe, edited by Wendy Bracewell and Alex Drace-Francis, 105–136. Oxford and New York: Berghahn Books, 2010.

Kovačević, Dusko M. *Srbiyâ i Rusiyâ 1878–1889. Od Berlinskog kongresa do abdikaciye Krayḷja Milana* [Serbia and Russia 1878–1889: from the Congress of Berlin until the abdication of King Milan]. Beograd: Istorijski in-t, 2003.

Kurjak, Jelica, Olga Popović-Obradović, and Milan Šuković. *Russia, Serbia, Montenegro.* Belgrade: Helsinki Committee for Human Rights in Serbia, 2000.

Leatherbarrow, William. "Conservatism in the Age of Alexander I and Nicholas I." In *A History of Russian Thought*, edited by William Leatherbarrow and Derek Offord, 95–115. New York: Cambridge University Press, 2010.

Malia, Martin. *Russia under Western Eyes: From the Bronze Horseman to the Lenin Mausoleum.* Cambridge-London: Belknap, 1999.

Mandic, Danilo. "Myths and Bombs: War, State Popularity and the Collapse of National Mythology." *Nationalities Papers* 36, no.1 (2008): 25–54.

Marriott, John Arthur Ransome. *The Eastern Question: An Historical Study in European Diplomacy.* The Clarendon Press: Oxford, 1917.

Masek, Miro. "Milos Crnjanski's Homecoming to a Migrating National Family." In *History of the Literary Cultures of East-Central Europe: Junctures and Disjunctures in the 19th and 20th Centuries*, edited by Marcel Cornis-Pope and John Neubauer. Vol. 4 of *Types and Stereotypes*, 211–219. Amsterdam and Philadelphia: John Benjamins Publishing Company, 2010.

Mitani, Keiko. "From Serbia with Love: Verbal Representation of Russia in Serbian Society." In *Beyond the Empire: Images of Russia in the Eurasian Cultural Context*, edited by Tetsuo Mochizuki, 353–372. Sapporo: Slavic Research Center Hokkaido University, 2008.

Neuburger, Mary. *The Orient Within: Muslim Minorities and the Negotiation of Nationhood of Modern Bulgaria.* New York: Cornell University Press, 2004.

Oroschakoff, Haralampi G. *Die Battenberg Affäre. Leben und Abenteuer des Gavriil Oroschakoff oder eine russische-europäische Geschichte.* Berlin: Berlin Verlag, 2007.

Peleva, Inna, and Joanna Spassova-Dikova. "Figuring the Motherland and Staging the Party Father in Bulgarian Literature." In *History of the Literary Cultures of East-Central Europe: Junctures and Disjunctures in the 19th and 20th Centuries*, edited by Marcel Cornis-Pope and John Neubauer. Vol. 4 of *Types and Stereotypes*, 176–82. Amsterdam and Philadelphia: John Benjamins Publishing Company, 2010.

Petrović, Aleksandar. *The Role of Banditry in the Creation of National States in the Central Balkans during the 19th Century: A Case Study, Serbia.* Master's thesis, Simon Fraser University, 2003. Accessed October 1, 2015. http://www.rastko.org.rs/istorija/xix/apetrovic-banditry_eng.html.

Petrovich, Michael Boro. *The Emergence of Russian Panslavism 1856–1870.* New York and London: Columbia University Press, 1966.

"Russia: Mythical Ally." *Helsinki Bulletin* 76 (2011): 1–5. Accessed August 1, 2012. www.helsinki.org.rs/doc/HB-No76.pdf.

Said, Edward. "Nationalism, Colonialism and Literature: Yeats and Colonization." *A Field Day Pamphlet* 15 (1988): 5–27.

"Serbiya i Rossiya posle Berlinskogo kongressa" [Serbia and Russia after the Congress of

Berlin]. Accessed July, 1, 2013. http://www.drugarstvo.ru/rus/serbia-russia-after-the-berlin-congress/.

Stamatopoulos, Dimitris. "From the Vyzantism of K. Leont'ev to the Vysantinism of I. I. Sokolov: The Byzantine Orthodox East as a Motif of the Russian Orientalism." In *Héritages de Byzance en Europe du Sud-Est à l'époque moderne et contemporaine,* edited by Olivier Delouis, Anne Couderc, and Petre Guran, 321–340. Athens: EFA, 2013.

Sukhorukov, Nikolay. "Russkiy konsul – v serbskoy pesne" [The Russian consul in Serbian songs]. Accessed August 1, 2012. http://serbska.org/serbia/ author/admin/page/ 2763/?nggpage=2.

Sundhausen, Holm. *Geschichte Serbiens. 19.-21. Jahrhundert.* Wien, Köln, Weimar: Böhlau Verlag, 2007.

Todorova, Maria. *Imagining the Balkans.* Oxford: Oxford University Press, 1997.

Tolstoy, Leo. *Anna Karenina.* Accessed August 1, 2012. http://www.cliffsnotes.com/ study_guide/literature/anna-karenina/summary-analysis/part-8/chapters-1-5/original-text.html.

Trifonov, Yurdan. "Istorichesko obyasneniena vyarata v 'Dyado Ivan' (Rusiya) u bŭlgarskiya narod" [A historical explanation of the belief in "Dyado Ivan" (Russia) by the Bulgarian people]. In *Izbrani studii.* Varna: LiterNet, 2006. Accessed August 1, 2012. http:// liternet.bg/publish17/iu_trifonov/izbrani /istorichesko.htm.

Vasov, Ivan. *Under the Yoke.* Accessed August 1, 2012. http://www.ebooksread.com /authors-eng/ivan-minchov-vazov/under-the-yoke-a-romance-of-bulgarian-liberty-hci/ page-7-under-the-yoke-a-romance-of-bulgarian-liberty-hci.shtml.

Veltman, Aleksandr F. "Rayna, korolevna Bolgarskaya" [Rayna, Bulgarian princess]. In *Romany.* Moskva: Sovremennik, 1985. Accessed August 1, 2012. http://ruslit.com.ua/russian_classic/veltman_af/rayna_korolevna_bolgarskaya.3192. https://www.litres.ru/ aleksandr-veltman/rayna-korolevna-bolgarskaya-631645/chitat-onlayn/.

Vlaykov, Todor. "Nay-poslerusiteidvati u nas" [Russians have come to us at last]. In *Prezhivyanoto* (1934, 1939, 1942). Accessed July 1, 2013. http://pravoslavie.domainbg. com/rus/15/vlajkov_bratushki.htm.

Wachtel, Andrew Baruch. *Making a Nation, Breaking a Nation: Literature and Cultural Politics in Yugoslavia.* Stanford: Stanford University Press, 1998.

Walicki, Andrzej. *Rosyjska filozofia i myśl społeczna od Oświecenia do marksizmu* [A history of Russian thought from the enlightenment to Marxism]. Warszawa: Wiedza Powszechna, 1973.

Włajkow, Todor. *Rosjanie wreszcie przybyli do nas* [The Russians have come to us at last]. In *Antologia noweli bułgarskiej,* 145–160. Translated by Bronisław Cirlić and Halina Kalita. Warsaw: Czytelnik, 1955.

Żakowska, Magdalena. "Niedźwiedź i zegarmistrz. U źródeł metafory 'rosyjskiego niedźwiedzia' w Szwajcarii w drugiej połowie XIX w." [A bear and a watchmaker: The sources of the "Russian bear" metaphor in Switzerland in the second half of the nineteenth century]. *Klio* 20, no. 1 (2012): 171–200.

———. "The Bear and His Protégés—Life in the Balkan Kettle According to the German-Language Caricatures of the Belle Epoque." In *Competing Eyes: Visual Encounters with Alterity in Central and Eastern Europe,* edited by Dagnosław Demski, Ildiko Sz. Kristóf, and Kamila Baraniecka-Olszewska, 304–329 Budapest: l'Harmattan, 2013.

Zieliński, Bogusław. *Serbska powieść historyczna. Studia nad źródłami, ideami i kierunkami rozwoju* [The Serbian historical novel: A study of sources, ideas, and trends in the development]. Poznań: Wydawnictwo Naukowe UAM, 1998.

Zlatar, Zdenko. "The Structure and Extent of the Pan-Slav Network in Imperial Russia 1910–1915: A Preliminary Survey." In *Approaches to Slavic Unity: Austro-Slavism, Pan-Slavism, Neo-Slavism, and Solidarity Among the Slavs Today*, edited by Krzysztof A. Makowski and Frank Hadler, 110–130. Poznań: Uniwersytet im. Adama Mickiewicza, 2013.

Lora Gerd

Russian View on Balkan Nationalism (1878–1914)

In the history of Southeastern Europe, the nineteenth century is usually referred to as the age of nationalism and the establishment of independent national states in the Balkans. One after another each of the peoples of the former Ottoman Empire acquired independence and formed a separate state—the Serbs, the Greeks, the Romanians, the Bulgarians.

Nationalism and religion in the Balkans were closely interconnected. Church independence either followed political independence, as in the case of Greece and Romania, or took place first, as in Bulgaria. This is rooted in the *millet* system traditional for the Ottoman Empire, whereby all non-Muslim nations were organized according to religious denomination. Up to the second half of the nineteenth century all the Orthodox peoples of the Ottoman Empire were included in the Rum, or Greek millet. With the rise of national movements of the Balkan peoples this religious principle was replaced by a national one.[1] Church affairs yielded to secular politics, and the domination of Constantinople in the Orthodox world was eroded step by step. The proclamation of the independent Greek church was not acknowledged by the Patriarchate of Constantinople until 1850, seventeen years later; the same was the fate of the Romanian autocephaly. Most dramatic were the events connected with Bulgarian ecclesiastical independence, where the church struggle was only a legal form for national and political struggle during many decades. In 1870

---

1   Arnakis, "The Role of Religion in the Development of Balkan Nationalism," 134–135; Karpat, *An Inquiry into the Social Foundations of Nationalism in the Ottoman State: From Social Estates to Classes, from Millets to Nations;* Clogg, "The Greek Millet in the Ottoman Empire," 185–207; Kitromilides, "Imagined Communities and the Origins of the National Question in the Balkans"; Makarova, *Bolgary i Tanzimat;* Petrunina, *Grecheskaya nacija i gosudarstvo v XVIII–XX vv,* 371–518.

the Bulgarians proclaimed their autonomous church, the Bulgarian Exarchate, which was accepted by the Ottoman government but condemned by Constantinople in 1872. The Bulgarian Schism was the background to events in the Ottoman part of the Balkans. The struggle between the Patriarchists and the Exarchists in European Turkey was to determine the future boarders of the Balkan states. The ecclesiastical struggle and the millet model served only as a cover for political ambitions.

The last decades of the nineteenth and the beginning of the twentieth centuries were the most difficult and turbulent period in the national struggles on the Balkan peninsula. The liberation movements of the Balkan nations against Ottoman rule were to a great degree complicated by the struggle of these nations with each other for control in the territories with mixed population, first and foremost in Macedonia. Greeks, Bulgarians and Serbs—each of these nations claimed this territory and found all possible historical and mythological justifications for doing so.[2] The supporters of the Greek Great Idea, and of the Bulgarian and the Serbian ideas of Greater Bulgaria and Greater Serbia, regarded Macedonia as originally belonging to each of their nations. The reason was that the population of the region was mixed: the Greeks lived more along the sea coast, while the Slavs inhabited the inner part of the country. Definitive distinctions between the Slavonic dialects did not exist, and their national self-identity depended on the propaganda of political agents and their church orientation.[3] So the activities of the Bulgarian, Serbian and Greek polit-

---

2   On the Greek Great Idea see: Augustinos, "The Dynamics of Modern Greek Nationalism: The 'Great Idea' and the Macedonian Problem," 444–53; Danova, *Nacionalnijat vâpros v grâckite politicheski programi prez XIX v*; Blinkhorn and Veremis, eds., *Modern Greece: Nationalism and Nationality*; Metallinos, *Orthodoxia kai Ellinikotita*; Traikov, *Nacionalnite doctrini na balkanskite strani*; Petrunina, *Grecheskaja nacija i gosudarstvo v XVIII–XX vv.*, 323–333.

3   The ethnic map of Macedonia was the subject of research of a series of Russian and European expeditions in the nineteenth century. In the 1880s most Slavs called themselves simply *raya*, subjects of the Sultan. One or two decades later their ethnic identity was determined by church borders; the Exarchists called themselves Bulgarians while the Patriarchists did not emphasize their ethnicity. See: Wilkinson, *Maps and Politics: A Review of the Ethnographic Cartography of Macedonia*; for the Bulgarian view, Brailsford, *Macedonia: Its Races and their Future*; for the Serbian view, Georgovitch, *Macedonia*; for the Greek view, Dakin, *The Greek Struggle in Macedonia, 1897–1913*. Also: Adanir, "The Socio-Economic Environment of Balkan Nationalism: The Case of Ottoman Macedonia 1856–1912," 221–254; Gounaris, "Social Cleavages and National 'Awakening' in Ottoman Macedonia," 409–427; Peckham, "Map Mania: Nationalism and the Politics of Place in Greece, 1870–1922," 7–95.

ical propagandists were aimed at the formation of their own nations in Macedonia and the promotion of nationalism in the interests of the corresponding political elites.

The Russian government did not have a firm opinion on the nationality of the Macedonian Slavs; it depended on the political situation of the moment. After the Russo-Turkish War of 1877–1878, Russia counted on the Bulgarian element in the Balkans for support while at the beginning of the twentieth century it was inclined to support the Serbs. The Russian Diplomat G. N. Trubetskoi asked:

Is Macedonia a Bulgarian province? For a long time Russia, Britain and other European countries responded with a positive answer to this question. However, many of our consuls who have studied this question in situ gave a different answer. Macedonia is neither a pure Bulgarian nor a Serbian region, but the Slavs who live there are a kind of raw material which can be transformed into either Serb and Bulgarian.[4]

At first the general population did not show much enthusiasm for the Bulgarian political propaganda, carried out by a narrow circle of priests, teachers and merchants. Later, however, it paid off, and by 1912, as Trubetskoi concluded, one could speak not about Macedonia, but about Bulgaro-Macedonia.

The tensions between the Greek and Slavonic population of Macedonia began in the first half of the nineteenth century with the rise of the national consciousness of the Balkan Slavs on one side, and the Greek Megali Idea, on the other. Later they grew into open conflicts. In the 1860–70s an independent Bulgarian church was established. According to the leaders of the Bulgarian liberation movement, who were supported by Count N. P. Ignatiev, the Russian ambassador to Constantinople, the Bulgarian Exarchate was supposed to include most of the Macedonian eparchies with mixed Greek and Slavonic populations. Following the Bulgarian Schism of 1872, these eparchies were considered independent both by

---

4   A note of G. Trubetskoi on the tasks of Russia in the World War: January 10, 1917, Archive of the Foreign Policy of the Russian Empire (AVPRI), f. Politarchiv, op. 482, d. 4313, l. 11. G. N. Trubetskoi was a vice-director of the First Department of the Ministry of Foreign Affairs at that time.

the Bulgarian Exarchate and the Patriarchate of Constantinople.[5] As the 1878 Congress of Berlin had ended the possibility of a "Greater Bulgaria" and Macedonia still remained in the Ottoman Empire, the struggle could be legally continued only at the ecclesiastical level, which disguised the national and political controversy. The Exarchists wanted to include the churches in those villages where the Slavonic element dominated and regarded them as potentially Bulgarian. The Patriarchists on the other hand tried to keep them under the control of Constantinople, which would ensure their future in the territory of the Greek kingdom. Uskub (Skopje), Bitola, Adrianople (Edirne), Drama, and Kavala became centers of the struggle. For two decades Macedonia was a battlefield of guerilla action between Bulgarian and Greek armed bands, who terrorized the peasants and demanded loyalty from them.

The second influential factor which determined the political picture in the region were the aspirations of the Great Powers for spheres of influence. The first of them which actively penetrated to the southeast was Austro-Hungary, which had designs on the port of Thessaloniki. Russian policy in the Balkan region at the end of the nineteenth century was reserved. The attention of the Russian politicians was diverted to the Far East. That is why Russia tried as long as possible to keep the status quo in Macedonia. Several treaties with the Habsburg monarchy since 1897 consolidated this situation. But after the defeat in the war with Japan in 1904–1905 and the revolution of 1905–1907 Russia was not able to pursue an active policy in the Near East. So it was forced to use the traditional ideological weapons, and especially religion.

The Orthodox faith shared by the peoples of the Ottoman Empire in the frame of the millet system was a strong advantage for Russian policy beginning with the seventeenth and eighteenth centuries. The Tanzimat movement, which was inspired by British policy, was to a great extent aimed at reducing of the extraordinary influence of Russia on the internal affairs of the Ottoman Empire, as proclaimed by the Kiuchuk-Kainardji treaty of 1774. After the Crimean War Russia's real power was weakened and hence its opportunity to influence the affairs in

---

5   Bylgarski Cyril, *Graf N. P. Ignatiev i Bâlgarskijat cârkoven vâpros*; Markova, *Bâlgarskata Ekzarhija. 1870–1879*; Boneva, *Bâlgarskoto cârkovno-nacionalno dvizhenie 1856–1870*; Stamatopoulos, "The Bulgarian Schism Revised," 105–125.

the Balkans was curtailed as well. In this new situation the government of Alexander II espoused Panslavism as a policy in the region. This did not mean that the old line of supporting all the Orthodox nationalities without respect for national difference was fully abandoned, but in the 1860s and 1870s, the focus on the Slavic population was prioritized. The anti-Slavonic trends in Greece and the orientation of its government to British policy contributed to this. Up until the middle of the nineteenth century, the Slavophile movement in Russia was a theoretical one, originating in German Romanticism. It was given no attention in the foreign policy of Nicolas I, since any proposal to liberate the Balkan nations would be seen as an encroachment upon the sovereignty of the Austrian or the Ottoman Empires. However, after Russia's defeat in the Crimean War the new tsar, Alexander II, adopted Slavophilism as the official ideology of Russian foreign policy. Sympathy for the South Slavs and the readiness of Russian society to help them were exploited by Russian officials. It was hoped that the nations which shared their faith and Slavonic origin with Russia would provide basic support in any future Russian activity. In 1858 the first Slavonic philanthropic committee was founded in Moscow; similar committees were organized in other Russian cities.[6] Panslavism reached its height in the 1870s, on the eve of the Russo-Turkish War. But the failure of Ignatiev to create a Greater Bulgaria, which had been intended to become a strong South Slav state under Russian control, resulted in Russian society's disappointment in Slavonic ideas. After 1880 it would be incorrect to speak of Panslavism as a Russian foreign policy ideology.

After the Russo-Turkish War and especially after the murder of Alexander II in 1881, Pan-Slavic ideology was replaced by a nationalis-

---

6   Tsimbaev, *Slavianophil'stvo. Iz istorii russkoj obshestvenno-politicheskoj mysli XIX veka;* Tatischev, *Imperator Alexandr II, ego zhizn' i carstvovanie;* Liluashvili, *Nacional'no-osvoboditel'naja bor'ba bolgarskogo naroda protiv fanariotskogo iga i Rossija;* Nikitin, *Slavianskije komitety v Rossii v 1858–1876 godah.* On the political side of Panslavism see: Pypin, *Panslavism v proshlom i nastojashem;* Kohn, *Panslavism: Its History and Ideology;* Fischel, *Der Pansalwismus bis zum Weltkrieg;* Sumner, *Russia and the Balkans 1870–1880;* Petrovich, *The Emergency of Russian Panslavism, 1856–1870;* Riasanovsky, *Russia and the West in the Teaching of the Slavophiles;* Fadner, *Seventy Years of Pan-Slavism in Russia: From Karamzin to Danilevsky, 1800–1870;* Walicki, *The Slavophile Controversy: History of the Conservative Utopia in Nineteenth-Century Russian Thought;* Milojkovoc-Djuric, *Panslavism and National Identity in Russia and in the Balkans, 1830–1880.*

tic one.[7] The pacifist, non-interference policy of the 1880s to 1890s was partly caused by the impossibility of immediate further actions towards a resolution of the Eastern Question. In the twenty years following 1878, Russia waited and prepared a more active policy—both diplomatic and ideological—which it expected to implement in the future. During this time, Russia also attempted to reverse some negative trends in the Orthodox East, primarily regarding the Bulgarian Schism. The religious factor played quite a strong role in this policy. In the 1880–1890s we may speak of a revival of the idea of Moscow the Third Rome on a new level, though these terms were never articulated officially up to the First World War. This ideology of Neo-Byzantinism was far from Panslavism; its main accent lay on Russian national interests and Pan-Orthodox unity. The disappointment with Bulgaria after 1885 and the policy of the Obrenovich house in Serbia only brought to further strengthening of the Pan-Orthodox universalist ideology.

Most important of the immediate precursors to the ideological developments of the 1880s and '90s was N. J. Danilevskii. His book, *Rossija i Evropa* [Russia and Europe], published in 1868 served as the basis for Russian imperialist ideology of the late nineteenth century.[8] Danilevskii's thesis, which concerns cultural-historical groups, sets him apart from other Slavophiles of his time. He did not advocate the superiority of the Slavonic world over other groups, but attempted only to explain its position in history. His main thesis—the necessity of countering Europe's influence in order to ensure Russian identity—coincided with the policy of Alexander III. The solution to the Eastern Question was for Danilevskii the creation of a Pan-Slavic federation under Russia with Constantinople as its capital.

On the eve of the Russo-Turkish War another voice spoke to the Eastern Question—that of the great writer, F. M. Dostoyevskii. Sooner or later Constantinople should become Russian, he wrote:

> So in the name of what moral right could Russia seek Constantinople?... As the leader of Orthodoxy, as its patron and protector—the role that had been assigned to it since Ivan III, who placed the two-

7 The ideology of this transformation is traced in Vovchenko, "Modernizing Orthodoxy: Russia and the Christian East (1856–1914)," 295–317.
8 Danilevskii, *Rossija i Evropa*.

headed eagle of Constantinople above the old emblem of Russia. It became possible to play this role only after Peter the Great, when Russia was strong enough to fulfill its assignment...The political relations of Russia with other nations would be clear: it should be their mother, but not owner. That would be the last word of Christ's truth.[9]

In the messianic dreams of Dostoyevskii, we can find neither a denial of the role of Peter I, which was characteristic of the old Slavophiles, nor a construction of "Pan-Slavic unity," but a broadly defined program, which as a whole coincides with ideas current in the 1880s and 1890s.

During the 1880s Neo-Byzantinism found its further development in the works of the famous philosopher and writer, Konstantin Leontiev.[10] He can be considered the most original Russian intellectual of his time. Leontiev was a professional diplomat; in the 1860s and 1870s he served as consul to Crete, Adrianople, Tulcea, Ioannina and Thessaloniki. His long term stay in the Orthodox East determined his character as a writer and politician. He realized the difficulty of implementing a peaceful solution to the national controversies in the Balkans. During his service in Ioannina, Leontiev came to the conclusion that a Russian consul to every Turkish town could result in Russia having much greater influence than the British, Austrian or French. Two conditions were necessary for this to work: good relations with the Ottoman authorities, and the ability to win over the Christians.[11] Leontiev himself demonstrated these skills in his relations with the Greek Metropolitan of Ioannina, Sophronios. Leontiev was one of the first among the Europeans to notice the religious indifference of the Balkan nations; Orthodoxy was first of all a vehicle for realizing their national ambitions. His ability to convey the esthetic beauty of certain facets of life in the Ottoman Empire together with his talent as a writer and his deep historic-philosophical thinking attracted the attention of the Russian reading public for several decades. In 1871, Leontiev

---

9 Dostoyevskii, "Dnevnik pisatelia. Ijun' 1876," 45–50.
10 The scholarship on Leontiev is extensive. See Dmitriev and Dmitrieva, eds., *Christianstvo I Novaja Russkaja Literatura. Biobibliograficheskij Ukazatel' 1800–2000*; on his "Byzantinism" see Stamatopoulos, *To Vyzantio meta to Ethnos*, 211–252.
11 Dolgov, ed., *Konstantin Nikolaevich Leontiev: Diplomaticheskie donesenija, pis'ma, zapiski, otchety, 1865–1872*, 253–257.

underwent a great emotional crisis and decided to become a monk on Mt. Athos. Due to his social status, not to mention his lack of spiritual conviction, he was not accepted; he spent the next few years in Constantinople in close contact with the clergy of the theological school on Chalki Island. It was here that Leontiev's views, which reflected his decision to support the Greek side in the ethnic confrontation, were formed. After the Russo-Turkish War, Leontiev, together with his friend Filippov, developed the idea of Byzantinism as the only possible basis for the future of the East European nations. For him Byzantinism was at the same time "our Russian Orthodoxy, our Russian autocracy, sanctified by Orthodoxy, and the many reflections of Orthodoxy and our Orthodox political system in literature, poetry, architecture and so on."[12]

In the 1880s and 1890s, the old Slavophiles were finally replaced by nationally orientated monarchists. One of the main politicians and ideologues during the rule of Alexander III was Michail Katkov (1818–1887). In Katkov's opinion, Russia would be saved only by strengthening absolutism, as no models of constitutional monarchy existed that would be suitable for Russia.[13] Whereas Leontiev treated the monarchist idea romantically, Katkov took it realistically.[14] In Katkov's articles we find a consistent reflection of the power of the state. He contrasted Russia, where trust and love for the tsar, a monarch appointed by God, motivated people's actions, with the West. In Russia every citizen was ready to serve the tsar, and this was the principle which united them; every service was a service to the monarch and by extension, the state. Such an ideology led to an idealization of Moscovian tsardom. Katkov's political sympathies with the pro-Peter period of Russian history were still more definitively reflected in his views on questions of church policy. Katkov, who did not separate church, faith and policy, revived the idea of the Third Rome on a new level and applied it to the political reality of his time.

Another theorist of Russian monarchism at the end of the nineteenth and the beginning of the twentieth century was Lev Tikhomirov (1852–1923). He began work as a publicist in the 1880s and developed a com-

---

12 Leontiev, "Pis'ma k V. S. Solovievu (o nacionalisme politicheskom i kul'turnom)," 273.

13 Katkov, "U groba imperatora Alexandra II. O vlasti," http://dugward.ru/library/alexandr2 / katkov_u_groba.html.

14 Berdiaev, "Konstantin Leontiev. Ocherk iz istorii russkoj religioznoj mysli," 107.

prehensive theory of the Russian monarchy with Byzantine monarchism as its immediate forerunner. At the end of the 1870s, Tikhomirov, who earlier had been a revolutionary (*narodnik*), adopted extreme conservative views; he became a regular contributor to *Moskovskie vedomosti* and wrote articles and books on monarchism. The government used his works to support its ideology in the 1880s and 90s. His book, *The Political System of the Monarchy*, was first published in 1905, although he formed the ideas for it during the last two decades of the nineteenth century.[15] Having studied the literature on Byzantinology, Tikhomirov proposed his own theory for why Byzantium fell. A strong independent church was needed as the basis of support of the monarch. Tikhomirov was a follower of Leontiev, and in his understanding Leontiev regarded Russia not as just an heir and restorer of Byzantium, but as a state in which byzantine ideas might serve as a model to be used to develop Russia's own type of empire. According to Tikhomirov, the Slavophiles marked the first phase of national revival and Leontiev the second.[16] So, while the liberals regarded Danilevskii and Leontiev as representatives of the end and decline of the Slavophile movement, in Tikhomirov's opinion their works were the next stage of the development of Russian national consciousness. In 1909 Tikhomirov became editor-in-chief of *Moskovskie vedomosti*, the mouthpiece of conservative Russian society.

The political course that aimed at preserving the status quo in the Balkans for some time arrested the development of messianic ideas in Russia. The stimuli to reverse this trend were the defeat in the war with Japan of 1904–1905 and the revolution in 1905–1907. The proclamation of freedom of print and speech, the appointment of Izvolskii as minister of foreign affairs—these events helped to revive the idea of Russian expansion in its former "historical ancestral lands," Constantinople. A new wave in the development of neo-Byzantinism came after the speech of Izvolskii in the *Duma* (Parliament) on April 4, 1908, in which he used for the first time, the term "national policy." The failure of Izvolskii in the matter of Bosnia and Herzegovina dampened for some time the development of hawkish policies. In April 1909, P. B. Mansurov, a diplomat and

---

15   Tikhomirov, *Monarchicheskaja gosudarstvennost'*.
16   Tikhomirov, "Russkie ideally I K. N. Leontiev," 515–516.

an authority on Russia's Near East policy, published an article in which he outlined the ideology of imperial Byzantinism and Russian policy in the Eastern Mediterranean in the first decades of the twentieth century. Russian society, wrote Mansurov, will not reconcile itself to diplomatic defeat and the humiliation of the motherland. Russia's first task at the moment, in his opinion, was to defend the Balkans and Asia Minor from German aggression. Mansurov paid special attention to the traditional direction Russian policy had taken, that is, union with all Orthodox nations of the Balkans. Directing the focus to Slavonic nations had been a mistake, as it turned away the sympathies of Orthodox Romania from Russia. Mansurov supported the idea of the primacy of the Greek nation among the Orthodox nations. He wrote: "The time is soon coming when the separate efforts of the churches will not be adequate to serve the truth of Orthodoxy." Thus, in his opinion, the need of an ecumenical council was obvious.[17]

Besides the dominant neo-Slavophile Russian nationalist views, there was also a pure pro-Greek trend in Russian political thought at the end of the nineteenth and the beginning of the twentieth centuries. It was introduced by A. S. Norov, a romantic and an admirer of Eastern Christianity, and developed by Tertii Ivanovich Filippov (1825–1899), state controller of Russia in the 1880s and '90s. Due to his high administrative position, Filippov could afford to take an independent pro-Greek stance in the Greek-Bulgarian ecclesiastical question. Even though the Russian government in the 1870s did not adopt them, he supported the decisions of the church council of 1872 which proclaimed the Bulgarian Schism. Filippov maintained extensive correspondence with the Greek Patriarchs of Constantinople and Jerusalem and was even given the honorary title of Guardian of the Holy Sepulchre.

The pro-Greek sentiment in Russian public opinion was picked up by I. I. Sokolov, a professor at St. Petersburg Theological Academy.[18] As a Byzantinologist and church historian, Sokolov concentrated on the history of

---

17 Mansurov, "Rossija i Blizhnij Vostok."
18 On the evolution of pro-Greek ideas in Russia from Leontiev to Sokolov see Stamatopoulos, "From the Vyzantism of K. Leont'ev to the Vyzantinism of I. I. Sokolov: the Byzantine Orthodox East as Motive of the Russian Orientalism," 329–348; idem, *To Vyzantio meta to Ethnos,* 244–252, 282–285.

the Patriarchate of Constantinople.[19] The credo of Sokolov's views was a revival of an ideal Orthodox monarchy after the model of Byzantium, a vision which he articulated in his introductory speech at the Department of History of the Eastern Greek Church, delivered at St. Petersburg Theological Academy on November 1, 1903.[20] Byzantium, an ideal state in his opinion, "embodied the idea of mutual dependence between the state and the church. Legally the church and the state in Byzantium were independent, but in fact they composed one body and were interconnected."[21]

Sokolov was editor-in-chief of the journal *Tserkovnyj vestnik* and for fifteen years regularly published notes and articles on the current events of church life in the Orthodox East. On the pages of *Tserkovnyj vestnik,* Sokolov often expressed ideas which did not coincide with the official line of the Holy Synod. After 1906, when Dmitrievskii was appointed secretary of the Imperial Palestine Society, Sokolov wrote extensively for its periodical, *Soobshchenija Imperatorskogo Pravoslavnogo Palestinskogo Obshchestva,* and the journal moved from its hitherto pro-Arabian position to one more sympathetic towards the Greeks. It was in this journal that Sokolov published the following words:

> We cannot help admiring the past glory of Byzantium! Everybody who knows the depth and strength of the national and political genius of Byzantium, the wonderful spirit of life, love, light, that the Byzantine church had, who has realized the bright ideas and universal ideals of Byzantine culture, the brilliance of which lit up both the West and the Orthodox Slavonic East—such a person cannot but help support the national-political aspirations of the Greeks.[22]

In all controversial matters concerning the national question of the Balkans or Palestine, Sokolov sided with the Greeks and their clergy. Thus

---

19 Sokolov, *Constantinopol'skaja cerkov' v XIX veke.* This fundamental research was a result of eight months' work in the archives of the Patriarchate. On Sokolov see: "25-letie uchenoj pedagogicheskoj dejatel'nosti prof. I. I. Sokolova" [The twenty-fifth anniversary of the pedagogical activity of I. I. Sokolov], *Cerkovnyj vestnik,* no. 33 (1915): 992–997; Lebedeva, "Iz istorii vizantinovedenija i neoellinistiki v Rossii: I. I. Sokolov," 229–246.

20 Sokolov, *O vizantinizme v cerkovno-istoricheskom otnoshenii.*

21 Sokolov, *O vizantinizme v cerkovno-istoricheskom otnoshenii,* 1–2.

22 Sokolov, "Vesti s Vostoka," 429.

he maintained the same attitude toward the Orthodox Greek East which had been held before by Norov and Filippov.[23] The dysfunction in church life in the East was seen by Sokolov to be a result of dynamics between the Western powers and the hostile Ottoman government, and not the result of its own internal dynamics. In his view, all aspirations of the Balkan peoples to create church autonomy were illegal and uncanonical. He could not help sympathizing with the Greek Great Idea, i.e. the union of all Greek lands into one kingdom. At the same time, he remained a Russian patriot and supported Russian aspirations in the Near East, dreamed about a Russian cross on St. Sofia and the union of all Orthodox nations under Russian domination.

Sokolov did not allow for conflict between the Greek and the Russian imperial aspirations, nor the possibility of Greek-Slavonic conflicts in the future ideal Empire of Christ on Earth. In his desire to see his Byzantine ideal fulfilled he sometimes overlooked historical facts, or misrepresented them. An example of such an interpretation is evident in his article on the liberated Mt. Athos (November 2, 1912):

> Hellenism, transformed by the genius of the people into Byzantinism, has reached a wonderful level on Mt. Athos... Hellenism reconciled all the inhabitants of Mt. Athos irrespective of their nationality, subordinated them to its stream, introduced them into the circle of common monastic ideals and motivated them to live and to pray according to rules and orders they established.[24]

Of course, Sokolov was aware of the ongoing controversies between the Greek and the Slavonic monks on Mt. Athos, and the conflicts between the Greeks and the Russians. In this case we have an example of the mythologizing of consciousness in which the desired is taken for—or at least represented as—real.

---

23 Sokolov had especially close relations with Patriarch Joachim III who granted him the title "archon and ieromnimon of the apostolic ecumenical *see.*" Patriarch Damian of Jerusalem granted him an additional title of "archon protonotarios of the apostolic patriarchal see of Jerusalem," and a golden cross with relics of the Holy Cross. The King of Greece awarded him the Order of Savior, third degree.

24 Sokolov, "Vesti s Afona" [News from Athos], *Tserkovnyj vestnik,* no. 42 (1912): 1317–1318.

The first Patriarch after the Russo-Turkish War was Joachim III (1878–1884).[25] Joachim had been metropolitan in Varna (Bulgaria) and Thessaloniki (Macedonia), so he was well acquainted with the national issues of church life. After the war he worked enthusiastically to improve the position of the church and addressed its difficulties, both financial and ethnic. Russia's place in the church was one of the important points in his political program. His pro-Russian position caused an open conflict with the Greek prime minister, Charilaos Trikoupis.[26] Russian diplomats, in turn, supported Joachim in his struggle against the Sublime Porte in support of the rights and privileges of the patriarchate. Despite the hopes of the Russian government and church that the Bulgarian Schism could be mended and the nationalist tendencies in the church overcome, they were not able to achieve these aims.

Just prior to the abdication of Joachim III, A. E. Vlangali, a member of the Russian foreign office, formulated Russia's position on Greek nationalism in the church:

Under the general name 'Greeks' we mean the Athens government, the inhabitants of Turkey of Greek origin, the patriarchate and the clergy, and finally the Greek monks of Mt. Athos... As for the patriarchate and the chief spiritual leaders of the Orthodox church, many times I had the opportunity to express my opinion in no uncertain terms. Our duty is to protect the rights and independence of the Eastern church. But we must draw a strict line of demarcation between the interests of this church and the national interests of the Greeks of Athens, because the Ecumenical Patriarch is not called to serve as a stronghold of Hellenism in any sense... Many of the high clergy here and many Greeks are infected by the ideas of Hellenism and are more attuned to the inspirations of the policy of Athens... Against these people we should fight, while defending the independence of the Ecumenical Church.[27]

25 Stauridou, *Oi oikoumenikoi patriarchai 1860-simeron*, 208–284; Gedeon, *Patriarchikai pinakes*, 626–628; Kardaras, *I politiki drasi tou patriarchi Ioakeim III: Proti patriarchia 1878–1884*; *Dimitria 27. Epistimoniko Symposio Christianiki Makedonia. O apo Thessalonikis Oikoumenikos Patriarkhis Ioakeim III o Megaloprepis*; *Ioakeim III o Megaloprepis. O apo Thessalonikis Oikoumenikos Patriarhis kai i epokhi tou*.

26 See the edition of their correspondence: Kardaras, *Ioakeim III-Charilaos Trikoupis. I antiparathesi. Apo tin anekdoti allilografia tou Oikoumenikou Patriarchi (1878–1884)*; Kofos, "Patriarch Joachim III (1878-1884) and the Irredentist Policy of the Greek State," 107–120.

27 December 28, 1883, No 238, AVPRI, f. 180 (Embassy in Constantinople), op. 517/2, d. 3212: 19–23.

After the abdication of Joachim in 1884 until the end of the nineteenth century, most patriarchs did not express any sympathy with Russian ambitions in the Near East. In 1886 Dionysios V was elected Ecumenical Patriarch. He was well known in Russia as the bishop who condemned the entry of Russian troops into Adrianople in 1877. So the contacts of the Russian diplomats with Dionysios were minimal. Again, the embassy would only be a passive observer of the events, without supporting either the Greeks or the Slavs. This mood is well reflected in one of the diplomatic notes, written on June 10, 1887.[28]

> Since the Treaty of Paris, our relations with the Christians in Turkey have changed radically, and we cannot influence them and their clergy at the level that we used to. Meanwhile, for political reasons and by habit we continue in our relations with them, supporting their proposals and at times asserting our support. Because of our position in relation to the Slavonic nations of the East, we have no means either to insist on the fulfillment of these demands, or to support them. The Constantinople church understands this very well and finds our tutelage cumbersome.[29]

As Greek nationalistic ideas prevail in the patriarchate, continues the note, Russia should change its strategy and strengthen relations with the Greek clergy, turning a blind eye to all their abuses. Thus peace would be maintained in the church and the support of the clergy ensured "at the moment of our historically inevitable confrontation with Hellenism on the ruins of Turkish domination."[30]

As noted above, Russian politicians did not have one definite opinion on Eastern church affairs and national policy. The difference in views in Russian society on Greek national trends in the Patriarchate can be vividly observed in the circumstances of the crisis at the end of 1890 in regard to the *Pronomiakon Zitima,* the struggle of the church to maintain its privileged position in the Ottoman Empire. In this situation the patriarchate counted on support from the Russians. However, the advisor to

---

28 AVPRI, F. Embassy in Constantinople, op. 517/2, d. 2923, ll. 6–16.
29 AVPRI, F. Embassy in Constantinople, op. 517/2, d. 2913, l. 13v.
30 Ibid., ll. 15v–16.

the Holy Synod, Professor I. E. Troitskii, counseled that Russia not be in a hurry to support the patriarchate and even called it an act of "national suicide," all for the sake of a nation which regarded Russia as the main obstacle to its restoration of the Byzantine Empire.[31] The Russian embassy in Constantinople, however, favored supporting the church.

In 1901, Joachim III was again elected Patriarch of Constantinople. In supporting his inauguration, the Russian diplomats hoped to have a Patriarch with "truly ecumenical" super-national views who would help overcome the ugly expressions of nationalism in the Balkan provinces. These hopes were based on the memory of the first patriarchate of Joachim (1878–1884), when he showed sympathy to Russian policy and seemed ready to conduct negotiations on the Bulgarian question. The Russian Synod welcomed the appeal of Joachim for closer relations between the independent churches, expressed in his Encyclical letter of 1902. But in the new political situation the Patriarch was much more dependent on Greek national ideas. The Bulgarian question was now regarded as a significant part of the *Pronomiakon Zitima*, the struggle of the Orthodox Church for preserving its traditional rights in the Ottoman Empire. So the attitude of the Russian government to Patriarch Joachim soon changed to a reserved and rather cool one. This can be traced in the answer of the Russian Synod to the second Encyclical letter of Joachim addressed to the autonomous churches in 1904. The spirit of national hatred and irreconcilability was dominant in the Orthodox East and this could be seen first and foremost in the case of the Bulgarian question, the authors of the answer stressed.

Despite the similarity of the topics of both circular messages, one can easily notice differences in the texts of the patriarch, but especially in the Russian answers. The first circular of 1904 was a programmatic document, marking the main directions of church administration, which were as a whole supported by Russia. The second was written two years later, when Russia was already somewhat disappointed in the policy of Joachim III. In the tense political and nationalistic atmosphere in the Balkans at the beginning of the twentieth century, he found it impossible to continue the same peacemaking agenda which was expected of him by the Russian

---

31   Troitskii, I. E., *Diary*, October 16, 1890, Central State Archives of St. Petersburg (CGIA SPb), f. 2182, op. 1, d. 1, l. 16.

government. Willing or not, Joachim had to support the Greek element and act against the Slavs in the growing nationalistic conflicts. Russia was not satisfied either by his position on the Antiocheian or on the Bulgarian question. Owing to Russia's political isolation in the Balkans at that time, the new policy of Joachim ruined Russia's hopes of influencing affairs through the patriarchate. That is why the tone of the answer of 1905 was cold and didactic, and the ideas expressed in it obviously did not take into consideration the dangerous situation in the Balkans at that time.[32]

After the Ilinden revolt and the Murzschteg agreement on reforms in Macedonia of 1903 both Austrian and Russian civil agents were sent to the province in order to oversee the implementation of the reforms. In 1904 a protest against the behavior of the Russian officers was received by the Russian Synod. Following the report of the Metropolitan of Voden, Stefanos, the Patriarch wrote that the Russian officers did not visit the Greek Metropolitan house in Voden, but were followed around town by one of the Bulgarians. They encouraged the activities of the Bulgarian committee in the villages of Vladovodon and Mesimerion as well, Joachim III wrote. This protest was received without any answer from the Russian government, but it provoked indignation in the Russian media. The Orthodox Russian officers know very well how to behave themselves, one of the journalists pointed out, and they are not obliged to indulge the national aspirations of either side. One shouldn't be surprised that the Russian government kept silent during the massacres of the Greek population in Bulgaria in 1906. In July–September 1906, Patriarch Joachim sent numerous memorandums to all the Great Powers where he described the horrors of the events in Anchialo, Varna, Stenimachos and other Bulgarian towns populated by Greeks. True to its neutral policy, the Russian diplomacy did not show any interest in supporting the Greeks, but neither did it exonerate the Bulgarians.

The Bulgarian schism continued to be a great problem and obstacle for Russian policy in the Balkans. Russian diplomats in the beginning of the twentieth century were by no means inclined to support the Bulgarian Exarchate, which was often used as a concealment for the extremists

---

32 On the difference between Joachim's policy during his first and second patriarchate see Stamato-poulos, "'…den ginetai na min einai Fanariotis stin psihi tou…' Oikoumenismos kai Ethnikismos apo tin proti sti deuteri patriarhia tou Ioakeim III," 189–224.

(*chetniks*). Both Bulgarian *chetniks* and Greek *antartes* were regarded by the Powers as illegal brigands. In the case of the inauguration of a Slavonic metropolitan in Skopje in 1903, the Russian embassy strongly supported the Serbian Firmilian, thus expressing both tolerance for the Patriarchate and sympathy for the Slavonic population of Macedonia. The Ilinden revolt of 1903, a purely Bulgarian one, received severe condemnation from Ambassador Zinoviev who called on the Ottoman government to take measures against the insurgents.

Another difficulty was connected with the prohibition of the con-celebration of the Holy Liturgy by Bulgarian and Russian clergy after the proclamation of the schism. This provoked a number of complicated situations affecting Bulgarian students in the Russian theological academies who were not allowed to take part in the church services in Russia. In 1904 the Russian church on Shipka had to be sanctified. Despite all of the precautions and preliminary negotiations, the concelebration of the Bulgarian metropolitan of Stara Zagora Methodius and the Russian clergy took place. This event provoked discussions and indignation among the members of the Patriarchal Synod, though no official protest followed.

Very often one could hear the Holy Mount Athos described as a Russian stronghold in the East Mediterranean. However, the archive sources demonstrate that the activities of the rich Russian *celliots* (the monk inhabitants of the small convents called cells) were not sanctioned by the government. Moreover, the instructions and opinions sent from Petersburg were contradictory and every diplomat visiting Athos acted on his own. The claims of the Greek media about a planned attack of Panslavism on Athos were completely false. On the contrary, we can read extensive opinions written by diplomats or state officials about the better application of Russian money inside the country. Russian monks were not involved in political affairs—that was many times affirmed by the Greek monks on the Holy Mount. The national controversies between Russians and Greeks on Athos in most cases had purely material reasons. Only as a result of conscious propaganda from outside could some small part of the Greek or Serbian monks oppose the Russians on nationalistic grounds. The Russian monks first appeared as a united political and national force only in 1912 when the question of the international status of the Holy Mount was discussed at the London Conferences. Their claim for the internationalization of Athos sounded like a political slogan in support of the demands of the Russian government.[33]

So, from the end of the nineteenth century up to 1910 the Russian church and government tried to remain aloof from any interference in the controversies of the Balkan nations of the Ottoman Empire. The main reason was the international isolation of Russia and its inability to undertake an active policy in the region. In this period, the moral authority of Russia in Balkan affairs was much stronger than its real force. The situation changed in the period of the formation of the Balkan League. Being interested in forming a coalition of the Balkan states to oppose Austro-Hungary, Russia first tried to construct a union including Turkey (the Charykov plan of 1910). When this project failed, the next steps were aimed at the formation of a league of Orthodox states. In this case the idea of Pan-Orthodox union under Russian guidance came into being. One of the main conditions of such a union was the mending of the Bulgarian schism. Endless negotiations with the Patriarch and the Bulgarian Exarch Joseph were held as well as with the representatives of the Bulgarian Synod in Sofia. As a result, the diplomats came to the bitter conclusion that the schism was regarded as advantageous by both Greek and Bulgarian national extremists. The secretary of the Bulgarian Synod Kostov told the Russian resident in Sofia that the Bulgarian church was born in struggle and he saw no reasons to seek peace with the Greeks. The situation did not move from stalemate until the beginning of the Balkan war of 1912. At the end of October when Bulgarian troops were ready to enter Constantinople, the best possible step for the Patriarch was to agree to mend the schism only in the capital for a short period of time, in order to prevent the service in St. Sofia by the Bulgarian Exarch. When the Russian government opposed itself to the further advance of the Bulgarian troops towards the Straits and Constantinople, the question of mending the schism was also immediately abandoned.

At the end of the nineteenth and the beginning of the twentieth century, the Russian government continued to send money to the Orthodox

33 On the Russians on Mt. Athos see: Fennell, *The Russians on Athos*; Troitskii, *Istoriia russkikh obitelei Afona v XIX–XX vekakh*; Gerd, *Russkii Afon 1878–1914. Ocherki tserkovno-politicheskoi istorii*; Fennell, Troitskii, and Talalai, *Il'inskii skit na Afone*; Gerd, "Rosika shedia gia to kathestos tou Agiou Orous sta hronia ton Balkanikon polemon," 87–96.

institutions of the Near East. Now these actions served first and foremost Russian national and colonial interests. Especially willingly it did it for the Greek monasteries of Eastern Turkey, as this territory was expected soon to come into Russian hands. On the eve of the First World War we find another characteristic example of the attitude of Russia to the national question in the Near East. Patriarch Joachim III several times had tried to obtain more Russian money for the Greek ecclesiastical school on Halki island. In 1902 he asked the Russian government for an additional subsidy of 25,000 rubles for the school. The request was sent again in 1904, when the Patriarch asked for an annual subsidy of 9,000 rubles.[34] The appeal was not supported by Ambassador Zinoviev, for the reason that the growing nationalism among the Greek clergy was leading to anti-Russian postures and most of the students of the Chalki school preferred to continue their studies at European universities, not in Russia. Under such conditions Russian aid would not lead to closer relations between the two churches.[35]

According to internal Synod correspondence, aid for the Chalki school should be sent only on the following conditions:

1) that a deputy of the Russian government would sit on the school committee;
2) that the Russian ambassador would have the right to appoint ten students, Russians and Slavs;
3) that students would thereafter be sent to Russian theological academies.[36]

Nevertheless, Ambassador Zinoviev rejected the request for a subsidy.[37] The final discussion on help for Chalki was held in the Russian embassy on March 7, 1913. An annual subsidy of 30,000 rubles was proposed on the following conditions:

34 Archim. Iacobos to the Minister of Foreign Affairs, July 24, 1904, AVPRI, f. Embassy in Constantinople, op. 517/2, d. 3476, ll. 2-2v.
35 I. A. Zinoviev to K. P. Pobedonostsev, November 27, 1904, No. 844, ibid.: 12-18; RGIA, f. 796, op. 185, 6 otd. 1 st., d. 5890, ll. 2–3.
36 AVPRI, f. Embassy in Constantinople, op. 517/2, d. 3476, ll. 19-20v.
37 K. P. Pobedonostsev to I. A. Zinoviev, January 28, 1905, no. 2772, AVPRI, f. Embassy in Constantinople, op. 517/2, d. 3476, ll. 10-10v.

1) 30 or 40 percent of the bursaries would be spent at the discretion of the embassy;

2) the embassy would control the program of the school;

3) the embassy would be involved in the finances of the school.[38]

It was felt that such a step would make for closer relations between the churches of Constantinople and Russia. On May 26, 1913 Patriarch Germanos wrote a note to the Russian embassy outlining the needs of the school, but further negotiations ceased because of the war.

During the beginning of the war, the main goal of Russian imperialism was Constantinople and the Straits. The messianic idea of a Christian cross over St. Sofia raised by the Russians came to its highest point in March 1915, when a secret agreement on the future partition of the Ottoman territories between Britain, France and Russia was signed. In April 1915, several secret notes were written by specialists in different fields, concerning education, church and national policy in the future "Russian Constantinople." Some of them have been edited, others remain in the archives. The most radical authors proposed a violent Russification of the area and the conversion of Constantinople into an eparchial Russian city with a Russian bishop at its head. Most, however, advocated restoration of the Ecumenical patriarchate in its Byzantine sense and the inclusion of a Russian bishop in the Holy Synod. There were also Greek supporters among the Russians who proposed to transfer the liberated Constantinople into the hands of the Greek king and to restore the Byzantine Empire. This would have been an act of gratitude for the baptism of Russia by the Greeks in the tenth century, they wrote. All these theories were an expression of political romanticism, a dream of the revival of the universal Orthodox state, Byzantium, at the beginning of the twentieth century. As they had nothing to do with reality, they were all too soon doomed to fail.

Conclusion

In Russian policy, Panslavism in the Balkans was replaced after 1878 by a nationalistic Pan-Orthodox model which can be regarded as a variant

---

38   RGIA, f. 796, op. 185, 6 otd. 1 st. D. 5890. 2-2v, 4-4v.

of colonial policy. The imperial aspirations of Russia in the East Mediterranean were achieved by different measures, and the ideological one was regarded as one of the most fruitful. The revival of a Neo-Byzantine ideology, with the union of the whole Orthodox world under Russian hegemony, seemed the most efficient and indeed the only possible ideology for achieving Russia's geopolitical goals and solving the Eastern Question. Nevertheless, at the beginning of the twentieth century, the realization of Russia's ambitions seemed unlikely. The political isolation of Russia in the Balkans and the need to keep the balance forced Russian politicians to be cautious and passive. The only time when a union of the Orthodox peoples of the Balkans was achieved with Russian help was on the eve of and during the First Balkan War of 1912–1913.

References

Adanir, F. "The Socio-Economic Environment of Balkan Nationalism: The Case of Ottoman Macedonia 1856–1912." In *Regional and National Identities in Europe in the XIXth and XXth Centuries,* edited by H. G. Haupt, M. Muller, and S. Woolf, 221–254. Boston: Kluwer Law International, 1998.

Arnakis, G. G. "The Role of Religion in the Development of Balkan Nationalism." In *The Balkans in Transition,* edited by B. and C. Jelavic. Berkeley: University of California Press, 1963: 115–145.

Augustinos, J. "The Dynamics of Modern Greek Nationalism: The 'Great Idea' and the Macedonian Problem." *East European Quarterly* 6 (January, 1973): 444–453

Berdiaev, N. A. "Konstantin Leontiev. Ocherk iz istorii russkoj religioznoj mysli" [Konstantin Leontiev: a sketch of Russian religious thought]. In *Konstantin Leontiev: pro et contra.* Vol. 2. St. Petersburg: RHGI Press, 1995.

Blinkhorn, M., and Veremis, T., eds. *Modern Greece: Nationalism and Nationality.* Athens: SAGE-ELIAMEP, 1990.

Boneva, Vera. *Bylgarskoto cyrkovno-nacionalno dvizhenie 1856–1870* [The Bulgarian Church-national movement 1856–1870)]. Veliko Tarnovo: Za bukvite-o pismenah, 2010.

Brailsford, H. N. *Macedonia: Its Races and their Future.* London: Methuen & Co., 1906.

Clogg, Richard. "The Greek Millet in the Ottoman Empire." In *Christians and Jews in the Ottoman Empire: The Functioning of a Plural Society,* edited by Benjamin Braude and Bernard Lewis. Vol. 1, *The Central Lands.* New York: Holmes and Meier Publishers, 1982: 185–207.

Cyril, Bylgarski. *Graf N. P. Ignatiev i Bylgarskijat cyrkoven vypros. Izsledvane i dokumenti* [Count N. P. Ignatiev and the question of the Bulgarian Church: research and documents]. Sofia: Sinodalno izadatelstvo, 1958.

Dakin, D. *The Greek Struggle in Macedonia, 1897–1913*. Thessaloniki: Institute for Balkan Studies, 1966.

Danilevskii, N. J. *Rossija i Evropa* [Russia and Europe]. St. Petersburg: Glagol, 1995.

Danova, Nadia. *Nacionalnijat vypros v gryckite poltiicheski programi prez XIX v* [The national question in Greek political programs in the nineteenth century]. Sofia: Nauka I izkustvo, 1980.

Dimitria 27. Epistimoniko Symposio Christianiki Makedonia. O apo Thessalonikis Oikoumenikos Patriarkhis Ioakeim III o Megaloprepis [A Scientific Symposium 'Christian Macedonia'. The Ecumenical Patriarch from Thessaloniki Joacheim III the Magnificent]. Thessaloniki: Dimos Thessalonikis, 1994.

Dmitriev, A. P., and L. V. Dmitrieva, eds. *Christianstvo i Novaja Russkaja Literatura. Bio-bibliograficheskij Ukazatel'1800–2000* [Christianity and the new Russian literature: biobibliographial index 1800–2000]. St. Petersburg: Nauka, 2002.

Dolgov, K. M., ed. *Konstantin Nikolaevich Leontiev: Diplomaticheskie donesenija, pis'ma, zapiski, otchety, 1865–1872* [Konstantin Nikolaevich Leontiev: diplomatic dispatches, letters, notes, reports, 1865–1872]. Moscow: Rosspen, 2003.

Dostoyevskii, F. M. "Dnevnik pisatelia. Ijun' 1876" [The diary of the writer, June 1876]. In *F. M. Dostoyevskii, Polnoe sobranie sochinenij* [Complete works], Vol. 23. Leningrad: Nauka, 1981.

Fadner, F. *Seventy Years of Pan-Slavism in Russia: From Karamzin to Danilevsky, 1800–1870*. Washington DC: Georgetown University Press, 1962.

Fennell, Nikolay, *The Russians on Athos*. Oxford: Berg, 2001.

Fennell, N., P. Troitskii, and M. Talalai. *Il'inskii skit na Afone* [The skete of St. Elias on Athos]. Moscow: Indrik, 2011.

Fischel, A. *Der Panslawismus bis zum Weltkrieg*. Stuttgart, 1919.

Gedeon, Manuel. *Patriarchikai pinakes* [Patriarchal tables]. Athens, 1996.

Georgovitch, T. R. *Macedonia*. London: Allen, 1918.

Gerd, Lora. "Rosika shedia gia to kathestos tou Agiou Orous sta hronia ton Balkanikon polemon" [Russian plans for the status of the Holy Mount during the Balkan Wars]. In *To Agion Oros sta hronia tis apeleutherosis* [The Holy Mount during the years of liberation], 87–96. Thessaloniki: Agioreitiki Estia, 2013.

———. *Russkii Afon 1878–1914. Ocherki tserkovno-politicheskoi istorii* [Russian Athos 1878–1914: sketches of church-political history]. Moscow: Indrik, 2010.

Gounaris, B. "Social Cleavages and National 'Awakening' in Ottoman Macedonia." *East European Quarterly* 29, no. 4 (1995): 409–426.

Ioakeim III o Megaloprepis. O apo Thessalonikis Oikoumenikos Patriarhis kai i epokhi tou [Joachim III the Magnificent. The Ecumenical Patriarch from Thessaloniki and his Times] Thessaloniki: Filoptohos Adelfotis Andron Thessalonikis, 2012.

Kardaras, C. *I politiki drasi tou patriarchi Ioakeim III: Proti patriarchia 1878–1884* [The political activity of Patriarch Joacheim III: first patriarchy, 1878–1884]. Ioannina: Ioannina University, 1993.

———. *Ioakeim III-Charilaos Trikoupis. I antiparathesi. Apo tin anekdoti allilografia tou Oikoumenikou Patriarchi (1878–1884)* [Joacheim III-Charilaos Trikoupis, the confrontation: from the unpublished correspondence of the ecumenical patriarch, 1878–1884]. Athens: Trohalia, 1998.

Karpat, K. *An Inquiry into the Social Foundations of Nationalism in the Ottoman State: From Social Estates to Classes, From Millets to Nations*. Princeton: Princeton University Press, 1973.

Katkov, M. N. "U groba imperatora Alexandra II. O vlasti" [By the tomb of Emperor Alexander II: concerning power]. http://dugward.ru/library/alexandr2 /katkov_u_groba.html.

Kitromilides, Paschalis M. "Imagined Communities and the Origins of the National Question in the Balkans." *European Historical Quarterly* 19, no. 2 (1989): 149–194.

Kofos, Evangelos. "Patriarch Joachim III (1878–1884) and the Irredentist Policy of the Greek State." *Journal of Modern Greek Studies* 4, no. 2 (1986): 107–120.

Kohn, H. *Panslavism: Its History and Ideology*. Notre Dame, IN.: University of Notre Dame Press, 1953.

Lebedeva, G. E. "Iz istorii vizantinovedenija i neoellinistiki v Rossii: I. I. Sokolov" [From the history of Byzantine and neohellenic studies in Russia: I. I. Sokolov]. In *Moskhovia. Problemy vizantijskoj i novogrecheskoj filologii* [Moskovia: problems of Byzantine and Neohellenic philology], edited by M. V. Bibikov, D. Gialamas, B. Fonkich, and M. Tsantsanoglou, 229–245. Moscow: Indrik, 2001.

Leontiev, Konstantin. "Pis'ma k V. S. Solovievu (o nacionalisme politicheskom i kul'turnom)" [Letters to V. S. Soloviev (on political and cultural nationalism)]. In *Sobranie sochinenij* [Complete works]. Vol. 6, 273–359. Moscow: V. M. Sablin Press, 1912.

Liluashvili, K. S. *Nacional'no-osvoboditel'naja bor'ba bolgarskogo naroda protiv fanariotskogo iga i Rossija* [The national liberation struggle of the Bulgarian People against the Phanariot yoke and Russia]. Tbilisi: Tbilisi University Press, 1978.

Makarova, I. F. *Bolgary i Tanzimat* [Bulgarians and the Tanzimat]. Moscow: URSS, 2010.

Mansurov, P. "Rossija i Blizhnij Vostok" [Russia and the near East]. *Moskovskie vedomosti* no. 90 (April 22, 1909), no. 92 and 93 (April 24 and 25, 1909).

Markova, Z. *Bylgarskata Ekzarhija. 1870–1879* [The Bulgarian Exarchate, 1870–1879]. Sofia: Izdatelstvo BAN, 1989.

Metallinos, G. *Orthodoxia kai Ellinikotita* [Orthodoxy and Hellenism]. Athens: Parousia, 1992.

Milojkovoc-Djuric, J. *Panslavism and National Identity in Russia and in the Balkans, 1830–1880: Images of the Self and Others*. Boulder: East European Monographs, 1994. Distributed by Columbia University Press.

Nikitin, S. A. *Slavianskije komitety v Rossii v 1858–1876 godah* [The Slavonic committees in Russia in the years 1858–1876]. Moscow: Moscow University Press, 1960.

Peckham, R. S. "Map Mania: Nationalism and the Politics of Place in Greece, 1870–1922." *Political Geography* 19:1 (2000): 77–95.

Petrovich, M. B. *The Emergency of Russian Panslavism, 1856–1870*. New York: Columbia University Press, 1956.

Petrunina, O. E. *Grecheskaya nacija i gosudarstvo v XVIII-XX vv.* [The Greek nation and state in the eighteenth–twentieth centuries]. Moscow: KDU, 2010.

Pypin, A. N. *Panslavism v proshlom i nastojashem* [Panslavism in past and present]. St. Petersburg: Kolos, 1913.

Riasanovsky, N. V. *Russia and the West in the Teaching of the Slavophiles*. Cambridge, MA: Harvard University Press, 1956.

Sokolov, I. I. "Vesti s Vostoka" [News from the East]. *Soobschenija Imperatorskogo Pravo-slavnogo Palestinskogo Obshestva* 16 (1905).

———. *Constantinopol'skaja cerkov' v XIX veke* [The Church of Constantinople in the nineteenth century]. St. Petersburg: M. Akinfiev, I. Leontiev Press, 1904.

———. *O vizantinizme v cerkovno-istoricheskom otnoshenii. Vstupitel'naja lekcija po kafedre istorii greko-vostochnoj cerkvi (ot razdelenija cerkvej), prochitannaja v Sankt-Peterburg-skoj Duhovnoj Academii 1go noajabr'a 1903 g.* [About Byzantinism in a church-histori-cal sense: an introductory lecture at the department of the history of the Greek-Eastern Church (after the splitting of the churches) read at St. Petersburg Theological Academy on the 1st of November 1903]. St. Petersburg: M. Merkushev Press, 1903.

"Vesti s Afona" [News from Athos], *Tserkovnyj vestnik*, no. 42 (1912): 1317–1318.

Stamatopoulos, Dimitris. "'…den ginetai na min einai Fanariotis stin psihi tou…' Oikou-menismos kai Ethnikismos apo tin proti sti deuteri patriarhia tou Ioakeim III" ["…it is impossible that he is not a Phanariot in his soul…": ecumenism and nationalism from the first to the second patriarchate of Joacheim III]. In *Ioakeim G' o Megaloprepis. O apo Thessalonikis Oikoumenikos Patriarhis kai I Epohi tou* [Joachim III the Magnifi-cent: the Ecumenical Patriarch Joachim III of Thessaloniki and his time]. Thessaloni-ki, Filoptohos Adelfotis Andron Thessalonikis, 2012.

———. "From the Vyzantism of K. Leont'ev to the Vyzantinism of I. I. Sokolov: The Byz-antine Orthodox East as motif of the Russian Orientalism." In *Héritages de Byzance en Europe du Sud-Est à l'époque moderne et contemporaine*, edited by Olivier Delouis, Anne Couderc, and Petre Guran, 321–340. Athens: EFA, 2013.

———. "The Bulgarian Schism Revisited." *Modern Greek Studies Yearbook* 24–25 (2008–2009): 105–125.

———. *To Vyzantio meta to Ethnos. To Problima tis Syneheias stis Balkanikes istoriografies* [Byzantium after the nation: the problem of continuity in Balkan historiographies]. Athens: Alexandria, 2009.

———. *Byzantium after the Nation: The Problem of Continuity in Balkan Historiographies.* Budapest: CEU Press, 2021.

Stauridou, B. T. *Oi oikoumenikoi patriarchai 1860–simeron* [The ecumenical patriarchs from 1860 to our days]. Thessaloniki: Etaireia Makedonikon Spoudon, 1977.

Sumner, B. H. *Russia and the Balkans 1870–1880.* Oxford: Clarendon Press, 1937.

Tatischev, S. S. *Imperator Alexandr II, ego zhizn' i carstvovanie* [Emperor Alexander II: his life and reign]. St. Petersburg: A. S. Suvorin Press, 1903.

Tikhomirov, L. A. *Monarchicheskaja gosudarstvennost'* [Monarchic state organization]. St. Petersburg: Rossijskii imperskii sojuz, 1992.

———. "Russkie ideally I K. N. Leontiev", in L. A. Tikhomirov, *Kritika demokratii* (Mos-cow: Moskva, 1997): 515–516.

Traikov, V. *Nacionalnite doctrini na balkanskite strani* [The national doctrines of the Bal-kan states]. Sofia: Znanie, 2000.

Troitskii, I. E. *Diary*, October 16, 1890. Central State Archives of St. Petersburg (CGIA SPb).

Troitskii, P. *Istoriia russkikh obitelei Afona v XIX–XX vekakh* [The history of the Russian monasteries on Mount Athos in the nineteenth and twentieth centuries]. Moscow: Indrik, 2008.

Tsimbaev, N. I., *Slavianophil'stvo. Iz istorii russkoj obshestvenno-politicheskoj mysli XIX veka* [Slavophilism: from the history of Russian socio-political thought in the nineteenth century]. Moscow: Moscow University Press, 1986.

Vovchenko, D. "Modernizing Orthodoxy: Russia and the Christian East (1856–1914)." *Journal of the History of Ideas* 73, no. 3 (April 2012): 295–317.

Walicki, A. *The Slavophile Controversy: History of the Conservative Utopia in Nineteenth-Century Russian Thought.* Oxford: Oxford University Press, 1975.

Wilkinson, H. R. *Maps and Politics: A Review of the Ethnographic Cartography of Macedonia.* Liverpool: Liverpool University Press, 1951.

Liliya Berezhnaya

Imagining the Third Rome and the New Jerusalem in the 16th–18th Century Polish-Lithuanian Commonwealth

*K*yiv Post wrote in April 2015, shortly after the outbreak of the Euro-maidan protests: "Kyiv may never become a 'New Jerusalem.' But it may well become a key player in the spiritual life of Eastern Europe; and, perhaps, a leader in the reunification of Orthodoxy and Catholicism."[1] In the same vein, the Russian politologist and journalist Andrei Okara published a number of articles years ago on the geopolitical and eschatological perspectives of the Ukrainian state. He devoted Ukraine, namely, its capital Kyiv, a particular role in the future development of the post-Soviet space. Okara appealed for the reconstruction of the spiritual hegemony of Kyiv as a leading center of the post-Byzantine Oikumena. This is interpreted as a union between Russia and Ukraine in which Moscow should play the role of the administrative center, the "Third Rome function," while Kyiv should occupy a significant position of the spiritual leader, the "New Jerusalem," in a fight with the "profanization" of the modern world. Okara writes about the new "Ukrainian imperialism" which has less to do with the issue of independence and more to do with the "self-perception of the elites and the Ukrainian public in general."[2]

Kyiv as the New Jerusalem as juxtaposed to Moscow (the Third Rome) is not a new idea, particularly in light of the recent reconceptualization of Russian and Ukrainian history after the collapse of the Soviet Union. Not only politologists, but also historians are taking active part in the reconsidering the idea of New Jerusalem in East European history. However,

---

1   Woloshyn, "The New Jerusalem."
2   Okara, *Ukraina v poiskach imperiskoi perspektivy. Suzhdeno li Kievu stat' tsentrom postviyantiiskoi tsivilizatsii?*

some of them consciously try to avoid political connotations. In the article of Gianfranco Giraudo, "The New Jerusalem Versus the Third Rome," the considerable number of studies on the topic of Moscow as the Third Rome are contrasted to the significantly fewer investigations on the Ukrainian Jerusalem. The reason for this disproportionate attention is explained by the unequal weight of Great Russian chauvinism and the Ukrainian independence movement. According to Giraudo, we are dealing with two myths that were used at different times for both domestic and interstate purposes.[3]

This argument is still valid today, since the topic of the "Ukrainian Zion" has yet to receive serious and ideologically neutral investigation.[4] Particularly, this observation refers to its early modern implementations, and to its essential context—the rise of the New Jerusalems in the Polish-Lithuanian Commonwealth at the end of the sixteenth through the beginning of the eighteenth centuries. This time period witnessed the competition between different Romes, namely of the Vatican, Cracow, and Warsaw with several New Jerusalems, like Vilnius, Mohylau, Luts'k, Raków, Zebrzydów, etc. Therefore, it is more appropriate to speak about the various entanglements and competitions between Catholic Romes and Orthodox, as well as Catholic, Protestant or Jewish Jerusalems in Poland-Lithuania. The juxtaposition of the Third Rome (Moscow) to the New Jerusalem (Kyiv) is less important in this context. To put it more precisely, for the early modern period the most valid ideological (as well as theological and imaginary) confrontation was between Cracow, Kyiv, Vilnius, Zebrzydów, and Raków as competing models in constructing sacral places.

---

3 Giraudo, "Vtoroi Ierusalim protiv Tretego Rima (k postanovke voprosa)," 264–265.

4 To name just a few most serious contributions: Stupperich, "Kiev–das Zweite Jerusalem. Ein Beitrag zur Geschichte des ukrainisch-russischen Nationalbewußtseins," 332–354; Danilevskij, "Mogli Kiev byt' Novym Ierusalimom?," 135–150; Pritsak, "Kiev and all of Rus: The Fate of a Sacral Idea," 279–300; Rychka, "Ideia Kyiva–drugoho Ierusalima v polityko-ideolohichnykh kontseptsiiach serednevichnoi Rusi," 72–81; Rychka, "Kyivski propilei (pro semiotychny status Zolotych Vorit)," 51–55; Rychka, *Kyiv- drugyi Ierusalym: z istorii politychoi dumky ta ideologii serednovichoi Rusi*; Lebedev, "Bogosloviie Russkoi zemli kak obraza Obetovannoi zemli Tsarstva Nebesnogo," 150–175; Iakovenko, "Simvol 'Bohokhranimoho hrada' u pamiatkach kyivs'koho kola (1620–1640-vi roky)," 296–332; Plokhy, "Two Capitals," 261–273. A Russian translation of the book fragment appeared in Iakovleva, *Ukraina i sosednie gosudarstva v XVII veke. Materialy mezhdunarodnoi konferentsii*, 125–144.

This confrontation and entanglement appeared during the times of confessionalization and was implemented in different forms of theological polemics as well as in attempts to present the ideas of the "true faith" on a visual level. One of such visual traces of *translatio loci* (translation of a site) on the Polish-Lithuanian landscape are modern Calvaries.

According to statistics, in present-day Poland there are 52 historical Calvaries, which are devotional complexes arranged on the slope of a mountain with a series of chapels or monuments (*aediculae*) containing paintings or sculptures representing scenes of the Life of Christ, Mary, or of the Saints. Reproductions of the New Jerusalem, the Sacred Mounts, offered pilgrims the ability to visit Holy places of a smaller scale than the places where the Passion of Christ took place. Often the ascents recall the Via Dolorosa, the road in Jerusalem that leads to the Calvary, followed by Christ carrying the Cross. The idea of Calvaries originated in fifteenth century Italy and found a fertile ground in the Polish-Lithuanian Commonwealth during confessionalization. Thirteen Polish-Lithuanian Calvaries were built in the seventeenth and eighteenth centuries.[5]

The situation here was complicated because the idea of symbolic transfer of the Holy City onto local ground was not foreign to other confessions and religions in the Polish-Lithuanian Commonwealth. Vilnius and Luts'k were called New Jerusalems not only by the Christians but by the Jews as well. The title of New Jerusalems for Jews in the Polish-Lithuanian Commonwealth marked not only the spiritual centers, but to places of education and settlement. This applied most of all during the second half of the seventeenth and the entire eighteenth century, when, after the mass pogroms of the Cossack wars, a new Jewish messianic movement found its roots on Polish-Lithuanian ground. The chiliasts of Sabbatai Zevi (1626–1676) "could hardly seek actively to build a 'new Jerusalem' in any part of the country they lived."[6] Not only *translatio Hierosolymi,* but also the later Hasidic schools, gave Vilnius the title of Jewish Jerusalem.[7] The same happened to Warsaw in the late eighteenth century, when the dense Jew-

5   Mitkowska, *Polskie Kalwarie.*

6   Weinryb, *The Jews of Poland: a Social and Economic History of the Jewish Community in Poland from 1100 to 1800,* 209.

7   Siauciunaite-Verbickiene, "Nasha obshhaja kul'tura: 'vyuchennaja pamjat' o litovskom Ierusalime," 155–166; Tymoshenko, *Rus'ka relihijna kultura Vil'na,* 525–542.

ish settlement beyond the city ramparts received the title of New Jerusalem. This title lasted for several decades until the Jews were expelled from Warsaw in 1775.[8]

Attempts to privatize "replica Jerusalems"[9] were made by different religious authorities during confessionalization. The competition between Catholic and Jewish New Jerusalems, as well as the traditional Christian anti-Semitism, led to the prohibition of Jews settling in Góra Kalwaria in the Mazovian voievodship in 1670 by the local Catholic bishop Stefan Wierzbowski (1620–1687).[10] It was also the case with the Kyivan Jerusalem in the time of the Cossack hetman Ivan Mazepa (1687–1708) that the very idea of reconstructing the spiritual significance of the city got new political connotations.

In the early modern Polish-Lithuanian Commonwealth, as in other regions of that time, where the *translatio loci* idea gained popularity, this topos was present in various genres of literature, particularly, in hagiographic and apocalyptic texts, chronicles, biographies, and religious polemics. Equally important for the circulation of the New Jerusalem and *Roma mobilis* (symbolic transfer of Rome) ideas were different sacral objects. According to Jelena Erdeljan, "*translatio Hierosolymi*, becomes the sacral counterpart of the idea of *Roma mobilis*, and is related to the phenomenon of *translation imperii* as its crucial precondition…. Those means… belong to the instruments of creating sacral space, in other words, to the sacralization of space—a phenomenon which was, in historical terms, recognized as *translatio Hierosolymi*."[11]

In what follows, I will trace the development of the idea of the *translatio loci* in the Polish-Lithuanian Commonwealth in two major parts. The first part deals with the ideas of the Polish Catholic New Jerusalems and New Romes as presented in the Catholic polemics of the Catholic Calvaries. The second part is devoted to the idea of the Ruthenian Zion (i.e. Kyiv) as a place of salvation in the Orthodox religious polemics.[12]

---

8   Dubnow, *History of the Jews in Russia and Poland*, 130.

9   Dubnow, *History of the Jews in Russia and Poland*, 29.

10   Shnayderman, *The River Remembers*, 133.

11   Erdeljan, *Chosen Places: Constructing New Jerusalems in Slavia Orthodoxa*, 2–3.

12   This part of the chapter is based upon my two articles: Berezhnaya, "Topography of Salvation," 246–271 and Berezhnaya, "'His Foundation is in the Holy Mountains.' Some Remarks on the New Jerusalem Symbolism in the Age of Mazepa," 71–82.

Polish Catholic Polemicists about the "Rome-Jerusalem" Dichotomy

The notion of a "spiritual Jerusalem" was accepted in all the Christian confessions, but it turned out to be of particular importance for the rise of early modern religious identities in eastern Slavic lands at the end of the sixteenth through the beginning of the seventeenth centuries. It is commonly accepted that the major impetus for the rise of interest in the issues of "true faith," "Rome versus Constantinople versus Jerusalem," came into the Polish-Lithuanian Commonwealth with the spread of the Reformation, Counterreformation, and the popularization of the Church Union idea in the elite circles, reflecting in the religious polemics of that time.

The debates involved mostly Orthodox and Uniate clerics. The Catholic side did not play a leading role in the discussion, even though it was the Jesuit Piotr Skarga (1536–1612) who fired one of the first shots in the polemics with his *On the Unity of God's Church* (first edition 1577).[13] The three camps of polemicists elaborated different approaches to the question of which Church maintains the true faith and how the East-West (Jerusalem-Rome) contradictions should be resolved. None of the camps was entirely unanimous. The variety of opinions gave rise to new interpretations of the old topos of the New Zion.

In the Catholic camp, Piotr Skarga's works were the most essential to understanding the position of Polish Catholic theologians on the Orthodox tradition.[14] For Skarga, the East comprises the Greeks (the patriarch-

---

13 Skarga, "O jedności Kościoła Bożego pod jednym Pasterzem i o greckim od tej jedności odstąpieniu," 223–580. In the second edition entitled *O rządzie i jedności Kościoła pod jednym pasterzem i o greckim i ruskim od tej jedności odstąpieniu* (Cracow, 1590), Skarga somewhat moderated his rhetoric and refrained from several accusations he had previously made against the Orthodox Church. For more on Piotr Skarga's role in the Union of Brest see: Grabowski, *Piotr Skarga na tle katolickiej literatury religijniej w Polsce wieku XVI*; Tazbir, *Piotr Skarga: szermierz kontrreformacji*; Rychcicki, *Piotr Skarga i jego wiek*; Tretjak, *Skarga w dziejach i literaturze Unii Brzeskiej*; Obirek, "Teologiczne podstawy pojęcia jedności w dziele ks. Piotra Skargi 'O Jedności Kościoła Bożego'," 183–199; Dmitriev, "Kontseptsii unii v tserkovnykh i derzhavnych kolakh Rechi Pospolytoi kintsia XVI st.," 39–73 (with discussion pp. 74–100).

14 The writings of the Jesuits Benedykt Herbest and Cardinal Stanisław Hosius (Hozjusz) were equally important for the Catholic polemics. Hosius in his famous *Confessio catholicae fidei Christiana* (Christian Confession of Catholic Faith), which appeared in 30 editions during his lifetime, denied any possibility for dialogue between Catholics and other Christian confessions. See Zdrodowski, *The Concept of Heresy According to Cardinal Hosius*; Halecki, *From Florence to Brest (1439–1596)*.

ate of Constantinople) and the Ruthenian lands ("the Ruthenian people, standing by the Greeks"). Skarga does not elaborate much on the Patriarchate of Jerusalem, nor on the other Orthodox administrative units. The major accentuated dichotomy corresponds with the axes of Rome versus Constantinople, Roman Church versus Greek Church, Catholicism versus Orthodoxy. Skarga places the Ruthenian Orthodox Church on the border between these sets of antipodes.[15] Jerusalem, for Skarga, was not the capital of the Orthodox Church of his days, nor the residence of one of its patriarchs. Rather it was the apocalyptic "Kingdom of Heaven,"[16] the City of God, and the ideal community for its citizens.

For Skarga, Jerusalem was only a metaphor, a symbolic place, an ideal city, although applicable to the realities of his times. The Polish Jesuit traced the signs of the Heavenly Jerusalem in two institutions—the Roman Catholic Church and the Polish-Lithuanian Commonwealth. For Skarga, it is crucially important to make visible the transcendental hierarchies in earthly reality, and to maintain the primacy of the Roman pope:

> The governing of God's Church here on earth is similar to that in Heaven. Just as there the angelic hierarchies gather in to one Lord, so also the visible earthly Kingdom of the same Lord God should assemble under the auspices of one vicar of God.[17]

Analogous parallels resonate in the famous *Diet Sermons* (1597), in which Skarga equates the szlachta's (gentry's) Polish-Lithuanian Commonwealth with Jerusalem.[18]

For Skarga, such a Jerusalem could be inhabited only by Roman Catholics. The others have no chance for salvation. Skarga differentiated between the heretics and schismatics, labeling the Protestants heretics and the Orthodox schismatics.[19] One of his arguments for Ruthenian Church unity

---

15 Skarga, "O jedności Kościoła Bożego," 385.
16 Matt. 25:1: "At that time the kingdom of heaven will be like ten virgins who took their lamps and went out to meet the bridegroom;" James 2:5: "Has not God chosen those who are poor in the eyes of the world to be rich in faith and to inherit the kingdom he promised those who love him?"
17 Skarga, "O jedności Kościoła Bożego," 278.
18 Skarga, *Kazania sejmowe*; Skarga, *Kazania sejmowe*, Biblioteka Narodowa, seria 1, no. 70, 39–40.
19 Skarga, "O jedności Kościoła Bożego," 332. See also Łużny, "Księdza Piotra Skargi S.J. widzenie Wschodu chrześcijańskiego," 71.

with Rome is the consequence of schism for other Orthodox peoples. The Patriarchate of Constantinople was conquered by the Turks, whereas the Muscovite Patriarch became totally dependent upon the Grand Prince.[20] The lost unity was once restored during the Council of Ferrara-Florence (1439), which Skarga often appeals to in his polemics.[21] For Skarga, neither Third Rome (Moscow), Second Rome (Constantinople), or Orthodox Jerusalem (Kyiv) existed. He does not juxtapose these sacral cities.

The "Polonization" of Christian imaginary encompassed not only the adaptation of the Polish-Lithuanian realities into the history of Jerusalem, but also used Old Testament terminology to describe the Commonwealth's past. Moreover, the juxtaposition of the Heavenly Jerusalem with the Christian Church had direct patristic reference. Several Church Fathers have emphasized this idea, which was accommodated by the Polish Jesuit to the standards of his times.[22]

POLISH-LITHUANIAN CATHOLIC CALVARIES—HOLY MEASURES OF JERUSALEM

Similar processes took place in the architectural landscape of the cities and villages of the Polish-Lithuanian Commonwealth and they were expressed in several different ways. One such way was by portraying Polish-Lithuanian cities and towns as New Jerusalems in the teaching and culture of European religious radicals, who often fled their cities to escape persecution. An example of one such settlement was the famous community of Raków (founded in 1569), the capital of Socinianism. The center of Polish Brethren, it was the ideal place for a real New Jerusalem.[23] Another paradigmatic example is the Italian radical New Jerusalem congregation

---

20 Skarga, "O jedności Kościoła Bożego," 327.
21 The place of the Council of Ferrara-Florence in the ideology of the Brest Union is a subject of historiographical debates. The best insights into this problem are the monographs of Gudziak, *Crisis and Reform. The Kievan Metropolinate, the Patriarchate of Constantinople and the Genesis of the Union of Brest*, esp. ch. 3 "The Union of Florence, the Greek East, and the Kyivan Metropolitanate"; and Mončak, *Florentine Ecumenism in the Kyivan Church*. See also Gudziak, "Grets'kyi Skhid, Kyivs'ka mytropoliia i Florentiiska unia," 48–64; Gudziak, "Unia florencka a metropolia kijowska," 19–32.
22 Hiliare de Poitiers, St. Augustine, pseudo-Denys, among others, wrote about this metaphor. *Dictionnaire de spiritualité, VIII*, 948–951. Bredero, "Jérusalem dans l'Occident médiéval," 259–271.
23 Wilczek, *Polonia Reformata: Essays on the Polish Reformation(s)*, 55–58; Tync, "Zarys dziejów wyższej szkoły Braci Polskich w Rakowie," 81–172.

that was established close to Pińczów under the protection of the local landlord *Mikołaj Oleśnicki* (1566–1567).[24]

A completely different form of the "material *translatio Hierosolymi*" in Poland-Lithuania was the Catholic Calvary. At approximately the same time that Skarga wrote his *Diet Sermons*, a Catholic Mikołaj Zebrzydowski (1553–1620), Voivode of Lublin and Cracow, erected a chapel on Żarek Hill (in the Żar Mountain) dedicated to the Crucifixion of Christ, following a model of the Chapel of the Holy Cross in Jerusalem.

Shortly thereafter, Zebrzydowski decided to build a chapel dedicated to the Tomb of Christ along with a convent designed by the architects Giovanni Maria Bernardoni (1541–1605) and Paolo Baudarth. This church, dedicated to the Madonna of the Angels, was consecrated by the Bishop of Cracow, Piotr Tylicki (1543–1616) in 1609. For the development of the Calvary, the decisive element was the writing of Christian Adrian Cruys (Christian Kruik van Adrichem), known as Adrichomius (1533–1585), particularly his treatise "Jerusalem sicut Christi Tempore floruit" (1584). This work described the Holy Land at the time of Jesus Christ and the 12 stations of the Cross[25] inspired Zebrzydowski to found new Calvaries.[26]

The influence of the Zebrzydowski's Calvary on the appearance of new New Jerusalems in the Polish-Lithuanian area from the seventeenth–eighteenth century is hard to overestimate.[27] Soon after Zebrzydów, many places in the Commonwealth tried to transfer the "Jerusalem measures" to the local region. Primarily Franciscans were involved in new construction. This feature bound the Polish-Lithuanian Calvaries to Italian ones.[28] The Jesuits were also active in constructing the "sacral mountains," par-

---

24 Another Italian émigré, Pietro Franco, a Venetian geographer at the court of King Zygmunt III Waza (1566–1632), prophesized the immediate restoration of the Heavenly City in Cracow. See Kostyło, "Commonwealth of All Faiths: Republican Myth and the Italian Diaspora in Sixteenth-Century Poland-Lithuania," 180–185.

25 Bania, *Kalwarie polskie w XVII wieku: dzieje stosowania w Europie od X do końca XVII wieku uświęconych Pasją Chrystusa miar jerozolimskich,* 58–61; Bania, "Tak zwany wpływ Adrychomiusza na XVII– wieczne kalwarie polskie," 257–262.

26 Rudyk, *Kalwaria Zebrzydowska: Passions-Mariensanktuarium: Vademecum*; Kowalczyk, *Kalwarja Zebrzydowska: (historia, cuda, obrzędy, odpusty, kaplice itd.) na podstawie najwiarygodniejszych źródeł.*

27 Bania, "Tak zwany wpływ Adrychomiusza na XVII–wieczne kalwarie polskie," 100–121.

28 Mitkowska, *Polskie Kalwarie,* 26–58; Cardini, Vannini, Smosarski, (AA. VV.) *Due casi paralleli: la Kalwaria Zebrzydowska in Polonia e la 'Gerusalemme' di San Vivaldo in Toscana*; Głowacki, "Miniaturowe Jerozolimy, czyli Polskie Kalwarie," 40–41; Prejs, "'Jerozolima Warmińska' w Głotowie wobec tradycji barokowych założeń kalwaryjskich," 363–379.

ticularly during later periods in the northeastern parts of the Common-wealth (Calvaria in Vilnius is a notable example). In most cases Jerusa-lem's sacral geography and architecture determined the program of the Polish-Lithuanian Calvaries. The Polish Catholic Church presented itself in these places as a direct heir of the Jerusalem tradition.

Only in one case was the Holy City of Rome used as a model for a Pol-ish-Lithuanian Calvary. This happened in the aforementioned Góra Kal-waria in the Mazovian voievodship, erected by the order of the Catho-lic Bishop Stefan Wierzbowski in the 1660s–70s. According to Zbigniew Bania, the inspiration of the bishop was to combine the major cultural features of the two Christian centers, Rome and Jerusalem, into a sin-gle urban program. He achieved this by using the proportions of Jerusa-lem (the distances between the holy places of Christ's Passions) and the design principle practiced during the construction of Rome, meaning ac-centuation of the major city's axes by building cathedrals upon its ends.[29] Of course, there should be no contradiction between the two concepts of Holy places, since Rome also aspired to be the Second Jerusalem. Howev-er, Wierzbowski's attempt was unique not only for the Polish-Lithuanian Commonwealth, but for the Catholic Calvary tradition in general. In this sense the Rome-Jerusalem dichotomy found its solution through visual and symbolic synthesis. The idea of *translatio Hierosolymi* did not contra-dict in this case with that of *Roma mobilis*.

RUTHENIAN ORTHODOX POLEMICISTS ON KYIV AS THE SECOND JERUSALEM

For the Orthodox Church the tradition of building Calvaries in a form of Via Doloris is rather unknown. Instead, there were several attempts to re-produce the Holy City of Jerusalem and its major cathedrals in the local forms.[30] According to the tradition which appeared in approximately the seventh century, when the eastern parts of the Roman Empire were con-quered by the Arabs, Constantinople acquired the name of the New Jeru-

---

29 Bania, "Tak zwany wpływ Adrychomiusza na XVII–wieczne kalwarie polskie," 116.
30 I have dwelt upon this issue more in detail in Berezhnaya, "Topography of Salvation," 246–271 and Berezhnaya, "'His Foundation is in the Holy Mountains.' Some Remarks on the New Jerusalem Symbolism in the Age of Mazepa," 71–82.

salem. Constantinople as a substitute for Jerusalem was interpreted in the Byzantine theology through the formula of the "God-saved city." It was considered to be a place created by the Lord Himself, founding the limit to chaos and ruin. The concept of "Constantinople's Jerusalemization" was implemented in the city planning and topography.[31]

There were, however, other claimants in the *Slavia Orthodoxa* to the fame of "God's city."[32] Among others (Tarnovo, later also Belgrade and Moscow),[33] Kyiv declared its right to the Constantinopolitan heritage. Igor Danilevski argues that already in the early eleventh century the idea of Constantinople that had lost its position as a center of salvation because of its citizens' sins, penetrated into the Rus' literary circles. Now it was also Kyiv that pretended for a glorious title of the "New Jerusalem of the Chosen Lands." For the first time this theory was declared in the metropolitan Hilarion's *Sermon on Law and Grace* (1049).[34]

Several publications of historians, art historians, and literary critics trace the notion of Kyiv as the New Jerusalem topos in the Old Kyivan tradition. The eleventh and twelfth century Kyivan architecture reflects transparent analogies with the Constantinopolitan topography, not only in the names of churches and fortifications, but also in the sacred meaning of its artistic implementations. For instance, the Golden Gates were treated as the entry to the Heavenly Jerusalem (as well as the Constantinopolitan and Jerusalem main gates). The same coordinates ruled the Saint Sophia Cathedral. All the major architectonical components find its parallel in the sanctuaries of the Holy City. At the beginning of the sixteenth century the jasper stone, the biblical symbol of the Heavenly Jerusalem, was set into St. Sophia's floor near the major altar.[35]

---

31 Flusin, "Construire une Nouvelle Jérusalem: Constantinople et les reliques," 51–70; Poirion, *Jerusalem, Rome, Constantinople. L'image et le mythe de la ville au Moyen Age. Colloque du Département d'Etudes Médiévales de l'université de Paris-Sorbonne (Paris IV)*; Erdeljan, *Chosen Places: Constructing New Jerusalems in Slavia Orthodoxa*, 52–62, 72–144.

32 Hengel, Mittmann and Schwemer, *La Cité de Dieu, die Stadt Gottes. 3. Symposium Strasbourg, Tübingen, Uppsala, 19–23 September 1998 in Tübingen*; Kühnel and Narkiss, *The Real and Ideal Jerusalem in Jewish, Christian and Islamic Art: Studies in Honor of Bezalel Narkiss on the Occasion of his Seventieth Birthday*; Kühnel, *From the Earthly to the Heavenly Jerusalem: Representations of the Holy City in Christian Art of the First Millennium*.

33 Erdeljan, *Chosen Places: Constructing New Jerusalems in Slavia Orthodoxa*, 154–221.

34 Danilevskij, "Mog li Kiev byt' Novym Ierusalimom?," 150.

35 Nikitenko, *Rus' i Vizantiia v monumentalnom komplekse Sofii Kyivskoi. Istoricheskaia problema-*

Kyivan Caves Lavra also bored the signs of the Heavenly City. Its sacred topography had clear parallels with the Constantinople city plan, but first and foremost with the Holy Land itself. Particularly it applies the Dormition Cathedral which was considered a guardian of the City of Kyiv, its inviolable Zion. According to the widely spread opinion, a pilgrim to Lavra turned to be an active participant of the Christ Passions. Since the territory of Lavra represented the Holy Land itself, entering its gates meant embarking on the path of salvation.[36]

This idea born in the Kyivan times was kept in the popular milieu for centuries. Folklore materials collected at the end of the nineteenth century provide evidence for the notion of Kyiv as a City of God, its monasteries and churches as holy places. It was often recognized as a gateway to Heaven.[37] As scrutinized by Elena Erdeljan, such beliefs meant "establishing a relation with an archetypal image."[38]

Kyiv as the New Jerusalem, presumed a heavenly place where souls are carried after death. Soteriological and eschatological parallels between Kyiv as a capital of the Ruthenian lands, and Jerusalem, an apocalyptic City of God, were clearly drawn in these texts. Kyiv-Jerusalem was a locus which occupied the highest position on the sacral scale.[39] The symbolic connotation present in the popular tradition was revived at the beginning of the seventeenth century by Kyivan literary clerics after a long period of silence caused by the Mongol invasion and a consequent city decline. The renaissance of the idea provided a ground for the rise of the con-

---

tika, 185–198; Rychka, "Ideia Kyiva—drugoho Ierusalima v polityko-ideolohichnykh kontseptsiiach seredniovichnoi Rusi," 72–81; Nikitenko, *Sviati gory kyivs'ki: pobudova sakral'noho prostoru ranniokhrystyians'koho Kyieva (kinets' X–pochatok XII st.).*

36 Nikitenko, "Obraz sviatoi zemli u sakralnii topografii Kyivo-Pechers'koi Lavry," 64–78.

37 In some texts Lavra was directly connected to the New Jerusalem. For instance, there is a recorded story that a woman being on a pilgrimage to the Kyivan Caves Lavra, got lost in the underground. After seven years of wandering, she met a monk who explained that she was in Jerusalem, in a foreign land. Soon this woman returned back to Kyiv. Hrushevs'kyi, *Istoriia ukrainskoi literatury*, vol.4, 218; Tchubinski, *Trudy etnografichesko-statisticheskoi ekspeditsii v Zapadnorusski krai*, 149. Noteworthy, in the variants coming from the territories of the nowadays Western Ukraine and Transcarpathian region, Kyiv is replaced by Rome. Holovatskii, *Narodnyie pesni Galickoi i Ugorskoi Rusi* 42, 39. Berezhnaya, "Ukrainian Millennialism: a Historical Overview," 259.

38 Erdeljan, *Chosen Places: Constructing New Jerusalems in Slavia Orthodoxa*, 151.

39 This applies also to other cities which pretended to the name of the Holy places in Slavic folklore: Tolstaia, "Ierusalim v slavianskoi folklornoi traditsii," 51–68, esp. 53. See also, Belova and Petrukhin, "'Sviatyie gory,'" 445–457.

cept of a "chosen people" and the notion of Kyiv as the mother of all Ruthenian cities.

Recently Natalia Iakovenko suggested that the metaphor of Kyiv as the New Jerusalem was first revived in the *Epistle* of the metropolitan Iov Borets'kyi (1621) with an appeal to the faithful of "Kyiv-God saved city, the second Jerusalem." And what is more, in *Paterikon* (1462) the term *bogoimenity* (God-named city) applied to Kyiv, whereas Constantinople carried the name of *bogospasaiemy* (God-saved city), but a century later in *Paterikon* (1554) Kyiv was already referred to as *bogospasaiemy*. Iakovenko put forth a hypothesis that the shift was determined by the borderland position of Kyiv in the Great Duchy of Lithuania, where the memory of the city's glorious past and its spiritual leadership was kept alive.[40]

However, there was another factor, namely the Brest Union (1596), which provoked discussions on the issues of the New Jerusalem, salvation, and spiritual continuity. Historians often connect the major impetus for the revival of such a discourse with the secret re-consecration of the Orthodox hierarchy in Kyiv by the Jerusalem patriarch Theophanes in 1620.[41] There were, however, several treatises which appear long before this event. These were primarily polemical texts.[42] One of the main emphases was placed upon the soteriological meaning of the contraposition of Jerusalem and Rome.[43] In turn, the Uniates after the Brest Union of 1596 renewed the old controversy with new arguments and topoi. One of the topics dis-

---

40 N. Iakovenko emphasizes another important impact that was connected with the rise of the Muscovite principality whose rulers often claimed the heritage of the Kyivan dynasty. In this respect, the concept of "Moscow-the second Kyiv" played an important role. Iakovenko, "Simvol 'Bohokhranimoho hrada' u pamiatkach kyivs'koho kola (1620–1640–vi roky)," 297 and 302; Danilevskij, "Mog li Kiev byt' Novym Ierusalimom?" 142. See the debates on the Moscovite nobility's awareness of the Kyivan past in Keenan, "Muscovite Perception of Other East Slavs before 1654—An Agenda for Historians," 20–38.

41 Iakovenko, "Simvol 'Bohokhranimoho hrada' u pamiatkach kyivs'koho kola (1620–1640–vi roky)," 303; Hrushevs'kyi, *Istoriia ukrainskoi literatury*, vol. 4, 142–144.

42 Ihor Ševčenko provides a periodization of the history of religious controversies in the Ruthenian lands over the Brest Union. The first period from the 1580s to about 1630s, was centered in Vilnius and Western Ruthenian lands; the second, from 1630 to the end of the seventeenth century, was centered in Kyiv. Ševčenko, "Religious Polemical Literature in the Ukrainian and Belarus' Lands in the Sixteenth and Seventeenth Centuries," 149–163. The full list of polemical treatises around the Union of Brest is available at: Gudziak and Turii, *Beresteis'ka unia i ukrains'ka kultura XVII stolittia. Materialy tretih "Beresteis'kykh chytan'." Lviv, Kyiv, Kharkiv, 20–23 chervnia 1995*, 161–176; see also Martel, *La langue polonaise dans les pays ruthénes, Ukraine et Russie Blanche. 1589–1667*, 132–141.

43 Shevchenko, *Pravoslavno-katolyts'ka polemika ta problemy uniinosti v zhytti Rusi-Ukrainy doberesteis'koho periodu*.

cussed in this context was the papal primacy. However, the terminology used in the discourse was much richer and included the notions of tradition, Jerusalem church, Roman church, old faith, sin, heresy, and schism, thus applying dogmatic terms to historical church events. Moreover, the polemicists operated with the eschatological vocabulary, since the New Jerusalem and the New Zion denotations had clearly apocalyptic meanings.[44]

Polemical sources of the sixteenth and seventeenth centuries allow for conclusions about the periodization in the formation of the Kyiv-Second Jerusalem topos. In the first stage, at the end of the sixteenth century, we do not find in the debates any direct connections of Kyiv with the New Jerusalem. Partly this was due to the fact that other Ruthenian cities were laying claim to the glorious title of the "God-saved city." Among them were Ostrih, L'viv, and Vilnius. In the next stage, the decision for the title of New Jerusalem was in favor of Kyiv in the 1620s, with a re-orientation of Orthodox clerical circles towards the idea of a single Orthodox capital of the Ruthenian lands.[45]

Jerusalem and Zion were understood to be a community of Orthodox believers, the true Church, both in the present and in the Other World. This unity was opposed to the sinful and schismatic Roman Church. This schema corresponds to the theological reflections found, for instance, in Kirill Trankvillion-Stavrovec'kyi's *A Mirror of Theology* (1618)[46] or in Ivan Vyshens'kyi's polemical *Book* (1598–1601). The latter was a Ruthenian monk residing Mt. Athos. Vyshens'kyi compared the behavior of the Roman Catholic hierarchs with the crimes of the biblical Nebuchadnezzar.[47] In contrast, Jerusalem, "the noblest city," was presented as a sym-

---

44 Gal. 4: 26: "But Jerusalem which is above is free, which is the mother of us all;" Heb. 12:22: "But ye are come unto mount Sion, and unto the city of the living God, the heavenly Jerusalem, and to an innumerable company of angels;" Rev. 3:12, 21: "and I will write upon him the name of my God, and the name of the city of my God, which is new Jerusalem, which cometh down out of heaven from my God: and I will write upon him my new name."

45 Besides Kyiv, Chyhyryn was a pretender to the capital role on the Ruthenian lands in the first half of the seventeenth century. Confrontations between the two cities lead to the different perceptions of the center in the Cossacks' eyes. While Kyiv was interpreted rather as a spiritual capital, Chyhyryn remained the Cossack administrative center. See Plokhy, "Two Capitals," 261–273.

46 Trankvillion-Stavrovec'kyi, *Zertsalo Bogosloviia*. On Trankvillion-Stavrovec'kyi's life and literary activity see, Maslov, *Tranquillion-Stavrovec'kyi i iego literaturnaia deiatel'nost'*.

47 Vyshens'kyi, "Knizhka... ot sviatyia Afonskiia gory v napominaniie vsekh pravoslavnykh khristian...," 97. George Grabowicz treats Vyshens'kyi as "the first major Ukrainian writer, the only writer from the entire middle period of Ukrainian literature." See, Grabowicz, "The Question of Authori-

bol of the Orthodox Church, the true victim of the crafty designs of the "proud bishops."[48]

The majority of polemical writings regularly presented the Ruthenian Orthodox Church as the direct heiress to the patrimony of Jerusalem. The *translatio* topos did not assume any intermediary stages; therefore, the topos of Constantinople as the New Jerusalem was excluded from this scheme. Consequently, the Orthodox clerics avoided answering the Catholic and Uniate argument that Constantinople had lost its spiritual significance after the fall of the city to the Turks. Of no lesser importance was another reason for the mystical interpretation of Jerusalem. In the majority of the Ruthenian Orthodox polemics from the period, Zion and Jerusalem were described as a community of believers, a "Cathedral not made by human hands" (*acheiropoietos*). The association of any earthly place with the heavenly kingdom was considered to be a serious error and a false statement—like in Zaxarija Kopystens'kyi's *Palinode, or Book of Defense* (1621–1622) which supported the idea that the Orthodox Church was the only canonical Church in the Ruthenian lands.[49]

These eschatological connotations, stimulated in part by Patriarch Theophanes's visit to Kyiv, received new forms and interpretations in a wider circle of Orthodox clerics. Theophanes's circular epistle, in which he exhorted the faithful, "...may your memory not relinquish the holy city of Jerusalem,"[50] and the re-consecration of the Orthodox hierarchy inspired several treatises in which the idea of the Ruthenian Zion was developed.

The reasons for the renaissance of the old concept in the Ruthenian Orthodox context cannot be reduced to the visit of the Patriarch of Jeru-

---

ty in Ivan Vyshens'kyi: a Dialectics of Absence," 781. A famous book by Ivan Franko on Vyshens'kyi that is often regarded as the height of Franko's literary achievement also places Vyshens'kyi as one of the major figures of early Ukrainian literary development. See Franko, *Ivan Vyshens'kyi*, 20–25. See also, Zema, "Seredniovichna tradytsiia slova, movy ta knyhy v tvorakh Vyshens'koho," 82–92.

48 Vyshens'kyi, "Knizhka... ot sviatyia Afonskiia gory v napominaniie vsekh pravoslavnykh khristian...," 106, 116.

49 Hrushevs'kyi argued that Kopystens'kyi continued to work on *Palinode* as late as 1623. See Hrushevs'kyi, *Istoriia ukrainskoi literatury*, vol. 6, 56. Omeljan Pritsak considers *Palinode* "simply the most comprehensive and erudite defense of Orthodoxy produced during the debate with the Uniates." See Pritsak and Strumiński, "Introduction." The best monograph on *Palinodiia* is Zavitnevich, *"Palinodiia" Zakharii Kopystenskogo i ieio mesto v istorii zapadno-russkoi polemiki XVI I XVII vv.*; Iakovenko, "Simvol 'Bohokhranimoho hrada' u pamiatkach kyivs'koho kola (1620–1640-vi roky)," 327.

50 Plokhy, "Two Capitals," 263.

salem alone. The revival of the tradition concerning the depiction of Kyiv as an Orthodox capital was also due to the growth of a new Polish historical narrative (for instance, the 1582 *Chronicle* of Maciej Stryjkowski),[51] as well as the revived Ruthenian annalistic tradition.[52]

The Orthodox Kyivan Archimadrite and later the Metropolitan Peter Mohyla (1596–1647) tried to give a new impetus in the formation of the idea of Ruthenian lands as the New Zion. This was mostly based upon the reanimation of the Kyivan Rus' tradition through the renovation of Kyivan cathedrals, the translation of the relics of Grand Prince Saint Volodymyr (958–1015), and the erection of a monument and a chapel devoted to Saint Volodymyr and his successor, Jaroslav the Wise (978–1054). The spiritual role of Kyiv as the New Jerusalem was perceived to be more important than its secular and historical value. Such an attitude was a specific feature of the seventeenth-century Ruthenian Orthodox tradition.[53]

INSTEAD OF A CONCLUSION: KYIV VERSUS MOSCOW, OR KYIV TOGETHER WITH MOSCOW?

It seems that the problem of juxtaposing Kyiv as New Jerusalem with Moscow as the Third Rome, posed at the beginning of this chapter, did not much interest early modern church hierarchs and secular leaders. Mohyla's efforts to renew the spiritual value of Kyiv never competed with Moscow's aspirations as the Third Rome. Partly this was due to the fact that the theory of the Third Rome as an "early justification for Russian expansionism is badly flawed"[54] and the idea of Moscow as the New Israel was much more popular among the Muscovite educated elites until the end of the seventeenth century. This preference resulted most vividly in the Patriarch Nikon's construction in 1652 of the New Jerusalem mon-

51 Stryjkowski, *Kronika polska, litewska, żmódzka i wszystkiej Rusi,* 128–134.
52 Plokhy, "Two Capitals," 262.
53 See also Brüning, "Peter Mohyla's Orthodox and Byzantine Heritage: Religion and Politics in the Kyivan Church Reconsidered," 83.
54 Rowland, "Moscow–The Third Rome or the New Israel?" 591. See also, Korpela, *Prince, Saint, and Apostle: Prince Vladimir Svjatoslavič of Kiev, His Posthumous Life, and the Religious Legitimization of the Russian Great Power,* 18–20.

astery on the Istra River northwest of Moscow.[55] The idea to build a precise copy of Jerusalem's Church of Holy Sepulcher and other Holy places was the culmination of the idea of the glory of the Muscovite Orthodox Church within the Christian oikumena and an attempt to elevate the Patriarch's position in it.[56]

Besides, the two ideas were not in opposition, to quote Daniel Rowland: "These were complimentary images, being part of the same idea of a series of Christian empires succeeding each other as prefiguration and fulfillment down to the Apocalypse."[57] For the Kyivan hierarchs Moscow couldn't be of any concurrence, since both cities were regarded as centers of Orthodox spirituality and revival. But this was true only for the Kyivan side. Muscovite church and state leaders neglected contemporary Kyiv and paid much attention to the history of the ancient one,[58] thus contesting the legacy of the Kyivan Rus' and the title of the New Jerusalem. The idea of the sixteenth–seventeenth century Kyiv as a spiritual capital, presented in the writings of the Ruthenian Orthodox polemicists, never received a significant response among eastern neighbors. Only at the second half of the seventeenth century together with the huge influx of the Ruthenian Orthodox clergy to Muscovy, did the situation change. The ideas of the common spiritual heritage, Kyiv as a cradle of both Ruthenians and Muscovites, eloquently presented in the Kyivan *Sinopsis* (1674), found keen repercussions in the Muscovite elite.[59] However, in the last quarter of the seventeenth century, according to Hans-Joachim Torke, the doctrine of Moscow as the New Jerusalem (as well as the Third Rome) was pushed aside. Both concepts were incompatible with ideas of political and spiritu-

---

55 Batalov, Viatchanina, "Ob ideinom znachenii i interpretatsii ierusalimskogo obraztsa v russkoi arhitekture XVI–XVII vekov," 22–42.
56 Ousterhout, "Flexible Geography and Transportable Topography," 403–404.
57 Rowland, "Moscow–The Third Rome or the New Israel?" 591, 613. See also, Kivelson, *Cartographies of Tsardom: The Land and Its Meanings in Seventeenth-Century Russia.*
58 Halperin, "Kiev and Moscow: An Aspect of Early Muscovite Thought," 312–321; Halperin, "Rus', Russia and National Identity," 157–174; Bushkovitch, review of *The Contest for the Legacy of Kyivan Rus'*, by Jaroslav Pelenski, *International History Review* 4, no. 21 (1998): 987–988; Plokhy, *The Origins of Slavic Nations: Premodern Identities in Russia, Ukraine, and Belarus*, 231–249.
59 "Sinopsis" was often reprinted in the seventeenth and eighteenth centuries. Kohut, "Origins of the Unity Paradigm: Ukraine and the Construction of Russian National History (1620s–1860s)," 72; Kohut, "From Japheth to Moscow: Narrating Biblical and Ethnic Origins of the Slavs in Polish, Ukrainian, and Russian Historiography (Sixteenth–Eighteenth Centuries)."

al expansionism. Instead, a new imperial ideology came into the picture, postulating ruler's exclusive role in the state.[60]

Although the Kyivan theologians were a part of these movements in all directions in the second half of the seventeenth century, they never appealed to construct something similar to the Catholic Calvary or the Patriarch Nikon's New Jerusalem monastery on Kyivan ground. In a way they remained faithful to the words of Kopystens'kyi about Heavenly Zion and Jerusalem as a community of believers, not as a particular earthly place.

In contrast, their counterparts on the Polish Catholic side often insisted upon the contraposition of Rome and Jerusalem. The problem of *translatio Hierusolymi* was mainly reduced to the opposition between the Polish Catholic and the Ruthenian Orthodox Churches. The main topoi in their polemics over the issues of sacral topography were necessary to overcome the schism and encourage the acceptance of the Catholic tenets and adherence to the decisions of the Council of Ferrara-Florence.

The dichotomy between *translatio Hierusolymi* and *Roma mobilis* was positively resolved only in the Calvary constructed upon the order of Bishop Wierzbowski. Numerous Catholic Calvaries were just one example of how to construct sacral space on the local ground. Another was suggested by Polish and other European radical Protestants that grounded their own New Jerusalem congregations in the Polish-Lithuanian Commonwealth, awaiting the Second Coming. All of these imagined and real ways of constructing New Jerusalems in Poland-Lithuania had archetypal common features referring to real Jerusalem.[61] At the same time these were competing projects that reflected the processes of confessional formation in early modern Poland-Lithuania.

Recently the idea of the New Jerusalem in former Polish-Lithuanian territories got new attention due to the outbreak of the Ukrainian crisis. As in early modern Poland-Lithuania, historians, politicians, and Church leaders debate the issue of whether Kyiv, Moscow, or other East Europe-

---

60 Torke, "The Unloved Alliance: Political Relations between Muscovy and Ukraine in the Seventeenth Century," 57.

61 Lidov, A. "Ierotopiia. Sozdaniie sakral'nykh prostranstv kak vid tvorchestva i predmet istoricheskogo issledovaniia," 25.

an cities deserve this sacral status.[62] In contrast to the sixteenth–seventeenth centuries, theological and mythical connotations are less important. Nowadays debates are heavily ideologically charged, serving the purposes of political and spiritual expansionism. In this way, the history of Eastern European New Jerusalems and its contemporary popularization deserve to be put anew on a research agenda.

REFERENCES

Bania, Zbigniew. *Kalwarie polskie w XVII wieku: dzieje stosowania w Europie od X do końca XVII wieku uświęconych Pasją Chrystusa miar jerozolimskich* [Polish calvaries in the seventeenth century: history of European applications of Jerusalem measures sanctified by Christ's Passions from the tenth until the end of the seventeenth centuries]. Warsaw: Akademia Teologii Katolickiej, 1993.

———. "Tak zwany wpływ Adrychomiusza na XVII-wieczne kalwarie polskie" [The so-called impact of Adrychomiusz on the seventeenth-century Polish calvaries]. In *Jerozolima w kulturze europejskiej* [Jerusalem in European culture], edited by Piotr Paszkiewicz and Tadeusz Zadrożny, 257–262. Warsaw: Instytut Sztuki Polskiej Akademii Nauk, 1997.

———. *Święte miary jerozolimskie. Grób Pański, Anastasis, Kalwaria* [Holy Jerusalem measures: the Holy Sepulcher, Anastasis, calvary]. Warsaw: Neriton, 1997.

Batalov, Andrei, and Tatiana Viatchanina. "Ob ideinom znachenii i interpretatsii ierusalimskogo obraztsa v russkoi arhitekture XVI–XVII vekov" [About the idea of meaning and interpretation of Jerusalem models in Russian architecture of the sixteenth–seventeenth centuries], *Architekturnoe nasledstvo* [Architectural heritage] 36 (1988): 22–42.

Belova, Olga, and Vladimir Petrukhin, "'Sviatyie gory,' Kiev i Ierusalim v slavianskoi mifopoeticheskoi traditsii" ['The Holy Hills,' Kyiv and Jerusalem in Slavic mythical-poetical tradition]. In *Novyie Ierusalimy: ierotopiia i ikonografiia sakral'nykh prostranstv* [New Jerusalems: hierotopy and iconography of sacred spaces], edited by Alexei Lidov, 445–457. Moscow: Indrik, 2009.

Berezhnaya, Lilya [Liliya]. "'His Foundation is in the Holy Mountains': Some Remarks on the New Jerusalem Symbolism in the Age of Mazepa." *Series Byzantina* 4 (2006): 71–82.

———. "Kiew–das 'Neue Jerusalem.'" In *Religiöse Erinnerungsorte in Ostmitteleuropa: Konstitution und Konkurrenz im nationen- und epochenübergreifenden Zugriff*, edited by Joachim Bahlcke, Stefan Rohdewald, and Thomas Wünsch, 37–51. Berlin: De Gruyter Verlag, 2013.

———. "Topography of Salvation. 'Kyiv-the New Jerusalem' in the Ruthenian Literary Polemics (End of the 16th–Beginning of the 17th Century)." In *Litauen und Ruthenien. Studien zu einer transkulturellen Kommunikationsregion (15.–18. Jahrhundert),*

---

62 Krawchuk, "Redefining Orthodox Identity in Ukraine after the Euromaidan," 175–202.

Forschungen zur osteuropäischen Geschichte, vol. 71, edited by David Frick, Stefan Rohdewald, and Stefan Wiederkehr, 246–271. Wiesbaden: Harrassowitz Verlag, 2007.

———. "Ukrainian Millennialism: A Historical Overview." In *The Apocalyptic Complex: Origins, Histories, Permanences*, edited by Nadia Al-Bagdadi, Mattias Riedl, and David Marno, 253–280. Budapest: CEU Press, 2018.

Bredero, Adriaan H. "Jérusalem dans l'Occident médiéval." In *Mélanges offerts à René Crozet à l'occasion de son soixante-dixième anniversaire*, vol. 1, edited by Pierre Gallais and Yves-Jean Rious, 259–271. Poitiers: Société d'Études Médiévales, 1966.

Brüning, Alfons. "Peter Mohyla's Orthodox and Byzantine heritage. Religion and Politics in the Kyivan Church Reconsidered." In *Von Moskau nach St. Petersburg. Das russische Reich im 17. Jahrhundert*, edited by Hans-Joachim Torke, 63–90. Wiesbaden: Harrassowitz Verlag, 2000.

Bushkovitch, Paul. Review of *The Contest for the Legacy of Kyivan Rus'*, by Jaroslav Pelenski. *International History Review* 4, vol. 21 (1999): 987–988.

Cardini, Franco, Guido Vannini, and Józef Smosarski. *Due casi paralleli: la Kalwaria Zebrzydowska in Polonia e la 'Gerusalemme' di San Vivaldo in Toscana*, Biblioteca della Miscellanea storica della Valdelsa, vol. 5. Florence: Società Storica della Valdelsa, 1983.

Danilevskij, Igor. "Mog li Kiev byt' Novym Ierusalimom?" [Could Kyiv be the New Jerusalem?] In *Odissej. Chelovek v istorii* [Odysseus: man in history], 135–150. Moscow: Nauka, 1999.

Dmitriev, Mikhail. "Kontseptsii unii v tserkovnykh i derzhavnykh kolakh Rechi Pospolytoi kintsia XVI st." [The Unity Conceptions in the church and state circles of the Polish-Lithuanian Commonwealth at the end of the sixteenth century]. In *Istorychny konytekst, ukladennia Beresteiskoi unii i pershe pouniine pokolinnia. Materialy pershych "Beresteiskikh chytan"* [Historic context of the Union of Brest and the first generation after the Union. Materials of the first "Brest proceedings"], edited by Boris Gudziak and Oleh Turii, 39–100. Lviv: Vydavnytstvo Instytutu Istorii Tserkvy L'vivkoi Bohoslovs'koi Akademii, 1995.

Dubnow, Simon M. *History of the Jews in Russia and Poland*, vol.1. New Haven: Jewish Publication Society of America, 2000.

Erdeljan, Jelena. *Chosen Places. Constructing New Jerusalems in Slavia Orthodoxa: Central and Eastern Europe in the Middle Ages (450–1450)*, vol. 45. Leiden–Boston: Brill, 2017.

Flusin, Bernard. "Construire une Nouvelle Jérusalem: Constantinople et les reliques." In *L'Orient dans l'histoire religieuse de l'Europe. L'invention des origines*, Bibliothéque de l'Ecole des Hautes Etudes et sciences religieuses, vol. 110, 51–70, edited by Mohammad Ali Amir-Moezzi, JohnScheid, and Jacques Le Brun. Turnhout: Brépols, 2000.

Franko, Ivan. *Ivan Vyshens'kyi*. Lviv: Drukarnia Shyjkovs'koho, no date.

Giraudo, Gianfranco. "Russkoie nastoiascheie i proshedsheie v tvorchestve Innokentiia Gizela" [Russian present and past in the works of Innokentii Gizel], *Mediaevalia Ucrainica: mentalnist ta istoria idei* [Mediaevalia Ucrainica: mentality and history of ideas] 1 (1992): 92–103.

———. "Vtoroi Ierusalim protiv Tretego Rima (k postanovke voprosa)" [The New Jerusalem versus the Third Rome (a research agenda)]. In *Jerusalem in Slavic Cultures, Jews and Slavs*, vol. 6, edited by Wolf Moskovich, Oto Luthar, and Samuel Schwarzband, 263–269. Jerusalem: Hebrew University, 1999.

Głowacki, Witold. "Miniaturowe Jerozolimy, czyli Polskie Kalwarie" [Miniature Jerusalems, or Polish Calvaries], *Polska* [Poland] 26 (2018): 40–4.

Grabowicz, George. "The Question of Authority in Ivan Vyshens'kyi: a Dialectics of Absence." In *Proceedings of the International Congress Commemorating the Millennium of Christianity in Rus'-Ukraine, Harvard Ukrainian Studies* (special issue), vol. 12–13, edited by Omeljan Pritsak, Ihor Ševčenko, and Miroslav Labunka, 780–794. Cambridge, MA: Harvard Ukrainian Research Institute, 1988–1989.

Grabowski, Tadeusz. *Piotr Skarga na tle katolickiej literatury religijniej w Polsce wieku XVI* [Piotr Skarga on the background of the Catholic literature in sixteenth-century Poland]. Cracow, 1913.

Gudziak, Boris and Oleh Turii, eds. *Beresteis'ka unia i ukrains'ka kultura XVII stolittia. Materialy tretih "Beresteis'kykh chytan'"Lviv, Kyiv, Kharkiv, 20–23 chervnia 1995* [The unity of Brest and the seventeenth-century Ukrainian culture. Materials of the third "Brest proceedings," Lviv, Kyiv, Kharkiv, 20–23 June 1995]. Lviv: Vydavnytstvo Instytutu Istorii Tserkvy L'vivkoi Bohoslovs'koi Akademii, 1996.

———. *Crisis and Reform. The Kievan Metropolinate, the Patriarchate of Constantinople and the Genesis of the Union of Brest.* Cambridge: Harvard University, 1996.

———. "Grets'kyi Skhid, Kyivs'ka mytropoliia i Florentiiska unia" [Greek East, Kyivan metropolia and the Unity of Florence]. In *Zapysky Natukovogo Tovarystva imeni Shevchenka. Pratsi Istorychno-filosofs'koi sektsii* [Proceedings of the Shevchenko Academic Society. Historical and philosophical section] vol. 28 (1994): 48–64.

———. "Unia florencka a metropolia kijowska" [The Unity of Florence and the Archdiocese of Kyiv]. In *Polska-Ukraina: 1000 lat sąsiedztwa* [Poland-Ukraine: 1000 years of neighborhood], edited by Stanisław Stępień, 19–32. Przemyśl: Południowo-Wschodni Instytut Naukowy w Przemyślu, 1994.

Halecki, Oskar. *From Florence to Brest (1439–1596)*. Rome: Sacrum Poloniae Millennium, 1958.

Halperin, Charles. "Kiev and Moscow: An Aspect of Early Muscovite Thought," *Russian History, Histoire russe* 7, no. 3 (1980): 312–321.

———. "Rus', Russia and National Identity." *Canadian Slavonic Papers* 1–2, vol. 48, (2006): 157–174.

Hengel, Martin, Siegfried Mittmann, and Anna Maria Schwemer, eds. *La Cité de Dieu, die Stadt Gottes. 3. Symposium Strasbourg, Tübingen, Uppsala, 19–23 September 1998 in Tübingen*. Tübingen: Siebeck, 2000.

Holovatskii, Iakov. *Narodnyie pesni Galickoi i Ugorskoi Rusi* [Folk songs of Galician and Hungarian Rus'], part 2. Moscow: V universitetskoi tipografii, 1878.

Hrushevs'kyi, Mykhailo. *Istoriia ukrainskoi literatury* [History of Ukrainian literature], vol. 4, book 2. Kyiv: AT "Oberehy," 1994.

———. *Istoriia ukrainskoi literatury* [History of Ukrainian literature], vol. 6, book 1. Kyiv: AT "Oberehy," 1995.

Iakovenko, Natalia. "Simvol "Bohokhranimoho hrada" u pamiatkach kyivs'koho kola (1620–1640-vi roky)" [The symbol of the God-saved city in the writings of the Kyivan circle (1620–1640s)]. In *Parallelny svit. Doslidzhennia z istorii uiavlen' ta idei v Ukraini XVI–XVII st.* [Parallel world: studies in the history of imagination and ideas in the sixteenth–seventeenth century Ukraine], 296–332. Kyiv: Krytyka, 2002.

Iakovleva, Tatiana. *Ukraina i sosednie gosudarstva v XVII veke. Materialy mezhdunarodnoi konferentsii* [Ukraine and the neighboring states in the seventeenth century. Proceedings of international conference]. St. Petersburg: Skif, 2004.

Keenan, Edward L. "Muscovite Perception of Other East Slavs before 1654—An Agenda for Historians." In *Ukraine and Russia in Their Historical Encounter*, edited by Peter Potichnyj, Marc Raeff, Jaroslaw Pelenski, Gleb N. Zekulin, 20–38. Edmonton: Canadian Institute of Ukrainian Studies Press, 1992.

Trankvillion-Stavrovec'kyi, Kiril. *Zertsalo Bogosloviia* [Theological mirror], 2nd ed. Pochaiv, 1790.

Kivelson, Valerie. *Cartographies of Tsardom: The Land and Its Meanings in Seventeenth-Century Russia*. Ithaca: Cornell University Press, 2006.

Kohut, Zenon. "Origins of the Unity Paradigm: Ukraine and the Construction of Russian National History (1620s–1860s)." *Eighteenth-Century Studies* 35, no. 1 (2001): 70–76.

———. "From Japheth to Moscow: Narrating Biblical and Ethnic Origins of the Slavs in Polish, Ukrainian, and Russian Historiography (Sixteenth–Eighteenth Centuries)." *Journal of Ukrainian Studies* 33–34 (2008–2009): 279–292.

Kostyło, Joanna. "Commonwealth of All Faiths: Republican Myth and the Italian Diaspora in Sixteenth-Century Poland-Lithuania." In *Citizenship and Identity in a Multinational Commonwealth: Poland-Lithuania in Context, 1569–1795*, edited by Karen Friedrich and Barbara M. Pendzich, 171–205. Leiden—Boston: Brill, 2009.

Kowalczyk, Walenty. *Kalwarja Zebrzydowska (historia, cuda, obrzędy, odpusty, kaplice itd.) na podstawie najwiarygodniejszych źródeł* [Zebrzydów Calvary (history, wonders, rituals, fair, chapel, etc.) on the basis of the most truthful sources]. Cracow: Gronuś, 1929.

Krawchuk, Andrii. "Redefining Orthodox Identity in Ukraine after the Euromaidan." In *Churches in the Ukrainian Crisis*, edited by Andrii Krawchuk and Thomas Bremer, 175–202. London: Palgrave, 2017.

Kühnel, Bianca. *From the Earthly to the Heavenly Jerusalem: Representations of the Holy City in Christian Art of the First Millennium*. Römische Quartalschrift für christliche Altertumskunde und Kirchengeschichte, Supplementheft 42. Rome–Freiburg: Herder Verlag, 1987.

———, and Bezalel Narkiss, eds. *The Real and Ideal Jerusalem in Jewish, Christian and Islamic Art: Studies in Honor of Bezalel Narkiss on the Occasion of his Seventieth Birthday*, Jewish Art, vol. 23–24. Jerusalem: Center for Jewish Art, 1998.

Lebedev, Lev. "Bogosloviie Russkoi zemli kak obraza Obetovannoi zemli Tsarstva Nebesnogo" [Theology of Russian land as an image of the Promised land of the Heavenly Kingdom]. In *Tysiacheletie kresheniia Rusi: Mezhdunarodnaia tserkovno-nauchnaia konferentsiia, Bogoslovie i dukhovnost, Moskva, 11–18 maia 1987* [Thousand anniversary of the baptism of Rus. International scientific and church conference. Theology and spirituality, Moscow 11–18 May 1987], 150–175. Moscow: Izdatelstvo Moskovskoi Patriarkhii, 1989.

Lidov, Alexei. "Ierotopiia. Sozdaniie sakral'nykh prostranstv kak vid tvorchestva i predmet istoricheskogo issledovaniia" [Hierotopy. The creation of sacred spaces as a form of creativity and subject of cultural history"]. In *Ierotopiia. Sozdaniie sakral'nykh prostranstv v Vizantii i Drevnei Rusi* [Hierotopy: the creation of sacred spaces in Byzantium and medieval Russia], edited by Alexei Lidov, 9–58. Moscow: Indrik, 2006.

Łużny, Ryszard. "Księdza Piotra Skargi S.J. widzenie Wschodu chrześcijańskiego" [Piotr Skarga's S.J. views of Eastern Christianity]. In *Polska-Ukraina: 1000 lat sąsiedztwa* [Poland–Ukraine: 1000 years of neighborhood], edited by Stanisław Stępień, 69–76. Przemyśl: Południowo-Wschodni Instytut Naukowy, 1994.

Martel, Antoine. *La langue polonaise dans les pays ruthénes, Ukraine et Russie Blanche. 1589–1667*. Lille: Université de Lille, 1938.

Maslov, Sergei. *K. Tranquillion-Stavrovec' kyi i iego literaturnaia deiatel'nost'* [Tranquillion-Stavrovec'kyi and his literary activity]. Kyiv: Naukova Dumka, 1984.

Mitkowska, Anna. *Polskie Kalwarie* [Polish calvaries]. Cracow: Ossolineum, 2003.

Mončak, Ihor. *Florentine Ecumenism in the Kyivan Church*. Romae: Universitatis Catholicae Ucrainorum S. Clementis Papae, 1987.

Nikitenko, Mariana. "Obraz sviatoi zemli u sakralnii topografii Kyivo-Pechers'koi Lavry" [The picture of Holy Land in the sacred topography of the Kyivan Caves Lavra]. *Proseminarij. Medievistyka, Istoriia tserkvy, nauky ta kultury* [Proseminar: medieval studies, church history, science and culture], vol. 5 (2005): 64–78.

———. *Sviati gory kyivs'ki: pobudova sakral'noho prostoru ranniokhrystyians'koho Kyieva (kinets' X–pochatok XII st.)* [Kyivan Holy Hills. The construction of sacral space in early medieval Kyiv (end of the tenth–beginning of the twelfth centuries]. Kyiv: Instytut arkheografii i dzhereloznavstva AN Ukrainy, 2013.

Nikitenko, Nadiia. *Rus' i Vizantiia v monumentalnom kompleksie Sofii Kyivskoi. Istoricheskaia problematika* [Rus' and Byzantium in the monumental complex of Kyivan St. Sophia Cathedral. Historical issues]. Kyiv: Slovo, 1999.

Obirek, Stanisław. "Teologiczne podstawy pojęcia jedności w dziele ks. Piotra Skargi 'O Jedności Kościoła Bożego'" [Theological basic of the Unity concept in Piotr Skarga's "About the Unity of God's Church"]. In *Unia Brzeska. Geneza, dzieje i konsekwencje w kulturze narodów słowiańskich* [The Union of Brest: genesis, history and consequences in Slavic cultures], edited by Ryszard Łużny, Franciszek Ziejka, and Andrzej Kępiński, 183–199. Cracow: Universitas, 1994.

Okara, Andrei. "Ukraina v poiskakh imperiskoi perspektivy. Suzhdeno li Kievu stat' tsentrom postviyantiiskoi tsivilizatsii?" [Ukraine in search of imperial perspective: was Kyiv predestined to be a center of a post-byzantine civilization?] *NG Sodruzhestvo* 9, no. 31, October 25, 2000. https://sites.ualberta.ca/~khineiko/NG_00_01/1151976.htm.

Oparina, Tatiana. "Chislo 1666 v russkoi knizhnosti serediny-tretiei chetverti XVII vieka" [The number 1666 in the Russian book culture of the mid–last quarter of the seventeenth century]. In *Chelovek mezhdu tsarstvom i imperiiei. Sbornik materialov mezhdunarodnoi konferentsii* [A man between the tsardom and empire. Proceedings of international conference], edited by Marina Kiseliova, 290–292. Moscow: Institut Cheloveka RAN, 2003.

Ousterhout, Robert. "Flexible Geography and Transportable Topography." In *The Real and Ideal Jerusalem in Jewish, Christian and Islamic Art: Studies in Honor of Bezalel Narkiss on the Occasion of his Seventieth Birthday*, Jewish Art 1997–1998, edited by Bianca Kühnel, 393–404. Jerusalem: Center for Jewish Art, 1998.

Plokhy, Serhii. *The Origins of Slavic Nations. Premodern Identities in Russia, Ukraine, and Belarus*. Cambridge: Cambridge University Press, 2006.

————. "Two Capitals." In *The Cossacks and Religion in Early Modern Ukraine*, 261–273. Oxford: Oxford University Press, 2001.

Poirion, Daniel, ed. *Jerusalem, Rome, Constantinople. L'image et le mythe de la ville au Moyen Age. Colloque du Département d'Etudes Médiévales de l'université de Paris-Sorbonne (Paris IV)*. Paris: Presses Paris Sorbonne, 1986.

Prejs, Marek. "'Jerozolima Warmińska' w Głotowie wobec tradycji barokowych założeń kalwaryjskich." In *Aplauz najzacniejszej damie: studia i szkice z kręgu literatury i kultury dawnej*, edited by Iwona Maciejewska and Agata Roćko, 363–379. Olsztyn: Wydawnictwo Uniwersytetu Warmińsko-Mazurskiego, 2017.

Pritsak, Omeljan. "Kiev and all of Rus': The Fate of a Sacral Idea." *Harvard Ukrainian Studies* 10 (1986): 279–300.

———— and Bohdan. Strumiński. "Introduction." In *Lev Krevza's Obrona iedności cerkiewney; and Zaxarija Kopystens'kyj's Palinodija, XVI* [Lev Krevza's defense of the church unity and Zaxarija Kopystens'kyj's Palinodija, XVI], edited by Omeljan Pritsak and Bohdan Strumiński. Cambridge: Harvard University Press for the Harvard Ukrainian Research Institute, 1995.

Rothe, Hans, ed. *Sinopsis*. Cologne: Böhlau, 1983.

Rowland, Daniel B. "Moscow—The Third Rome or the New Israel?" *The Russian Review* 55, no. 4 (1996): 591–614.

Rudyk, Mikołaj. *Kalwaria Zebrzydowska: Passions-Mariensanktuarium: Vademecum*. Kalwaria Zebrzydowska, 2004.

Rychcicki, Maurycy. *Piotr Skarga i jego wiek* [Piotr Skarga and his times], vol.1–2. Cracow: Zakład wydawnictwa dzieł katolickich, 1850.

Rychka, Volodymyr. "Ideia Kyiva—drugoho Ierusalyma v polityko-ideolohichnykh kontseptsiiach seredniovichnoi Rusi" [The idea of Kyiv—the second Jerusalem in political and ideological conceptions of medieval Rus'] *Archeologia* 2 (1998): 72–81.

————. "Kyivski propilei (pro semiotychny status Zolotych Vorit)" [Kyivan propileas (about semiotic status of Golden Gates)]. In *Kyivs'ka starovyna* 2 (2002): 51–55.

————. *Kyiv—drugyi Ierusalym: z istorii politychoi dumky ta idelogii seredniovichoi Rusi* [Kyiv—the second Jerusalem: from the history of political thought and ideology of medieval Rus']. Kyiv: Instytut Istorii Ukrainy AN Ukrainy, 2005.

Scheidegger, Gabriele. *Endzeit. Russland am Ende des 17. Jahrhundert*. Bern: P. Lang, 1999.

Ševčenko, Ihor. "Religious Polemical Literature in the Ukrainian and Belarus' Lands in the Sixteenth and Seventeenth Centuries." In *Ukraine between East and West. Essays on Cultural History to the Early Eighteenth Century*, edited by Ihor Ševčenko, 149–163. Edmonton–Toronto: Canadian Institute of Ukrainian Studies Press, 1996.

Shevchenko, Vitalii. *Pravoslavno-katolyts'ka polemika ta problemy uniinosti v zhytti Rusi-Ukrainy doberesteis'koho periodu* [Orthodox-Catholic polemics and the problems of union in Ukrainian-Rus' life before the Union of Brest]. Kyiv: Presa Ukrainy, 2001.

Shnayderman, Shemu'el-Leyb. *The River Remembers*. New York: Horizon, 1978.

Siauciunaite-Verbickiene, Jurgita. "Nasha obshhaja kul'tura: 'vyuchennaja pamjat' o litovskom Ierusalime" [Our common culture: "the learnt memory" of Lithuanian Jerusalem]. *Ab Imperio* 4 (2004) 155–166.

Skarga, Piotr. *Kazania sejmowe* [Parliamentary sermons] (first edition, 1597), *Biblioteka Narodowa* [National Library], seria 1, no. 70, 4th ed. Wrocław, 1984.

———. "O jedności Kościoła Bożego pod jednym Pasterzem i o greckim od tej jedności odstąpieniu" [About the unity of God's Church under one shepherd and about the Greek's apostasy from this union]. In *Pamiatniki polemicheskoi literatury v zapadnoi Rusi* [Monuments of the polemical literature in Western Russia], vol. 2, 223–580. St. Petersburg: Arkheograficheskaia komissiia, 1882.

Stryjkowski, Maciej. *Kronika polska, litewska, żmódzka i wszystkiej Rusi* [Polish, Lithuanian, Żmódź and the whole Rus' Chronicle], vol. 1. Warsaw: Nakładem G.L. Glüksverga, 1846. First published 1582.

Stupperich, Robert. "Kiev–das Zweite Jerusalem. Ein Beitrag zur Geschichte des ukrainisch-russischen Nationalbewußtseins." *Zeitschrift für slavische Philologie* 12, no. 3–4 (1935): 332–354.

Tazbir, Janusz. *Piotr Skarga: szermierz kontrreformacji* [Piotr Skarga: fencer of counterreformation]. Warsaw: Wiedza Powszechna, 1978.

Tchubinski, Pavel. *Trudy etnografichesko-statisticheskoi ekspeditsii v Zapadnorusski krai* [Proceedings of ethnographic and statistic expeditions in Western Russia], vol. 1. St. Petersburg: P.A. Gildebrandt, 1872.

Tolstaia, Svetlana. "Ierusalim v slavianskoi folklornoi traditsii" [Jerusalem in Slavic and folkloristic traditions]. In *Jerusalem in Slavic Culture, Jews and Slavs*, special issue, vol. 6, edited by Wolf Moskovich, Oto Luthar, and Samuel Schwarzband, 51–68. Jerusalem–Ljubljana: Hebrew University of Jerusalem, 1999.

Torke, Hans-Joachim. "The Unloved Alliance: Political Relations between Muscovy and Ukraine in the Seventeenth Century." In *Ukraine and Russia in Their Historical Encounter*, edited by Peter J. Potichnyj, 39–66. Edmonton: Canadian Institute of Ukrainian Studies Press, 1992.

Tretjak, Józef. *Skarga w dziejach i literaturze Unii Brzeskiej* [Skarga in the history and literature of the Union of Brest]. Cracow: Akademia Umiejętności, 1912.

Tymoshenko, Leonid. *Rus'ka relihijna kultura Vil'na. Kontekst doby. Oseredky. Literatura ta knyzhnist' (XVI – persha tretyna XVII st.)* [Ruthenian religious culture of Vilnius. Context of the period. Centers. Literature and book culture (XVIth – first third of the XVIIth centuries)]. Drohobych: Kolo, 2020.

Tync, Stanisław. "Zarys dziejów wyższej szkoły Braci Polskich w Rakowie" [Outline of the history of the Raków Polish Brethren Highschool]. In *Raków–ognisko arianizmu* [Raków–the bonfire of Arianism], edited by Stanisław Cynarski, 81–172. Cracow: Państwowe Wydawnictwo Naukowe, Oddział w Krakowie, 1968.

Vyshens'kyi, Ivan. "Knizhka... ot sviatyia Afonskiia gory v napominaniie vsekh pravoslavnykh khristian...," [Book... from the Holy Athos mountain in the memory of all the Orthodox Christians]. In *Tvory* [Works], edited by Valerii Shevchuk. Kyiv: Dnipro, 1986.

Weinryb, Bernard Dov. *The Jews of Poland: a Social and Economic History of the Jewish Community in Poland from 1100 to 1800*. Philadelphia: Jewish Publication Society, 1973.

Wilczek, Piotr. *Polonia Reformata: Essays on the Polish Reformation(s)*. Göttingen: Vandenhoeck & Ruprecht, 2016.

Woloshyn, George. "The New Jerusalem," *Kyiv Post*, April 26, 2015. https://www.kyivpost.com/article/opinion/op-ed/george-woloshyn-the-new-jerusalem-387133.html.

Zavitnevich, Vladimir. *"Palinodiia" Zakharii Kopystenskogo i ieio mesto v istorii zapadnorusskoi polemiki XVI I XVII vv.* [The "Palinodiia" of Zakharii Kopystens'kyj and its place in the history of the Western Russian polemics (sixteenth and seventeenth centuries)]. Warsaw: Tipografiia Varshavskogo uchebnogo okruga, 1883.

Zdrodowski, Francis J. *The Concept of Heresy According to Cardinal Hosius*. Washington: LLC, 1947.

Zema, Valerii. "Seredniovichna tradytsiia slova, movy ta knyhy v tvorakh Vyshens'koho" [Medieval tradition of word, language, and book in the writings of Vyshens'kyi]. *Mediaevalia Ucrainica: Mental'nist' ta istoriia idei* 5 (1998): 82–92.

Zhilenko, Irina, ed. *Synopsis Kyivs'kyi* [Kyivan sinopsis]. Kyiv: VIPOL, 2002.

Part IV
Ottoman Utopias and Dystopias

Maro Kalantzopoulou

Balkan Nationalisms Against the Oriental Empire:
Balkan National Poetry and the Disavowal of a Literary System

Literatures of the Balkans have usually met with the reluctance of scholarship to examine the literary cultures of the region in any systemic terms, that is, as a network of literatures which bear some kind of relations with one another. This is true even in the few cases of scholars who have taken the literary cultures of Southeastern Europe as their object of study, since such works tend to juxtapose the separate histories of the different Balkan literatures rather than seeing them as sharing a number of features which unite them into a coherent whole. Significantly, studies on the overall literary history of the region tend to be the work of Western rather than local scholars, and consist of some distinct overviews of the literary histories of Yugoslavia, Romania, Bulgaria, Greece and Albania, generally abstaining from any attempt at conceptualizing a kind of system which would include the different literary cultures in question.[1]

What is more, this unsystematic approach which focus on the literary history of Southeastern Europe is also to be found in the accounts of the literatures of Yugoslavia, perhaps the only case of Balkan literatures to be viewed as part of a whole. Indeed, if scholars have examined the literary cultures of the Yugoslav peoples in a combined manner, they have generally done so by juxtaposing rather than systematizing the main currents of the literatures of the Serbs, Croats, and Slovenes, remaining perplexed as to what place to ascribe to the literary histories of the Bosnians and Mace-

---

[1] This is, for example, the case with one of the rare books on the literatures of the Balkans as a whole: Graciotti et al., *Storia delle letterature del sud-est europeo*.

donians, and disavowing any idea of a system consisting in the common literary history of these peoples since the demise of Yugoslavia at the end of the twentieth century.[2]

Balkan Orientalism and the Disavowal of the Balkan Interliterary System

The dismissal of the idea of a possible Balkan interliterary network characterized by the common and systematizable features of the different literary cultures of the region is somehow connected to what recent scholarship has discussed as the Balkan variant of Said's Orientalism, that is, as Balkanism, and, more precisely, as it will be argued, to a kind of internal Balkanism. In other words, the reluctance of scholarship to see the Balkan literary cultures as linked by a certain kind of relations and thus contributing to a supranational literary system should be examined by means of a discussion of the Balkan colonial and postcolonial, or rather, of the Balkan imperial and post-imperial, condition. This last approach involves the examination of the position of the Balkans within a multilevel network of relations, namely, of the relations between East and West, between the Balkans and the East, between the Balkans and the West, and within the Balkans themselves.

To begin with, it is a particular analysis of the relations between East and West that underlies Said's conceptualization of Orientalism.[3] The concept refers to the representation of the East by the West, and more precisely, to the negative representations of the East as the locus of backwardness and irrationalism, as part of a discourse that takes the historical development of the West as a coherent and canonical model, and which accounted for the interests of three Western imperial forces, namely the British, French and American empires. At this level of the discussion of the relations between East and West, the Balkans are assimilated to the East which is objectified by the powerful subject that is the West. Following Said's conceptualization of Orientalism, Balkanism has thus been described as the negative, reductive and Western-centric representations of

2   See Barac, Antun, *Jugoslavenska književnost*; Meriggi, *Le letterature della Jugoslavia*; Cronia, *Storia della letteratura serbo-croata*.
3   Said, *Orientalism*.

the peoples living in a region of Southeastern Europe which is historically characterized by backwardness, irrationalism and an incomplete adherence to modernity, and more recently by a violent and unintelligible split into small, powerless, and underdeveloped states.[4]

An analysis of the other levels to be taken into account in the discussion of the network of relations in which the Balkans are involved raises several questions with regard to the conceptualization of a Balkanism based upon the assimilation of the Balkans to an East which is negatively objectified by the West.[5] While Orientalism involves a relation of inequality between the dominant colonizer and the dominated colonized in the objectification of the East by the West, the same does not apply to the case of the Balkans: the negative representation of the Balkan peoples is not the work of the dominant Ottoman imperial center, but again of the West, which is not in this case the colonizing subject. Contrary to the East involved in Said's Orientalism, the Balkans, rather than making part of the Western empire, have been dominated by a political and cultural center which itself belongs to the Saidian East. The same would largely apply to the imperial center that the Balkans had depended on before submitting to the Ottomans, specifically the Byzantine Empire.

Contrary to the categories involved in Said's conceptualization of Orientalism, the Balkans did not become the object of a negative criticism on the part of the imperial center by which they were dominated, nor did this center belong to a West which was seeking to construct the Other. What is more, this Ottoman imperial center significantly differed from Western colonial empires. In contrast to its contemporary, the Spanish empire, the Ottoman empire, did not apply any generalized policy of linguistic, religious and overall cultural assimilation of its Balkan subjects. This condition made so that the Balkan peoples, with the exception of the Islamized Bosnians and Albanians, did not fully integrate into Ottoman culture and, even if various aspects of their popular cultures shared much in common with their Ottoman counterparts, their cultural elites evolved largely independently of Ottoman influence.

---

4 Todorova, *Imagining the Balkans*.
5 On this debate see Fleming, "Orientalism, the Balkans, and Balkan Historiography," 1218–33; Goldsworthy, *Inventing Ruritania: The Imperialism of the Imagination*; Stamatopoulos and Tsimbiridou, eds., *Orientalismos sta oria. Apo ta othomanika Valkania sti synchroni Mesi Anatoli*.

The view according to which the Ottoman empire, on which the Balkans depended—varyingly until the beginning, the middle or the end of the nineteenth century—is part of what Said problematizes as the East, is held not only by the West but also by the peoples of the Balkans themselves. This means that while the postcolonial condition of the former subjects of the Western colonial empires involves a dimension of hegemony,[6] in the sense that the colonized themselves internalized the idea of their inferiority to the colonizing Western culture, the peoples of the Balkans largely based their national discourse on their differentiation from the Eastern imperial center on which they depended. The Balkan peoples, often under the influence of their compatriots of the diaspora, finally opposed what they saw as an obscurantist and premodern Ottoman imperial center, their submission to which was blamed for their belatedness with respect to the flourishing West.

Having thus examined the Balkan imperial and post-imperial condition in the light of the discussion of the relations between East and West, as well as of the relations by which the Balkans are linked to each one of them, let us now turn to the relations between the different Balkan peoples themselves. If, as we saw, the Balkan peoples somewhere in the nineteenth century constructed their national discourse based on their opposition to what they considered as a backward and premodern—as an Eastern, in Said's sense—imperial center, they progressively also differentiated themselves from what they described as their premodern and barbarous neighbor.[7] Nineteenth-century nationalism of the ethnic and perennialist[8] rather than the civic and modernist[9] variant, early twentieth-century warfare, post-1945 nationalism within the socialist framework and, in the Greek case, the opposition to communism, all incited the Balkan peoples to develop negative views of their neighbors, to whom they ascribed an essentially Balkan character that they denied for themselves. More recently, the progressive adherence of some of the Balkan states to the structures of the European Union intensified the distance between those who considered themselves as part of the West and those who they saw as their underdeveloped, truly Balkan neighbors.

---

6   Gramsci, *Prison Notebooks*.
7   Bakić-Hayden, "Nesting Orientalisms: The Case of Former Yugoslavia," 917–31.
8   Smith, *National Identity*; Smith, *Nations and Nationalism in a Global Era*.
9   Anderson, *Imagined Communities: Reflections on the Origin and Spread of Nationalism*.

At the level of the intra-Balkan relations, there is, on the part of each one of the peoples of the region, a double questioning of the validity of their neighbors as acceptable partners. On the one hand, there is Orientalism as a discourse which is articulated by the peoples of the Balkans themselves, consisting in a negative representation of their Ottoman past, and accounting for the Orientalist representations made of the Balkan neighbor, who is disqualified by having a strong Ottoman legacy, as being belated and premodern, as belonging to the East rather than to the West, that is, as merely being Balkan. On the other hand, there is a kind of internal Balkanism which additionally causes the different cultures of the region to reject one another as being violent, oppressive and authoritarian, or, from the point of view of the non-socialist Greece, as being an enemy to Western progressive social-democracy and capitalism, as irrationally and unintelligibly splitting into minuscule powerless states, and, more recently, as still being Balkan when other states of the region culturally and institutionally belong to the West.

The Balkan imperial and post-imperial condition, as it has been so far argued, involves the historical development of certain political and ideological processes which prevented not only the Balkan peoples in general, but also their scholarship, from conceiving of the different cultures of the region as part of a common system. As far as literary studies are concerned, in symbolic and ideological terms, the widespread view according to which one's neighboring Balkan state was characterized by belatedness, backwardness and an essentially Oriental character accounts for the underestimation of the numerous features shared by the different literary cultures of the region. Thus, the Balkan variant of Said's Orientalism as discussed previously, that is, Orientalism as invoked not by Western but by Balkan subjects, explains, together with other factors, the reluctance of scholarship to examine a given Balkan national literature in its relations with other literatures of the region that were considered to be part of an Oriental, negatively connoted culture.

If scholars thus discarded any idea of studying a given Balkan literature in its connections with its counterparts in the region, they did, however, insist on the relations it established with Western, namely French, Italian and German, literatures.[10] This concern, on the one hand, is indicative of a

10 This is illustrated in the writings of some of the most distinguished scholars in the literary studies of

strong historical movement whose outcome was that the Balkan cultures, by the end of the eighteenth century, began to fall increasingly under the influence of the cultural evolutions taking place in the West. On the other hand, it illustrates the determination with which the different Balkan cultures, in an Orientalist manner, rejected the Ottoman/Oriental tradition as culturally ineffective, and blamed it for what they saw as their own lack of progress in their endeavor to catch up with the Western centers. It is not without significance, in this sense, that, while the Balkan peoples, at least at first, tended to develop the ethnic and perennialist rather than the civic and modernist variant of nationalist discourse, seeking to trace their origins back to antiquity and the medieval times, they were nevertheless concerned with aligning themselves with the accomplishments of the Western centers.

From this point of view, what differentiates in symbolic and ideological terms Balkan from, say, Latin American scholarship in relation to their attitudes with respect to the totality of the cultures of their respective regions, is the representation that each one of them makes of both the imperial center on which they depend—significantly, for roughly the same period going from the fifteenth to the nineteenth centuries—and of their neighbors. In other words, if scholarship refused to identify a Balkan interliterary network while it did see one in the case of Spanish Latin America,[11] it is due to the fact that the Balkan peoples developed an Orientalist view with respect to the Ottoman empire and their Balkan fellows, while Latin Americans had based their cultural development on the ideal of their assimilation to the culture of the empire—a Western empire, to be sure.

The ideological processes discussed previously, consisting in the disavowal of the idea of a Balkan interliterary network as linked to the negative views that the Balkans peoples held of the Ottoman imperial center and their Balkan fellows, cannot be dissociated from the political processes that determined the Balkan imperial and post-imperial condition. Orientalism as practiced by the Balkan peoples, with the rejection of the Ot-

their respective Balkan countries. On the Greek case, see Dimaras, *A History of Modern Greek Literature*; on the Croatian case, see Barac, *Hrvatska književnost od Preporoda do stvaranja Jugoslavij.*

11 See Ureña, *Literary Currents in Hispanic America*; Coutinho, *Literatura comparada na América Latina. Ensaios.*

toman in favor of Western culture, is in this sense linked to the fact that the Balkan cultures did not generally integrate into the culture of the empire; and this relative Balkan cultural autonomy is due to the fact that the Ottoman center did not, for the most part, implement policies aiming for the linguistic, religious and overall cultural assimilation of its subjects.

The cultural policy of the Ottoman empire allowed for the development and expression of the different Balkan cultures, and this had two intertwined outcomes. On the symbolic side, as has already been discussed, the Balkan peoples, rather than adhering to the culture of the empire, sought to reinforce their national identity, among other means, by producing negative images of the Ottomans. From a more pragmatic point of view, the material conditions, among which is notably the condition of linguistic unity, were not fulfilled in order for the Balkan peoples to regard themselves as part of a common cultural system. In contrast with Latin American subjects of the Spanish empire, the indifference of the Ottoman center towards the issue of the acculturation of its subjects had as a consequence not only that the Balkan peoples did not abandon their national languages in favor of the language of the empire, but also that they remained linguistically isolated from one another.

FROM THE EMPIRE TO THE NATION: ASPECTS OF THE BALKAN INTERLITERARY SYSTEM

The dismissal of the idea of a network of connected Balkan literatures is linked to certain symbolic factors and a historical material reality which explains, not only in ideological but also in practical terms, the reluctance of scholarship to undertake this task. Under these circumstances, criticism privileged the study of the Balkan literary cultures at the level of the different national literatures, or otherwise sought to explore the links between these national literatures and the literatures of the West, in an asymmetrical relation where the latter served as a canonical influence for the former. By doing that, scholars opted for a reductive conceptualization of Balkan literature, which they saw either as a sum of unconnected national literatures or as a series of literatures at the European periphery which had to be examined from the point of view of their capacity to catch up with developments in the Western centers.

The study of Balkan literatures either at the national level or in their relations exclusively with the literatures of the West involved a certain interpretation of historical reality, which refused to take into account the numerous features that suggested the existence of a common Balkan interliterary network. Criticism of the last decades has stressed the historicized character of such perceptions and has suggested alternative interpretations for non-Western literary cultures, often seeking to explore the literary manifestations of processes that gave rise to hybrid and transculturated identities.[12] This kind of criticism opted, in various cases, for the conceptualization of supranational interliterary communities, the constituent parts of which shared a common culture and had to be studied jointly.

Scholarship that has systematically dealt with the theorization of the concept of interliterary networks has identified several factors which account for the conceptualization of a given interliterary community, like geography, ethnicity, language, religion, political and administrative organization and ideology.[13] Among these factors some could probably be discarded and others could be added; the idea, however, remains that interliterary networks should be seen as historical processes rather than static totals of literatures. As historical categories, cultural—and literary—communities are constituted based upon political and cultural factors such as the ones identified here. However, the particular configurations these factors may take depending on historical processes which are specific to the context in question, may account for the invisibility of cultural networks that could be otherwise identified, as is the case with the Balkan literatures we have been discussing.

Taking the case of what would be a Balkan interliterary community as a historical category diachronically determined by cultural and political factors, the specific configurations that these have taken may explain why the literary cultures of the region have not generally been seen as such. Taking the factors which have been identified by scholarship in the matter, the Balkan peoples have been ethnically diverse and, more importantly, have never attained linguistic unity. At the same time, the political and administrative entity on which they depended from the fifteenth

---

12   See Glissant, *Introduction à une poétique du divers*; Canclini, *Culturas híbridas. Estrategias para entrar y salir de la modernidad*; Rama, *Transculturación narrativa en América Latina*.
13   Ďurišin, *Theory of Literary Comparatistics*.

to the nineteenth centuries (the Ottoman empire) imposed a kind of unity based upon the economic obligations of its subjects towards the central state, but allowed for relative political autonomy, and ascribe a great deal of authority to the religious community that was the basis of the administrative system. Even under the socialist order, the political organization of the different Balkan states—let alone the tension between non-socialist Greece and the rest of the Balkans—was characterized by a significant nationalist concern, and did not allow for the development of the idea of belonging to a common cultural system.

These obstacles to the idea of Balkan cultural unity notwithstanding, an alternative interpretation of the specific configurations of the same cultural and political factors would allow us to discern the points where the cultures of the region did converge. With respect to the linguistic factor, the Balkan peoples never formed a homogeneous linguistic community, but there are some aspects of linguistic unity which can be observed. On the one hand, at the level of the Balkan vernaculars, there was the group of peoples who were speakers of the different South Slavic languages. On the other hand, and what is more important for the Balkan peoples as a whole, was that a Balkan-wide elite had established itself since the centuries of the Byzantine domination in the region which used Greek as the language of the church, higher education and literature, a tendency which was still strong in nineteenth-century Bulgaria and Albania. There was also the Greek-speaking elite of the Phanariots, who assumed authority in the religious matters of Greek Christianity in the external affairs of the Ottoman empire, as well as in the government of the Danubian principalities.

The political organizations of which the Balkans became part in different periods of history were thus the common framework within which the Balkan cultures evolved over the course of the centuries, and this coexistence led to the configuration of a shared cultural heritage. The aforementioned establishment of certain Balkan Greek-speaking elites is an example of these common cultural developments that are linked to specific historico-political processes, which goes back to the period of Byzantine domination in the region. An important Bulgarian, Greek-speaking elite was formed under the pressure of the policies of acculturation employed by the Byzantine Empire, and its continuous presence until the nineteenth century is further linked to the establishment of a flourishing Greek bourgeoisie in the eighteenth century, to the existence of important Greek-speaking educational institutions which received students from all over the Balkans, to the role of Greek intellectuals as carriers of ideas of Enlightenment and revolution, and to the advent of the Greek national and independence movements several decades before the Bulgarian ones.

The historico-political processes and their associated cultural developments had as a consequence the configuration of a cultural network which, to an important extent, was common to the Balkans. To stay with our previous example, the policies of acculturation which were implemented by the Byzantine Empire led not only to the establishment of Greek as the erudite language of the Balkan elites, as we have already seen, but also to important literary developments which were largely common to the peoples of the Balkans. Such developments include the emergence of the Bulgarian,[14] Macedonian, and Serbian[15] medieval literatures, after the introduction of the Christian written heritage by Cyril and Methodius, based upon the translation and adaptation of Byzantine Greek texts, notably the writings of Church Fathers such as John Chrysostom, Gregory of Nazianzus, Basil of Caesarea and John Damascene. The literary cultures of the Balkans evolved in parallel ways during the medieval period, with the use of the same source materials and the cultivation of common genres, which consisted in pieces of writing of religious and non-religious character, the former including hymns, lives of Saints, panegyrics and apocrypha, and the latter, panegyrics of cosmic persons, chronicles, philosophical treatises, poetry, epistolary literature, epitaphs and legal literature.

Some further important parallels in the development of the Balkan literatures can be observed during the post-Byzantine Ottoman period until the end of the eighteenth century, when the influence of Greek literature continued to be strong, at least in the Bulgarian case, with respect to both religious and secular literature. This shared tradition involved a lasting Greek influence within Balkan literary cultures and is illustrated by the example of the *damaskini*—a sixteenth-century collection of predica-

---

14 Moser, *A History of Bulgarian Literature, 865–1944*; Castellan and Vrinat-Nikolov, *Histoire de la Bulgarie: au pays des roses*; Igov, *Kratka istorija na bălgarskata literatura*. For all subsequent references to Bulgarian literature, refer to these sources.

15 Barac, *A History of Yugoslav Literature*; Deretić, *Kratka istorija srpske književnosti*. For all subsequent references to Serbian literature, refer to these sources.

tions by Damaskinos Stoudites, a Greek associated with the circle of the Venetian diaspora, which was translated and repeatedly copied since the sixteenth century, and remained popular in eighteenth-century Bulgaria. Part of the same tradition were numerous translations and copies of both older and more contemporary Greek texts which continued to circulate until the latter part of the eighteenth century within the same Bulgarian cultural context.

Apart from the kind of formal literature that has already been mentioned, the Balkan peoples shared an interest in a popular literature consisting in translations, mostly from intermediary Greek versions, of texts whose popularity was enormous until the end of the nineteenth century. This popular literature includes texts of Oriental—but usually not Ottoman—origin, as well as of medieval romances and tales, such as *Syntipas*, *Barlaam and Ioasaph*, *Stephanites and Ichnelates*, the *Arabian Nights*, the stories of Nasreddin Hodja, Alexander the Great, The Trojan War, and the Empress Theophana. In the field of popular literature, the other genre which developed in strikingly similar ways throughout the Balkan literary cultures, and which, contrary to other aspects of the Balkan interliterary system, has sometimes been studied in its inter-Balkan dimension, is oral popular poetry or the folksong, together with the associated traditions of folk tales and other orally transmitted literary materials.

So far we have discussed aspects of a Balkan interliterary network consisting in common developments as linked to influences whose source is internal to the Balkan region. Toward the end of the eighteenth and during the nineteenth centuries, however, there was a shift in the orientation of the Balkan interliterary system. Often under the guidance of intellectuals based outside of the frontiers of their future national states, in the Austro-Hungarian Empire, France, or the Danubian principalities, the Balkan literary cultures by that time became increasingly influenced by political and cultural evolutions in Western Europe. The ideas of the Enlightenment, mostly in its French version, then the philosophical and literary doctrines of Romanticism, in its German, English and French versions, together with elements of the European Neoclassicism of an earlier period, and finally Realism and the currents of the second half of the nineteenth century, became the sources of inspiration for Balkan literatures at the time of nationalisms. Interestingly, Ottoman literary culture, which, for the historico-political reasons that have already been invoked, had virtually no connection with Balkan literatures during the long period of the Ottoman domination in the region, was also radically transformed in the second half of the nineteenth-century, abandoning the traditionally cultivated forms in favor of the nineteenth century Western European genres.[16]

Having examined certain aspects of the Balkan interliterary network, which, we have to emphasize, constitute but a partial account of a complex and scarcely, if at all, studied phenomenon, we shall make some remarks concerning the body of literatures in question. We have seen that the literary cultures of the Balkans, broadly speaking, received no influence from the Ottoman center on which they depended from roughly the fifteenth to the nineteenth centuries, and we have noted that even the widely circulated popular Oriental literature was usually not of Ottoman origin. However, this does not apply in the cases of Bosnia[17] and partly of Albania,[18] whose populations, having converted to Islam, had to an important extent integrated into Ottoman culture. The literary cultures of these parts of the Ottoman Empire developed under the influence of the imperial center, and cultivated the Ottoman literary forms, and featured texts written in the local languages but using the Ottoman script of the time, or the development of Balkan versions of the Ottoman genre of divan poetry.

Another precision should be made with regard to the Balkan cases which were not controlled by the Ottomans but by other imperial forces, and whose literary cultures developed independently of the evolutions in the Ottoman-dominated Balkans. Such cases are Slovenian literature, which developed under the influences of the Holy Roman Empire, then the Habsburg Monarchy, and the literatures of Crete[19] or Dalmatia,[20] both influenced by the literature of the Republic of Venice. The importance of such cases of Balkan literary cultures under Western, for instance Frankish or Venetian, rule, is such that literatures of this kind is often considered as the only valuable pieces of writing in the otherwise Otto-

16 Bombaci, *Storia della letteratura turca.*
17 Rizvić, *Književno stvaranje muslimanskih pisaca u Bosni i Hercegovini u doba Austrougarske vladavine.*
18 Elsie, *History of Albanian Literature*; idem, *Albanian Literature: A Short History.*
19 Holton, *Literature and Society in Renaissance Crete.*
20 Jelčić, *Povijest hrvatske književnosti.*

man-dominated, and for this reason culturally underdeveloped, respective future national territories. Importantly, these cases of Balkan cultures which developed under the influence of a non-Ottoman, Western imperial power, are indicative of tendencies within the Balkan interliterary network which also present significant systematicity, and should for this reason be examined within the framework of a common Balkan cultural system.

National Identity, Western Culture and Anti-Ottomanism in Solomos, Mažuranić and Njegoš

The nineteenth century was for the Balkan peoples a period of radical transformations, in terms both of political and cultural history. On the political side, historical evolutions include the nationalist movements of the Serbs and Greeks against the Ottoman Empire at the beginning of the century, those of the Slovenes, Croats and Romanians against the Austro-Hungarian Empire around the revolutionary year 1848, then, in the latter part of the nineteenth century, those of the Bulgarians and Bosnians, and later (and perhaps more reluctantly), those of the Albanians and Macedonians against the declining Ottoman empire.[21] Linked to these political evolutions are certain cultural developments whose manifestations are strikingly analogous to different European cultures, both of the center and the periphery. A major tendency among these developments was Romanticism, a heterogeneous movement which is closely tied to political upheavals of the time, in Western Europe and the Balkans alike. In what follows we shall focus on three major expressions of the Balkan version of Romanticism, namely on the major compositions by Dionysios Solomos, Ivan Mažuranić and Petar Petrović-Njegoš. The three poems suggest a specific conceptualization of national identity which is based on the construction of a national space-time of an idealized local Christian community in opposition to an essentially Oriental, Ottoman/Muslim, imperial factor.

---

21 Jelavich and Jelavich, *The Establishment of the Balkan National States, 1804–1920*; Jelavich, *History of the Balkans*, Vol. 1, *Eighteenth and Nineteenth Centuries* and Vol. 2, *Twentieth Century*.

Idealizing the Nation: Between the People and the West

Dionysios Solomos's "The Free Besieged"[22] (1826–1849), Ivan Mažuranić's *The Death of Smail-Aga Čengić*[23] (1846) and Petar Petrović-Njegoš's *The Mountain Wreath*[24] (1847), have been unanimously qualified by criticism of different historical periods as the masterpieces of the authors, who are considered as the respective national poets of the Greeks, Croats and Serbs. At the core of the three poems is a local Balkan people's struggle against the representatives of the Ottoman forces, depicted through the representation of a single specific episode which opposes the two sides. Solomos's text is inspired by a historical event which took place in the first half of the nineteen century, during the Greek war of independence, namely the second siege of the Greek town of Missolonghi by the allied Ottoman and Egyptian forces, and of the heroic exodus of its inhabitants. Mažuranić's poem represents a historical event of the first half of the nineteen century, when Muslim Herzegovinian Smail-aga Čengić was killed in an ambush organized by Montenegrin Christians. And Njegoš's poem depicts an event supposed to have occurred at the end of the seventeenth century, which resulted in the massacre of the Montenegrin Muslims by Montenegrin Christians of the region.

Thus the three poems feature an important nationalist concern, and a patriotic subject matter which is characteristic of much nineteenth-century Balkan literary writing—even if, in the case of the Balkans, national questions are often associated with broader social and political concerns, as it is illustrated by the internal conflicts during the Greek war of independence, by the fact that the first Serbian revolt broke out as an opposition not to the Ottoman center but to Ottoman notables who had recently established themselves in the region and whose actions were directed to counter central Ottoman power, or by the fact that the claims of the 1848 Croat national movement, rather than aiming at national independence, included the use of Croatian rather than the newly introduced Hungarian as an official language and the end of feudal obligations towards the Hun-

---

22 The consulted edition is Solomos, *Poiimata kai peza*.

23 We have used the French translation: Mažuranić, *La mort de Smaïl-aga Tchenguitch*.

24 We have used the French translation: Petrović Njegoš, *La couronne de montagne: épisode historique vers la fin du XVII siècle*, trans. Antoine Sidoti and Christian Cheminade (Paris: Non Lieu, 2010).

garian crown. From this point of view, as far as literature is concerned, the nationalist component seems to be a particular characteristic of what would be a Balkan version of the dominating movement of Romanticism. The poems that we are currently concerned with are inscribed in this literary framework, and are in this sense characteristic of the realizations of the Romantic movement in the Greek, Croatian and Serbian contexts.

Let us recall that Greek Romanticism developed in two different variants: one around the Athenian capital, and the other in the Ionian Islands. The former, traditionally referred to as the Romantic school of Greek literature, engages in a nationalist discourse of a mostly perennialist character, invoking the ancient Greek tradition and using the archaic language or *katharevousa*. It features a concern with the classical past which on the one hand could be ascribed to Neoclassicism, but which on the other hand can be seen as the Greek expression of the Romantic quest for the national past. The latter, whose leading figure is Solomos himself, is traditionally discussed as merely the poetry of the Seven Islands, but has more recently[25] been seen as Romantic in character, in spite of the fact that Andreas Kalvos (the second major poet of the region) is Neoclassicist in tone and certain Neoclassicist tendencies can be found in some of the early poems by Solomos. The Romanticism of the Seven Islands involves the use of the vernacular language or *demotike* and the exploration of the popular literary tradition, thus subscribing to the Western Romantic concern with the concept of the people and its cultural achievements. At the same time, Romantic (and Classico-Romantic)[26] authors of both the Athenian center and the Ionian Islands, shared an interest in broader social and political issues, the former often explicitly opposed to the Bavarian government of the newly founded independent Greek state, and the latter sometimes criticizing the British ruling class which replaced Venetian, then short-lived Napoleonic, domination in the islands.

Nineteenth-century Croatian literature was marked by the ideas of Illyrism,[27] a movement which sought to link the Croats and South Slavs with the ancient Illyrians, supported the idea of the unity of the South

---

25 Veloudis, "O eptanisiakos, o athinaikos kai o europaikos romantismos," 97–124; Garantoudis, "I logotechnia 1830–1880," 195–210.

26 Ibid.

27 On the Croatian Illyrist movement, see Frangeš and Živančević, *Ilirizam, realizam*.

Slavs and studied their cultural traditions, demanded the use of Croatian rather than the newly imposed Hungarian as the language of administration and culture in the Croatian lands, opposed the Hungarian rule as well that of the Ottomans who dominated their fellow South Slavic peoples, and promoted the cause of Croatian national identity. The concerns of Illyrism, of which Mažuranić himself was a major proponent, were to be maintained in literature of the latter part of the nineteenth century, which is characterized by a more accentuated Romantic interest in both the Croatian past and the living traditions of the Croatian people. Nineteenth-century Serbian literature,[28] on the other hand, evolved through the transition from a Neoclassicist tone to a more Romantic writing—a transition which can be observed in Njegoš's writing as well—which refers equally either to the Serbian medieval past or to the idea of the Serbian people, its cultural tradition and its struggles against the Turks. As in the Greek case, there is also a special concern with the language question, which consists in the gradual abandonment of the archaic Slavo-Serb in favor of the vernacular.[29]

Situating themselves within the context of these broader intellectual movements, Solomos,[30] Mažuranić[31] and Njegoš[32] present some important similarities in their use of specific aspects of the cultural production of what they conceive as the people, as is illustrated, importantly, by the choice they make in terms of linguistic and stylistic devices. Solomos opted for the use of the vernacular as opposed to the archaic register, and so did Njegoš, as opposed to the formal Slavo-Serb of the time, while both feature elements of their local dialects, of the Ionian Islands and Montenegro respectively. Mažuranić, on the other hand, had close links with Ljudevit Gaj, the major intellectual of the Illyrian movement, which established, among others, the use of the *štokavski* variant, the most popular dialect of the Croatian and the Serbian tongue, which was by this point largely unified. As far as versification is concerned, the first draft of "The

---

28 On the Serbian Romantic movement, see Popović, *Romantizam*.

29 Interestingly, the question of the language register does not seem to have been an issue for Croats, since the use of Latin as the language not only of the Church but also of the administration within the framework of the Hungarian crownlands until the end of the eighteenth century prevented the configuration of an archaizing Croatian variant.

30 As a general introduction to Solomos's life and work see Mackridge, *Dionysios Solomos*.

31 On Mažuranić's life and work see Barac, *Mažuranić*.

32 On Njegoš's life and work see Popović, Latković and Deretić, *P. P. Njegoš: 1813–1963*.

Free Besieged" was planned to be written in the form of eight-line lyric stanzas, while the more important and later composed second and third drafts are characterized by the use of the fifteen-syllable verse of Greek folksong. *The Mountain Wreath* is for the most part written in the ten-syllable verse of the Serbian epic oral popular poetry, and *The Death of Smail-Aga Čengić* features both ten-syllable and eight-syllable verses.

These linguistic and stylistic choices of the three poets are indicative of a common concern with the idea of the people and of their interest in aligning themselves with the popular literary cultures of their contexts. The poets' contact with the literary traditions of their respective peoples has anyway been repeatedly underlined by scholarship.[33] Solomos had become acquainted with Greek literature which had been written in the vernacular, especially the Byzantine novel and the literature of Renaissance Crete, and Mažuranić had extensively studied the literature of seventeenth-century Dubrovnik, and had even been asked to complete, by adding two stanzas, the most important work of Ivan Gundulić, this movement's major representative. Interestingly, both poets were in close contact with earlier writing of their respective literary cultures which developed under the influence of the Western, and notably the Italian, context.

The three were also familiar with the tradition of oral popular poetry of their peoples, which presented a great deal of common features. This popular tradition had by the beginning of the nineteen century become an object of study for local and Western intellectuals. In Serbia, Vuk Karadžić, who is also largely responsible for the abandonment of the Slavo-Serb and the foundation of the modern Serbian literary language based upon the spoken vernacular, undertook the task of collecting oral folk poetic material, and the same was done in the Croatian case by the representatives of the Illyrian movement, while Greek folk poetry was by that time being collected and published according to different methodologies which served different political and cultural interests. This oral popular tradition profoundly influenced Solomos, Mažuranić and Njegoš, and various features of their works have been linked to their use of precisely this kind of material.

---

33   On Solomos and the Greek cultural tradition see Kapsomenos, *O Solomos kai i elliniki politismiki paradosi.*

The concern with the manifestations of an older literary tradition written in the vernacular as well as with folk poetry, however, does not only illustrate the poets' interest in the specific traditions of the people of their local context; rather, it is indicative of the poets' adherence to a more general Romantic tendency, which by that time privileged the idea of the people and the study of their cultural achievements. Indeed, this tendency was a strong component of Western (particularly German) Romanticism, and was linked to the quest for what would constitute the national identity of a people whose unification into a national state was to take place some decades later. The concept of the people was used in this context to forge a common national consciousness, and this had as a consequence an increasing interest in the exploration of popular tradition, and a concern with the people's origins, which had to be sought in a period as far in the past as possible. As far as the three poets we are currently discussing are concerned, their interest in the culture of their respective peoples is linked not only to a preoccupation with locality and the national questions of their contexts, but also with their adherence precisely to a Western cultural movement.

If thus Solomos, Mažuranić and Njegoš seem to inscribe themselves in a Romantic tradition which involves a specific use of the idea of the people, they also share an interest in nineteenth-century philosophical ideas, and especially in German idealism,[34] as linked to the education they received that allowed them a more or less direct contact with intellectual evolutions in the West. Solomos was educated in the Italian context, and studied Western literature and philosophy in its Italian, English, French and German versions. Mažuranić received an Italian education too, studied philosophy, and became familiar with French, English, Slavic, and classic literatures. Njegoš, although he did not receive the same quality of education as the other two poets, also studied Italian, and be-

---

34 On Solomos's contact with the ideas of German idealism, see Veloudis, *Dionysios Solomos: Romantiki poiisi kai poiitiki. Oi germanikes piges*; idem, *Dionysiou Solomou "Stochasmoi" stous "Eleutherous Poliorkismenous"*; and idem, "O eptanisiakos, o athinaikos kai o europaikos romantismos," 79–96. On Njegoš's philosophical and political ideas we have consulted, apart from the above cited works, Aubin, *Visions historiques et politiques dans l'œuvre poétique de P. P. Njegoš*; Prulovich, *Religious Philosophy of Prince-Bishop Njegosh of Montenegro, 1813–1851*; Petronijević, *Filozofija u "Gorskom vijencu"*; Marković, ed., *Društveno-politička misao Njegoša: Primljeno na VI skupu Odeljenja društvenih nauka od. 20. septembra 2005. godine.*

came acquainted with the ideas of the Enlightenment and German idealism, as well as with French, English and Russian nineteenth-century literatures and the Greek classics. As far as the German philosophical context
is concerned, Solomos had become familiar with these ideas through the
translations which were prepared for him by people of his circle, and importantly Ermannos Lountzis, who had studied in Germany and was connected with some of the major representatives of the philosophical movements of the period. Njegoš, likewise, became acquainted with the ideas
of German idealism through his tutor Sima Milutinović Sarajlija, a Serbian intellectual who had studied for some time in Germany, where he met
important figures of the philosophical circles of the time.

The poems of Solomos, Mažuranić and Njegoš feature various elements of German idealism, including, importantly, several elements of
the philosophical thought of Hegel. The three poems evolve around an
episode which illustrates the fight between a national community and its
enemy, the identity of the former depending on the oppositional relation
that it bears with the latter. In Solomos's poem, the people of Missolonghi are besieged by the Ottoman and Egyptian armies and doomed to be
defeated by their allied forces, in Mažuranić's poem Christian Montenegrins are faced with extreme violence inflicted by the forces of the Herzegovinian Muslim Smail-Aga Čengić, and *The Mountain Wreath* depicts
the opposition between Christian and Muslim Montenegrins. In the idealistic universe of the three poems, this opposition is not limited to the
material relation between two national communities, but rather, the entities in question are taken to incarnate, at a more abstract level, different
moral qualities. The Christian communities of the three poems represent
the good and fair and while Muslims are associated with the evil and cruel, as it is illustrated by the suffering that the latter inflict to the former in
Solomos's and Mažuranić's poems, and by the mere description of the latter as the personification of evil in Njegoš's case.

This subject matter of a dialectics tending to the observation of some
universal moral qualities is nevertheless situated in a clearly designated
historical context, which is the framework of the historical—or supposedly historical, in Njegoš's case—events which are at the core of the three
poems, namely the exodus of the people of Missolonghi while the city is
under siege, the assassination of Smail-Aga Čengić and the massacre of

the Muslim Montenegrins, respectively. The first two constitute major events that marked the national life of the Greeks and Yugoslavs and the reader can easily situate them in their historical context of the first half of the nineteenth century; and Njegoš clearly designates, in the full title of his poem, the seventeenth century as the temporal framework of the events he describes. In this sense, what ascribes to the material oppositions between Christians and Muslims the aspiration to universality is not a supposed lack of temporal and spatial indications, but rather the description of a historical context which allows one to observe the moral superiority of the former as opposed to the moral insufficiency of the latter. History is furthermore seen as a process towards a kind of idealistic end which coincides with the ideal of freedom. This is perhaps clearest in Solomos's poem, where the besieged are increasingly faced with suffering, against which they gradually develop an apparatus of moral defense which allows them to attain freedom by opting for death. Indeed, the people of Missolonghi are subject to physical and moral suffering, as they have no provisions, have to fight against the temptation of nature in springtime, are conscious of the superiority of the enemy forces, and have complete certainty that they are bound to be killed while attempting their exodus. In response to this, their initial uncertainty is replaced by increasing determination to go towards death, a decision which is hailed by the symbols of the nation and Orthodoxy. The act will be finally acknowledged by Greece herself, in a scene which is replaced in the third draft by the description of a state of serenity in the face of imminent death.

A similar framework can be found in Mažuranić's and Njegoš's poems. As in "The Free Besieged," in *The Death of Smail-Aga Čengić* Christian Montenegrins are submitted to the violence inflicted by the forces of the aga, against which they progressively develop a mechanism of defense which goes from submission and suffering to forms of defying and questioning the aga's power, and finally to the decision to kill him, with a view to defending religious and moral values and attaining freedom. Njegoš's poem has a quite different organization, since it is the collective subject of the Christian Montenegrins who decide to exterminate Montenegrins who have converted to Islam; there too, however, an idealistic dimension is ascribed to the opposition between Christian Montenegrins and their Islamized compatriots. The initial dilemma of *vladika* Danilo with respect to the utility of an act of violence is transformed into determination after a series of interventions by different characters who expose the moral differences which separate them from the Muslims, and, once the attempt to persuade the latter to reconvert to Christianity has failed, the extermination of Muslim Montenegrins finally takes place with a view to defending Serbdom and Christianity and to attaining freedom.

Orientalizing the Nation's Enemy: National Space-Time and Anti-Ottomanism

The opposition between a Christian community of the Balkans and the representatives of Ottoman rule, the latter including members of the community who converted to Islam, is, as we have seen, a central idea in the major poetic compositions of Solomos, Mažuranić and Njegoš. In spite of the idealistic dimensions that can be ascribed to it, the choice of this opposition as the subject matter illustrates the poets' concern with designating a national community whose identity is structured through its political and cultural/religious opposition to another community.

The opposition of the Christian community to the representatives of the Ottoman/Muslim factor evolves in the three poems in distinct ways, which can be seen as a gradual movement from defense to revenge and from there to aggression and offense. In Solomos's poem the decision of the people of Missolonghi to venture their exodus and die is presented as a means of defense against the allied Ottoman and Egyptian forces who maintain them under siege. In Mažuranić's poem the murder of Muslim Smail-Aga Čengić is seen as an act of revenge undertaken by Christian Montenegrins who are subject to the atrocities of the aga, and to which they are incited by a Muslim whose father has been killed after his disagreement with respect to the violent repression of the Christians. In Njegoš's poem the decision of Christian Montenegrins to banish native Muslims from the country is presented as an act of aggression and offense which takes the form of an attack which is not a response to violence or to a process of subjection of the former to the latter; rather, it is justified by the need to fight against a religious community which is seen as an obstacle to national unity and to the establishment of a national identity based upon the invocation of the idea of a Christian Serbdom going back to medieval times.

We have seen that a fundamental position is ascribed by Solomos, Mažuranić and Njegoš to the opposition of a Balkan Christian community to the representatives of the Ottoman/Muslim forces, the latter being taken either as an external or internal enemy. There are several other indications of the poets' concern with expressing the constitutive elements of their peoples' national identity, among them their interest in structuring a universe of national symbols to be recognized by a public whose national consciousness was by that time increasingly gaining force. The emphasis put by the three poets on this kind of national symbolism is illustrated by the construction of a national space-time which includes the places that serve as the setting of events of a distant or more recent national history, and the dates when such events took place, as well as important days of the religious calendar, the latter often being assumed to coincide with the former. The configuration of a system of national symbols is further illustrated by the invocation of key figures of the national history of each one of the peoples in question, who are taken as points of reference of a mythological dimension.

With respect to the configuration of a national space-time, Solomos's poem is set in Missolonghi, the place of the well-known event of the exodus of its inhabitants during the second siege of the town, which is the central theme of "The Free Besieged"; it is also the place of an important Greek victory during the first years of the war of independence, as well as the place where Byron died, both events being referred to in the poem. In *The Death of Smail-Aga Čengić* the events described are located in places of symbolical value, the poet even providing settings of national prestige for events that did not really happen there, and reiteratively referring to Kosovo, the mythical place of the battle that marked the submission of the South Slavs to the Ottoman empire. Njegoš also locates events in places which acquire a symbolic dimension, and the invocation of Kosovo is recurrent in this poem too. The temporal indications are also symbolically significant, and, if no precise dates are provided, the background of the events consists of important holidays of the Christian religious calendar. In Solomos's poem the events take place on Palm Sunday, while Easter is approaching, and the events described by Njegoš are supposed to have happened on the Eve of Pentecost, on the day of the Nativity of Virgin Mary, on Christmas Eve, Christmas Day, and finally on New Year's Day.

The nationalist concern of the poems can be observed not only in the designation of a framework which consists in the spatial and temporal coordinates of particular events of the national life of the Balkan peoples, but also in the invocation of figures which are important to the respective national narratives. In "The Free Besieged" there are references to Markos Botsaris, a well-known figure of the Greek war of independence, and Byron, who died in Missolonghi some years before the composition of the poem, while Njegoš reiteratively refers to Prince Lazar and Miloš Obilić, emblematic figures of the battle of Kosovo, and dedicates his poem to Karađorđe, leader of the Serbian revolt. Moreover, in the three poems the decisions made with regard to the action to be undertaken by the collective subjects have to be confirmed by figures who represent the political and religious components of the national narrative. In "The Free Besieged," the decision of the people of Missolonghi to undertake the exodus is hailed by the figure of Mother Greece, who appears to be sure of their determination to choose spiritual freedom over the temptations of an earthly life of slavery. In *The Death of Smail-Aga Čengić* and *The Mountain Wreath*, likewise, a monk and the blind abbot Stefan bless the ventures undertaken by Christian Montenegrins against Smail-Aga Čengić and the Turkicized Montenegrins respectively.

If the idea of a Christian national community whose integrity is preserved through its opposition to the representatives of the Ottoman/Muslim forces is common to the three poems, some divergences arise not only with respect to the motivation behind this opposition, as has been already discussed, but also to the purported limits of the respective communities. In "The Free Besieged," Christian Greeks and Muslim Turks form two distinct communities whose positions vis-à-vis each other are clearly delineated and invariable, and whose members are only bound to meet while in battle. In Mažuranić's and Njegoš's poems, on the contrary, the world of Muslims permeates that of Christians, and people often move from one religion to another. In *The Death of Smail-Aga Čengić*, the murder of Bauk, the Muslim servant of Smail-Aga who, anticipating the reaction of the aga's subjects, advises him to release the prisoners, encourages his son Novica to join the Christians seeking revenge for his father's death, and even to ask to receive Christian baptism. In *The Mountain Wreath*, part of the Montenegrin population has converted to Islam and their Christian compatriots assume that an open conflict could be prevented in the event they decided to return to the Christian faith.

We have seen that, while the community described in "The Free Besieged" is quite homogeneous, the world depicted in Mažuranić's and Njegoš's poems is one of ambiguous and shifting identities. The action undertaken by Christian Montenegrins in these poems is precisely intended to establish unity among a heterogeneous community whose members now have to conceive of themselves as belonging to a unified national community. The different forms that the opposition between Christians and the Ottomans/Muslims take in the three poems present in this sense some analogies with the different degrees of homogeneity that can be observed among the respective communities. In Solomos's poem, the people of Missolonghi are the members of a solid Greek Christian community, and their decision to venture their exodus and die is seen as an act of defense vis-à-vis the Ottoman and Egyptian forces who maintain them under siege and the state of political and moral slavery to which this is equated. In *The Death of Smail-Aga Čengić*, the Christian Montenegrins form a unified community, to which even Muslims can belong provided that they get baptized and develop a proper national identity. The action that is undertaken by Christian Montenegrins is depicted as an act of revenge for the violence inflicted by the forces of a Muslim Herzegovinian aga, as well as for the assassination of one of their Islamized compatriots whose son reconverts to the Christian faith. In *The Mountain Wreath*, the limits of the community are even more blurred, since Muslim Montenegrins are taken to be the compatriots of the Christian inhabitants of the region, and it is for this reason that the members of the latter consider the possibility of a compromise on the basis of the former's reconversion to Christianity. Their decision to banish Muslim Montenegrins from the country comes as an aggressive act of offense whose aim is to establish unity and to forge a national identity based upon religion and the invocation of a culturally unified past which goes back to the origins of Serbdom in medieval times.

A central theme in the three poems is the representation of the community, its constituent parts and its limits. From this point of view, the poems represent the process of development of a national identity which came to replace the religious identity that had been dominant among the Balkan peoples during the previous centuries. Overall, there is a tension between the category of religion and that of political history as far as the construction of the new national identity is concerned, and this is expressed in the three poems in different ways. There is Njegoš, the prince-bishop or *vladika*, the head of Montenegro, who has to ensure his control over a society characterized by tribal organization and the presence of both Christian and Muslim populations. As the ruler of nineteenth-century Montenegro, Njegoš opts for the idea of a national community which could replace the inhabitants' identification with different clans, and, although members of the same clan can be Christian or Muslim, this national community is intended to exclude the Muslim element. On the other hand, Mažuranić's and Solomos's poems present an interesting particularity as far as their conception of national belonging is concerned. "The Free Besieged" and *The Death of Smail-aga Čengić*, just as *The Mountain Wreath*, deal with the idea of a national consciousness which is based upon the opposition between a Christian—Greek and Montenegrin, respectively—community of the Ottoman territory and the Ottoman/Muslim factor. However, neither Solomos nor Mažuranić can be seen as representing this community whose fight against the Ottoman/Muslim element they discuss in their poems. Solomos lived and wrote his poems in the Ionian Islands, a zone which was from the beginning of the thirteenth until the end of the eighteenth centuries under the rule of the Republic of Venice, then passed for a while under French, and finally British control, until it became part of the independent Greek state several decades after this had been established, in the latter half of the nineteenth century. Similarly, Mažuranić was born in Dalmatia, a zone which was historically associated with the Republic of Venice, had a short period of French rule, then passed to the Austrian Empire and finally to the Hungarian crown. In the latter part of the nineteenth century he served as governor or *ban* of the kingdom of Croatia-Slavonia, which had been under Austrian, and was by that time under Hungarian, rule.

It is thus striking that, while both Solomos and Mažuranić were involved in the cultural and political life of zones which never experienced Ottoman domination, they nevertheless based the subject matter of their masterpieces on an episode which illustrates the opposition between a Christian community living in the Ottoman territory and the representatives of the Ottoman empire. The two poets dedicate their compositions to the opposition between Greeks and South Slavs of the Ottoman territories on the one hand, and the representatives of the Ottoman empire on the other, while disavowing any depiction of an opposition between Greeks and Croats of the non-Ottoman Ionian Islands and Croatia-Slavonia or Dalmatia on the one hand, and the representatives of the British and Hungarian empires on the other. Both poets are members of the elite of zones under the domination of a Western imperial force, vis-à-vis which important political claims are made by the time of the composition of the poems with which we are concerned; their authors nevertheless choose to talk about a national identity based upon the opposition to the Ottoman/Muslim Empire. Similarly, Njegoš is member of the elite of a zone whose inhabitants are both Christian and Muslims; he nevertheless chooses to talk about a national identity which is based upon the opposition of the Christian to the Muslim factor.

The choice of our poets is indicative of the strong political component of the cultural and literary evolutions in the nineteenth-century Balkans, and precisely in the Greek and Croatian case with which we are concerned. The interest of the Balkan intellectuals of zones which were under Western rule in the political claims of their compatriots of the Ottoman territories must be linked, in Mažuranić's case, to the concern of the Illyrian movement with the idea of a South Slavic unity which could develop under the leadership of the Croats as well as to the rising national conscience among South Slavs of both the Ottoman and the Austro-Hungarian Empire, and, in Solomos's case, to the increasing discontent towards the British government of the Ionian islands and to the growing desire of their people to become part of the independent Greek state, the people of which had already affirmed their opposition to the Ottoman imperial center since the time of the revolution. From another point of view, one could see in the three cases an Orientalist point of view which makes of the Eastern, in the Saidian sense, force (that is, the Ottoman/Muslim empire) the entity against which the discourse of the cultural and political elites of the Balkans is to be articulated. The national identities that we have been discussing so far are thus finally constructed on the basis of an Orientalist discourse which evolves more clearly in the nineteenth century, and which involves the dismissal of the Ottoman element and, in historical terms, the disavowal of the respective Balkan peoples' Ottoman past, and their political and cultural reorientation towards the West. If the three poets set an idealistic framework in which the opposing sides are to be seen as representing opposing moral stances, the choice of the Ottoman/Muslim factor as the entity against which their heroes have to fight is indicative of a specific ideological choice: the disqualification of the Ottoman/Muslim political and cultural factor in such abstract terms as the ones described by Said. The three poets opt for the expression of their opposition to a center of power other than the one under which they, as well as the people they represent in political, social and cultural terms, live, conceiving of the Ottoman/Muslim rule as abstractly unworthy and evil, that is, as essentially Oriental. If the opposition precisely to this, essentially Oriental, Ottoman/Muslim factor is the basic material to which the three poets intend to ascribe an idealized, universal dimension, this claim finally equates with the aspiration to ascribe an idealized, universalizable value to what is thus taken as a binary opposition between the Christian/Western locus of the good and fair and the Muslim/Oriental locus of oppression, obscurantism and evil, in an Orientalist manner which has been much appreciated by the intellectual elites of the Balkan region ever since that time.

References

Anderson, Benedict. *Imagined Communities: Reflections on the Origin and Spread of Nationalism*. London: Verso, 1991.

Aubin, Michel. *Visions historiques et politiques dans l'œuvre poétique de P. P. Njegoš*. Paris: Université de Paris-Sorbonne; Belgrade: Faculté de philologie, 1972.

Bakić-Hayden, Milica. "Nesting Orientalisms: The Case of Former Yugoslavia." *Slavic Review* 54 no. 4 (1995): 917–931.

Barac, Antun. *A History of Yugoslav Literature*. Beograd: Committee for Foreign Cultural Relations of Yugoslavia, 1955.

———. *Hrvatska književnost od Preporada do stvaranja Jugoslavij* [Croatian literature from the Renaissance to the creation of Yugoslavia]. *Knjiga I, Književnost ilirizma* [Volume I, the literature of Illyrism]. Zagreb: Jugoslovenska akademija znatnosti i umjetnosti, 1954–60.

———. *Jugoslavenska književnost* [Yugoslav literature]. Zagreb: Matica Hrvatska, 1959.

———. *Mažuranić*. Zagreb: Matica Hrvatska, 1945.

Bombaci, Alessio. *Storia della letteratura turca*. Milan: Nuova Accademia, 1956.

Canclini, Néstor García. *Culturas híbridas. Estrategias para entrar y salir de la modernidad*. México, DF: Editorial Grijalbo, 1990.

Castellan, Georges, and Marie Vrinat-Nikolov. *Histoire de la Bulgarie: au pays des roses.* Brest: Ameline, 2007.

Coutinho, Eduardo. *Literatura comparada na América Latina. Ensaios.* Rio de Janeiro: Editora da Universidade do Estado do Rio de Janeiro, 2003.

Cronia, Arturo. *Storia della letteratura serbocroata.* Milan: Nuova Accademia, 1956.

Deretić, Jovan. *Kratka istorija srpske književnosti* [A short history of Serbian literature]. Novi Sad: Adresa, 2007.

Dimaras, C. Th. *A History of Modern Greek Literature.* Albany: State University of New York Press, 1972.

Ďurišin, Dionýz. *Communautés interlittéraires spécifiques.* Bratislava: Institut de littérature mondiale, Académie slovaque des sciences, 1993.

———. *Théorie du processus interlittéraire I.* Bratislava: Institut de littérature mondiale. Académie slovaque des sciences, 1995.

———. *Theory of Literary Comparatistics.* Bratislava: Veda, 1984.

Elsie, Robert. *Albanian Literature: A Short History,* London and New York: Tauris, 2005.

———. *History of Albanian Literature.* New York: Columbia University Press, 1995.

Fleming, K. E. "Orientalism, the Balkans, and Balkan Historiography." *The American Historical Review* 105, no. 4 (2000): 1218–33.

Frangeš, Ivo, and Milorad Živančević. *Ilirizam, realizam* [Illyrism, realism]. Zagreb: Liber, Mladost, 1975.

Garantoudis, Euripidis. "I logotechnia 1830–1880" [Literature, 1830–1880]. In *Istoria tou neou ellinismou 1770–2000* [History of modern Hellenism 1770–2000], t. 4 [vol. 4]. Athens: Ellinika Grammata, 2004.

Glissant, Édouard. *Introduction à une poétique du divers.* Paris: Gallimard, 1995.

Goldsworthy, Vesna. *Inventing Ruritania: The Imperialism of the Imagination.* New Haven and London: Yale University Press, 1998.

Graciotti, S., M. Popescu, S. Karadgiov, F. Màspero, and N. Ressuli. *Storia delle letterature del sud-est europeo.* Milan: Fabbri, 1970.

Gramsci, Antonio. *Prison Notebooks.* Edited by J. Buttigieg. New York: Columbia University Press, 1992.

Henríquez-Ureña, Pedro. *Literary Currents in Hispanic America.* Cambridge: Harvard University Press, 1945.

Holton, David. *Literature and Society in Renaissance Crete.* Cambridge: Cambridge University Press, 1991.

Igov, Svetlozar. *Kratka istorija na bălgarskata literatura* [A short history of Bulgarian literature]. Sofia: Zahari Stojanov, Sv Klimnet Ohridski, 2005.

Jelavich, Barbara. *History of the Balkans.* Vol. 1, *Eighteenth and Nineteenth Centuries,* and Vol. 2, *Twentieth Century.* Cambridge: Cambridge University Press, 1983.

Jelavich, Charles, and Barbara Jelavich. *The Establishment of the Balkan National States, 1804–1920.* Seattle and London: University of Washington Press, 1977.

Jelčić, Dubravko. *Povijest hrvatske književnosti* [History of Croatian literature]. Zagreb: P.I.P, 1997.

Kapsomenos, Eratosthenis. *O Solomos kai i elliniki politismiki paradosi* [Solomos and the Greek cultural tradition]. Athens: Vouli ton Ellinon, 1998.

Mackridge, Peter. *Dionysios Solomos.* Bristol: Bristol Classical Press, 1989.

Marković, Mihailo, ed. *Društveno-politička misao Njegoša: Primljeno na VI skupu Odeljenja društvenih nauka od. 20. septembra 2005. godine* [The socio-political thought of Njegoš: proceedings of the sixth meeting of the department of social sciences, 20 September 2005]. Beograd: SANU, 2006.

Mažuranić, Ivan. *La mort de Smaïl-aga Tchenguitch*. Translated by Antoine Sidoti. Paris: Non Lieu, 2011.

Meriggi, Bruno. *Le letterature della Jugoslavia*. Florence: Sansoni, 1970.

Moser, Charles. *A History of Bulgarian Literature, 865–1944*. The Hague: Mouton, 1972.

Petronijević, Branislav. *Filozofija u "Gorskom vijencu"* [Philosophy in "The Mountain Wreath"]. Beograd: Izd. S. B. Cvijanovića, 1920.

Petrović Njegoš II, Pierre. *La couronne de montagne: épisode historique vers la fin du XVII siècle*. Translated by Antoine Sidoti and Christian Cheminade. Paris: Non Lieu, 2010.

Popović, Miodrag. *Romantizam* [Romanticism]. Beograd: Nolit, 1975.

———, Vido Latković, and Jovan Deretić. *P. P. Njegoš: 1813–1963*. Beograd: Nolit, 1963.

Prvulovich, Žika Rad. *Religious Philosophy of Prince-Bishop Njegosh of Montenegro, 1813–1851*. Birmingham: Ž.R. Prvulovich, 1984.

Rama, Angel. *Transculturación narrativa en América Latina*. Buenos Aires: Andariego, 2007.

Rizvić, Muhsin. *Književno stvaranje muslimanskih pisaca u Bosni i Hercegovini u doba Austrougarske vladavine* [The literature of Muslim writers in Bosnia and Herzegovina during the Austro-Hungarian rule]. Sarajevo: Akademija nauka i umjetnosti Bosne i Hercegovine, 1973.

Said, Edward W. *Orientalism*. New York: Vintage Books, 1978.

Smith, Anthony. *National Identity*. London: Penguin, 1991.

———. *Nations and Nationalism in a Global Era*. Cambridge: Polity Press, 1995.

Solomos, Dionysios. *Poiimata kai peza* [Poetry and prose]. Edited by Stylianos Alexiou. Athens: Stigmi, 1994.

Stamatopoulos, Dimitris, and Foteini Tsimbiridou, eds. *Orientalismos sta oria. Apo ta othomanika Valkania sti synchroni Mesi Anatoli* [Orientalism at the limits: from the Ottoman Balkans to the contemporary Middle East]. Athens: Kritiki, 2008.

Todorova, Maria. *Imagining the Balkans*. New York: Oxford University Press, 1997.

Veloudis, Giorgos. *Dionysios Solomos: Romantiki poiisi kai poiitiki. Oi germanikes piges* [Dionysios Solomos, romantic poetry and poetics: the German sources]. Athens: Gnosi, 1989.

———. *Dionysiou Solomou "Stochasmoi" stous "Eleutherous Poliorkismenous"* [Dionysios Solomos's "reflections" on "The Free Besieged"]. Athens: Periplous, 1997.

———. *Deka neoellinika meletimata* [Odds and evens: ten studies on modern Greek literature]. Athens: Gnosi, 1992.

———. "O eptanisiakos egelianismos" [The Ionian-Island Hegelianism]. In *Mona-zyga. Deka neoellinika meletimata* [Odds and evens: ten studies on modern Greek literature], 79–96 Athens: Gnosi, 1992.

———. "O eptanisiakos, o athinaikos kai o europaikos romantismos" [Ionian-Island, Athenian and European romanticism]. In *Mona-zyga. Deka neoellinika meletimata* [Odds and evens: ten studies on modern Greek literature], 97–124. Athens: Gnosi, 1992.

Eleonora Naxidou

Differing Perceptions of Ottoman Rule in the Bulgarian Ethnic Narrative of the Revival

The prevalence of nationalism in the Balkans during the nineteenth century led to the gradual transformation of ethnic communities into nations and the concomitant replacement of the Ottoman imperial structure by national political organizations. Given that the Balkan nations, at least in their early form, were mainly based on cultural traits,[1] in the way that is best described by Anthony Smith,[2] one of the major strategies that the respective intelligentsias adopted in order to mold national identities was the creation of ethnic narratives.[3] During this process of narrative creation within each ethnic group, diverging representations of the past were put forward[4] before one finally prevailed.[5] These differing

---

[1] Recent studies have disputed the clear-cut distinction between a Western-civic and Eastern-cultural concept of nation as these are usually referred to. See Brubaker, "The Manichean Myth: Rethinking the Distinction between 'Civic' and 'Ethnic' Nationalism," 55–71; Iordachi, "The Ottoman Empire: Syncretic Nationalism and Citizenship in the Balkans," 120–151; Reeskens and Hooghe, "Beyond the Civic–ethnic Dichotomy: Investigating the Structure of Citizenship Concepts Across Thirty-three Countries," 579–597. Although the matter is still open to discussion, ethnic groups in the Balkans were initially differentiated on the basis of their cultural features since the sense of belonging to a community of citizens and the sharing of a common political culture was non-existent.

[2] According to Smith the elements of the ethnic conception of the nation are genealogy and presumed descent ties, popular mobilization, vernacular languages, and customs and traditions. See Smith, *National Identity*, 12.

[3] This strategy was applied all over Europe. See Berger and Lorenz, eds., *Nationalizing the Past: Historians as Nation Builders in Modern Europe*.

[4] This issue is dealt with by Dimitris Stamatopoulos in his remarkable book *To Vyzantio meta to Ethnos. To Provlima tis Sineheias stis Valkanikes Istoriographies*, (published in English as *Byzantium after the Nation: The Problem of Continuity in Balkan Historiographies*), which compares the diverging ways that Byzantium was perceived in the context of the Greek, the Bulgarian, the Albanian, the Turkish and the Rumanian national historiographies.

[5] After the establishment of nation-states, the task of "nationalizing" the past was undertaken and methodically promoted by both political and intellectual elites which sought to develop national

and often conflicting narrations were on the one hand due to the "multiple nature of the past,"[6] and on the other to the multifariousness of the Balkan national movements, each of which embraced a variety of ideological trends, courses of action and aspirations, whose common denominator was the cultivation of a distinct national character. Such divergences were only natural if one takes into account the fact that the proponents of national ideals did not have the same political, socio-economic or educational background, which determined both their stances and methods of operating.[7]

Focusing on the Bulgarian case, the present paper examines alternative interpretations of the ethnic past which were proposed by prominent intellectuals and political figures of the Bulgarian national mobilization. It aims to shed light on the process of the formation of the Bulgarian ethnic narration from the period of the Revival[8] up until the establishment of the autonomous principality in 1878.

Despite the divergences, all versions of the Bulgarian historiographical scheme were constructed on a linear pattern which consisted of four main stages: birth, growth or golden age, decline, and rebirth.[9] The first stage concerned the quest for the ethnic origins of the Bulgarian people; the second corresponded to the development of the Medieval Bulgarian kingdom in the Balkans, which was described as a glorious era of national prosperity in all domains of public and private life; the third coincided with the period of Ottoman domination; and the fourth stage was associ-

---

homogeneity among citizens. This is how the dominant national discourse has been created and reproduced up to the present.

6 Smith, *The Ethnic Origins of Nations*, 179. Smith points out that "Very rarely, is it possible to speak of a 'single' past of any ethnie; rather, each ethnie possesses a series of pasts, which modern secular intellectuals attempt to interrelate in a coherent and purposive manner." Ibid.

7 Focusing on Albanian nationalism, Nathalie Clayer points out that "divergences are to be seen at the level of the intellectual building of the national identity, not only in terms of an alterity vis-à-vis other national groups, but also in terms of a variety of ways of building a nation." See Clayer, "Convergences and Divergences in Nationalism through the Albanian Example," 214.

8 In Bulgarian historiography the term Revival (*Vâzrazdane*) denotes not only the socio-political, economic and ideological process of the creation of the Bulgarian nation, but also a certain period of modern Bulgarian history i.e. the last 100 years of the Ottoman dominion in the Bulgarian lands, although there is no consensus as to its exact beginning and end. However, the main phase of the Revival is usually thought to have started after the Treaty of Adrianople (1829) and ended with the establishment of the Bulgarian Principality in 1878. For this issue see Daskalov, *The Making of a Nation in the Balkans: Historiography of the Bulgarian Revival*, 11ff.

9 For the linear development of ethnic narratives see Smith, *The Ethnic Origins of Nations*, 191–192.

ated with the Revival which was expected to take place and restore the nation to its former greatness.

In this context two variant readings of the third stage will be discussed and related to different national milieus. On the one hand, is the perception of Ottoman rule as the "Turkish yoke" which was seen by the national activists of the diaspora as a time of oppression and decline due to Turkish backwardness and barbarism. For this reason, they espoused political emancipation mostly by means of armed revolt. On the other hand, is the description of the Ottoman era simply as Ottoman domination—a view held mainly by the national elite who lived within the borders of the Empire. Even though they too considered this period to be a time of suffering and regression, they attributed it to the ecclesiastical subordination of the Bulgarians to foreign (Greek) high clergy. In summary, each of the two readings resulted from differing perceptions of Ottoman rule and Bulgarian national aspirations: the one advocated the political principle of nationalism that each nation was entitled to independent political status,[10] while the other sought ecclesiastical self-government and the perpetuation of the Ottoman regime.

"POLITICAL NATIONALISM" AND THE CONCEPT OF THE "TURKISH YOKE"

The Revival, which began as a form of "cultural nationalism," was promoted through the establishment of schools, the written use of the Bulgarian language and the publication of newspapers, journals, and historical, ethnographic and folkloric works.[11] This soon took a more radical turn that can be labeled as "ecclesiastical nationalism" which demanded the formation of a separate church on a national basis. Yet a third trend of the Revival, developed in the 1860s, was that of "political nationalism," which was the call for political liberation primarily through revolutionary

---

10   For the political dimension of the nation which became the main driving force of Balkan nationalisms see Anderson, *Imagined Communities: Reflections on the Origins and Spread of Nationalism*, 6; Gellner, *Nations and Nationalism*, 1.

11   See Meininger, "The Formation of a Nationalist Bulgarian Intelligentsia 1835–1878"; Aretov, *Bâlgarskoto Vâzrazdane i Evropa*; Boneva, *Vâzrazdane: Bâlgariia i Bâlgarite v Prehod kâm Novoto Vreme*; Sampimon, *Becoming Bulgarian*.

action.[12] The main supporters of this approach were the national leaders of the diaspora living in the Danubian Principalities, as well as in Serbia and Russia. It should be noted that despite certain similarities, the key figures of the various Bulgarian communities abroad did not have a common profile, though most of them were engaged in all kinds of national work simultaneously promoting cultural, educational, ecclesiastical and political aspirations. Although in principle they agreed on the adoption of revolutionary methods in order to gain political independence, they were not able to coordinate their activities, largely because they shared neither the same attitudes nor objectives. Two main groups emerged roughly based on their pursued policies. The Moderates, or the "Old" as they were nicknamed by their contemporaries, were pro-Russian, adherents of ecclesiastical emancipation from the Patriarchate of Constantinople, and approved of the prospect of an armed uprising only with Russian consent and support. In contradistinction, the Liberals or the "Young" distrusted Russia, were pro-Western, proponents of ecclesiastical nationalism and political liberation by solitary revolutionary action. This second group was further divided into various factions, each of which belonged to a different organization. Nevertheless, the Old and some members of the Young were not opposed to the likelihood of a peaceful solution to the Bulgarian national problem by attaining political autonomy within the Ottoman Empire.

During the fifteen-year period of 1860–1875 the diaspora of both groups formed committees, the most influential of which were established in Bucharest. The Old founded the Benevolent Society (*Dobrodetelna Druzhina*) and published their views in the newspaper *Otechestvo* (Homeland). In 1867 they proposed a plan, with Russian instructions, for the creation of a Serbo-Bulgarian (or Bulgaro-Serbian) state that would be under the rule of the Obrenovich dynasty, which although initially approved by the Serbian government was never really put into practice.[13] The most important organizations of the Young were the Bulgarian Revolutionary Central Committee under Liuben Karavelov, editor of the newspapers *Freedom* (Svoboda) and *Independence* (Nezavisimost), and Vasil

---

12 For the different routes taken by the Bulgarian national movement see Naxidou, "The Routes to the Bulgarian National Movement: Simultaneously Homogenous and Polymorphous," 25–42.

13 Peev, "Dobrodetelnata Druzhina i Pregovorite sâs Sârbiia prez 1867–1868 g.," 115ff.

Levski and the Bulgarian Secret Central Committee under Pantelei Ki-
simov, which published the newspaper *Narodnost* (Nationality). Its conservative wing submitted a *Report* to the Sultan in 1867 proposing the
restructuring of the Ottoman Empire into a Turko-Bulgarian dual monarchy. Such a plan was also later welcomed by the Old. [14]

It was in this environment that the concept of the "Turkish yoke," [15]
which became dominant after Bulgarian political liberation, was developed and fervently propagated. This was not a new idea as it dated back
to the end of the eighteenth century. It had been introduced by the monk
Paisii Hilendarski, the forerunner of the cultural expressions of the Bulgarian Revival, as early as 1762 in his *Slavo-Bulgarian History*. Paisii narrated that Bulgarians, after having suffered many defeats on the battlefield, were eventually enslaved by the Turks in 1370 when Tarnovo, the
capital of the medieval Bulgarian kingdom, fell. [16] From then, he continued, the Bulgarians were subdued to the arbitrary rule of the fierce and ra-
pacious Turks, which under the influence of Christian ethics did gradually become milder. According to Paisii, justice was, however, still an
unknown virtue to the Turks. [17] All in all, he perceived Ottoman rule in
the Bulgarian lands as a time of slavery.

Paisii was also the first to criticize the ecclesiastical administration
of the Bulgarians during the long period of Ottoman domination. He
claimed that, having illegally subordinated them to his jurisdiction, the
Patriarch of Constantinople usually appointed to the Bulgarian provinces
high clergy of Greek origins who not only tried to impose Greek culture
on the Bulgarian people but exploited them financially as well. Therefore,
Paisii blamed the ecclesiastical authorities for Bulgarian illiteracy and the
neglect of Bulgarian education and language. [18]

Paisii's comprehension of his compatriots' political and ecclesiastical
situation lay at the core of the ethnic narrative, which was composed by

---

14 See Genchev, *Bǎlgarsko Vǎzrazdane*, 358ff.
15 Mary Neuburger argues that the concept of the Turkish yoke was inspired by the Russian idea of the
    "Tatar yoke" which held the two centuries of Mongolian-Tatar rule responsible for Russian back-
    wardness and their being distanced from "civilized Europe." See Neuburger, *The Orient Within:
    Muslim Minorities and the Negotiation of Nationhood in Modern Bulgaria*, 24–25.
16 Paisii Hilendarski, "Istoria Slavianobolgarskaia," 58.
17 Paisii Hilendarski, "Istoria Slavianobolgarskaia," 60.
18 Paisii Hilendarski, "Istoria Slavianobolgarskaia," 73–74.

the Bulgarian émigrés of liberal, revolutionary orientation. The notion of the Turkish yoke was fully embraced and advocated in their printed works and newspapers, serving as a major argument for claiming political liberation. At the same time, the idea of Greek ecclesiastical oppression justified the demand for ecclesiastical emancipation. Despite agreeing with the plans for ecclesiastical and political independence, the moderates were in favor of milder tactics and thus abstained from making any negative descriptions or comments to either the Bulgarian ecclesiastical or political administration.[19]

The Liberals, on the other hand, described Ottoman rule in their writings by using such expressions as Turkish, Ottoman, foreign or Asiatic yoke, or a barbarian and inhuman yoke, a devastating yoke, the yoke of the infidels, tyranny, despotism and so on.[20] In the same vein, the Turks were characterized as merciless tyrants, a barbarian tribe, enemies of the Bulgarians, fanatical barbarians who hated Christians, inhuman, cruel, cunning, uncivilized, bloodthirsty, torturers, infidels, and so on.[21] Perhaps this image is best encapsulated in the phrase by Liuben Karavelov: "the Turk is a Turk, neither God nor the Devil can make a human out of him."[22] Elsewhere, Georgi Rakovski claimed that no other race had caused greater suffering, more human disasters or devastation, or treated the people they had conquered so mercilessly as the Turks.[23] It is difficult to find words to express the horror at the magnitude of the Turks' malice when the blood of innocents shed or the grave ills inflicted on the people that they had subjugated in Asia, Africa and Europe are brought to mind, he asserted.[24]

---

19   This policy is evident in the contents of their newspaper *Otechestvo*.

20   It should be noted that they mostly used the terms Turk or Turkish rather than Ottoman.

21   The Liberals' views were set forth mainly in the various published works by Georgi Rakovski, for example the poems "Gorski Putnik" [Forest traveler], "Iztuplenii Dervish ili Vâstochnii Vâpros" [The exultant dervish or the eastern question] and many others, as well as in his newspaper *Dunavski Lebed* [Danube swan] which he edited in Belgrade (1860–1861); also in the newspapers *Narodnost* (1867–1869) by Ivan Kasabov, *Svoboda* (1869–1872) and *Nezavisimost* (1873–1874) by Liuben Karavelov, and *Zname* [Flag] (1874–1875) by Hristo Botev. For a complete overview of Bulgarian newspapers during the Revival see Borshukov, *Istoriia na Bâlgarskata Zhurnalistika 1844–1877, 1878–1885*.

22   Karavelov, "Moi Bratia."

23   Rakovski, *Sâchineniia III*, 400.

24   Rakovski, *Sâchineniia III*, 400.

The Liberals likewise had an extremely negative and derogatory opinion about the Ottoman administration. In contrast with the civilized European governments, they considered the Turkish authorities backward and arbitrary, accusing them of abusing their power, not respecting the law and violating human and civil rights. Under such circumstances, it was declared, progress was completely unattainable in education and science, cultural development, peace, freedom, security or prosperity. According to Hristo Botev, all living things were already in the deadly clutches of Turkey, and nothing survived but fire and the sword.[25] An article in the *Narodnost* newspaper maintained that the Turkish government was indifferent to the welfare of its subjects and treated them as if they were foreigners. The people were expected to work in order to pay taxes that financed the government officials, who did not perform their duties and whose only interest was to collect money. The article also claimed that order was imposed by force while a person's life, property and honor were not protected.[26] Elsewhere it was stated that justice was nonexistent. Judges ruled as they pleased or decided in favor of the party who paid the highest bribe.[27] In addition, the laws were subject to continuous change.[28]

At the time the common view among the Liberals was that decay had set in too far in the Turkish political structure and that the reforms announced by the sultans could by no means remedy it. It was argued that the Turkish Empire could not be revived and thus, collapse was inevitable.[29] The proclaimed reformation (*Tanzimat*) was nothing more than a farce, whose sole intent was to throw dust in the eyes of the Europeans.[30] In practice, it was impossible to implement equality between Muslims and Christians.[31] Indeed, the Tanzimat reforms were disadvantageous for the Christian communities, which saw their autonomy and privileges diminish at the expense of more centralized power.[32] Both the Europeans and

---

25 *Zname,* January 5, 1875, No 4.
26 "Bâlgarski Vâpros," *Narodnost,* December 1, 1867, no. 8.
27 Rakovski, *Sâchineniia III,* 45.
28 Karavelov, "Moi Bratia."
29 *Zname,* February 2, 1875, no. 8.
30 *Svoboda,* November 26, 1869, no. 4.
31 *Narodnost,* November 3, 1867, no. 3.
32 *Narodnost,* November 3, 1867, no. 3.

the Bulgarians who believed that the Ottoman Empire could be transformed into a modern European state were, therefore, sharply criticized.[33]

In this context, the Liberals considered the fate of the Bulgarian people as deplorable and in their writings depicted it in very dark colors. This is clearly illustrated in the following description by Karavelov: Bulgarian miseries were due to the physical slavery imposed on them by the Turks and the moral hardships by the Greek/Phanariot clergy.[34] This double enslavement was also compared to two mortal wounds that threatened Bulgarian nationality, of which the first was the more polluted and dangerous.[35]

Initially, it was asserted that if the Bulgarians had possessed their own kingdom, church and schools, their political system would have developed and they would have become a European nation. Instead, they had been subdued to the Turkish tyrannical yoke which had turned them into animals.[36] According to this interpretation, in the course of the more than 400 years of Turkish domination, the Bulgarians had endured arbitrariness, injustices, oppression, military abuses, financial exploitation, theft and anarchy, and were deprived of both their political rights and their national leaders who had been put to death. In this way they had been reduced to the status of slaves.[37] In a nutshell, it was claimed that they had been ethically degraded to the level of beasts, materially to the position of ancient helots, financially to that of beggars and mentally to a state of stupidity.[38]

"ECCLESIASTICAL NATIONALISM" AND THE IDEA OF OTTOMAN DOMINATION

At the same time, the Bulgarian elite who resided within the Ottoman Empire promoted what could be called a more "modest" national agenda in the sense that while they too pursued an initially "cultural" and lat-

---

33 Rakovski, *Sâchineniia III*, 334; *Svoboda*, December 3, 1869, no. 5; December 24, 1869, no. 8 and January 4, 1870, no. 9.

34 *Otechestvo*, July 25, 1869, no. 1. This is an article written by Karavelov, who was offered the post as the newspaper's editor. Although Karavelov initially accepted, he did not commence the job because of the considerable differences between the attitudes and aims of the Benevolent Society and his own.

35 Rakovski, *Sâchineniia III*, 471.

36 *Narodnost*, November 11, 1867, no. 4.

37 *Narodnost*, October 27, 1867, no. 2.

38 *Zname*, February 16, 1875, no. 9.

er "ecclesiastical nationalism," they were, nevertheless, opposed to any revolutionary plans or the prospect of immediate political secession. In this context, they provided a different interpretation of the Ottoman era. Even though they also described it as a period of decay and regression for the Bulgarian people, they maintained that this situation was not due to Ottoman administration, which was both just and respectful to the rights of all subjects, but it was brought about due to Bulgarian ecclesiastical dependence on foreign, Greek clergy and lack of autonomy.

Ecclesiastical nationalism—that is, the demand for ecclesiastical independence—led to a major conflict between the Bulgarians and the Patriarchate of Constantinople in the 1860s. The outcome of this was the establishment of a Bulgarian Church in 1870 by decree of the Sultan without the consent of the Patriarch.[39] Most of the national leaders in this endeavour were members of the Bulgarian community of Constantinople[40] which had already developed a strong sense of Bulgarianness and had differentiated itself from the Rum millet.[41] In spite of their common aspirations, these national figures were not unanimous either in the actual content of their claims or in the strategies to achieve them. In line with

---

39   For the Bulgarian ecclesiastical issue see Matalas, *Ethnos kai Orthodoksia. Oi peripeteies mias shesis. Apo to "Elladiko" sto Voulgariko Shisma*; Markova, "Bâlgarskoto Cârkovno-Nacionalno Dvizhenie do Krimskata Voina"; Nikov, *Vâzrazhdane na Bâlgarskiia Narod. Cârkovno-Nacionalni Borbi i Postizheniia;* Stamatopoulos, "The Bulgarian Schism Revisited,"105–125; Boneva, *Bâlgarskoto Cârkovnonacionalno Dvizhenie 1856–1870.*

40   The Bulgarian community in Constantinople had approximately 20,000–30,000 members, many of whom belonged to the affluent, expanding bourgeoisie. Most were merchants and professionals organized into guilds, while the one thousand or so Bulgarian workers in the state military uniform factory enjoyed financial privileges. Several intellectuals such as Georgi Rakovski, Gavril Krâstevich, Ivan Bogorov, Petko Slaveikov, Marko Balabanov and others had settled permanently or temporarily in the Ottoman capital. See Markova, "Bâlgarskoto Cârkovno-Nacionalno Dvizhenie do Krimskata Voina," 119–121; Genchev, *Bâlgarsko Vâzrazhdane,* 222–225; Bozhinov, *Carigradskite Bâlgari mezhdu Reformite i Revoluciiata 1875–1877 g.,* 26–86.

41   Until the 1830s, the Bulgarians and the Greeks belonged to the unified Orthodox community which is usually called the Rum millet. In line with the Ottoman administration, this included all Orthodox subjects in the Empire, irrespective of ethnic, linguistic, cultural or other differences, under a common ecclesiastical organization headed by the Patriarchate of Constantinople. See Braude and Lewis, eds., *Christians and Jews in the Ottoman Empire Vol. 1*; Konortas, "From Ta'ife to Millet: Ottoman Terms for the Ottoman Greek Orthodox Community," 169–179. The breakup was brought about by the prevalence of national ideology and the formation of national identities, which rendered the previous model unviable and led to differentiation within the population on the basis of national rather than religious criteria. See Stamatopoulos, "From Millets to Minorities in the 19th Century Ottoman Empire: An Ambiguous Modernization," 253–273.

the views and methods applied to further their cause, they can be catego-
rized into three main groups: the Moderates or the Old, the Radicals or
the Young,[42] and the proponents of the formation of a Bulgarian Uniate
Church. The first group, headed by Gavril Krastevic and Todor Bourmov,
through the publication of their newspapers *Savetnik* (Advisor) 1863–
1865, *Vreme* (Time) 1865–1866 and *Pravo* (Law) 1869–1873,[43] advocated
a compromise solution of common consensus with the Patriarchate following the path of discourse with no intervention from the High Porte.
They shared the Russian concern that the unity of the Eastern Orthodox
Church should not be endangered under any circumstances.[44] For this
reason, they were in close contact with the Russian ambassador to Constantinople who acted as an unofficial mediator.[45]

The second group, headed by the representative of the Bulgarian community of Philipoupolis (modern day Plovdiv) in the Ottoman capital,
Stoian Chomakov, and the publicist of the newspaper *Makedoniia* (Macedonia) 1866–1872, Petko Slaveikov, were more interested in the national
dimension of the issue. Their unwavering demand was that all the Bulgarian populations in the Balkans were included in the jurisdiction of a separate Bulgarian Church created on a national basis. Hence, in 1867 they
requested the restoration of the Archbishopric of Ohrid in order to nul-
lify the Patriarch's plan for the formation of a Bulgarian Exarchate in the
region between the Danube and the Haemus mountains.[46] In addition,
they believed that the prospect of an ecclesiastical schism would facilitate
the bolstering of national cohesion, opposing, therefore, Russia's concilia-
tory stance and seeking instead the support of the Ottoman political authority.[47] Thus, their leaders communicated with state officials, not only

---

42 Despite the common name, the groups of the Old and the Young of the Bulgarian elite in Constantinople did not have the same profile with their compatriots of the diaspora, as it is shown in this
paper. However, they did share some ideological orientations. The Old in both cases were moderate
and Pro-Russian, whereas the Young were more radical, anti-Russian and pro-Western.
43 For the editors and the program of all the Bulgarian newspapers in Constantinople during this period see Borshukov, *Istoriia na Bǎlgarskata Zhurnalistika 1844–1877, 1878–1885.*
44 Markova, "Bǎlgarskata Ekzarhiia 1870–1879," 260; Naxidou, "The Routes," 33.
45 For Ignatiev's role and Russian policy see Meininger, *Ignatiev and the Establishment of the Bulgarian Exarchate 1864–1872*; Markova, "Rusiia i Bǎlgarskiiat Cǎrkovno-Nacionalen Vǎpros 1856–1864,"
165–247.
46 Shopov, "Dr. Stojan Chomakov, Zhivot, Deinost i Arhiva," 443–446.
47 Markova, "Bǎlgarskata Ekzarhiia 1870–1879," 260; Naxidou, "The Routes," 33–34.

making goodwill gestures, but also yielding obedience to the Ottoman government.[48]

Finally, the third, less influential faction, under the leadership of Dragan Cankov, editor of the newspaper *Balgariia* (Bulgaria) 1859–1863, encouraged Bulgarian affiliation with the Catholic Church in order to obtain ecclesiastical independence. Their attempts to realize such a scheme were unsuccessful.[49]

Despite their differences, all sides declared their respect for and subservience to the Sultan whom they praised for his generosity and aspired to gain his favor to their cause. Unlike their compatriots abroad, in their writings they most often used the adjective Ottoman instead of Turkish when they referred to the Empire, while they usually employed the terms Government, Honorable Government, Imperial or Royal Government, Turkish Government, or Sublime Porte when denoting the administration, and Sultan or His Imperial Majesty the Sultan, our Ruler, and so forth, when referring to the head of the Empire.[50] This choice of wording was in keeping with the group's favorable inclinations towards Ottoman political rule, of which a most indicative example is the declaration published in the newspaper *Savetnik*. It read that the Sultan kindly demonstrated his interest for the material and moral wellbeing of all his subjects without making any distinctions concerning nationality or faith. Along these lines the text also affirmed that Bulgarians should be thankful for the Sultan's love and benevolence, which they should reward with their devotion and loyalty.[51]

The Bulgarian national leaders argued, however, that their people were not able to benefit from such generous political conditions due entirely to their having been subordinated to the ecclesiastical patronage of foreigners which was the primary cause for their suffering and underdevelopment. These attitudes about the miserable status of Bulgarians and their

---

48 Todev, *Dr. Stoian Chomakov (1819–1893): Zhivot, Delo, Potomci*, Part 1, 189ff.

49 On the relationship between the Bulgarians and the Catholic Church see Kiril, *Katolicheskata propaganda sred Bâlgarite prez vtorata polovina na XIX vek*.

50 These expressions appear in the articles of the Bulgarian press in Constantinople and the writings of Stoian Chomakov. It should be noted that the Bulgarian newspaper *Turciia* (Turkey) 1864–1873 was not taken into account because it is considered Turkophilic by Bulgarian historiography and not in service of national interests. See Borshukov, *Istoriia na Bâlgarskata Zhurnalistika*, 160–164.

51 *Sâvetnik* no. 1, March 25, 1863.

exploitation by the alien Greek clergy during the Ottoman period con-
curred with those of the émigrés, the only difference being that the former
used less sharp language and far gentler expressions. The terms "yoke" and
"slavery" to depict the Bulgarians' fate were seldom employed.

It was within this ideological framework that the Radicals (the second of the three groups) expressed the above-mentioned ideas more openly and explicitly, constructing in this way a differing ethnic narrative according to which the Ottoman Empire had been the "protective shield"
for Bulgarians and their national character over the course of many centuries. For them, continuation of Ottoman rule was in the interest of the
Bulgarians on condition that they were allowed to establish their national
church within the context of a process of reformation and modernization.
The Radicals' assessment of the Ottoman past is best summarized in the
Address to the Sultan, which was published in the Constantinople press in
December 1866 immediately following the outbreak of the Cretan uprising. It was, in fact, a public declaration of allegiance to the Ottoman ruler on behalf of the Bulgarian people, which was inspired by Chomakov
and signed by the national leaders. In the *Address* it was stated that the
Bulgarians wished to express their devotion and gratitude to their bene-
factor, the Sultan, who for almost five centuries had protected their lives
and property against internal and external enemies. Due to Ottoman generosity the Bulgarians were able to safeguard their language, religion and
nationality, despite Greek efforts to Hellenize them. Finally, this act was
meant to affirm the subservience of the Bulgarians to the Sultan and con-
demn the irrational and ungrateful conduct of the Cretans who took up
arms against what they termed their generous ruler.[52]

The Radicals promoted their views not only at home, mainly with articles in the *Makedoniia* newspaper but also in Europe, largely through
the English press.[53] They characterized Ottoman rule as Ottoman domination and contended that Bulgarian socio-economic and cultural prog-

---

[52] *Makedoniia* no. 6, December 31, 1866.

[53] In 1868, Stoian Chomakov sent for publication at least three articles about the Bulgarian issue in the
newspaper *The Pall Mall Gazette* in London. In the same year he also edited a brochure in French
entitled *La Question Bulgare* which he passed on to important personalities in Europe. See Todev,
Dr. Stoian Chomakov, part 1, 277. These documents are included in Chomakov's personal archive
which was published by Todev, *Dr. Stoian Chomakov*, part 2.

ress was not hindered by the political regime as such but by the lack of a separate ecclesiastical organization through which Bulgarians would have been able to enjoy a sort of political autonomy.[54] More specifically, their account of events went as follows: the Ottoman Emperors had always respected the law, which contributed to their victories during the period of conquests. Even before the Ottomans had settled in European territories, many Christians would visit Bursa and Nice in order to submit their disputes to the judgment of the Ottoman monarch. When later the Ottoman Empire was formed, its political administration did not interfere with the internal affairs of the various religious communities and could not therefore be held responsible for the injustices that were inflicted upon the Bulgarians.[55] The source of all their miseries was due to the fact that the Bulgarians as Orthodox Christians were placed together in the same religious group as the Greeks. Being subordinated to foreign (Greek) hierarchy, they were deprived of their own national development and at the same time were exposed to the risks of becoming Hellenized.[56] This could happen because the power of the clergy was not restricted to religious and spiritual duties. In essence, it went far beyond this to the direct or indirect control of the moral, civil and financial activities of their flock. In other words, it was the ecclesiastical authorities who were in charge of education, judged secular cases, conducted marriages, executed wills, gathered taxes and represented the people before the government.[57]

Being fully convinced of the sincerity of the Sublime Porte's intentions to improve all the domains of public life by reforms, the Radicals maintained that they, the Bulgarians, describing themselves as a peaceful and conservative people, had no intention of revolting against the Ottoman scepter. On the contrary, they were determined to serve the interests of the Empire on the condition that they were granted internal autonomy to develop their individual national character, i.e. language, religion, ethics, and way of life. In fact, all they asked for was to be recognized as a separate millet under the leadership of their own national clergy.[58] According

---

54 Todev, *Dr. Stoian Chomakov*, part 2, 374–376.
55 *Makedoniia* no. 18, April 1, 1867.
56 Todev, *Dr. Stoian Chomakov*, part 2, 390ff.
57 *Makedoniia* no. 22, April 29, 1867.
58 Todev, *Dr. Stoian Chomakov*, part 2, 388.

to Chomakov, the integrity of the Ottoman Empire depended on the respect for the nationality of each of the various peoples who lived within the borders of this multiethnic state: "Variété au sein de l'unité, liberté au sein de l'ordre."[59] Moreover, the Radicals were concerned about the Bulgarian political future and the possibility of being brought under foreign (Russian or Greek) rule once again, should the Empire dissolve.[60]

CONCLUSIONS

Both of the abovementioned readings concerning Ottoman rule emerged mostly in the years 1860–1875 when the Bulgarian national movement grew stronger and raised specific demands for the political and ecclesiastical status quo in the Balkans to be revised. Such national claims were formulated and propagated by a considerable number of publications and newspapers which appeared during this period. It was also then that the dichotomy between the national leaders who preferred immediate revolutionary action and those who favored gradual national development through ecclesiastical autonomy, education, and cultural progress solidified. In Bulgarian historiography the former are called revolutionaries, whereas the latter are characterized as evolutionists.[61] In this context, the revolutionaries believed that Turkish subjugation hindered the national, political and cultural development of the Bulgarians, who were forced to remain illiterate, poor and backward. So long as the unfavorable conditions of the lack of political freedom and civil rights existed, they could not be a part of European civilization, and progress and prosperity would continue to elude them. This is why, for them, the only alternative was political emancipation by the extreme act of a revolution. If armed struggle was not feasible, then they would settle for full autonomy under the Sublime Porte. In contradistinction, the evolutionists fully exculpated the Ottoman state for the ill-fate of the Bulgarians. Their argumentation rested on the claim that the Sultan was a wise and well-intentioned ruler who had the welfare of all his subjects at heart. In addition, of the evolutionists, the Radicals claimed that Turko-Bulgarian collaboration and co-existence within a multiethnic

---

59 Todev, *Dr. Stoian Chomakov*, part 2, 420. Chomakov was quoting an unspecified German philosopher.
60 *Makedoniia* no. 12, February 18, 1867.
61 See Daskalov, *The Making of a Nation in the Balkans*, 162ff.

political entity were much more preferable to the uncertainty and danger which lay in any form of modification to the status quo.

Recounting different stories to convey Ottoman reality, it becomes apparent that each side endeavored to serve their own particular national goals and support diverse positions through their specific arguments. Their motives were closely intertwined with their differing ideological orientations, socio-economic positions and even personal interests. On the one hand, the Liberals and revolutionaries of the diaspora adopted and fervently promoted the "yoke" version of Turkish rule in order to emphasize the necessity of creating an independent nation-state in which they aspired to assume a dominant political and intellectual role. Moreover, being in close contact with Western Europe, they were not only attracted to, but also highly influenced by the political and ideological trends that had originated and become popular in that part of the continent. Espousing liberal political ideals,[62] they placed great emphasis on respect for civil, human and national rights while severely criticizing absolutism.[63] The progressive model of governance that they embraced was totally incompatible with the Ottoman political system, meaning that under no circumstances could they tolerate the preservation of an autocratic regime in Southeastern Europe. In addition, living in the newly-formed states of Serbia and Romania, it was natural for them to be inspired by the paradigm of these Balkan nations that had already acquired independence or autonomy. One important point to be taken into account is that the Bulgarians abroad were able to publicly express their views against the Ottomans with little or no restrictions, taking advantage of the freedom of speech which they were afforded in their host countries.

On the other hand, the Bulgarian elite of Constantinople—the evolutionists—appeared favorably inclined towards the Ottoman regime, providing a very different reading of Ottoman rule. At this point two factors should also be taken into consideration: first of all, public criticism against

---

62 For this issue see Naxidou, "National Interpretations of Misfortune and Welfare: The Paradigm of the Intellectuals of the Bulgarian Revival," 189–204.

63 Karavelov and Botev were the most fervent opponents of autocracy, advocating mainly through their newspapers the principles of the French revolution. Freedom was not to abolish the Turkish or German tyrants and replace them with national leaders who had the same absolutist outlook and conduct, stated Karavelov. His conviction was that the government should exist for the sake of the people and not the reverse. See *Publicistikata na Liuben Karavelov*, 459.

the authorities was not possible due mainly to press censorship; and second, Bulgarian newspapers circulated under official license were granted financial privileges. For example, *Savetnik* was initially exempt from post taxes.[64] But there was certainly more to it than that. The foremost priority of the Bulgarian Ottomans, and more specifically the radical faction, was ecclesiastical independence which would place the Bulgarians in a separate millet. In this national battle, they very much counted on the aid of the Sultan against the Patriarchate, which refused to make any concessions. Besides the evident expediencies, however, their stance was also related to their close political and financial affiliations with the Ottoman authorities. Holding high administrative posts and undertaking profitable enterprises that contributed to, and at the same time depended on, the state's economy, they identified their privileged socio-economic status and welfare with the durability of the Ottoman Empire.[65] What is more, they were fully convinced that the imperial environment was the most suitable for the cultivation of Bulgarian national consciousness and the suppression of the assimilationist aspirations of rival nationalisms. Being deeply concerned about Hellenization in the event that the Ottomans dissolved and the Balkan provinces were annexed to a rival nation-state, they were adherents of all-inclusive or maximalist nationalism. They strongly opposed the establishment of a small, incomplete state which did not contain within its borders the Bulgarian populations of Macedonia and Thrace, that is, the entire nation. Rather, they preferred autonomy under the auspices of the Sublime Porte, which, according to them, would enable the territorial and national unification of all Bulgarians.

When the Bulgarian ecclesiastical issue was settled in 1870, the main goal of the Bulgarian leadership in Constantinople was accomplished. In this way they were called to reconsider their national program and re-

---

64 *Sâvetnik* no. 1, March 25, 1863.

65 Influential Bulgarian merchant families such as the Tâptsilestovs were members of the multi-ethnic Ottoman aristocracy in the nineteenth century, as were noted Bulgarians who held high positions in the Ottoman bureaucracy, such as Gavril Krâstevich and the Bogoridi and Chalikov families. See Davidova, *Balkan Transitions to Modernity and Nation-States: Through the Eyes of Three Generations of Merchants (1780s–1890s)*; Boneva, *Vâzrozhdenecât Gavril Krâstevich*; Philliou, *Biography of an Empire: Governing Ottomans in the Age of Revolution*; Lyberatos, "Men of the Sultan: the Beğlik Sheep Tax Collection System and the Rise of a Bulgarian National Bourgeoisie in Nineteenth-Century Plovdiv," 55–85.

schedule their next steps. Adhering to the preservation of the Empire, however, was becoming all the more difficult because the promising reforms had already proved fruitless, while there was growing discontent and tension among the various nationalities. Under such circumstances the plans for political liberation and their proponents gradually gained ground. The Balkan crisis of 1875, the Bulgarian uprising in April of 1876 and the Russo-Turkish war of 1877–1878 led to the redrawing of the political map in Southeastern Europe. By decree of the Congress of Berlin, an autonomous Bulgarian Principality was established, realizing the main claim of Bulgarian political nationalism. It appears then that the revolutionaries and their ideals had prevailed. Having the first say in the political and intellectual affairs of the newborn state, their ethnic representation of the "Turkish yoke" was turned into the main national discourse.[66]

All in all, the emergence of differing, conflicting representations of the ethnic past (and present) during the period of the Revival clearly shows how the creation of the Bulgarian ethnic narrative that was still in the making was a process affected by the interplay of various ideological, political and socio-economic factors against a national background.

References

Anderson, Benedict. *Imagined Communities: Reflections on the Origins and Spread of Nationalism*. London: Verso, 1991.

Aretov, Nikolai. *Bâlgarskoto Vâzrazhdane i Evropa* [The Bulgarian revival and Europe]. Sofia: Izdatelstvo 'Kralica Mab,' 1995.

Bell, John D. "The 'Revival Process': The Turkish and Pomak Minorities in Bulgarian Politics." In *Ethnicity and Nationalism in East Central Europe and the Balkans*, edited by Thanasis Sfikas and Christopher Williams, 237–268. Aldershot: Ashgate, 1999.

Berger, Stefan, and Chris Lorenz, eds. *Nationalizing the Past: Historians as Nation Builders in Modern Europe*. London: Palgrave Macmillan, 2010.

Boneva, Vera. *Bâlgarskoto Cârkovnonacionalno Dvizhenie 1856–1870* [The Bulgarian National Church Movement 1856–1870]. Sofia: Za Bukvite, 2010.

———. *Vâzrazhdane: Bâlgaria i Bâlgarite v Prehod kâm Novoto Vreme* [Revival: Bulgaria and the Bulgarians during the transition to the new age]. Shumen: Universitetsko Izdatelstvo Episkop Konstantin Preslavski, 2005.

---

66 Bell, "The 'Revival Process': The Turkish and Pomak Minorities in Bulgarian Politics," 238.

———. *Vâzrozhdenecât Gavril Krâstevich* [The national leader Gavril Krâstevich]. Shumen: Helion, 2000.

Borshukov, Georgi. *Istoriia na Bâlgarskata Zhurnalistika 1844–1877, 1878–1885* [History of Bulgarian journalism 1844–1877, 1878–1885]. Sofia: Izdatelstvo Paradoks & Sv. Kliment Ohridski, 2003.

Bozhinov, Plamen. *Carigradskite Bâlgari mezhdu Reformite i Revoluciiata 1875–1877 g.* [Bulgarians in Constantinople: between reforms and revolution 1875–1877]. Sofia: Prof. Marin Drinov, 2012.

Braude, Benjamin, and Bernard Lewis, eds. *Christians and Jews in the Ottoman Empire.* Vol. 1. New York: Holmes and Meier Publishers, 1982.

Brubaker, Rogers. "The Manichean Myth: Rethinking the Distinction between 'Civic' and 'Ethnic' Nationalism." In *Nation and National Identity: The European Experience in Perspective*, edited by Hanspeter Kriesi, Klaus Armingeon, Hannes Siegrist, and Andreas Wimmer, 55–71. West Lafayette, IN: Purdue University Press, 2004.

Clayer, Nathalie. "Convergences and Divergences in Nationalism through the Albanian Example." In *Developing Cultural Identity in the Balkans: Convergence vs. Divergence*, edited by Raymond Detrez and Pieter Plas, 213–225. Brussels: Peter Lang, 2005.

Daskalov, Rumen. *The Making of a Nation in the Balkans: Historiography of the Bulgarian Revival*. Budapest—New York: CEU Press, 2004.

Davidova, Evguenia. *Balkan Transitions to Modernity and Nation-States: Through the Eyes of Three Generations of Merchants (1780s–1890s)*. Leiden and Boston: Brill, 2013.

Gellner, Ernest. *Nations and Nationalism*. Oxford: Blackwell, 1994.

Genchev, Nikolai. *Bâlgarsko Vâzrazhdane* [The Bulgarian Revival]. Sofia: Iztok Zapad, 1991.

Iordachi, Constantin. "The Ottoman Empire: Syncretic Nationalism and Citizenship in the Balkans." In *What is a Nation? Europe 1789–1914*, edited by Timothy Baycroft and Mark Hewitson, 120–151. Oxford: Oxford University Press, 2006.

Karavelov, Liuben. "Moi Bratia" [My brothers]. *Narodnost* no. 16, March 9, 1869.

Kiril, Patriarh Bâlgarski. *Katolicheskata propaganda sred Bâlgarite prez vtorata polovina na XIX vek* [Catholic propaganda to the Bulgarians during the second half of the nineteenth century]. Sofia: Sinodalno Izdatelstvo, 1962.

Konortas, Paraskevas. "From Ta'ife to Millet: Ottoman Terms for the Ottoman Greek Orthodox Community." In *Ottoman Greeks in the Age of Nationalism: Politics, Economy, and Society in the Nineteenth Century*, edited by Dimitri Gondicas and Charles Issawi, 169–179. Princeton, NJ: The Darwin Press, 1999.

Lyberatos, Andreas. "Men of the Sultan: The *Beğlik* Sheep Tax Collection System and the Rise of a Bulgarian National Bourgeoisie in Nineteenth-Century Plovdiv." *Turkish Historical Review* 1 (2010): 55–85.

Markova, Zina. "Bâlgarskata Ekzarhiia 1870–1879" [The Bulgarian Exarchate 1870–1879]. In *Izbrani Sâchneniia*. Vol. 1, 233–634 Sofia: Prof. Marin Drinov, 2007.

———. "Bâlgarskoto Cârkovno-Nacionalno Dvizhenie do Krimskata Voina" [The Bulgarian Ecclesiastical-National Movement up to the Crimean War]. In *Izbrani Sâchnenia*. Vol. 1, 13–232 Sofia: Prof. Marin Drinov, 2007.

———. "Rusiia i Bâlgarskiiat Cârkovno-Nacionalen Vâpros 1856–1864" [Russia and the Bulgarian Ecclesiastical-National issue 1856–1864]. In *Izbrani Sâchineniia*. Vol. 2, Studii i Statii, 165–249. Sofia: Prof. Marin Drinov, 2008.

Matalas, Paraskevas. *Ethnos kai Orthodoksia. Oi peripeteies mias shesis. Apo to "Elladiko" sto Voulgariko Shisma* [Nation and Orthodoxy, the adventures of a relationship: from the "Greek" to the Bulgarian schism]. Heraklion: Cretan University Press, 2003.

Meininger, Thomas. "The Formation of a Nationalist Bulgarian Intelligentsia 1835–1878." PhD diss., University of Wisconsin, 1974.

———. *Ignatiev and the Establishment of the Bulgarian Exarchate 1864–1872.* Madison: University of Wisconsin, 1970.

Naxidou, Eleonora. "National Interpretations of Misfortune and Welfare: The Paradigm of the Intellectuals of the Bulgarian Revival." In *Wealth in the Ottoman and Post-Ottoman Balkans: a Socio-Economic History,* edited by Evguenia Davidova, 189–204. London: Tauris, 2015.

———. "The Routes to the Bulgarian National Movement: Simultaneously Homogenous and Polymorphous." *ADAM Akademi Sosyal Bilimler Dergisi* 2, no. 1 (2012): 25–42.

Neuburger, Mary. *The Orient Within: Muslim Minorities and the Negotiation of Nationhood in Modern Bulgaria.* Ithaca and London: Cornell University Press, 2004.

Nikov, Petar. *Vâzrazhdane na Bâlgarskiia Narod. Cârkovno-Nacionalni Borbi i Postizheniia* [The revival of the Bulgarian nation: ecclesiastical-national struggles and attainments]. Sofia: Prof. Marin Drinov, 2008.

Paisii, Hilendarski. "Istoria Slavianobolgarskaia." In *Literatura na Bâlgarskoto Vââzrazhdane XVIII-XIX vek* [Literature of the Bulgarian Revival eighteenth–nineteenth century]. Tom Vtori. I Chast [Second volume. Part one], edited by Hristo Slavov, 9–84. Sofia: Misal & Prof. Marin Drinov, 2002.

Peev, Vladimir. "Dobrodetelnata Druzhina i Pregovorite sâs Sârbiia prez 1867–1868 g." [The benevolent society and the negotiations with Serbia in 1867–1868]. In *Vremeto na Levski,* edited by Plamen Mitev, 88–144. Sofia: Kulturno-prosvetno Druzhestvo Rodno Ludogorie, 2010.

Philliou, Christine M. *Biography of an Empire: Governing Ottomans in the Age of Revolution.* Los Angeles: University of California Press, 2011.

Publicistikata na Liuben Karavelov [Journalistic Works of Liuben Karavelov]. Vol. 1, edited by Mihail Dimitrov. Sofia: BAN, 1957.

Rakovski, Georgi Stoikov. *Sâchineniia III* [Works III], edited by Veselin Traikov. Sofia: Bâlgarski Pisatel, 1984.

Reeskens, Tim, and Marc Hooghe. "Beyond the Civic–ethnic Dichotomy: Investigating the Structure of Citizenship Concepts Across Thirty-three Countries." *Nations and Nationalism* 16, no. 4 (2010): 579–597.

Sampimon, Janette. *Becoming Bulgarian.* Amsterdam: Pegasus, 2006.

Shopov, Anton. "Dr. Stojan Chomakov, Zhivot, Deinost i Arhiva" [Dr. Stojan Chomakov: life, activities and archive]. *Sbornikna BAN XII Klon Istoriko-Filologicheni Filosofsko-Obshtestven.* Sofia, 1919.

Smith, Anthony. *National Identity.* London: Penguin, 1991.

———. *The Ethnic Origins of Nations.* Oxford: Blackwell Publishing, 2008.

Stamatopoulos, Dimitris. "From Millets to Minorities in the 19th Century Ottoman Empire: An Ambiguous Modernization." In *Citizenship in Historical Perspective,* edited by S. Ellis, G. Halfdanarson and A. K. Isaacs, 253–273. Piza: Piza University Press, 2006.

———. *To Vyzantio meta to Ethnos. To Provlima tis Sineheias stis Valkanikes Istoriogra-*

phies [Byzantium after the nation: the problem of continuity in Balkan historiographies]. Athens: Alexandreia, 2009.

———. "The Bulgarian Schism Revisited." *Modern Greek Studies Yearbook* 24–25 (2008–2009): 105–125.

———. *Byzantium after the Nation: The Problem of Continuity in Balkan Historiographies.* Budapest: CEU Press, 2021.

Todev, Iliia. *Dr. Stoian Chomakov (1819–1893): Zhivot, Delo, Potomci* [Dr. Stoian Chomakov (1813–1893): life, activity and descendants]. *Chast Parva: Izsledvane* [Part 1, study]. Sofia: Prof. Marin Drinov, 2003.

———. *Dr. Stoian Chomakov (1819–1893): Zhivot, Delo, Potomci* [Dr. Stoian Chomakov (1813–1893): life, activity and descendants]. *Chast Vtora: Dokumenti* [Part 2, documents]. Sofia: Prof. Marin Drinov, 2003.

Konstantinos Giakoumis

Against the Imperial Past: The Perception of the Turk and the Greek "Enemy" in the Albanian National Identity-Building Process

A significant body of literature on the birth and development of Albanian nationalism focuses mostly on the role of elites in the establishment and spread of Albanian nationalism. This trend can be found both in older Albanian historiography in Albania[1] and abroad,[2] both of which emphasized the cultural activities of Naum Veqilharxhi in the 1830s and '40s, and the political initiatives of the League of Prizren in the international context of the Treaty of San Stefano and the Congress of Berlin. Tajar Zavalani[3] and recently Dritan Egro[4] shifted the beginning of the movement back in 1829, to the aftermath of the Greek Revolution, yet they still single out the role of the elites. International scholars, such as Nuray Bozbora[5] and Nathalie Clayer,[6] emphasize the role of the Albanian diaspora in the rise of Albanian nationalism.

Besides the Marxist portrayal of the Albanian national awakening movement in terms of the struggle of classes by the communist Albanian historiography[7], little attention has been paid, however, to how the Alba-

---

1   For example, Frashëri, *The History of Albania*, 120–122, 126–179; Zavalani, *History of Albania*, 138–155; Thëngjilli, Buda, "Lëvizja Kombëtare;" Buda, "Mendimi Politik;" Frashëri, "Lidhja Shqiptare e Prizrenit;" Myzyri, "Zhvillimi;" Prifti, "Ngritja e Lëvizjes" and "Rritja e Lëvizjes".
2   Skëndi, *Albanian Political Thought and Revolutionary Activity, 1881–1912*.
3   Zavalani, "Albanian Nationalism."
4   Egro, "Disa të Dhëna të Reja mbi Fillimet e Nacionalizmit Shqiptar," 5–17.
5   Bozbora, *Osmanlı Yönetiminde Arnavutluk ve Arnavut Ulusçuluğunun Doğuşu*.
6   Clayer, *Aux Origines du Nationalisme Albanais. La Naissance d'une nation majoritairement Musulmane en Europe*.
7   Cf. the 1984 edition of the *History of Albanian People* in Pollo, Stefanaq, Aleks Buda, Kristaq Prifti, Kristo Frashëri, *History of Albania*.

nian nationalist movement gained the necessary critical mass of popular momentum to manifest itself as a forceful divisive thrust. While the role and influence of elites to elicit popular support in a movement is not to be doubted, the assertive power of nationalism is related to people's wider identification shifts that proved capable of eventually severing the strong imperial and religious universalist thrusts of the Ottoman Empire that had managed to maintain group solidarity in an ethnically diverse empire. This paper investigates from a worm's-eye view one aspect of this lacuna, namely the role of elites in molding perceptive "filters" in national terms, and the image such filters attributed to the "Other" prior to and shortly after the establishment of the Albanian state, in the hope of thereby casting light onto an important aspect of the formative process of the engineering of an Albanian national identity.

The matter at hand is tightly linked with identities. Identity, according to Jeffrey Weeks, "is about belonging, about what you have in common with some people and what differentiates you from others."[8] As an individual entity experiencing a group setting, considering the impossibility of getting to know all of the members of the group one does or does not feel one belongs to, the perception of in-group and out-group, in other words, the "imagined community,"[9] to use Benedict Anderson's term, is of paramount significance to identity and group formation. Socio-psychological research has concluded that "the centre invests the Other with its terrors. It is the threat of the Other that ignites the irrational hatred and hostility as the centre struggles to assert and secure its boundaries, that construct self from not-self."[10] If one defines ethnic identity as "allegiance to a group—large or small, dominant or subordinate—with which one [perceives that one] has ancestral links," where "there is no necessity for a continuation, over generations, of the same socialisation or cultural patterns, but some sense of a group boundary must persist... sustained by shared objective characteristics (language, religion, etc.), or by more subjective contributions to a sense of 'groupness,' or by some combination of both," and where "symbolic or subjective attachments must relate, at how-

8 Weeks, "The Value of Difference," 88.
9 Anderson, *Imagined Communities*.
10 Rutherford, "A Place Called Home: Identity and the Cultural Politics of Difference," 11.

ever distant a remove, to an observably real past,"[11] the importance of the group's perception of the "Self" and the "Other" in the ethnic and national identification process thus becomes apparent.

The dynamics of the perception of the "Self" and the "Other" can be so powerful as to make groups that have identified themselves for hundreds of years in one way to shift their loyalty to some other constructed in-group in the course of a very short time. In the cases studied here, no longer than three months before declaring independence from the Ottoman state, the Albanian Assembly in Vlora sent the Ottoman authorities a memorandum, in which it demanded autonomy, though not independence.[12]

In a 2008 German film directed by Dennis Gansel, titled *Die Welle* (The wave), the forceful impact of the perception of the "Other" as an enemy is made manifest. The high school where Wenger teaches has a project week and Wenger sets autocracy as the topic with his class. His students, third generation Germans since World War Two, do not believe that a dictatorship could be established in modern Germany, so Wenger starts an experiment to demonstrate how easily the masses can be manipulated by selecting two classes to represent "autocracy" and "anarchy." The film shows, how in a matter of one or two weeks, social groups can be created, and by way of in-group alliances and out-group enmities, they can strongly impact individual identities. The film was inspired by Ron Jones' social experiment of the same name carried out in the 1960s, an experiment that triggered further research in the '70s by the social psychologist Henri Tajfel with his students and colleagues. They investigated the formation and maintenance of *minimal groups*. Their research demonstrated "just how easy it is to divide people into groups on the basis of unimportant criteria, and how subsequent behavior is affected by this," and how, once new demarcations have been created, "group membership *per se* becomes important."[13] Adopting Edwards' interpretation of what in-group allegiance is and why it occurs:

---

11 Edwards, *Language and Identity: An Introduction*, 162.
12 Despot, *The Balkan Wars in the Eyes of the Warring Parties: Perceptions and Interpretations*, 262–3.
13 Edwards, *Language and Identity*, 25; cf. Tajfel, ed., *Differentiation Between Social Groups: Studies in the Social Psychology of Intergroup Relations*, 33–4.

...The apparent ease and "minimality" associated with group formation are the interesting matters; the bonding, the solidarity and the
rivalries that follow are quite predictable... As to *what in-group allegiance is all about*, for instance, the answer is *in-group favouritism*: we
favour those with whom we are associated or aligned, our hopes and
expectations are often higher for them, we bleed when they bleed, and
so on. This can take place very rapidly, once "us and them" borders
have been established, once some social categorisation has occurred.
It is not difficult, as well, to understand how the same sense of belonging that creates favouritism can also lead to the formation of stereotypes—blunt characterisations that can be either positive or negative, depending upon which group you are describing... According to
the [social identity] theory, it follows that within-group favouritism is
predictable since it reflects and supports the particular "us and them"
boundaries that can heighten feelings of individual worth.[14]

I have repeatedly emphasized the role of *perception* in the processes of
identification and identity shifts. As a filter through which sensory data
are strained, "it is obvious that the establishment and maintenance of this
filter are culturally specific and—within social groupings—personalized
to a greater or lesser extent."[15] The role of elites in molding perceptive filters of their groups is therefore self-evident.

The way the ontological categories of the Self and the Other and their
perceptions translate into political reality has been treated by Jeismann in
his realist theory of political identification. Jeismann examined national aggression and investigated the way in which it has been explained to
date, i.e., by focusing either on foreign policy (which is thereby considered
as additional element in the ongoing rivalry between European states), or
on elites, thereby viewing national enmities by way of "negative integration" as fueled and exploited by ruling elites in safeguarding their power.
He concluded that both explanatory models focus on the instrumentalization of nationalism, but fail to identify the causes for national aggression.[16] In his attempt to enquire onto the causes of national aggression,

---

14   Edwards, *Language and Identity*, 25–6.
15   Edwards, *Language and Identity*, 154.
16   Jeismann, "Nation, Identity, and Enmity: Towards a Theory of Political Identification," 17.

he identified that a "more compelling concept of the nation can be seen to have developed out of an oscillation between two poles: national self-definition, on the one hand, and the image and idea of the enemy, on the other."[17] Consequently, Jeismann viewed nationalism as "a symbiotic relationship in which the 'national' as a foundation represents the value of collectivity, characterized by relatively unchangeable attributes, grounded in dualistic and polarized friend-foe models which then had to be furnished with specific colorings."[18] Contextualizing the concept of "political religion," where national enemies were simultaneously "enemies of God,"[19] Jeismann concluded:

> The emotional and irrational quality of nationalism rendered it protean and, as is evident from a reading of nineteenth-century history, pushes it beyond a dichotomy of (largely rational) civic and (substantively irrational) ethnic types. Nationalism was not merely orchestrated by states and elites. Rather, the emotional and irrational mechanisms of national identification and alienation were related to long-established cultural and religious sources, but could also be activated by short-term enmities and conflicts, which themselves were a product—at least in part—of particular political interests. Such emotional and irrational mechanisms or sources have still not been explored in sufficient detail.[20]

Jeismin's views oppose those of Benedict Anderson, who appears to have underestimated the role of enmity towards the Other in national identity formation, when he wrote that "truly rare it is to find... nationalist products expressing fear and loathing..."[21] In spite of Abizadeh's criticism of the necessity of the Other in the modern era,[22] Jeismann's thesis does seem to fit for the period of the present study.

---

17 Jeismann, "Nation, Identity, and Enmity," 19.
18 Jeismann, "Nation, Identity, and Enmity," 20.
19 Jeismann, "Nation, Identity, and Enmity," 26.
20 Jeismann, "Nation, Identity, and Enmity," 26.
21 Anderson, *Imagined Communities: Reflection on the Origins and Spread of Nationalism*, 141–2.
22 Abizadeh, "Does Collective Identity Presuppose an Other? On the Alleged Incoherence of Global Solidarity," 45–60.

From the early Middle Ages and throughout the Ottoman rule the Balkans was a terrain in which diverse ethno-cultural groups peacefully co-existed, identifying themselves primarily in terms of religion (cf. the Ottoman *millet* system). The territory of modern-day Albania was no exception; such ethnic groups as Albanians, Greeks, Turks, Vlachs, and Jews lived together and formed in-group or out-group identification alliances in terms of religion. For example, in eighteenth- and nineteenth-century ecclesiastical documents from Gjirokastra, Ottoman Muslims and Ottoman authorities are more often than not collectively referred to as members of the out-group, the "out-siders" (Gk. ἐξωτερικοί/exoterikoi)[23] with their "external force" (Gk. ἐξωτερικὴ βία/exoteriki via)[24] and "external law" (Gk. ἐξωτερικὸς νόμος/exoterikos nomos).[25] Scarce and unsystematic is the use of ethnic or racial names, such as "Albanian," "Turk," "Ottoman," "of other race," "gypsy," or "national."[26] Such a reality was as common in the Balkans as the meaning of the words "giaour" and "Turk," which, in Albanian as in all Balkan languages, denoted the Christian and the Muslim respectively.

It is interesting to note that, once in the diaspora and together with other Christian subjects of the Ottoman Empire, members of the in-group identify themselves as "Romans" or "Romans from the places of Turkey."[27] The will of Hadji Leontios Chrēstou from Gjirokastra who died in Vienna on July 11, 1778 records his donation of the amount of 100 florins to Saint George's chapel of the ʻτουρκομερητῶν Ῥωμαίωνʼ (*Tourkomeriton Romaion*, Romans from the places of Turkey) in Vienna and 50 florins to the church ʻτῶν Ῥωμαίωνʼ (*ton Romaion*, of the Romans) in Trieste.[28] Beyond the Ottoman territory, eighteenth-century Christian

23 Giakoumis, "Dialectics of Pragmatism in Ottoman Domestic Interreligious Affairs: Reflections on the Ottoman Legal Framework of Church Confiscation and Construction and a 1741 Firman for Ardenicë Monastery," 118–25; Giakoumis and Egro, "Ottoman Pragmatism in Domestic Inter-Religious Affairs: The Legal Framework of Church Construction in the Ottoman Empire and the 1741 Firman of Ardenicë Monastery," 111–7.
24 A. Q. Sh. F. Arkivi Qëndror i Shtetit / Central Archives of the State (Tirana, Albania) 139, D. 2, f. 13r.
25 A. Q. Sh. F. 139, D. 2, f. 20v.
26 Giakoumis, "A Preliminary Linguistic Approach of the 'Codex of Dositheos,' Bishop of Dryinoupolis and Gjirokastra, (1760–1858)," 167–174.
27 A. Q. Sh. F. 139, D. 2, ff. 32v-34r.
28 A. Q. Sh. F. 139, D. 2, ff. 32v-34r.

scholars or merchants from Gjirokastra appeared to identify the city of their descent in geographical terms. Hence, Gjirokastra is located in "European Albania" (ἐξ Ἀργυροκάστρου τῆς Εὐρωπαίας Ἀλβανίας; ex Europea Albania), according to a hidalgo scholar named Georgios Dimitriou, author of a Greek-Latin grammar book published in Vienna;[29] in Macedonia, according to Kyriakis Vasileiou and Ioannis Poulios in the 1767 census of Ottoman merchants in Vienna;[30] or in Epiros, according to Themelēs Chrēstou, who was also recorded in the same census.[31] All three merchants were recorded as "non-Uniate Greek," apparently denoting religious identity rather than ethnicity. Hence, national identification concerns still appear to be irrelevant in the course of the eighteenth-century configurations of the in-group or the out-group.

Yet mainstream Albanian historiography has claimed that the rise of an Albanian national identity occurred much earlier. Pëllumb Xhufi, for example, viewed the late Byzantine rise of Albanian principalities as a movement of distancing themselves from the Empire.[32] Others have viewed the Scanderbeg insurrections,[33] Ali Pasha's separatist stance,[34] and regional unrest caused by the Tanzimat Reforms in nationalist terms. Yet a growing body of evidence, dating as late as the nineteenth and early twentieth century, does not vindicate such views. Instead, they are ascribed to some sort of identity lability.[35] Indeed, even in the nineteenth century when European and Balkan nationalist currents were at their strongest, the constructions of Albanian identification were unfixed, with no instrumentalization of the language issue, which was later turned with such vehemence into a tool of forceful differentiation of the Other.[36]

---

29 Dimitriou, *Grammatiki Ellinolatinis ek Diaforon Syllechteisa*, frontispiece.

30 David do Paço "L'Orient à Vienne: L'Integration des Marchands et des Diplomates Ottomanes dans la Ville et la Résidence Impériale," 513, 531.

31 Do Paço, "L'Orient à Vienne," 530.

32 Xhufi, *Dilemat e Arbërit. Studime mbi Shqipërinë Mesjetare*; idem, *Nga Paleologët te Muzakajt: Berati dhe Vlora në Shekujt XII-XV. Me një Botim Kritik të Kronikës së Gjon Muzakës (1510)*; idem, *Ikje nga Bizanti*.

33 Misha, "Invention of a Nationalism: Myth and Amnesia," 43–5.

34 Clayer, *Aux Origines du Nationalisme Albanais*, 131–3.

35 Kalemaj and Giakoumis, "Oscillating between Inclusionary Autonomy and Secessionist Independence: Identification Shifts and the Dynamics of Albanian Perceptions of the Young Turks Movement," 155–71.

36 Giakoumis, "Relativizmi i identifikimit ideologjiko-politiko-gjeografik të shqiptarëve dhe i trevave shqipfolëse prej vetes dhe prej të tjerëve në '*Longue Durée*'" 71–89.

Several nineteenth century records from the so-called "Great Codex" of the Metropolis of Korça demonstrate that a renowned representative of the Albanian Enlightenment movement (Alb. Rilindja / Renaissance) like Thimio Mitko,[37] or the ancestors of others, like Mihal Grameno[38] and Themistokli Gjërmeni,[39] signed themselves in Greek, recording their names in their Hellenized forms, while others whose family names are not known in literature for patriotic actions rendered them in their Albanian forms.[40] This is not different from the way that anthroponyms were recorded in Gjirokastra, although the matter there is more difficult to analyze, because, in spite of certain Arabic or Albanian names pointing to persons of Albanian descent, such as Hena (meaning health or blessing in Arabic; or moon in Albanian) given to a girl, a number of Albanian versions of anthroponyms was on occasion recorded in Greek. For example, the first name of a 1780 archon of the city of Gjirokastra named George Alexiou is recorded by the same scribe at one time as 'Γεώργιος' (Georgios) and at another instance as 'Γκιέργκης' (Gkiergkis / Alb. Gjergji).[41] The unfixedness of identification is evidenced also by public benefactors of Albanian descent in Greece (e.g. Arsakis and Sinas from Korça; Zappas from Labova, etc.), who, in their wills, identified their origin in regional/ local rather than ethnic terms, similar to pre-independence Albanian immigrants in the US, who often did not identify themselves as Albanians.[42] These inconsistencies in identification reflected the linguistic reality on the ground, where cultural bilingualism or multilingualism was more often the case than not, it is not surprising that even at the turn of the twen-

---

37 A.Q.Sh. F. 141, D. 2, f. 68r. In 23.09.1864 the well-known author of the *Albanian Bee* (Alb. Bleta Shqiptare) signs as "Εὐθύμιος Μῆτκος" (Euthymios Mētkos).

38 A.Q.Sh. F. 141, D. 2, f. 69v, 72r, 80r; here in 04.01.1866, 21.09.1868 and in 16.05.1893 Mihal Grameno's ancestor, Kosta Grameno, signs himself "Κῶτζης Γραμμένος" or "Κῶτζις Γραμμένος" or "Κῶτσις Γραμμένος" (Kōtzēs, Kōtzis and Kōtsis Grammenos, respectively).

39 A.Q.Sh. F. 141, D. 2, f. 72r; here in 21.09.1868 his ancestor, Mitro Gjërmeni, signs himself "Μητρης Γερμενης" (Mētrēs Yermenis).

40 For example, in a decision of the noblemen of Korça's Varosh quarter dated May 8, 1811, the following noblemen record their names in their Albanian pronunciation: "Χαράλαμπος ἱερεὺς τοῦ Πάντζα Γκέτζο" (priest Charalambos, [son] of Pantza Gketzo / Alb. Panxha Gjënxho), "Τζίτζο Φίλιος" (Tzitzo Philios / Alb. Xhixho Filjo), "Βασίλ Κόστα Μάκο" (Vasil Kosta Mako). A.Q.Sh. F. 141, D. 2, f. 72r; cf. Andi Rëmbeci, "O kodikas Mitropoleos Koritsas. Ekdosi kai Istoriki Tekmiriosi (170s-190s aionas)," 233.

41 Giakoumis, "A Preliminary Linguistic Approach," 170.

42 Thernstrom, Orlov, and Handlin, eds., *Harvard Encyclopedia of American Ethnic Groups*, 23–8.

tieth century, a number of Albanian nationalist intellectuals communicated with their readers in Greek or Turkish,[43] since Albanian was not yet a standardized written language. As has been shown elsewhere, the unfixedness of identification constructions led some Albanians to remain loyal servants of an Empire that was later doomed.[44] Such unfixedness is expressly recorded in "the most influential and perhaps the most popular poem ever written in Albanian, that has ensured [the author] his deserved place in Albanian literary history: the famous "O moj Shqypni, e mjera Shqypni" (Oh Albania, poor Albania),"[45] written by Pashko Vasa. In his stirring appeal for national awakening, believed to be written between 1878 and 1880, Vasa exclaims:[46]

...Sa thonë kemi fe, sa thonë kemi din,	...Some say we have faith, others say we have knowledge,
njeni thotë jam turk, tjetri jam latin,	One says "I am Turk," another "I am Latin"
do quhen grek, shqeh disa tjerë,	[Some] will be called Greek, some others Slav,
por jeni vllazën gjithë, mor të mjerë!	but you are all brothers, [you oh] poor [fellows]

It is thus evident that as late as at the turn of the twentieth century many Albanians did not identify themselves as such or, at most, had just started a process of national identification shift. The question of the social spread of national identification and the unfixedness of identifications in diverse social strata is addressed in a play by Namik Delvina[47] entitled "Dashuria e Mëmëdheut" (The love for the motherland), staged in Thessaloniki shortly before the outbreak of the 1908 Young Turks Revolution. The play aimed to raise nationalist awareness, as well as to promote

---

43 Giakoumis, "The Policy of the Orthodox Patriarchate Toward the Use of Albanian in Church Services," 146–54.

44 Kalemaj and Giakoumis, "Oscillating between Inclusionary Autonomy and Secessionist Independence."

45 Elsie, *Historical Dictionary of Albania*, 467. For the mythistorical value of national poetics, see Aleksić, "Introduction: Mythistorical Genres of the Nation," 1–11.

46 Vasa, *E Verteta mbi Shqipërinë dhe Shqiptarët (Një Studim Kritik Historik)*, 39.

47 Delvina, *Dashuria e Mëmëdheut. Thjatro me Tetë Pamje.*

Albanian education and learning. It indicated that nationalist identification appealed mostly to the younger generation, the older generation being largely characterized by uniform ignorance, or even indifference to
such matters.[48] Yet the rise of Balkan nationalisms in the nineteenth century (and Albanian nationalism especially during the last three decades of
the nineteenth century) applied a powerfully divisive elite-driven thrust
to wider social strata. In the spirit of the Romantic exaltation of nationalism, the leaders of the Albanian national movement who were intellectually nourished in Turkish or Greek schools felt the urge to sever their educational and intellectual roots, and devoted their energies to transform
a "low" Albanian culture to a "high" culture (in the Gellnerian sense),[49]
and demonized Turks and Greeks alike as "enemies" in order to achieve a
shift towards national means of identification. This was not an unknown
trajectory, since other ethnic groups, like the Finns and the Estonians,
developed their low culture to a high culture by severing the umbilical
cord from the German and Russian high cultures, respectively.[50] From the
multiplicity of factors that agents applied or utilized to serve this shift of
identification, I shall delve into one specifically: the identification of the
in-group's common enemies, both from within as well as from without,
that is, the construction of a myth about the Other, whereby myths are
not traced solely for the purpose of debunking them and uncovering historical truth, but also for placing them as sources of discourse, "an object
of study in and of themselves," as well as a process of identification.[51]

The absence of religious uniformity in Albania compelled the nascent
Albanian state to engage in a conscious and concentrated endeavor to
eradicate linguistic pluralism in the process of homogenization and craft-
ing of a national identity for the Albanian people. It is noteworthy that as
late as the 1930s, elites often communicated in foreign (i.e. non-Albanian)
languages to each other, even in casual everyday settings, both in cities

48   Clayer, *Aux Origines du Nationalisme Albanais*, 341–3.
49   Gellner, *Nations and Nationalism*, 8–38.
50   Gellner, "'Do Nations have Navels?'" *Reply to A. Smith's Opening Statement to the Warwick Debates*,
     1995, http://gellnerpage.tripod.com/Warwick2.html, accessed March 25, 2013; cf. Hall, "National-
     isms: Classified and Explained"; and Smith, "Memory and Modernity: Reflections on Ernest Gell-
     ner's Theory of Nationalism."
51   Cruz and Frijhoff, "Myth in History, History in Myth," Introduction, 1–2; for the study of politi-
     cal myth as a process, see Bottici, *A Philosophy of Political Myth*.

and in provinces,[52] even though after 1926 the last bulwark of resistance against the generalized use of Albanian in the newly-founded Albanian state, the Orthodox Church, had already adopted Albanian as the exclusive liturgical language in church services.[53] In this context, the identification of such heroes as Father Stathi Melani, Kristo Negovani and others,[54] who died for the cause of language, was accompanied by the identification of traitors or enemies from within—whoever did not share the linguistic views of Albanian patriots was either Grecoman ("grekoman") or Turcoman.[55] Thus, those Qestorat peasants who did not like Koto Hoxhi's patriotic views were "grekomanosur," according to Guri Sevo.[56] Furthermore, according to Petro Luarasi, those who admitted one mother tongue (Albanian) and one father tongue (Greek) were moved to do so "by a third language, that of interest, which they kept for themselves," thereby betraying the national cause with childish fabrications in the service of foreign ends.[57]

In this ideological frame it is not strange that the enemies within were often countered violently. Guri Sevo recorded a shocking event related to the use of violence against those who disagreed with the mainstream linguistic policies and practices of the nationalists. A certain Papa Stefan Kici, a priest from Petro Luarasi's native village, Luarasi, took the side of the Metropolitan of Kastoria in the case of Luarasi's excommunication.[58]

---

52 Giakoumis, "The Policy of the Orthodox Patriarchate Toward the Use of Albanian in Church Services," 147–8; notes 31 & 32.

53 Xhuvanni, *Çashtie Politiko-Religjoze, Konstandinopoli-Tiranë*, 12.

54 The primary sources were primarily based on the cases of: 1) Petro Luarasi: see Grameno, *Mallkimi i Gjuhës Shqipe. Komodi në Vjershë me Tre Pamje, Ngjarë në Korçë më 1886*; Luarasi, *Mallkimi i Shkronjave Shqipe dhe Çpërfolja e Shqiptarit*, also available in Greek as *To Epitimion ton Alvanikon Grammaton kai i Apologia tou Alvanou*; Sevo, *Petro Luarasi, Mësonjësi im i Shqipes*. 2) Papa Stathi Melani: For his life and murder, with the related literature, see Clayer, "Le Meurtre du Prêtre. Acte Fondateur de la Mobilisation Nationaliste Albanaise à l'Aube de la Revolution Jeune Turke," 3) Fr. Kristo Negovani: for a basic account see Jacques, *The Albanians: An Ethnic History from Prehistoric Times to the Present*, 315; to illustrate how reality became a myth by way of instrumentalization, cf. Logori, "Lament," 4. 4) Fr. Pano Gjirokastra, see Jani, "Papapano Gjirokastra—Figurë e Shquar e Kishës Shqiptare," 88–92; and others, such as Fr. Vasil Negovani, Fr. Llambro Ballamaçi, etc.

55 From the plethora of sources, both primary and secondary, on this matter, see Sevo, *Petro*, 53.

56 Among others, see Sevo, *Petro*, 11, 23; comparable with "the bad Grecoman Albanians of Kolonja (Luarasi, *To Epitimion ton Alvanikon Grammaton kai i Apologia tou Alvanou*, 25, 42).

57 Luarasi, *Mallkimi i Shkronjave Shqipe dhe Çpërfolja e Shqiptarit*, 70–71; Luarasi, *To Epitimion ton Alvanikon Grammaton kai i Apologia tou Alvanou*, 95–96.

58 Sevo, *Petro*, 23.

In 1896, when Luarasi became *muftar* (administrator), Papa Stefani, "the brave Albanian priest," in Sevo's words, was forced to flee the village when the villagers punished him on allegations of accepting the standard presents for marriages ("Fshati e dënoi...").[59] The indicated omission of words leave no doubt that it referred to corporal punishment. Threats of violence were also raised in the case of the use of Greek in Church services in Korça in 1909.[60]

The demonization of the enemy from without followed a similar path of instrumentalization. The role of the enemy from without in linguistic matters was assigned primarily to the Ecumenical Patriarchate and its "agents" in the region, the nascent Greek state with its irredentist plans, but also the Serbian and the Romanian Churches, whose presence in Albania, in the words of Bishop Vissarion Xhuvanni, "offended the national dignity of the Albanian Church."[61] The Ecumenical Patriarchate was blamed systematically by the representatives of Albanian Renaissance as an instrument of Greek nationalism.[62] Members of the higher clergy dispatched to Albania were considered to be agents of the Ecumenical Patriarchate. The assassination of Metropolitan Photios in September 1906 by an Albanian *çeta* (band) in retaliation for the assassination of papa Kristo Negovani and his brother, who was also a priest, and the displacement of Greek Metropolitans from their jurisdiction in Albania[63] were culminating events in this process of demonizing "the enemy."

I have elsewhere analyzed the way in which Luarasi demonized the three Metropolitans of Kastoria who excommunicated him, especially Philaretos, who in Luarasi's work acquired the attributes of evil, who "not daring to tell the truth, demonstrates his soul's weakness, which, lacking the bravery to endure the bitterness of truth, always lies"; a "tyrant and anti-gospel" hierarch, engaging in "intrigues," he was portrayed as the prosecutor, judge, legal advisor and witness of a "trial" against Luarasi and Albanian learning.[64] Metropolitan Philaretos was not satisfied by excom-

---

59 Sevo, *Petro*, 60–1.

60 Sevo, *Petro*, 97.

61 Xhuvanni, *Çashtie Politiko-Religjoze, Konstandinopoli-Tiranë*, 10.

62 Cf. Luarasi, *Mallkimi i Shkronjave Shqipe dhe Çpërfolja e Shqiptarit*, in various passages throughout the work.

63 Clayer, "Le Meurtre du Prêtre."

64 Luarasi, *Mallkimi i Shkronjave Shqipe dhe Çpërfolja e Shqiptarit*, 28, 81, 86.

municating Luarasi but "wished to sow his evil weeds to Petro's family as well," by preventing his family from participating in church services.[65] These same agents were stereotypically portrayed as enemies with an evil profile in later historiography. The demonization of these enemies passed into the realm of fiction and a play by Mihal Grameno.[66] Such views were stereotypically reproduced even as recently as in the latest edition of the History of the Albanian State in 2002, where the advent of the Albanian Enlightenment is claimed to have been accompanied by a war waged against the protagonists of the Albanian Enlightenment by the Greek Patriarchate, which "used religion for its political ends."[67]

The demonization of Greeks and Turks was also pursued internationally by Albanian scholars living in the U.S., as Noel Malcolm has demonstrated.[68] In *Albania's Rights and Claim for Independence* Kristo Dako[69] states that the Ottomans:

inaugurated a system of oppression and persecution, and deprived [our people] of the sacred right to educate themselves in their own language, while foreign propaganda and intrigue had a wide open door and a free hand to divide and denationalize the Albanian nation. This foreign propaganda and intrigue was of such a nature that it has not disappeared entirely from amongst us, even in this country [i.e. the USA].[70]

Chekrezi[71] demonizes Sultan Abdülhamid II when he describes his relations to the Albanians in the following way: "Abdülhamid II favored the Albanians as individuals; as a nation, however, he attacked them with the rage and bitterness that characterized his criminal propensities"; while elsewhere in his book he describes the Young Turks in similar terms.[72] Last but not least, similar tones of demonization can also be

---

65 Luarasi, *Mallkimi i Shkronjave Shqipe dhe Çpërfolja e Shqiptarit*, 87.
66 Grameno, *Mallkimi i Gjuhës Shqipe. Komodi në Vjershë me Tre Pamje, Ngjarë në Korçë më 1886.*
67 Pollo and Prifti, "Rilindja Kombëtare Shqiptare dhe Veçoritë e Saj Dalluese," 26–7.
68 Malcolm, "Myths of Albanian National Identity," 70–87.
69 Dako and Grameno, *Albania's Rights and Claims to Independence*, 4–5.
70 Dako and Grameno, *Albania's Rights and Claims to Independence*, 4–5.
71 Chekrezi, *Albania: Past and Present*, 64, 67.
72 Chekrezi, *Albania: Past and Present*, 66–7.

found, among others, in the *Adriatic Review*, a journal published by Albanians in the U.S.

In this case, the demonization of the enemy involved processes of dissociation from a community of individuals formerly identified as members of the in-group and their dehumanization, which aimed at instilling fear and loathing of the "enemy" into members of the in-group. As I shall show below, on the basis of the histories produced by prominent Albanian nationalists whose writings were taught in schools after the establishment of an independent Albanian state, this dissociation involved strategies like abnegation, distancing, compartmentalization, rationalization and scapegoating. Dehumanization entailed compartmentalizing and reproducing, or simply forging, a past of terror.

Denial or abnegation is a psychological defense mechanism, in which a subject faced with an uncomfortable reality either rejects it altogether or minimizes its importance. Such was often the reaction of prominent Albanian nationalists when confronted with the existence of a rich tangible, and intangible, heritage in Albania that was claimed by neighboring countries as theirs. The presence of several, "civilized, half-civilized, or barbarian," "invaders" to Albania "in the course of her long history"[73] left imprints in the country's cultural heritage. Yet, according to Constantine Chekrezi:

> The Gauls, the Romans, the Goths, the Slavs, the Normans, the Venetians, and, finally, the Turks, successively set their foot on, and obtained temporary mastery over, the Albanian territory. But, in the course of time, the natives have gradually driven out or assimilated the invaders. So many invasions and influences have left hardly any appreciable traces, least of all on the national characteristics, traditions, customs, and language of the Albanian people.[74]

Similar abnegation is also to be traced elsewhere, for example, in the works of Vasa.[75] Centuries of inclusion of Albanian-speaking territories in the Byzantine state left no heritage, according to Chekrezi, who claims

---

73 Chekrezi, *Albania: Past and Present*, 10.
74 Chekrezi, *Albania: Past and Present*, 10.
75 Vasa, *E Verteta mbi Shqipërinë dhe Shqiptarët (Një Studim Kritik Historik)*, 11–3.

that "Greek Byzantine influence is nil on the intellectual side,"[76] thereby implying that the Byzantines were nothing but another invader. With such views, it is no surprise that Vasa, although referring only to antiquity, maintains that Albania is "a place belonging to the Albanian race, which has nothing in common with Greece."[77] It is interesting to note that, considering that such views did not quite fit with the material culture of the wider Graeco-Roman heritage found in Albania, it was claimed that they were forged by Greeks: "The Greek authorities planted deep into the soil a number of stones on which they wrote Greek inscriptions—in ancient Greek, of course,—so that they may create a new title to their claims on Southern Albania."[78]

Compartmentalization is another psychological defense mechanism for coping with disconcerting situations, whereby a subject partitions an integrated part of their life or knowledge into diverse compartments, disassociated from each other. The previous example of the instrumentalization of the language issue in Church services, and the alleged excommunication of the Albanian language and learning, serve as an example of compartmentalization.[79] On occasion, a compartmentalized part of a memory is over-generalized, thereby acquiring the power of a quasi-axiom. In the course of the five-centuries-long Ottoman rule over Albania the historian can find traces of Bektashi veneration of certain Christian saints, as well as examples of Albanian Muslims acting in favor of Christian Albanians, but also evidence for the contrary, i.e. Albanian Muslims acting against their Christian fellows, such as in the case of Voskopoja's (Moschopolis') destruction. In such aspects of interreligious relations, the Albanian-speaking territories of the West Balkans were similar to other provinces of the Ottoman empire. Yet, according to Chekrezi:

the Albanian Moslem has never forgotten ... his former religion to some of the saints of which he still pays tribute, such as St. George, in memory of George Castriota Scanderbeg, and to St. Demeter. More-

76 Chekrezi, *Albania: Past and Present*, 19–20.
77 Vasa, *E Verteta mbi Shqipërinë dhe Shqiptarët (Një Studim Kritik Historik)*, 10.
78 Chekrezi, *Albania: Past and Present*, 132.
79 Giakoumis, "The Policy of the Orthodox Patriarchate Toward the Use of Albanian in Church Services."

over, he has always protected his weaker brethren, the Christian Albanians, against the brutalities of the Turk.[80]

Distancing is another psychological strategy of dissociation, through which a subject seeks to clearly demarcate their separateness from everything around them. In the context discussed here, some of the evidence provided above in the frame of denial could also be understood as a form of distancing. Vasa provides an example of this in the ways he takes the pains to insist, in the frame of an alleged Albanian indifference towards religion, that Albanians remain pagan in their beliefs and in the ways they commit themselves to their communities (oath-taking),[81] thereby distancing themselves from Muslims (associated with the Turks), or Christians (associated with Greeks, Serbs, or others). In view of the poor support for the claim of a pagan Albania in the nineteenth century, it was eventually replaced by the much celebrated religious indifference of the Albanians, propagated by Vasa's "the religion of the Albanian is Albanianism,"[82] and reinforced by others, such as Chekrezi,[83] a myth extensively discussed by Noel Malcolm.[84] Albanian indifference towards religion can be classified as evidence of distancing, a strategy of dissociation later also used by the communist regime for other reasons.

Rationalization is applied when controversial actions or feelings necessitate logical justifications. Albanian aggression or irredentist claims were initially grounded on the theory of the Pelasgian origin of the Albanians, thereby raising primordialist claims of precedency over disputed territories.[85] These claims were not confirmed by any archaeological, epigraphic or historical evidence, thereby causing another controversy. Rationalization was also applied to produce responses to claims that the Albanian na-

---

80   Chekrezi, *Albania: Past and Present*, 202.
81   Vasa, *E Verteta mbi Shqipërinë dhe Shqiptarët (Një Studim Kritik Historik)*, 14–5.
82   Vasa, *E Verteta mbi Shqipërinë dhe Shqiptarët (Një Studim Kritik Historik)*, 40.
83   "The truth is that the Albanian is not fanatical; on the contrary, it may be said that, mi fonds, he is indifferent in religious matters. Toleration exists in Albania as nowhere in the Balkans and as it does not exist even in some more advanced sections of Europe." Chekrezi, *Albania: Past and Present*, 201.
84   Malcolm, "Myths."
85   Chekrezi, *Albania*, 3–18; Malcolm, "Myths of Albanian National Identity"; Ilir Kalemaj, "Visualizing Virtual Borders: Identity Territorialization Shifts and 'Imagined Geographies' in the Albanian Case."

tion had no deep historical roots.[86] The origin of the ancient Greek pantheon was said to be "borrowed":

> The Albanian language affords the only available means for a rational explanation of the meaning of the names of the ancient Greek gods as well as of the rest of the mythological creations, so as exactly to correspond with the faculties attributed to these deities by the men of those times. The explanations are so convincing as to confirm the opinion that the ancient Greek mythology had been borrowed, in its entirety, from the Illyrian-Pelasgians.[87]

According to this line of thinking, since the ancient pantheon was handed to Greeks by the Illyrian-Pelasgians, then ancient Greek mythology must have also been borrowed because "the principal legends of ancient Greece are still alive in the popular myths of the Albanian people."[88] After all, forging an ancient past by planting "deep under the ground inscriptions [in] ancient Greek"[89] could explain the absence of archaeological evidence for such Pelasgian-Albanian continuity.[90] Such alleged fabrications were central to the Albanian inter-war anxiety to purge toponymy in Albania from any foreign influences and Albanize it.[91]

Last but not least, scapegoating was also practiced to single out a group of people, or a country, to blame for unpleasant matters within the ingroup. Portraying Albanian history as a succession of destructive foreign invasions and occupations necessitating permanent national struggle[92] provided a pool of scapegoats to blame with relative ease. At different periods of time different countries assumed the role of the scapegoat, not least Greece, Turkey and Serbia.

---

86 Dako, *Albania's Rights, Hopes and Aspirations*, 5.
87 Chekrezi, *Albania: Past and Present*, 6; Vasa, *E Verteta mbi Shqipërinë dhe Shqiptarët (Një Studim Kritik Historik)*, 11–3.
88 Chekrezi, *Albania: Past and Present*, 7–8.
89 Chekrezi, *Albania: Past and Present*, 132.
90 Malcolm, "Myths of Albanian National Identity."
91 Clayer, Nathalie, "L'Albanization des Toponymes dans l'Albanie de l'Entre-Deux Guerres ou les Meanders d'une Lente Construction Étatique," 237–55.
92 Chekrezi, *Albania: Past and Present, passim*.

Finally, the process of demonization of the enemy was the next stage of dehumanization. Thus, Greeks and Turks, as was observed above, acquired the image of evil, on occasion collaborating to counter

> the progress of popular Albanian education… Consequently, in 1886, the Albanian schools were closed by order of Sultan Abdülhamid II, and publications in the Albanian language were suppressed. A supplementary decree was issued by the Greek Patriarch of Constantinople by which Orthodox Albanians were threatened with excommunication in case they used the "accursed" Albanian language in the schools and churches.[93]

This is the subject of an entire play written by Mihal Grameno,[94] regarding the instrumentalization of the Albanian language matter.[95] The reality on the ground, however, indicated that even in inscriptions of ecclesiastical items written in Greek, Albanian patrons or artists found no obstacle in celebrating their Albanian identity and contesting some space of the sacred locale of these inscriptions by having their names commemorated in their Albanian version.[96]

In the work of Chekrezi, Greeks are portrayed as "cunning,"[97] engaging in "machinations,"[98] and spreading terror.[99] The most palpable element of this dehumanization process by Chekrezi is his implicit reference

---

93 Chekrezi, *Albania: Past and Present*, 216.

94 Grameno, *Mallkimi i Gjuhës Shqipe. Komodi në Vjershë me Tre Pamje, Ngjarë në Korçë më 1886*.

95 Giakoumis, "The Policy of the Orthodox Patriarchate Toward the Use of Albanian in Church Services."

96 Giakoumis, "Contesting the Sacred: Albanian Anthroponymy in Votive Inscriptions of 18th to 20th Century Artworks at the Onufri Museum, Berat."

97 "The Conference had to deal now with no less cunning a nation than the Greeks." Chekrezi, *Albania: Past and Present*, 96.

98 Among others: "In their zeal to present to the International Commission an entirely Greek-speaking population, the Greek authorities saw to it that only Greek-speaking people be allowed to circulate in the streets during the passage of, or to come into contact with, the Commission. In places where no Greek-speaking persons could be had, Greek colonists and refugees from Asia Minor imported ad hoc were to figure as natives." Chekrezi, *Albania: Past and Present*, 111–123.

99 "The third move of the Greek authorities was to terrorize and cow the population. The prisons of Korcha, Janina, Fiorina, Salonica and of other Greek cities were crowded with prisoners from the places which were to be visited by the Commission. The avowed Albanian patriots had earlier found places in the damp dungeons of the former Turkish prisons which were now honored by Greek guards." Chekrezi, *Albania: Past and Present*, 116.

to an alleged mass murder (or genocide) of almost half a million Albanians committed by Greeks in the summer of 1914:

> The nearest estimate of the number of people of Albanian race is between three and three and a half million, of which nearly two million inhabit the Albania of the London Conference. Taking, however, into account the ravages of the recent wars and especially the losses in human lives resulting from the devastation of Southern Albania by the Greeks in the summer of 1914, it will be nearer the truth to say that Albania has now a population of about 1,500,000.[100]

Needless to say, such mass killings have not been documented. Claims that Luarasi did not die of natural causes but was poisoned by agents of the "Greek" Patriarchate[101] gave rise to a series of alleged murders by Greeks by way of poisoning.[102] Strategies to dehumanize Greeks as enemies were further fostered, for a different set of reasons, by the communist regime of Enver Hoxha, in spite of his popular writings about two friendly peoples,[103] as evidenced by the multitude of bunkers facing Greece and aimed at countering a potential invasion from Greece, or by films like the *Mesonjëtorja* (1980) by M. Fejzo, and to some extent they persist to this day.[104]

Although not as detailed, the description of the Turk is no better. In Chekrezi's attempt to play down concerns regarding the establishment of a predominantly Muslim state in Christian Europe, he resorts to a language of distaste for Muslims, as he speaks of the Turks in the following way: "By the force of circumstances, a Moslem generally implies a Turk, and the Turk is rightly considered a beast, a pitiless persecutor and butch-

---

100 Chekrezi, *Albania: Past and Present*, 186.
101 Giakoumis, "The Policy of the Orthodox Patriarchate Toward the Use of Albanian in Church Services."
102 See popular blog writings indicative of the matter, such as http://kosovare.forumotion.com/t254-nje-tufe-lule-mbi-varrin-e-aristidh-koles, accessed January 27, 2014.
103 Hoxha, *Dy Popuj Miq: Pjesë nga Ditari Politik dhe Dokumente të Tjera për Marrëdhëniet Shqiptaro-Greke, 1941–1984.*
104 This is the overall impression provided by a first reading of the impressive survey results conducted by the University of Oslo and the University of Rijeka across the Balkans, including Albania, in the research project titled "Strategies of Symbolic Nation-building in West Balkan States: Intents and Results," http://www.hf.uio.no/ilos/english/research/projects/nation-w-balkan/. The results for Albania still echo such biases against Greeks. See http://www.hf.uio.no/ilos/forskning/prosjekter/nation-w-balkan/dokumenter/nb_albania-wine-summer.pdf, accessed January 27, 2014, Tables 60–62, 70–72 and 73–75.

er of Christians."[105] The Ottoman rule in Albania is described as "the occupation of... [the] country by the fanatical Asiatic hordes..."[106]

To conclude, I have attempted to demonstrate the role of the "Other"
in national identification shifts, and the Albanian perception of the
Greek and the Turk as part of the ontological category of the Other, as a
demonized enemy. In the course of the Albanian national identity-build-
ing process before and after Albania's independence, the Albanian state
had, in schools and the military, two powerful instruments to steer society and to construct and consolidate an exclusive, national Albanian
identity. This chapter has argued that as far as documentary and narrative sources permit us to sense from the worm's-eye view how the lower
middle and lower strata of local communities felt, acted, interacted with
other ethno-cultural groups, and identified themselves. The centuries-
old symbiosis of diverse ethno-cultural communities identifying themselves as members of an in-group was still deeply rooted in Albania at
the beginning of the twentieth century, until the centralized nation-state
national-identity building processes maximized divisive thrusts by demonizing the Greek and Turkish "enemies" and led to a certain degree of
homogenization of the region's population. It is noteworthy that for different reasons demonization stereotypes persisted throughout communist times, almost until today.

REFERENCES

Abizadeh, Arash. "Does Collective Identity Presuppose an Other? On the Alleged Incoher-
ence of Global Solidarity." *American Political Science Review* 99, no. 1 (2005): 45–60.
Aleksić, Tatjana. "Introduction: Mythistorical Genres of the Nation." In *Mythistory and
Narratives of the Nation in the Balkans*, edited by Tatjana Aleksić, 1–11. Newcastle:
Cambridge Scholars Publishing, 2007.
Anderson, Benedict. *Imagined Communities: Reflection on the Origins and Spread of Na-
tionalism*. London and New York: Verso Books, 1991.
Bottici, Chiara. *A Philosophy of Political Myth*. New York: Cambridge University Press,
2007.

105 Chekrezi, *Albania: Past and Present*, 201.
106 Chekrezi, *Albania: Past and Present*, 200–2.

Bozbora, Nuray. *Osmanlı Yönetiminde Arnavutluk ve Arnavut Ulusçuluğunun Doğuşu* [The emergence of Ottoman Albania and the management of Albanian nationalism]. Istanbul: Boyut Kitapları, 1997.

Buda, Aleks. "Mendimi Politik dhe Kultura Kombëtare në Vitet 50-70 të Shek. XIX" [The Political Thought and National Culture in the Years '50–'70 of the Nineteenth Century]. In *Historia e Popullit Shqiuptar*. Vol. 2, edited by Kristaq Prifti, 121–131. Tirana: Toena, 2002.

Chekrezi, Constantine. *Albania: Past and Present*. New York: McMillan, 1919.

Clayer, Nathalie. "The Myth of Ali Pasha and the Bektashis: The Construction of an 'Albanian Bektashi National History.'" In *Albanian Identities: Myth and History*, edited by Stephanie Schwandner-Sievers and Bernd J. Fischer, 127–33. Bloomington & Indianapolis: Indiana University Press, 2002.

———. "Le Meurtre du Prêtre. Acte Fondateur de la Mobilisation Nationaliste Albanaise à l'Aube de la Revolution Jeune Turke." *Balkanologie–Revue d'Études Pluridisciplinaires* 9, no. 1–2 (December 2005). Accessed January 13, 2010. http://balkanologie.revues.org/index575.html.

———. *Aux Origines du Nationalisme Albanais. La Naissance d'une nation majoritairement Musulmane en Europe*. Paris: Karthala, 2007.

———. "L'Albanization des Toponymes dans l'Albanie de l'Entre-Deux Guerres ou les Meanders d'une Lente Construction Étatique." In *Nommer et Classer dans les Balkans*, edited by Gilles de Rapper and Pierre Sintès, 237–55. Athens: École Française d'Athènes, 2008.

Cruz, Laura, and Willem Frijhoff, eds. *Myth in History, History in Myth*. Leiden and Boston: Brill, 2009.

Dako, Christo A. *Albania's Rights, Hopes and Aspirations. The Strength of the National Consciousness of the Albanian People*. Boston: s.n., 1918.

Dako, Christo A., and Mihal Grameno. *Albania's Rights and Claims to Independence*. Boston: s.n., 1918.

Delvina, Namik. *Dashuria e Mëmëdheut. Thjatro me Tetë Pamje* [The love for the motherland: a theatrical piece in eight acts]. Thessaloniki: Mbrothësia-Kristo Luarasi, 1909.

Despot, Igor. *The Balkan Wars in the Eyes of the Warring Parties: Perceptions and Interpretations*. Bloomington: iUniverse, 2012.

Dimitriou, Georgios. *Grammatiki Ellinolatinis ek Diaforon Syllechteisa* [Greek-Latin grammar: a compilation]. Vienna: Josip Baumeiste, 1785.

do Paço, David, "L'Orient à Vienne: L'Integration des Marchands et des Diplomates Ottomanes dans la Ville et la Résidence Impériale." PhD diss., Université Paris 1-Sorbonne, 2012.

Edwards, Jacques. *Language and Identity: An Introduction*. Cambridge: CUP, 2009.

Egro, Dritan. "Disa të Dhëna të Reja mbi Fillimet e Nacionalizmit Shqiptar" [Some data on the beginnings of Albanian nationalism]. *Studime Historike* 3–4 (2010): 5–17.

Elsie, Robert. *Historical Dictionary of Albania*. 2nd ed. Plymouth: Scarecrow Press, 2010.

Frashëri, Kristo. *The History of Albania (A Brief Survey)*. Tirana: s.n., 1964.

Frashëri, Kristo. "Lidhja Shqiptare e Prizrenit (1878-1881)" [The Albanian League of Prizren (1878–1881)]. In *Historia e Popullit Shqiuptar*. Vol. 2, edited by Kristaq Prifti, 132–228. Tirana: Toena, 2002.

Gellner, Ernst. "'Do Nations have Navels?'" *Reply to A. Smith's Opening Statement to the Warwick Debates*, 1995. Accessed March 25, 2013. http://gellnerpage.tripod.com/Warwick2.html.

———. *Nations and Nationalism*. Oxford: Blackwell, 1983.

Giakoumis, Konstantinos. "Dialectics of Pragmatism in Ottoman Domestic Interreligious Affairs: Reflections on the Ottoman Legal Framework of Church Confiscation and Construction and a 1741 Firman for Ardenicë Monastery." *Balkan Studies* 47 (2013): 73–132.

———. "The Policy of the Orthodox Patriarchate Toward the Use of Albanian in Church Services." *Albanohellenica* 4 (2011): 137–171.

———. "A Preliminary Linguistic Approach of the 'Codex of Dositheos', Bishop of Dryinoupolis and Gjirokastra, (1760–1858)." *Albanohellenica* 5 (2013): 167–174.

———. "Relativizmi i identifikimit ideologjiko-politiko-gjeografik të shqiptarëve dhe i trevave shqipfolëse prej vetes dhe prej të tjerëve në *'Longue Durée'*" [The ideological, political and geographical identification of the relativism of Albanians and Albanian-speaking regions from the self and the others in the *Longue Durée*]. In *Shqipëria mes Lindjes dhe Perëndimit. Aktet e Konferencës Shkencore Ndërkombëtare*, edited by Andi Rëmbeci, 71–89. Tirana: Universiteti i Tiranës, 2014.

———. "Contesting the Sacred: Albanian Anthroponymy in Votive Inscriptions of 18th to 20th Century Artworks at the Onufri Museum, Berat." *Albanohellenica* 6. http://albanohellenica.wix.com/greekalbanianstudies #!albanohellenica-6-contents/c1md3.

Giakoumis, Konstantinos, and Dritan Egro. "Ottoman Pragmatism in Domestic Inter-Religious Affairs: The Legal Framework of Church Construction in the Ottoman Empire and the 1741 Firman of Ardenicë Monastery." *Epirotika Chronika* 44 (2010): 73–127.

Grameno, Mihal. *Mallkimi i Gjuhës Shqipe. Komodi në Vjershë me Tre Pamje, Ngjarë në Korçë më 1886* [The curse of the Albanian language: a comedy in verses with three acts]. Bucharest: N.N. Voicu, 1905; Korçë: Dhori Koti, 1921.

Hall, John A. "Nationalisms: Classified and Explained." *Daedalus* 122, no. 31 (1993): 1–28.

Hoxha, Enver. *Dy Popuj Miq: Pjesë nga Ditari Politik dhe Dokumente të Tjera për Marrëdhëniet Shqiptaro-Greke, 1941–1984* [Two friendly people: parts from a political diary and other documents on Albanian-Greek relations, 1941–1984]. Tirana: 8 Nëntori, 1985.

Jacques, Edwin E. *The Albanians: An Ethnic History from Prehistoric Times to the Present*. Jefferson, NC: McFarland, 1995.

Jani, Alqi. "Papapano Gjirokastra—Figurë e Shquar e Kishës Shqiptare" [Father Pano Gjirokastra: renowned figure of the Albanian Church]. In *70 Vjet të Kishës Ortodokse Autoqefale Shqiptare*, 88–92. Tirana: Akademia e Shkencave-Instituti i Historisë, 1993.

Jeismann, Michael. *La patrie de l'ennemi. La notion d'ennemi national et la représentation de la nation en Allemagne et en France de 1792–1918*. Paris: CNRS Editions, 1997.

———. "Nation, Identity, and Enmity: Towards a Theory of Political Identification." In *What is a Nation? Europe, 1789–1914*, edited by Timothy Baycroft and Mark Hewitson, 17–27. London: OUP, 2006.

Kalemaj, Ilir. "Visualizing Virtual Borders: Identity Territorialization Shifts and 'Imagined Geographies' in the Albanian Case." PhD diss., Central European University, 2013.

—―—. *Contested Borders: Territorialization of National Identity and Shifts of "Imagined Geographies" in Albania*. Oxford: Peter Lang Ltd., 2014.

Kalemaj, Ilir, and Konstantinos Giakoumis. "Oscillating between Inclusionary Autonomy and Secessionist Independence: Identification Shifts and the Dynamics of Albanian Perceptions of the Young Turks Movement." In *Balkan Nationalism(s) and the Ottoman Empire*. Vol. 3 of *The Young Turk Revolution and Ethnic Groups*, edited by Dimitris Stamatopoulos, 155–171. Istanbul: Isis Press, 2015.

Logori, Loni. "Lament." *Liria* 25 (1980): 4.

Luarasi, Petro Nini. *Mallkimi i Shkronjave Shqipe dhe Çpërfolja e Shqiptarit* [The curse of Albanian letters and the apology of the Albanian]. Manastir: Shtypshkronja Tregëtare nëkombëtare, 1911.

—―—. *To Epitimion ton Alvanikon Grammaton kai i Apologia tou Alvanou* [The curse of Albanian letters and the apology of the Albanian]. Manastir: Shtypshkronja Tregëtare nëkombëtare, 1911.

Malcolm, Noel. "Myths of Albanian National Identity." In *Albanian Identities: Myth & History*, edited by Stephanie Schandner-Sievers and Bernd J. Fischer, 70–87. Bloomington & Indianapolis: Indiana University Press, 2002.

Misha, Piro. "Invention of a Nationalism: Myth and Amnesia." In *Albanian Identities: Myth & History*, edited by Stephanie Schandner-Sievers and Bernd J. Fischer, 33–48. Bloomington & Indianapolis: Indiana University Press, 2002.

Myzyri, Hysni. "Zhvillimi i Lëvizjes Kombëtare në Shqipëri në Vitet 1882–1895" [The Development of the National Movement in Albanian during the Years 1882–1895]. In *Historia e Popullit Shqiuptar*. Vol. 2, edited by Kristaq Prifti, 229–256. Tirana: Toena, 2002.

Pollo, Stefanaq, Aleks Buda, Kristaq Prifti, Kristo Frashëri. Eds. *Historia e Shqipërisë* [History of Albania]. Vol 2 (Years '30 of the Nineteenth Century–1912), Tirana: Akademia e Shkencave e RPS të Shqipërisë – Instituti i Historisë, 1984.

Pollo, Stefanaq, and Kristaq Prifti. "Rilindja Kombëtare Shqiptare dhe Veçoritë e Saj Dalluese" [The Albanian national renaissance and its distinct particularities]. In *Historia e Popullit Shqiptar*. Vol. 2, edited by Kristaq Prifti, 17–33. Tirana: Toena, 2002.

Prifti, Kristaq. "Ngritja e Lëvizjes për Autonomi (1896–1900). Lidhja Shqiptare e Pejës (1899–1900)" [The rise of the movement for autonomy (1896–1900). The Albanian League of Peja [n.a. Serb. Peć] (1899–1900). In *Historia e Popullit Shqiuptar*. Vol. 2, edited by Kristaq Prifti, 257–297. Tirana: Toena, 2002.

Prifti, Kristaq. "Rritja e Lëvizjes Kombëtare në Shqipëri në Vitet 1901–1908 [The development of national movement in Albania during the years 1901–1908]. In *Historia e Popullit Shqiuptar*. Vol. 2, edited by Kristaq Prifti, 298–336. Tirana: Toena, 2002.

Rembeci, Andi. "O Kodikas Mitropoleos Koritsas. Ekdosi kai Istoriki Tekmiriosi (17os–19os aionas)" [The codex of the Korça metropolis: publication and historical documentation, 17th–19th centuries]. Master's thesis, Ionian University, 2009.

Rutherford, Jonathan. "A Place Called Home: Identity and the Cultural Politics of Difference." In *Identity: Community, Culture, Difference*, edited by Jonathan Rutherford, 9–27. London: Lawrence & Wishart, 1990.

Sevo, Guri. *Petro Luarasi, Mësonjësi im i Shqipes* [Petro Luarasi, my Albanian language teacher]. Tirana: Shtypshkronja Tirasna, 1936.

Skëndi, Stavro. *Albanian Political Thought and Revolutionary Activity, 1881–1912.* München: M. Schick, 1954.

Smith, Anthony. "Memory and Modernity: Reflections on Ernest Gellner's Theory of Nationalism." The Ernest Gellner Memorial Lecture, LSE, 1996. Accessed November 2, 2013. http://gellnerpage.tripod.com/SmithLec.html.

Tajfel, Henri, ed. *Differentiation between Social Groups: Studies in the Social Psychology of Intergroup Relations.* London: Academic Press, 1978.

Thëngjilli, Petrika and Aleks Buda. "Lëvizja Kombëtare Shqiptare në Vitet 30–70 të Shek. XIX" [The Albanian national movement in the years '30 –'70 of the Nineteenth Century]. In *Historia e Popullit Shqiuptar.* Vol. 2, edited by Kristaq Prifti, 75–125. Tirana: Toena, 2002.

Thernstrom, Stephan, Ann Orlov, and Oscar Handlin, eds. *Harvard Encyclopedia of American Ethnic Groups.* Cambridge & London: Harvard University Press, 1980.

Wassa Effendi [Pashko]. *Albanien und die Albanesen. Eine Historisch-Kritische Studie.* Berlin: Verlag von Julius Springer, 1879; in Albanian, Vasa, Pashko. *E Verteta mbi Shqipërinë dhe Shqiptarët (Një Studim Kritik Historik)* [The truth on Albania and Albanians (a critical historical study)]. Translated from German by Skënder Maçi. Tiranë: Naim Frashëri, 1988.

Weeks, Jeffrey. "The Value of Difference." In *Identity: Community, Culture, Difference,* edited by Jonathan Rutherford, 88–100. London: Lawrence & Wishart, 1990.

Xhufi, Pëllumb. *Dilemat e Arbërit. Studime mbi Shqipërinë Mesjetare* [The dilemmas of Arbër: studies on medieval Albania]. Tirana: Pegi, 2006.

———. *Nga Paleologët te Muzakajt: Berati dhe Vlora në Shekujt XII-XV. Me një Botim Kritik të Kronikës së Gjon Muzakës (1510)* [From the Palaeologans to the Musacchi: Berat and Vlora from the 12th to the 15th century. With a critical publication of the John Musacchi chronicle (1510)]. Tirana: Shtëpia Botuese 55, 2009.

———. *Ikje nga Bizanti* [Departures from Byzantium]. Tirana: Dituria, 2009.

Xhuvanni, Vissarion. *Çashtie Politiko-Religjoze, Konstandinopoli-Tiranë* [Political-religious issues]. Tirana: Shtypshkronja Tirana, 1926.

Zavalani, Tajar. "Albanian Nationalism." In *Nationalism in Eastern Europe.* 2nd ed., edited by Peter F. Sugar and Ivo John Lederer, 5–92. Seattle–London: University of Washington Press, 1971.

Zavalani, Tajar. *History of Albania.* Edited by Robert Elsie and Bejtullah Destani. London: Centre for Albanian Studies, 2015.

DR HAB. NIKOLAI ARETOV is Professor at the Institute for Literature, Bulgarian Academy of Sciences, and Deputy Editor-in-chief of *Literaturna misal* journal. He is also lecturer at Sofia University and New Bulgarian University. The author of several books published in Bulgarian, among them *The Translated Prose from the First Half of 19th Century* (1990), *The Bulgarian Murder: Plots with Crimes in Bulgarian Literature* (1994, 2nd revised ed. 2007), *Bulgarian National Revival and Europe* (1995; 2nd ed. 2001), *National Mythology and National Literature* (2006), as well as editor of several collections of articles on Bulgarian and Balkan culture. Dr. Aretov is the coordinator of several interdisciplinary projects on different aspects of collective identities and their representations in culture (balkansbg.eu). His fields of interest focus on Bulgarian literature of the eighteenth to twentieth centuries, comparative literature, cultural studies, crime literature, nationalism and national mythology.

DR LILIYA BEREZHNAYA is an Associate Professor at University of Münster's "Religion and Politics" Cluster of Excellence in Germany. She earned her MA degree from the Moscow Lomonosov State University, and her second MA and PhD in history from the Central European University. Her research interests are focused on comparative borderland studies, imperial and national discourses in Eastern European religious and cultural history, symbolic geography and the construction of "the other," as well as on eschatological notions in Christian traditions. She has co-edited (together with Christian Schmitt) *Iconic Turns: Nation and Religion in Eastern European Cinema since 1989* (Leiden: Brill, 2013) and (together with Heidi Hein-Kircher) *Rampart Nations: Bulwark Myths of East European Multiconfessional Societies in the Age of Nationalism* (Oxford and New

York: Berghahn Books, 2019). *Her The World to Come. Ukrainian Images of the Last Judgment*, co-written with John-Paul Himka, was published in 2015 by Harvard University Press.

LORA GERD was born in St. Petersburg (Leningrad) in 1970. In 1994 she defended her PhD thesis "Questions of Canon Law in the Tactikon of Nikon of Black Mountain, 11th Cent," and in 2006 defended her Doctoral (Hab.) thesis "Constantinople and Petersburg: Russian Church Policy in the Orthodox East (1878–1898)." She is the author of more than forty-five articles and five books on Byzantine and Post-byzantine canon law, history of Byzantine studies, Church history, relations between Russia and the Greek world of the nineteenth through the beginning of the twentieth centuries. She is a senior researcher at St. Petersburg Institute of History, Russian Academy of Sciences (since 1994) and Professor at St. Petersburg University (Ancient Greek, Greek paleography, Greek history of the Turkish and Modern periods, 1453–1821, 1821–1923, since 1999) and at the Theological Academy (Russia and the Orthodox East, Byzantine law, since 2009).

DR KONSTANTINOS GIAKOUMIS holds a PhD from the Centre for Byzantine, Ottoman and Modern Greek Studies, at the University of Birmingham, U.K. and Associate Professor of World Civilizations and Art History at the University of New York in Tirana, Albania. His research interests center on late medieval and modern political, social, economic and cultural history of the Balkans, including the rise of nationalism. His research on interethnic relations, ethnicity and nationalism range from the politics and pragmatics of the veneration and pilgrimage of medieval saints utilized for the purpose of enhancing interethnic coherence in areas inhabited by an ethnically mixed population, to studies on the volatility of identifications from the Self and the Other in the late eighteenth, nineteenth, and twentieth centuries, as well as the role and the demonization of the Other in the construction of national identities.

MARO KALANTZPOULOU is completing her PhD in Greek and Comparative Literature at the Ecole des Hautes Etudes en Sciences Sociales (EHESS) and the Université Paris III-Sorbonne Nouvelle, where she is teaching as *chargée de cours*. She has studied Greek, Balkan and Comparative Literature in Athens, Paris, New York and São Paulo. Her research focuses on the literary representations of the post-imperialist condition and transition to modernity in the Balkan and Latin American contexts. She has published articles on nineteenth-century Greek and Balkan prose writing, the relations of Greek literature to its Occidental and Oriental contexts, the idea of a Balkan interliterary system, and the scales of literary study varying from the national to the transnational and the world-level with a view to questioning the idea of a center-periphery model for the world-system of literature and culture.

NAOUM KAYTCHEV is Associate Professor in Modern History of the Balkans in the Sofia University "St. Kliment Ohridski," Bulgaria. His main research interests are focused on problems of nation-building and nationalism, as well as on history of education and textbook research in the context of nineteenth-century intellectual and social history of Croatia, Serbia and Bulgaria. His publications include *Illyria from Varna to Villach: Croatian National Revival, Serbs and Bulgarians (until 1848)*, (Sofia 2015), *Desired Macedonia: Army, School and Nation-Building in Serbia and Bulgaria, 1878–1912* (Sofia, 2003), both in Bulgarian, as well as an edited volume on the Miladinov brothers and Grigor Părlicev.

DR ARIADNI MOUTAFIDOU is adjunct professor at the Hellenic Open University (European History, Studies in European Civilization) and is cooperating with the Haifa University within the framework of the project *The Greek Big Merchant Houses in the Ottoman Empire*. She is the author of a book titled *Beitrag zur Konflikt- und Allianzforschung vor dem Ersten Weltkrieg. Die Politik Österreich-Ungarns gegenüber dem osmanisch-griechischen Krieg von 1897* [A contribution to the research of conflicts and alliances before the First World War: the policy of Austria-Hungary towards the Greek-Ottoman war of 1897] (Hamburg, 2003). She published numerous articles on European, Greek and Ottoman History in international academic journals. Her recent research focuses on Italian Philhellenism and state politics at the end of the nineteenth century, on the Patrona Halil revolt as reflected in the European travel accounts, as well as on Greek Big Merchants and entrepreneurs in the Mediterranean economic world in the nineteenth century.

ELEONORA NAXIDOU is Assistant Professor of Modern History of South-eastern Europe at Democritus University of Thrace, Komotini, Greece. Her research area is the Balkans and her research interests include nationalism, national identity, church and national ideology, and ethnic minorities. She is currently working on the Bulgarian national movement during the nineteenth century. Among her recent publications are: "Traditional Aspects of Modernity in the Nineteenth-Century Balkans: The Ecclesiastical Dimensions of the Bulgarian National Movement," in *Power and Influence in South-Eastern Europe 16th–19th Century*, ed. Maria Baramova, Plamen Mitev, Ivan Parvev, and Vania Racheva (Berlin: LIT, 2013), 425–439, and "Competing Representations of Shared Legacies: Greek and Bulgarian Narratives in the 19th Century," *Nationalism and Ethnic Politics* 21, no. 3 (2015): 357–373.

FUJINAMI NOBUYOSHI holds a PhD in Area Studies 2010, at the University of Tokyo, and is associate professor at the TSUDA College, Tokyo. His main research topic is the political and intellectual developments in the late Ottoman Empire. He is the author of *The Ottomans and Constitutionalism: Politics, Religion, and Communities in the Young Turk Revolution* (Nagoya: The University of Nagoya Press, 2011, in Japanese). His recent articles include "Privileged but Equal: The Privilege Question in the Context of Ottoman Constitutionalism," in *Balkan Nationalism(s) and the Ottoman Empire Vol. III: The Young Turk Revolution and Ethnic Groups*, ed. Dimitris Stamatopoulos (İstanbul: Isis, 2015); "The Patriarchal Crisis of 1910 and Constitutional Logic: Ottoman Greeks' Dual Role in the Second Constitutional Politics," *Journal of Modern Greek Studies* 27, no.1 (2009); and "'Church Law' and Ottoman-Greeks in the Second Constitutional Politics, 1910," *Études Balkaniques* 43, no. 1 (2007).

DR. DIMITRIS STAMATOPOULOS is Professor in Balkan and Late Ottoman History in the Department of Balkan, Slavic and Oriental Studies at the University of Macedonia, Thessaloniki. He was member of the School of Historical Studies in the Institute for Advanced Study in Princeton for the academic year 2010–11. He wrote many articles on the history of the Greek Orthodox populations in the Ottoman Balkans. His current interests focus on the relationship between religion and politics in the Balkans and more specifically on the process of secularization and the rise of civil society.

Bogdan Trifunović is a graduate of the University of Belgrade in Modern History and a PhD in Cultural Studies, University of Warsaw (2015). His PhD thesis "Collective Memory and the Sites of Memory in the Serbian Discourse of Old Serbia" investigates the culture of memory which influenced development of the Serbian national identity in the nineteenth and early-twentieth century. He has also vocational degree in Library and Information Science and over a decade of experience in digitization and digital preservation of library material. Bogdan's academic interests include the fields of social and cultural history of the Balkans and Europe in the nineteenth and the twentieth centuries, the First World War, interdisciplinary collaboration, and digital humanities.

Dr Magdalena Żakowska is an assistant professor at the Faculty of International and Political Studies at the University of Lodz, Poland. She examines the image of Russia in West European cultures, as well as the history and cultural identity of Central, East and South European countries. She wrote *Russian and Polish German: Cultural Programming of German "Late Uut-settlers" from Russia and Poland* (in Polish, Łódź 2011) and, with A. de Lazari and O. Ryabov, *Europe and a Bear* (in Polish, Warsaw 2013) about the image of Russia-the-bear in European cultures.

INDEX